STUDIES IN HISTORY, ECONOMICS AND PUBLIC LAW

Edited by the
FACULTY OF POLITICAL SCIENCE
OF COLUMBIA UNIVERSITY

NUMBER 386

NATIONAL ROMANTICISM IN NORWAY

BY

OSCAR J. FALNES

NATIONAL ROMANTICISM IN NORWAY

BY

OSCAR J. FALNES, Ph.D.

Department of History
New York University

NEW YORK
COLUMBIA UNIVERSITY PRESS
LONDON: P. S. KING & SON, LTD.
1933

To
AUGUSTA JOHNSON FALNES

PREFACE

THIS book is devoted to an investigation of Norwegian nationalism during the period of romanticism. In seeking to present the nationalist and romanticist views that were characteristic of the scholars and publicists of that period, the writer has examined not only their larger works but also most of their contributions to the newspaper and periodical literature of the mid-century. The task of locating these contributions was facilitated through the use of the bibliography of Norwegian authors by J. B. Halvorsen, entitled *Norsk Forfatter-Lexikon 1814-1880*. The major portion of the material for the study was gathered at the University Library in Oslo; this has been supplemented with data available in the Library of Columbia University and the New York Public Library. Through its inter-library loan service the Washington Square College Library of New York University has made available individual items from the Widener Library at Harvard University and from the Library of the University of Illinois.

The progress of the study was facilitated financially by the writer's appointment as a University Fellow in History in Columbia University for the year 1925-26, and as a Traveling Fellow of the American-Scandinavian Foundation in 1926-27.

The study owes its inception and no small part of its finished form to Professor Carlton J. H. Hayes of Columbia University. His lectures on nationalism during a summer session in 1923 at the University of California aroused the writer's first interest in nationalism, and his seminar at Columbia University later served to give that interest more

definite form.   His careful reading of the manuscript led to
several improvements in organization and to innumerable
improvements in form and expression.   For equally numerous suggestions to better the literary form and for calling in
question several matters of organization, the writer is deeply
indebted also to Professor Geroid T. Robinson of Columbia
University, who painstakingly read the study both in manuscript form and in proof.   The writer also received certain
specific suggestions from other members of the History Department of Columbia University, and particularly from Dr.
John H. Wuorinen.   When still in its earlier stages the work
elicited the sympathetic interest of several Norwegian
scholars, especially Professor Oscar Albert Johnsen and Professor Edvard Bull, the latter since deceased.   Finally, the
writer is deeply grateful to Wilhelm Munthe, Chief Librarian
at the University Library in Oslo and to several members of
its staff for meeting his frequent queries and requests with
unfailing courtesy and helpfulness.

O. J. F.

New York University
May, 1933

TABLE OF CONTENTS

9

LIST OF ABBREVIATIONS USED IN FOOTNOTES

Aftbl.—Aftenbladet.

Alm. n. Maanedskr.—Almindelig norsk Maanedskrift.

Ann. f. n. Oldk.—Annaler for nordisk Oldkyndighed.

Chra.—Christiania.

Chra.-Post.—Christiania-Posten.

Den Const.—Den Constitutionelle.

Dept. Tid.—Departements-Tidende.

Efterl. Skr.—Efterladte Skrifter.

For. t. n. Fortidsm. Bev.—Foreningen til norske Fortidsmindersmærkers Bevaring.

Forn-Swenskans . . . Språkbygnad. — Forn-Swenskans (Swaensku ok Gözku) och Forn-Norskans (Norroenu) Språkbygnad.

Hist. Tidsskr.—Historisk Tidsskrift.

Ill. Nyhbl.—Illustreret Nyhedsblad.

Det kgl. Fred. Univ.—Det Kongelige Fredriks Universitet.

Det kgl. n. Vid.-Selsk. Skr.—Det kongelige norske Videnskabers-Selskabs Skrifter.

Maanedskr. f. Litt.—Maanedskrift for Litteratur.

Morgbl.—Morgenbladet.

Nordm. i det nit. Aarh.—Nordmænd i det nittende Aarhundrede.

Norges Konst. His.—Norges Konstitutions Historie.

Norsk Biog. Leks.—Norsk Biografisk Leksikon.

Norsk Forf.-Lex.—Norsk Forfatter-Lexikon.

N. Tids. f. Vid. og Litt.—Norsk Tidsskrift for Videnskab og Litteratur.

Nor. Univ. og Sk. Annaler.—Norske Universitets- og Skole-Annaler.

Det n. Folkspr. Gram.—Det norske Folkesprogs Grammatik.

NFH.—Det Norske Folks Historie.

Den nor. Rigstid.—Den norske Rigstidende.

Saml. Afh.—Samlede Afhandlinger.

Saml. Skr.—Samlede Skrifter.

Saml. t. d. N. F. Spr. og Hist.—Samlinger til det Norske Folks Sprog og Historie.

Skr. i Saml.—Skrifter i Samling.

Skr. i Udv.—Skrifter i Udvalg.

Spd.—Speciedaler.

Stort. Forh.—Stortings Forhandlinger.

Udv. Skr.—Udvalgte Skrifter.

14

PART I

GENERAL BACKGROUND

INTRODUCTION

MODERN nations of the western world owe many of their nationalist attitudes to the period of romanticism. In its broader aspects the romantic movement imparted a pronounced nationalist impulse to several fields of culture.[1] It influenced especially the work of the scholar, the littérateur and the publicist, partly because romanticism was less critical than it was emotional and even sentimental. The cultivation of history, for instance, profited greatly though unevenly from its stimulus; interest was apt to be concentrated upon the most brilliant period of a people's past to the neglect of more prosaic eras. Its concern for folk-lore and folk-culture helped to emphasize the peculiarities of individual groups while much of its philosophic speculation was but the intellectual justification for its faith in the basic uniqueness of every people. Each nation seemed a unity unto itself, indivisible and self-sufficient, fully able to develop in isolation all the potentialities of its being.

Because it helped to center attention upon the individual folk personality, romanticism had a separatist influence on racial and national groups. This was most true of its contributions to political nationalism. Many nationalists of the period, resting their arguments largely on romanticist premises, formulated programs that aimed at national independence for their respective peoples—programs which, in the imperialized condition of nineteenth-century eastern and central Europe, were bound to be revolutionary and highly

[1] *Cf.* Carlton J. H. Hayes, *Essays on Nationalism* (New York, 1926), pp. 52-5, 62-9.

provocative. A Norwegian writer has aptly said that the nineteenth century, heralded so jauntily with the tones of *" Des Knaben Wunderhorn "* retired to the strains of the trumpets of Mars.[2]

In this study we are to observe how romanticist scholarship in Norway, too, busied itself with national history, folk-literature and folk-language, seeking justification for its faith in political independence and a national culture. It is worth noting at the outset that here the larger outcome of the period was a fatal legacy of social cleavage; in this instance romanticism left behind it a long heritage of social strife. Since that day there have been, in a sense, two Norways invariably at odds; only of late have the more optimistic with some reason dared hope for eventual harmony.

Some say this friction is merely the perpetuation of a hoary antagonism in Norwegian society—that it is but the centuries—old rivalry between peasant and upper classes. Perhaps so, but then it must be recognized that romanticism gave that rivalry new bearings and new weapons. Romanticist scholarship consolidated the peasant's position and gave his cause new strength by furnishing it with a broad justification, at once historical, philosophical and cultural.

We shall concentrate our attention more particularly upon the Norwegian scholars and publicists of the four mid-century decades. The opening chapters of this study will deal with the historical background and with nationalism and romanticism in some of their more general aspects. Later sections will give detailed attention to the historians, the folklorists and the philologists. Then the concluding chapter will point to some of the more obvious manifestations of the romanticist influence that continue beyond the strict

[2] Gunnar Reiss-Andersen, *" Ormen Lange og Målormen," Samtiden,* vol. xli, p. 506.

limits of the period and complicate Norwegian public life today.[3]

[3] For general accounts of the period of this study the reader is referred to: the large coöperative work by Alexander Bugge, E. Hertzberg, A. Taranger, Y. Nielsen, O. A. Johnsen and J. E. Sars, *Norges Historie fremstillet for det norske Folk* (6 vols., Chra., 1908-17), especially vol. v, part ii by O. A. Johnsen, and vol. vi, part i by J. E. Sars; the more popular work by Edvard Bull, Wilhelm Keilhau, Haakon Shetelig and Sverre Steen, *Det norske folks Liv og Historie gjennem ·Tiderne* (projected in ten volumes of which six have appeared. Oslo, 1929———). The background of the period is treated quite extensively in Fredrik Paasche's work (available to me after this study was completed) entitled *Norges Litteratur fra 1814 til 1850-aarene* (1932) which forms volume iii of the joint work by Francis Bull and Fredrik Paasche, *Norsk Litteraturhistorie* (Oslo, 1923—). A convenient survey of Norwegian nationalism from 1750 to 1850 is the study by Andreas Elviken, *Die Entwicklung des norwegischen Nationalismus* (Berlin, 1930). The English reader may consult: K. Gjerset, *History of the Norwegian People* (2 vols., New York, 1915. Printed in one volume, New York, 1927), vol. ii, pp. 446-534; G. Gathorne Hardy, *Norway* (London, 1925), pp. 145-91; A. Elviken, "The Genesis of Norwegian Nationalism," *The Journal of Modern History* (Chicago, 1929—), vol. iii, pp. 365-91; and, for the literary background, the study just published by Theodore Jørgenson, *History of Norwegian Literature* (New York, 1933), chaps. x–xiii.

CHAPTER I

CERTAIN ASPECTS OF NORWEGIAN NATIONALISM
TO 1870

THE word nationalism will be used in this study to denote the attitude of mind which exalts nationality and impels the members of a national group to devote their highest loyalty to their nationality as this expresses itself in a national culture and frequently also in the political organization of a national state. Even in the instances where such a culture and such a national state are yet non-existent in fact, they may be important as ideals to be realized. When members of a nationality subscribe to these ideals they are moved by the force we call nationalism.[1]

* * * * *

Modern nationalism was in its formative period in the eighteenth century and naturally it was affected by the ideals of the " Enlightenment." The age of rationalism did not have the same influence upon nationalism as did the period of romanticism, and we may understand the latter's influence from a brief reference to that of the earlier period. In the case of Norwegian nationalism, it will serve our purpose to refer briefly to certain ambiguities which in the age of rationalism characterized Dano-Norwegian concepts of patriotism and fatherland, ambiguities that were natural enough in the state of Denmark-Norway where a common government ruled over more than one nationality.

Take first the word fatherland. In the eighteenth century

[1] *Cf.* C. J. H. Hayes, *Essays on Nationalism*, p. 6; C. J. H. Hayes, *The Historical Evolution of Modern Nationalism* (New York, 1931), p. 6.

this word was used in a sense that bore certain Greek and Roman connotations. The fatherland came to be thought of largely in terms of the ancient city-state, particularly in regard to ceremonials. It was proposed, for example, that the youth of the country be admitted to political life through elaborate initiatory rites, which might be given the solemnity of political or national " confirmations." [2] There were references to " the altar of the fatherland," [3] and for those who made the supreme sacrifice in time of war, funeral ceremonies were arranged in imitation of the classic processionals [4] of pagan antiquity.

Just what did the fatherland include in political scope and territorial extent? For Danes in particular and even for all subjects of the realm, it was natural and in line with traditional ways of thinking, to equate the fatherland with the sovereign state [5] which ruled Denmark, Norway, the German Duchies, and the islands in the west. Even as late as 1812, the fiery Nicolai Wergeland, after writing his spirited essay on the need for a separate Norwegian University, when accused by Ørsted of restricting the concept " fatherland " to Norway alone, stoutly rejoined that he regarded the state of Norway and Denmark as " my fatherland." [6]

Yet an occasional voice let the concept of fatherland take a more restricted meaning and applied it only to Norway. Hans Arentz, writing for a prize competition arranged in 1786 by *Det nordiske Selskab* (" The Northern Society ")

[2] L. Engelstoft, *Tanker om National Opdragelsen* (Copenhagen, 1808), p. 224.

[3] *Indbydelse til Et Corresponderende Topographisk Selskab for Norge* (Chra., 1791), p. 11.

[4] *Budstikken*, 1808, p. 113.

[5] J. Baden, *Forsög til en moralsk og politisk Catechismus for Bönderbörn* (Copenhagen, 1766), p. 34.

[6] *Dansk Literatur Tidende*, 1812, p. 103; *cf.* also *ibid.*, 1811, p. 596.

in London, denied that the central idea in the concept of
fatherland was the political union of several countries and
peoples, and boldly announced that the Norwegian fatherland
was Norway alone.[7] This implied that Denmark-Norway
was a case of two or more fatherlands within the same state.
Arentz' ideas evoked no particular comment at the time, but
a generation later the experiences of the Napoleonic Wars
led many to the same point of view when geographical
separation taught the bureaucracy and the prosperous middle
class many lessons in initiative and self reliance.[8]

The word patriot also was used with various meanings.
In a restricted sense [9] it was applied only to those who had
distinguished themselves in some public service.   Thus it
was used to honor a local agriculturalist or the promoter of
some new process in the extractive industries.[10]   The improvement of soil fertilization, the clearing of forest land,
the breeding of better livestock, any of these might be
known as the contributions of a patriot.[11]

Such a usage tended to make the term patriotism synony-
mous with public spirit, yet there were writers who made a
distinction between the two.   Public spirit, they said, was a
matter of reason, while patriotism sprang from emotion and

[7] Hans Arentz, *Grundtegning af den fornuftige norske Patriotisme*
(Bergen, 1787), pp. 18-19, 27.

[8] In the *Indbydelse til et Selskab for Norges Vel* (Chra., 1809), the
use of the term "fatherland" is at times ambiguous but in some instances it clearly refers to Norway proper rather than to the Dano-
Norwegian state at large.

[9] *Cf.* J. Rosted, *Om patriotismens Væsen og Begreb* (Chra., 1811), p. 4;
Engelstoft, *op. cit.*, p. 21.

[10] *Cf. Tiden*, 1808, p. 57 *et seq.*

[11] In this connection one may find many interesting pages both in
Danmarks og Norges oekonomiske Magazin (8 vols., Copenhagen, 1757-
64), especially vol. i, pp. iv-v, and in the *Topographisk Journal for Norge*
(10 vols., Chra., 1792-1808).

instinct,[12] though they admitted that reason might govern patriotism.[13]   Virtue and public spirit might properly be the objects of moral precept, but not so the love of fatherland; as an emotion it was outside the realm of moral values and no one could command another who lacked it to acquire it.[14]

The stirring events of 1814 removed for all Norwegians any ambiguity left in the territorial meaning of the word fatherland.   Complete national independence once having been proclaimed, the term could henceforth refer only to Norway.   The entry upon the dynastic union with Sweden failed to renew the ambiguity and at no time was there any thought that the term included Sweden.[15]   So far as patriotism was identified with public spirit or civic virtue, however, it retained some of the rationalist connotation for a longer time.   There are some good instances of this usage in the works of Wergeland.   As late as 1834, he dealt with the saga period in a spirit much akin to eighteenth-century didacticism.[16]

*   *   *   *   *

Norwegian national feeling, stimulated to the highest intensity in Napoleonic days, and made articulate and effective especially through the many plans and projects of *Selskabet for Norges Vel* (" The Society for Norway's Welfare "), founded in 1809, was left somewhat deflated soon after 1814; the dramatic events of that year had inspired many rosy dreams that were quickly dissipated by the new realities.

[12] Rosted, *op. cit.*, pp. 2, 4.

[13] Arentz, *op. cit.*, pp. 12, 21-2, 24-5; *cf.* also Engelstoft, *op. cit.*, p. 14.

[14] M. G. Birckner, *Samlede Skrifter* (4 vols., Copenhagen, 1798-1800), pp. 46-7.

[15] *Cf.* N. Wergeland, *En sandfærdig Beretning om Danmarks politiske Forbrydelse imod Kongeriget Norge fra Aar 995 indtil 1814* (Christianssand, 1816), p. 145.

[16] *Cf.* "*Tale ved en Borgerfest i Eidsvoll til Fædrenes Minde*," *Digterværker og prosaiske Skrifter* (6 vols., Copenhagen, 1882-4), vol. v, pp. 164-183.

Hardly had the nation won its independence before its freedom passed into a partial eclipse, as Norway entered a new political union, this time with Sweden. For some years the general European situation was most unfavorable. The directive minds of the Metternichian era who were busy ferreting out liberalism and any nationalism that might threaten the status quo, expected Karl XIV Johan, a parvenue who needed their favors, to deal accordingly with the revolutionary forces that then were refuged in his second kingdom. Liberal and patriotic Norway was lonely and suspect in Restoration Europe, and waited for Karl Johan to strike, but when his threatened blow did not fall in 1821,[17] Norwegian national feeling felt somewhat easier.

As the 'twenties wore on that feeling became mildly aggressive and before the decade was over it had dedicated a national holiday and consecrated a national song. The latter was evoked somewhat artificially at the opening of the decade, a time it may be noted, when tension with Karl Johan was growing. *Selskabet for Norges Vel* through the generosity of Marcus Pløen, a Christiania wholesaler, offered a hundred *Speciedaler*[18] for the best national poem. There were twenty-two entries in the competition and the first prize was awarded to H. A. Bjerregaard for his "*Sønner af Norge, det ældgamle Rige*" (Sons of Norway, the Age-Old Kingdom ").[19] Pløen later offered a similar prize for a melody to accompany the poem.[20]

[17] He had ordered some mysterious army manoeuvres to take place near Christiania. Norwegian opinion was hostile to him due to the debt settlement with Denmark and because of the Bodö case in which the Department of Foreign Affairs at Stockholm seemed to have been unduly lax in handling a matter of Norwegian import.

[18] The old *speciedaler* amounted to a trifle more than an American dollar.

[19] *Norraena, En Samling af forsøg til Norske National Sange* (Chra., 1821).

[20] Composed by Chr. Blom, a music teacher in Drammen. *Cf.* H.

The day that was to become a national holiday was the 17th of May, the anniversary marking the formal completion of the constitution at Eidsvold in 1814. At first no one, save an occasional person like Peterson [21] in Trondhjem, a man of Slesvigian birth, made any ado about the day. But on the approach of the tenth anniversary plans were afoot, especially among the students in Christiania,[22] to observe the day in a fitting manner. The king showed his displeasure and for some years discouraged any celebrations but in 1829 the unexpected developments in connection with *Torvslaget* (" The Battle of the Market Place ") [23] forever consecrated the day for Norwegian nationalism. An incident growing out of *Torvslaget* brought a young student named Henrik Wergeland into trouble with the authorities and made him something of a hero among certain elements. He had begun his versatile career as a littérateur and publicist two or three years earlier, and with his unceasing efforts to stimulate national energies in many fields he was soon to become the foremost patriot of his generation.

The Revolutions of 1830 greatly improved the situation for Norwegian liberals and patriots; the Holy Alliance was thwarted and large breaches were torn in the walls of the Metternichian system.[24] Of a sudden the atmosphere had grown freer; Norway's position had become respectable and even enviable, and that without any change on her part. Europe had faced about to march in Norway's direction.

Jæger, *Illustreret norsk Literaturhistorie* (2 vols., Chra., 1892-96), vol. ii, pp. 68-70.

[21] *Ibid.*, vol. ii, p. 98.

[22] H. Bjerregaard, *Den 17de Mai 1824.* Reprinted from *Morgenbladet,* 1859, no. 236.

[23] *Cf.*, for instance, Edv. Bull, *et al., Det norske folks Liv og Historie gjennem Tiderne*, vol. viii, pp. 276-82.

[24] *Cf.* H. Wergeland's poem *" Det befriede Europa "* (1831), reprinted in his *Digterværker og prosaiske Skrifter*, vol. i, p. 85.

Instead of being under surveillance, Norway was now in the vanguard. Her liberalism and constitutionalism, as embodied in the great work at Eidsvold in 1814, apparently would have the sanction of history. Stimulated by the revolutionary impulses from abroad, Norwegian nationalism in the early 'thirties made a notable forward thrust in connection with *Norskheds-bevægelsen,* that is, the movement for "Norwegianness." This aggressive trend was noticeable in all fields of national endeavor—in politics and economics, in social affairs as well as literature. Everywhere it forced sharper antagonisms — between liberal and conservative, peasant and bureaucrat, commoner and aristocrat, even in a vague way between rationalist and romanticist.

On its political side the movement involved an attempt to fulfill a sweeping promise of 1814. For at Eidsvold, under the prevailing Rousseauean infatuation with rusticity, the framers of the constitution, many of them bureaucrats, had most magnanimously assigned a very spacious rôle to the Norwegian *bonde.*[25] This adulation for the peasant and his idyllic life had lived on among patriots and liberals, but little had been done to make the concessions of 1814 effective. Quite naturally the peasant in time took himself seriously and began to challenge official control of local affairs. After making sizable gains in two successive *Storting* (*i.e.,* parliamentary) elections, the *bønder* forced through in 1837 their program for reform in local government.

A striking aspect of *Norskheds-bevægelsen* was its econ-

[25] The word *bonde* is best translated as peasant though the latter term is somewhat inadequate. The word has two shades of meaning depending upon the context. In this study, when speaking of the political challenge to the bureaucracy, "peasant" will refer particularly to the freeholding, and usually wealthier, part of the rural population, the element of some importance politically, but when treating of the romanticist interest in the "peasant," the term will apply loosely to the rural population at large.

omic nationalism. In the name of a proper national spirit
it discouraged the use of foreign products in favor of
domestic wares.[26] It developed an ambitious anti-luxury
program aimed to encourage extreme simplicity in habit and
dress. Societies were organized [27] and by-laws drawn in
which men and women, with a restraint little less than
Spartan, pledged themselves to wear coarse homespun and
to buy no such " finery ", for instance, as silk ribbon or
cotton stockings.[28]

One distinctive feature of the broader movement, much
in line with traditions of the eighteenth century, was the
interest in popular, and more particularly rural, enlightenment, an interest which found expression through the
characteristic agency of the reading society. Usually each
local society was equipped with the rudiments of a book
collection, and organized to carry on discussions devoted
mainly to the improvement of agriculture and of transporta-
tion, though there were efforts to include also broader
cultural matters. Some persons entertained high hopes for
a general elevation of rural well-being. The normal unit
for this activity was the parish. The movement spread
rapidly and in the first two or three years of the decade
more than fifty societies were founded.[29]

The intellectual leaders of *Norskheds-bevægelsen* directed
their attacks particularly at the ubiquitous Danish influence,
which seemed as firmly entrenched as ever, though fifteen
years had passed since the separation from Denmark. In
speech, in belles-lettres, in official circles, in the halls of
learning, on the stage, everywhere, social standards and

[26] *Cf. Statsborgeren*, vol. i, p. 198; *Tilskueren*, 1824, no. 74.

[27] *Folkebladet*, 1831, no. 22.

[28] For a brief discussion and a good bibliography of the anti-luxury
movement see G. Gran, *Norges Dæmring* (Bergen, 1899), pp. 189-93.

[29] *Budstikken, Ny Samling*, Deel 2, pp. 229-33; Deel 3, pp. 34-5.

cultural traditions were Danish. The complicated ties of centuries-old union could not all be snapped in the wrench of political separation. Burghers and bureaucrats most frequently were well rooted in Danish traditions.[30] Books, newspapers, magazines, school texts, every variety of printed matter came mainly from Copenhagen. In 1814 there was not a single independent book dealer in the country, according to a later writer, though it is true that several Danish firms had branches there.[31] On the stage, Danish influence tended rather to increase with the passing of time. At the University the teachers, trained in Copenhagen, passed on to the second generation many of their academic attachments and sympathies. In the 'forties, P. A. Munch, whose training was wholly native, wrote that "Danish scholars ought actually to control our University."[32] In the realm of language, the Danish hegemony was decisive; Danish had been the medium of administration and culture for several centuries until it was inextricably woven into the warp and woof of Norwegian public life. Many a Norwegian was no doubt surprised later to learn that the language of public intercourse was "alien." The events of 1814 involved little threat to its hold, and in some quarters conditions after the separation may have improved its position.[33]

*   *   *   *   *

One patriot, conspicuous above all others for his attack on the Danish influence, was Henrik Wergeland, and we turn here to notice his overshadowing controversy with

[30] Many, of course, were of Danish descent.

[31] Mart. Nissen, "*Statistisk Udsigt over den norske Litteratur fra 1814 til 1847*," *Norsk Tidsskrift for Videnskab og Litteratur*, vol. iii, p. 204.

[32] P. A. Munch, *Lærde Brev* (Chra., 1924), vol. i, p. 73. June 9, 1843 to Chr. Molbech.

[33] *Cf.* A. Burgun, *Le Développement linguistique en Norvége depuis 1814* (2 vols., Chra., 1919-21), vol. i, p. 93.

Johan S. Welhaven. On the surface, the controversy was highly personal, for the two men were opposites in background and temperament. Welhaven was prim, decorous,[34] fastidious, attuned to balance and harmony. Wergeland, marked with a touch of genius, was rough, rugged, and undisciplined;[35] ideas and literary images often sputtered from his pen in very impromptu fashion.

Henrik Arnold Wergeland (1808-45) came of peasant stock, although the father was a pastor and the mother had traces of Danish and Scottish blood. The boy grew up in close intimacy with the countryside and when he was nine the family moved from Christianssand to Eidsvold, by then a place rich in the memories of 1814. Henrik was precocious; he published his first poem at fourteen, entered the University five years later, and at twenty-one began work on a great epic poem. He wrote incessantly as a poet and publicist, and from the outset his rugged and boisterous personality made him a storm center in public life. He once sought an appointment to a pastorate, but in vain. For a time he was a copyist at the University Library and in 1840 he was appointed the country's chief archivist (*Riksarkivar*). A lingering illness brought his crowded life to a close in 1845.

Johan Sebastian Cammermeyer Welhaven (1807-73) was urban born and bred; what is more, some of his antecedents were foreign. A paternal grandfather was a Mecklenburger, while his mother was a cousin of the distinguished Danish critic, P. A. Heiberg. At first Welhaven was attracted to painting as a career, but he became, instead, a publicist, littérateur and academician. At the mid-century he was the

---

[34] Though Laura Larsen-Naur has related that on occasion he could be very rude. See her *P. A. Munchs Levnet og Breve* (Chra., 1901), p. 32.

[35] But see H. Beyer's contrast of the two men in *Edda*, vol. xxx, pp. 269-80.

country's outstanding poet. In 1842 he had been appointed to teach philosophy at the University, a position he held until his retirement in 1868.

Since both men aspired to cultural leadership, there was bound to be a clash. We can here refer to the controversy [36] only in briefest outline. Wergeland in 1830 made a bid for leadership with his epic poem, *Skabelsen, Mennesket og Messias* ("Creation, Man and the Messiah"), and Welhaven refused to accept this effort as in any sense a serious contribution to Norway's puny young literature. Gradually he broadened his criticism to include the pretensions of *Norskhedspartiet* ("The Party of Norwegianness") at large and claimed to be the spokesman of a truer national tradition. He drew support from the cultured and bureaucratic circles and his followers became known as *Intelligentspartiet* ("The Party of the Intelligentsia"). These created a schism in the Students' Union in 1832 and withdrew to form *Studenterforbundet* ("The Students' Alliance"), launching their own organ, *Vidar*.

The controversy flared up vigorously again in 1834 when Welhaven published his long critical poem, *Norges Dæmring*.[37] In it he ruthlessly impugned what he considered the superficial patriotism of his countrymen, especially that prevailing in *Norskhedspartiet*. He railed at the spirit of braggadocio, ever ready to throw itself into unrestrained

[36] The literature on this controversy is voluminous, but aside from biographies and sketches of the two personalities see especially: G. Gran, *Norges Dæmring*; A. Bugge, *et al., Norges Historie fremstillet for det norske Folk*, vol. vi, pt. i, pp. 238-84; Y. Nielsen, *Norges Historie efter 1814* (3 vols., Chra., 1880-91), vol. iii, pp. 268-315; H. Jæger, *Illustreret norsk Literaturhistorie*, vol. ii, p. 87 *et seq.*; K. Elster, *Illustreret norsk Literaturhistorie* (2 vols., Chra., 1923-24), vol. ii, pp. 1-208; L. Heber, *Norsk Realisme i 1830- og 40-aarene* (Chra., 1914); "*En Selvbiografi af Welhaven*," *Samtiden*, vol. xii, pp. 296-301.

[37] "Norway's Dawnlight." It ran to a length of 75 laborious sonnets. *Cf.* his *Samlede Skrifter* (8 vols., Copenhagen, 1867-69), vol. i, pp. 173-249.

self-congratulation over Norway's marvellous freedom.   In
paying his respects to each of the larger towns he vented
his spleen especially on particularism and local pride.
Christianssand was but " a whale half-dead, yawning lazily
on land."   At Christiania they prated much about liberty
in the manner of the " Enlightenment " but

> In spite of all the Freedom here proclaimed,
> The spirit truly regnant
> Is but a whiff from powdered wig of yore.

His home town, Bergen, was thoroughly absorbed in the
affairs of the counting house.   Trondhjem gloated over its
once great Cathedral, but how, he asked ironically, had
it cared for

> That vandalized temple
> Which heroes arched to a marbled heaven,
> Which the Swede plundered, and which you have—
>   whitewashed.

Nothing held in honor by the self-styled patriots was spared
the acerbity of his pen.
    The storm of disapproval that arose was well-nigh uni-
versal.   Welhaven was threatened with personal injury, and
at a gathering in Øvre Romerike on the 17th of May,
1835, several copies of his poem were formally burned.[38]
Even among his friends in *Intelligentspartiet* only a few
remained steadfast.   Among these was P. A. Munch, whose
career we are to follow in some detail later.   Munch pointed
out that Welhaven had made clear what the prerequisites
for freedom were, and somewhat tauntingly he suggested to
the patriots that Norway may have been unripe for freedom
when it came.   He urged Welhaven to keep on lashing " the

[38] A. Bugge, *et al.*, *Norges Historie fremstillet for det norske Folk*,
vol. vi, pt. i, p. 271.

viper brood " of *Norskhedspartiet* with " whips and scorpions." [39]

Beyond the chief personalities in the controversy we may discern the traditional antagonism in Norwegian life—the old cleavage between *bonde* and bureaucrat.[40] Welhaven and his followers spoke for the burgher and the official, whose cultural roots reached far outside, usually to Denmark, but who — though some were of Danish descent — nevertheless felt themselves to be indisputably Norwegian. It was their traditions Welhaven would respect and preserve; in them he would seek the rudiments with which to help build the culture of the new independent Norway. From this point of view he rejected the uprooting tendencies of his opponents and claimed to be pleading the cause of historical continuity.[41]

Wergeland and his supporters, many of them in *Norskhedspartiet,* spoke for the tradition best represented by the *bonde,* which felt itself more indigenous. The burgher and official classes, thought Wergeland, had given to Danish influence an overwhelming importance in Norwegian life, a circumstance that was particularly unfortunate now when the new national culture was still in a formative period. This culture, according to Wergeland, needed a chance to grow and develop by itself so that it might appropriate more freely and equitably what it desired from various foreign

[39] *Morgenbladet,* 1835, no. 77.

[40] In Norwegian writings there are frequent references to the antagonism between the *bønder* and the bureaucracy (*"Embedsstanden"*) in which the latter term includes not only the civil service proper, but the clergy, the professional groups, and the intelligentsia generally. Collectively and more especially before the rapid growth of modern urban populations, these upper-class elements seemed to the peasant an order generally unsympathetic with his interests; in a measure they were all " bureaucrats " to him.

[41] See his " *Selvbiografi,*" *Samtiden,* vol. xii, p. 300.

influences.   Both Wergeland and Welhaven, it is evident,
were primarily concerned about the best conditions in which
to develop a national culture and both thought a foreign
stimulus desirable.   But Welhaven would approve no violent
break with Danish tradition, while Wergeland felt that the
imperative need was to reduce the scope of the Danish in
favor of other foreign influences.[42]

*   *   *   *   *

The nature of the union of Norway with Sweden in
1814-5 gave the Norwegian patriots much concern from
time to time.   In the new arrangement the foremost symbol
of independence, monarchy itself, had to be shared.   Ostensibly the union was entered upon terms of equality, but there
were reasons to fear that Sweden with her superior power
and resources might contemplate the ultimate absorption of
her weaker colleague.   Norway ought to be on her guard,
it was felt, especially after it became clear that some of the
clauses in the arrangements of 1814-5 were ambiguous.

On several occasions before 1870, Norwegian patriots
sought to guard against the danger of closer union with
Sweden.   In the second regular *Storting* (1818) Flor of
Drammen had taken steps to assert Norway's position of
equality within the union, and the question came prominently to the fore in the 'thirties.   Jonas A. Hielm, a publicist and lawyer, who was sympathetic with *Norskhedspartiet,*
presented several national demands, regarding larger Norwegian representation on the ministerial council at Stockholm and separate consuls to look after Norwegian trading
interests.   He supported the agitation for a separate
merchant flag and for certain insignia in the union flag to
indicate more clearly Norway's position of equality with
Sweden.

---

[42] It is interesting to note that on his foreign tour, Wergeland visited,
not Denmark and Germany, but England and France.

In 1836 Karl Johan lent some color to Hielm's fears of Swedish encroachment when he precipitated a crisis by unexpectedly dissolving the *Storting* (in the face of foreign complications).[43]   At its next session this body successfully impeached Minister Løvenskiold for not opposing the dissolution, and there loomed ahead the possibility of a long parliamentary struggle.   But the *Storting's* assertiveness subsided, and in his closing years the king got along much better with his Norwegian subjects.   Oscar I, on his accession in 1844, further conciliated Norwegian feeling by his choice of several liberal ministers and by making concessions on the flag issue and on the question of diplomatic procedure.

The *Storting's* tractability after 1837 grew out of a domestic realignment.   Since 1814 the leading element in the *Storting,* the bureaucracy, had guarded the constitution and objected to any royal encroachment.   The crisis of 1836-7 seemed to demand the keenest vigilance.   But at this very moment, as we have seen, the *bønder* wrested from official hands the control of local government (1837).   Now the bureaucracy began to tone down its opposition to the king, and even sought the aid of his ministers to check the turbulent "Norwegianness" of the *bønder.*   Concerned about the danger to their entrenched position, the upper classes showed a willingness to help sabotage parts of the constitution.   There developed a tendency, well expressed in the writings of men like Dunker and Ræder, to exalt the power of the monarchy.   Very striking was the change in attitude toward paragraph 79 in the constitution, a section which made a proposal law in spite of the royal veto if it were passed by three successive *Stortings.*   Where formerly this clause had stood as a bulwark against royal encroachment it now seemed an unwarranted check on the monarchy.   It is worth noting that when Minister Vogt was charged with

[43] Bull, *et al., Det norske folks Liv og Historie,* vol. viii, pp. 408-9.

transgressing on the power of the *Storting,* some of the results of his impeachment (1845) were quite repugnant to many in the upper classes. The report of a joint committee on union affairs (1844) also showed a desire to work more closely with Swedish authorities, a tendency now accentuated by the growing movement of Scandinavianism.

*   *   *   *   *

Scandinavianism, the movement to promote more intimate cultural ties and draw somewhat closer the political bonds between the several northern peoples,[44] had its center of gravity in Denmark and was brought on by the Schleswig-Holstein question. Scandinavianism like nationalism, benefitted from the romantic movement of which we are to speak in the next chapter. Romanticism often extolled the antiquity of the north as an undifferentiated unity. To take a single instance: the opening number of *Nordisk Literatur-Tidende* (" Northern Literary Tidings ") at Copenhagen in 1846 addressed itself to " all men of the north " and proposed as a rallying standard the glorious old *norrøn* tongue. Scandinavianism flourished most among university circles [45] and at first it was pretty much restricted to these, but as the question of the Duchies became more acute it took on a political tinge and statesmen of the three northern countries had to take cognizance of it.

Norwegian patriots could not help but feel that Scandinavianism involved a threat to national self-sufficiency and national independence. The existence of three separate peoples in the north was an artificiality if the true nationality was a unity of the three. J. Dahl's periodical, *Idun,* recognized that the three northern peoples had some, though

[44] For a general treatment of it see J. Clausen, *Skandinavismen historisk fremstillet* (Copenhagen, 1900).

[45] It inspired in 1854 the scholarly organ, *Nordisk Universitets-Tidsskrift. Cf.* vol. i, pt. iii, p. 75.

not all, things in common, and took pains to say at the
outset that no one nationality was sufficient unto itself.[46]
In the same vein August Sohlman, eager to promote the
" spiritual " unity of the north, urged each people to gather
strength from the root of the common " northern "
nationality.[47]

The nonchalance with which the proponents of Scandinavianism designated certain matters as " northern " tended
to annoy the more patriotic Norwegian scholars, and their
support of the movement was less hearty than that of
colleagues in Sweden and Denmark.   They disliked to have
Scandinavianism, or Swedish and Danish romanticism too
for that matter, extol the primitive life of the north as one
undifferentiated entity; they resented having the prized old
Eddic poetry and the venerable sagas lumped together under
the generic term " northern " literature.   Even the rich
folklore just being recovered in Norway might have to be
shared with others.   A Danish reviewer, commenting favor-
ably on Asbjørnsen's Fairy Tales, called them " a product
of the popular-northern (*folkelig-nordiske*) spirit "[48] and a
Swedish opinion two decades later observed that Asbjørnsen's stories seemed to suggest " not the relationship, but the
essential identity," of the two northern peoples.[49]

For a brief period Norwegian intellectuals and publicists
did take wholeheartedly to Scandinavianism, namely in connection with the Dano-German crisis of 1848-9.[50]   Most of
them then dropped their anti-Danish apprehensions, realized
more keenly the unity of the north, and came to feel that

[46] " *Det nationale i Literaturen,*" *Idun,* 1851, no. 1.

[47] *Nordisk Tidsskrift,* 1852-3, p. 233.

[48] *Nordisk Literatur-Tidende,* 1846, p. 156.

[49] " *Det Svenske Aftonblad og Asbjørnsens Huldre-eventyr,*" *Vort
Land,* 1867, no. 15.

[50] *Cf.* the example of P. A. Munch. *Infra,* pp. 147-50.

Denmark was fighting the cause of all.[51]   But when the crisis had passed their interest in Scandinavianism declined. At all times, even when giving it most support, they were apt to think of Scandinavianism in terms of coöperation rather than of union, for they were reluctant to have national lines erased.   Hence they were concerned to justify a measure of diversity [52] and to urge a mutual respect for the characteristic in each nation.[53]   Possibly there did actually exist a common northern folk spirit, wrote Sophus Bugge, but if so it had at least manifested itself uniquely in each of the three peoples.[54]

*   *   *   *   *

The sentiment favoring closer political and cultural ties between Norway and Sweden, while it was really as old as the political union, had at first not been influential in Norway.   We have noted above what apprehensions it aroused in Norwegian circles in the first decades of the new arrangement.   But toward the mid-century the sentiment took a somewhat practical turn—promoted in the late 'thirties by the realignment in Norwegian domestic politics,[55] and later by the vogue of romanticism and Scandinavianism—and for a time it took on the formality of an organized movement, which we shall call unionism.   Naturally it centered in Swedish circles but it gained many adherents also among the official classes at Christiania.   Its point of departure was the dynastic tie between the two countries and when some of

[51] *Cf.* A. Krogvig, *Fra det nationale gjennembruds Tid* (Chra., 1915), p. 267. Jørgen Moe to his brother, Ole, April 17, 1848; *Chra.-Post.*, 1848, no. 11.

[52] J. S. Welhaven, "*For Samhold i Norden*," *Saml. Skr.*, vol. vi, p. 302.

[53] *Cf.* P. A. Munch, *Samlede Afhandlinger* (4 vols., Chra., 1873-76), vol. ii, pp. 42, 55, 58; vol. iii, p. 215; Munch, *Lærde Brev*, vol. i, pp. 153, 159, 211, 230, 353. See also *Stort. Forh.*, 1857, vol. i, no. 3, pp. 121-2.

[54] *Maal og Minne*, 1909, p. 55. Sept. 4, 1856 to Sv. Grundtvig.

[55] *Supra*, pp. 35-6.

its energies crystallized into a regular organization in 1851 the latter was named *Karl Johansforbundet* ("The Karl Johan's Alliance"), in honor of Bernadotte who had established the union in 1814-5. Its members met from time to time to extol his work. In 1858, on the initiative of P. A. Munch, a branch of the society was established in Christiania.

In 1859, unionist sentiment became deeply involved in the *statholder* question. That office bore a stigma of inferiority to many Norwegians who had long been anxious to abolish it. A new proposal to that effect was passed that year and the general expectation was that the king would sign it. But Karl XV, being something of a militarist and a unionist, failed to do so when certain acrimonious objections were suddenly raised in the Swedish *Rigsdag* (Parliament). The *Storting* in turn was aroused and there loomed a crisis of the first magnitude. But Frederik Stang was chosen minister (1861) and did much to quiet the situation.

The zealous Norwegian patriot of the mid-century was bound to view any growth in unionist sentiment with some apprehension. If the ties between Sweden and Norway became too close, Sweden's influence would surely predominate. What readjustments a patriot might make may be seen in the case of P. A. Munch. As a good liberal, he thought Sweden's constitution the most medieval in Europe [56] and he opposed particularly the "egoistic, antiquated, ultra-conservative" Swedish nobility.[57] Apropos of Scandinavianism he thought the abolition of the Swedish nobility might well be the prerequisite to any closer coöpera-

[56] Munch, *Saml. Afh.*, vol. iii, p. 575.

[57] K. H. Hermes, *De europæiske Staters Historie* (2 vols., Chra., 1847-8), vol. ii, p. 523. Munch wrote pages 511-28 on the three northern kingdoms.

tion among the three northern kingdoms.[58]   But a certain shift in the European diplomatic situation by the middle of the 'fifties forced a reconsideration of the attitude toward Sweden.   The Crimean War aroused the traditional hostility to Russia and many feared lest the colossus of the east, balked in the Black Sea, might strike for an ice-free port through Finmark and violate Norwegian territory.[59]   This was no time for national assertiveness and some Norwegians now saw more clearly " their relations with other peoples." [60] Among them was P. A. Munch, and while he preferred to have Norway and Sweden remain distinct and fight side by side against the eastern despotism, he conceded that under certain safeguards he might favor a " real " union of Scandinavian states.[61] A closer rapprochement with Swedish circles then seemed desirable ; Munch spoke in flattering terms of the ruling dynasty,[62] and became actively interested, as we have noted, in *Karl Johansforbundet.*

Munch's case was by no means an isolated one.   Whenever Scandinavianism or unionism flourished, things appeared rather confused to Norwegian patriots.   While many of their countrymen were proclaiming that Norway must lose herself in a larger unity, the patriots could not help but feel that she needed most to develop every possible confidence in her newly-won national independence.[63]   Then too, material

[58] Munch, *Lærde Brev,* vol. i, p. 286.   May 31, 1848 to Krieger.

[59] The western Powers were interested, and lengthy negotiations in 1855 led them to guarantee the neutrality of Sweden-Norway.   *Cf.* P. Knaplund, " *Nye oplysninger om novembertraktatens forhistorie,*" (*norsk) Historisk Tidsskrift,* vol. v, pt. vi, pp. 213-58.

[60] *Aftenbladet,* 1855, no. 1.

[61] Munch, *Saml. Afh.,* vol. iii, p. 600.

[62] *Cf.* the dedicatory page of his *Norges Konge-Sagaer* (Chra., 1857-59).

[63] In the nineteenth century, Norwegians spoke quite freely of their country as independent, having in mind the circumstances that when the tie with Denmark was dissolved, a national regeneration led to the

progress had become the order of the day and its promotion seemed to depend not so much on the development of what was indigenous as on the facility with which the latest mechanical advances were appropriated, no matter whether their origins were domestic or alien. The basic trend might well be toward the cosmopolitan and there was talk of keeping the struggle for nationality within limits. M. J. Monrad, in his authoritative voice, spoke of being shut out from humanity by the "one-sidedness" of national-ity.[64] In the face of such sentiment it was rather puzzling to know whether Fate had intended that the final nationality in the north should be Norwegian or Scandinavian.

In the 'sixties Scandinavianism (at any rate until 1864) and unionism came to be matters of first importance. Political life seemed to be moving in the direction of unifica-tion or federalism. Italy proceeded along that road in 1859-60 and 1866 and the Germanies took the same path in 1864 and 1866. In America, the national union triumphed in the Civil War of 1861-5. Two years later, Austria and Hungary, in much the same position as Norway and Sweden, arranged their *Ausgleich*. What about Scandinavia?

Prominent voices in Norway too spoke in terms of a larger consolidation and thus helped to undermine confidence in national independence. In 1864 Schweigaard, the fore-most economist, believed Destiny intended that related nations should combine,[65] and certainly that was the drift of sentiment in the *Storting* committee on union affairs which

proclamation of independence and the choice of a king, and when the country entered the union with Sweden it did so, they felt, without im-pairing the essentials of its independence. In this study we shall occa-sionally employ the word independence as they used it.

[64] "*Om Theater og Nationalitet,*" *Norsk Tidsskrift for Videnskab og Litteratur*, vol. vii, pp. 9-10.

[65] E. Hertzberg, *Professor Schweigaard i hans offentlige Virksomhed 1832-70* (Chra., 1883), p. 50.

in 1867 reported a project favoring closer ties with Sweden.
Likewise some of the newer historians — particularly T.
H. Aschehoug and M. Birkeland — developed a positive
interest in the oft-maligned centuries of the Danish union
and took the attitude that their influence on Norway had been
in some ways distinctly beneficial.[66]

* * * * *

But while the enervating tendencies of Scandinavianism
and unionism were prominently to the fore, there were in the
latter ' fifties and in the 'sixties many pronounced manifestations of Norwegian national feeling.   The national
spirit, remarked Vinje, was now awakened with all " good
folk; " [67] in the words of another, there was then a craving
in the Norwegian people, " a striving toward its own which
demands satisfaction." [68]   Some of its urge was directed
against the foreign influence, Swedish as well as Danish.
A little manifesto,[69] appearing in 1859, called upon Norwegians to realize clearly that they were a distinct nation
possessing their own customs, their own language, and a
distinctive folk character.   The pamphlet sounded a call to
action; it was time to press for the elimination of all foreign
elements from Norway's public life.   The sponsors of this
brochure came from circles similar to those which in
November of the same year organized *Det Norske Selskab*
(" The Norwegian Society ") to encourage " nationalism in
literature and art "—more specifically, to oppose the Düssel-
dorf tradition in painting and the Danish influence on the
stage.[70]   The initiative in forming this society had been

---

[66] T. H. Aschehoug, *Statsforfatningen i Norge og Danmark indtil 1814*
(Chra., 1866), p. 592 *et seq.*; M. Birkeland, *Historiske Skrifter* (3 vols.,
Chra., 1919-25), vol. i, pp. 101-113.

[67] *Nordmandsforbundet*, 1926, p. 458.

[68] *Chra.-Post.*, 1858, no. 320.

[69] *Det Unge Norge, 17de Mai, 1859.*

[70] *Cf.* H. Jæger, *The Life of Henrik Ibsen* (London, 1890), pp. 111-12.

taken by Bjørnson and Ibsen, the former becoming president, the latter vice-president. Enthusiasm ran high for a time and there were plans to have branches in Bergen and Trondhjem.[71] While the organization never became as important as the founders had hoped it would, it took a decisive part in the final successful assault on the Danish theater in Christiania. In 1859 also, Bjørnson penned his *Ja, vi elsker dette Landet* ("Yes, we Love this Country") which, somewhat modified later, became universally preferred as Norway's national song.

At the close of the decade there was a strong nationalist current also in the *Storting*. In 1857 this body rejected two projects—one regarding tariffs and the other pertaining to judicial decisions—intended to draw a bit closer the bonds of union with Sweden. In the fall of 1859 (the *statholder* question was an issue) some of the liberal members in the *Storting* formed the short-lived organization called *Reformforeningen* ("The Reform Association"), which sought among other things to promote Norway's national interests and maintain her equality within the union.[72]

When unionist tendencies proved strong again in the 'sixties, a group of younger patriots at Christiania were emboldened to assert renewed confidence in their nationality. Ludvig Daae admitted that the smaller states felt very much depressed, but he held that their feeling was not justified. Norway would again, as of old, he felt certain, take her respected place among the nations, provided she did not lose confidence in herself.[73] It was not necessary, wrote Ludvig Kr. Daa, to regard political consolidation as inevitable. The folk uniquenesses were beyond the reach of human will; fashioned basically by natural environment, they were not

[71] Ludvig Daae, *Stortingserindringer* (Oslo, 1930—), p. 62.

[72] *Ibid.*, p. 15 *et seq.*

[73] *Ill. Nyhbl.*, 1866, p. 142.

erasable by the arrangements of man. Daa consoled his countrymen with the thought that as long as Dovre Mountain and the Northern Sea existed the people of Norway would not cease to be Norwegian.[74]   J. E. Sars set to work on the Danish period which the romanticists had largely avoided, insisting that it be studied as a very important period of national growth.   Sars was one of that group of younger spirits,[75] who in 1867 gathered up the traditions from 1859 of *Det Unge Norge* and *Det Norske Selskab* and launched the short-lived patriotic organ, *Vort Land* ("Our Country"), to champion a more assertive national stand in public affairs.   The patriotic and liberal elements helped to arouse the opposition groups generally to a sense of the danger that the project of 1867 for closer union with Sweden might pass, and in the face of a strong nationalist opposition the proposal was decisively defeated in 1871.

The broader national developments in Norway after 1870 are beyond the limits of our study.   In retrospect we may observe that whenever romanticism was in the ascendant it gave direct stimulus to Norwegian national feeling, and also to Scandinavianism and unionism.   These served directly to confuse Norwegian national feeling, but in so far as they operated to place that feeling on the defensive, they ultimately helped to develop its power to resist any threatened encroachment by the stronger kingdom in the Suedo-Norwegian union.

[74] L. K. Daa, *Om Nationaliteternes Udvikling* (Chra., 1869), pp. 224-5.
[75] The others were Carl and H. E. Berner, J. C. Krogh and W. Werenskjold.

CHAPTER II

ROMANTICISM IN NORWAY

ANYONE who has to be concerned with romanticism is soon aware that this comprehensive movement is not readily defined in a brief statement.[1] It is of interest to remember that Fr. Schlegel, one of the great romanticists, wasted 125 pages of manuscript in trying to explain the word romantic.[2] The difficulties connected therewith arise because romanticism affected so many phases of cultural life and implied such widely different things to different people.

Romanticism is very broadly defined as the cultural movement which was in the ascendant during the interval between the "Enlightenment" of the eighteenth century and the realism and naturalism of the latter portion of the nineteenth century. It was a reaction against the ideals and the attitudes of the age of rationalism and therefore it rejected the unquestioned dominance of reason, and exalted emotion. It developed a deep sentimental attachment to nature and interested itself in common men and common things. It felt drawn to the life of childhood, a world of memories and of longing. It idealized certain periods of history, especially the Middle Ages. In facing the deeper problems of life, it turned from the rational approach to place more confidence in imagination, intuition and faith.

[1] There are two compilations of definitions from the literary standpoint by A. O. Lovejoy, "On the Discrimination of Romanticisms," *Publications of the Modern Language Association*, vol. xxxix, pp. 229-53 and P. Kaufman, "Defining Romanticism: A Survey and a Program," *Modern Language Notes*, vol. xl, pp. 193-204.

[2] *Cambridge Modern History*, vol. x, p. 396.

The aspect of romanticism of most concern to us—since we are to deal primarily with the works of scholars and publicists—is the philosophical. So far as it was a philosophy, romanticism aimed to synthesize the diverse phenomena of life and to find an all-embracing unity. Its greatest desire, as Coleridge put it, was " to behold and know something *great,* something *one* and *indivisible.*" [3] In line with this desire it premised the immanent and transcendant Idea as a vast connective, interpenetrating all existence, and assigning every phenomenon of life to its proper place. But the realm of the Idea could be apprehended fully only through the non-rational faculties.

From this premise of the Idea, in part, romanticism came to have a very high regard for history and the great heroic figures of the past, and for poetry, especially folk poetry. The poet and the hero were the seers who relayed revelation from on high, the intermediaries through whom, as one writer put it, the Idea entered the realm of the human. [4] The world of Idea was disclosed to the bard and the poet in a measure denied to more ordinary men, and its demands were most adequately fulfilled by the great hero. [5] In a sense, history was but the story of the heroes; Fr. Schlegel thought it could be written in the biographies of the great human figures, and Carlyle actually made the attempt in his *Heroes and Hero Worship.* The rise and the fall of historical forces were but the pulsation of the great Idea, " the peaceful measured breathing of the world spirit." [6] From it came the " inner drive " which prepared the great

[3] A. E. Powell, *The Romantic Theory of Poetry* (London, 1926), p. 4.

[4] K. Borries, *Die Romantik und die Geschichte* (Berlin, 1925), pp. 6, 151.

[5] Otto Sylwan, *et al., Svenska Litteraturens Historia* (2nd ed., Stockholm, 1929), vol. ii, p. 6.

[6] K. Borries, *op. cit.,* p. 216.

events and epochs.[7]   Everything had its intended form, its
Idea, and toward this norm it kept striving.   All creation,
wrote the folklorist, Jørgen Moe, in a somewhat revealing
context, was enchained but struggling to develop in forms
that might correspond to their intention, that is, to the Idea.[8]
We must mention briefly how the romantic interest in
history gave further impetus to nationalism.   Where the
eighteenth century thought of historical forces in terms of
the sudden and cataclysmic, romanticism viewed them as
organic, and developed an appreciation of historical continuity.   This thought could be applied to individual nationalities to give them the dignity of a long historical tradition.
As previously noted, romanticism tended to center attention
upon the most brilliant period of a nation's past; it might
seem that at such a time the Idea of the nationality had
attained its most adequate expression.   Then we note also
that the premise of the Idea supplied a profound intellectual
justification for nationalism.   For a nationality, like any
other thing, had its Idea, its norm, whose perfection it strove
to fulfill, and that perfection required, of course, the status
of freedom.   How comforting then, especially in the case
of suppressed nationalities, to know that their struggles for
freedom were part of the Great Plan contemplated by the
all-embracing Idea.

In speaking of our period as that of romanticism and of
certain individuals as romanticists, we do not wish to imply
that the age was entirely lacking in other intellectual currents.
We mean only that among educated and cultured people
generally, the widely prevailing interpretation of the facts of
life, the one that gave the age its tone and color, was
romantic.   Relatively few individuals worked out to com-

[7] *Ibid.*, p. 147 *et seq.*

[8] A. Krogvig, *Fra det nationale gjennembruds Tid*, pp. 176-77.   Letter
in the autumn of 1839 to Asbjørnsen.

pleteness the romantic interpretation, but most intellectuals of the period accepted in varying degree the fundamental premises of romanticism and helped themselves to what they needed, much or little, of its logic.   In this regard our study will present wide personal differences.   Jørgen Moe and Rudolf Keyser were thoroughly imbued with the romanticist ideology, and one should perhaps add to this group also P. A. Munch.   Aasen too had much of it, though discernibly less.   Although Asbjørnsen had relatively little of it, some of the results of his labors were widely acclaimed by romanticists and his works often were important for romanticism.

*   *   *   *   *

A number of romanticist tendencies developed even in the eighteenth century.   The age which so exalted reason did not on that account always starve the emotions or shun the mysterious.   It is sufficient to recall the widespread interest in free-masonry, in mesmerism, in animal magnetism, or the ever-widening emotional stream of pietism, which influenced several who later became conspicuous as romanticists, for example, Tieck, Steffens, Oehlenschlæger and Herder.   There was an unmistakable romanticist trend in many eighteenth-century phenomena such as the Rousseauean yearning for the primitive simplicity of a "state of nature," the admiration for the life of the noble savage, the flutter of interest in Percy's *Reliques* and in medieval minstrelsy, Horace Walpole's revival of Gothic architecture, Beckford's *Vathek* with its rank orientalism and—the thing that most interests us here since it directly anticipated an important aspect of romanticism in Norway—a lively concern for the ancient Norse mythology which has been expressively spoken of as a " northern " renaissance.[9]

[9] A. Blanck, *Den nordiska renässansen i sjuttonhundratalets litteratur* (Stockholm, 1911) ; P. Van Tiegham, " *La mythologie et l'ancienne poésie*

The interest in this mythology became widespread. In England, Gray, Warton and Percy in making fragments of Old Norse poetry known to their readers, opened a fresh field to English literature. / A general interest in the antiquity of the north was aroused by the Genevan-born Paul Henri Mallet (1730-1807) with his *Introduction a l'histoire de Dannemarc* (1755).[10] Mallet prepared his work when he lived for some years at Copenhagen, which, with its abundance of records from Iceland, became the center of interest in Scandinavian antiquities. There developed a lively activity in transcribing and editing Old Norse records. In 1757 Markussøn put out a smaller saga collection and in 1775 came an edition of *Gunlaugsaga;* Snorre's great work, for which Gerhard Schøning prepared the Latin and Jon Olafsen the Danish text, appeared in 1776; two years later Jon Erichsen arranged the Danish version for H. Einarsson's edition of *Kongs-skugg-sio* ("The King's Mirror"). A definitive edition of the Edda began to appear in 1787 (completed in 1828). In 1786 Thorkelin made transcriptions of the Anglo-Saxon work, *Beowulf,*[11] and the same year Johnstone published *The Chronicle of Man.* The story of the north was becoming known also through the ambitious histories by Suhm, Schøning and Lagerbring.

This revival of interest in the saga period beyond a doubt recovered a distinguished cultural inheritance, about which the ideas were at first very hazy. It was, to begin with, an undifferentiated "northern" revival; Mallet wrote rather loosely (1756) on the mythology and the poetry of "the Celts and particularly the ancient Scandinavians." Klop-

---

scandinaves dans la littérature européenne au XVIIIe siécle," Edda, vol. xiii, pp. 38-65.

[10] Percy later issued an English translation with notes, entitled *Northern Antiquities* (London, 1770).

[11] Though he did not publish any of it before 1815.

stock and other German writers entered upon this terrain with only the vaguest distinctions between a Celtic and a Germanic element. The first person to perceive clearly that it was necessary to separate out a British (Celtic), an Anglo-Saxon, a German, and a Scandinavian heritage was Herder, and to him more than to anyone else the north is indebted for being the first to see the narrower but more definite outline of a northern mythology proper.[12]

This enthusiastic interest in the antiquity of the north foreshadowed a trait that was to characterize romanticism in general, namely, a dislike for the Latin tradition. It is interesting to note that Herder at Weimar took steps to reduce the scope of that tradition in the curriculums of the elementary schools.[13] This antipathy became so marked a feature of the later movement that some have characterized romanticism as the great emancipation of the German spirit from "the alien world of Latin classicism." [14] This interpretation has been voiced from time to time in Scandinavia,[15] occasionally in the modified form of an hostility to the "French" spirit and to the dominance of "French" taste.[16]

*   *   *   *   *

When romanticism from the Germanies reached the north, Copenhagen was the political capital of Denmark-Norway

[12] F. Paasche, "*Herder og den Norröne Digtning,*" *Maal og Minne,* vol. ii, pp. 121-2.

[13] C. J. H. Hayes, "Contributions of Herder to the Doctrine of Nationalism," *American Historical Review,* vol. xxxii, pp. 732-33.

[14] *Cambridge Modern History,* vol. x, p. 395; cf. L. Reynaud, *Le Romantisme: Ses origines anglo-germaniques* (Paris, 1926), pp. 114-5.

[15] Cf. Welhaven, *Saml. Skr.,* vol. ii, pp. 67-68 and for a more recent example, C. D. Marcus, "*Romantikkens filosofi,*" *Nordisk Tidsskrift,* 1907, p. 499.

[16] Munch, *Saml. Afh.,* vol. ii, p. 302; L. Eskeland, "Ole Vig," *Syn og Segn,* vol. xxx, p. 54.

and the cultural center of both kingdoms. There Norwegians and Danes participated indiscriminately in the political and cultural life of the realm. If Oehlenschlæger and Grundtvig were Danes, Henrich Steffens, who brought German romanticism fullblown to the Danish capital with his lectures (1802-3) on Schelling's *Naturphilosophie,* was a Norwegian. Nevertheless, romanticism penetrated very gradually into Norway proper. For a time after the separation from Denmark her littérateurs were only of second or third rank and there was no outstanding figure whose prestige and influence could place romanticism indisputably in the ascendant. Side by side with the newer tendencies, the traditions of the " Enlightenment " lingered on—in fact the liberal impulses released in the early 'thirties may temporarily have strengthened those traditions.

While romanticism registered no spectacular overturn, it was making its way. The reading public apparently read many works of Danish and German romanticists.[17] It was in their spirit that Mauritz Hansen, the country's lone novelist of any talent, wrote a number of entertaining and popular historical novels. Meanwhile Jacob Aall, in some ways a noble example of what was best in the ideals of the " Enlightenment," showed that he was responsive to romanticist influence in connection with his growing interest in saga history. In the decade of the 'thirties evidences of the new influence became more pronounced. Its manifestations in the field of historical scholarship we are later to observe in the work of the new historians, Keyser and Munch. In literature too it was more positively represented. Henrik Wergeland, brought up in a home with a pronounced eighteenth-century atmosphere, was, in his formative years very deeply influenced by romanticism.[18] In his literary

[17] *Cf.* Edv. Bull, *et al., Det norske folks Liv og Historie,* vol. ix, p. 272.
[18] *Cf.* H. Beyer, *Henrik Wergeland og Henrich Steffens* (Chra., 1920) ;

works, rationalism and romanticism were often blended
(though the proportions from one time to another were not
necessarily equal or constant) ; in one passage he could be
as representative of the earlier movement, as he was of the
later in another.   Likewise, the leaders of *Intelligentspartiet*
were influenced by romanticism — some in the following
decade became distinguished as romantic littérateurs, and
this was true in spite of their professed determination to
get away from the unrealities of the older romanticism in
favor of a pronounced empiricism.[19]   It may be noted that
they felt much akin to the " Young Germany " of Heine's
day, but the realism they professed was the " realism of
romanticism;" it was not naturalism, not the portrayal of the
real in its several phases, but a disregard of " incidentals,"
and an emphasis upon those aspects which seemed a part of
the " essential," the " ideal."   It should be recalled that in
some of its phases romanticism was quite concerned about
the real and the concrete, though it be only to exalt
" characteristic " qualities.

*   *   *   *   *

However, romanticism in Norway was to be most distinguished, not as literary but as national romanticism—to
borrow the expressive phrase of the original, as *national-
romantikken*. National romanticism, being vitally concerned
with the nation, its past as well as its present, and seeking,
in conformity with the romanticist ideology, to determine
(and also to extol) the " primeval " or the " characteristic "
—this national romanticism was no quixotic *ritter-romantik*

Valborg Erichsen, *Henrik Wergeland i hans forhold til Henrich Steffens*
(Chra., 1920) ; cf. A. H. Winsness, " *Wergeland og Stagnelius*," *Edda*,
vol. xiii, pp. 161-80; A. H. Winsness, " *Var Wergeland Rationalist?* "
Edda, vol. xx, pp. 215-23.

[19] Cf. L. Heber, *Norsk realisme i 1830- og 40-aarene, passim*; " *Dansk
og norsk æstetik fra 1830-aarene i europæisk belysning*," *Edda*, vol.
viii, pp. 288-324.

and no mere dilettante search for literary themes among the common people, but a broad cultural movement that concentrated attention on the folk or nation. In point of time the literary phase of romanticism in Norway was somewhat ahead of the pronounced national phase. In the same way it seems also to have been the first to show signs of recession; at any rate there are forewarnings of the realism that was to flourish after the 'sixties, in Camilla Collett's *Amtmandens Døtre* ("The Governor's Daughters") which appeared in 1854-5 and in Olaf Skavlan's parody (1857) of Ibsen's national romanticist treatment in *Gildet paa Solhoug* ("The Feast at Solhoug").

National romanticism rose to remarkable intensity in the 'forties. Its interest in the nation implied an interest in the Norwegian peasant, and the suddenness and completeness with which this interest spread among the cultured elements was surprising in view of the widespread renewed hostility toward the peasant after 1837 when the latter had successfully challenged official control of the local government. Nevertheless in the first half of the 'forties the cultured groups generally turned about to bestow their sympathetic attention upon the *bonde*. The occasion for this turncoating was the work of the folklorists; Jørgen Moe published a collection of ballads in 1840, and in conjunction with Asbjørnsen he edited a series of folk tales (1841-44). The reorientation turned largely on the fact that through the folklore the cultured were learning to know a new peasant. Instead of the boisterous boor, whom they had been accustomed to hear challenging traditional authority in the *Storting* they became acquainted with a different peasant, a gentle creature who was the heir of ancient song and story, the faithful conserver of popular traditions (though in actual fact it seems that the conservation of the traditions was due less to the superior *bønder* as a class, than to the inferior servants and cotters).[20]

A serious interest in the peasant was typical of romanticism generally. The peasant's life, to the romanticist, seemed philosophically and esthetically complete in the circle of tradition, intuition and faith. He had that quality which the romanticists so often acclaimed—the naïveté of the child-like mind that saw everything simply and directly.[21] Little given to rationalness and without sophistication, he knew nothing of the "prosaic and mathematical laws" that governed natural phenomena.[22] Hence it was that he created a world of fancy, the world of folklore, enjoyed by the child mind and the romanticist alike. Unable to account rationally for the eerie wastes of the high plateau or the queer reverberating voices among the mountains, the peasant peopled these regions with elves and fairies and monsters, some good, others evil, according to the forbidding mien of this towering mountain or the placid vista of yon winding valley. This world, simple and direct, was without the subtleties of reason. The folk tales, wrote Moe, "scorn reflection;" in them all was graphic and their ability to objectify was exceeded only by their "moving naïveté."[23]

Convinced that in their own day the nation was most adequately represented in the peasant, the intellectuals of the mid-century made a serious effort to understand better his ways and traditions. Artists, authors and collectors, as if they were a troop under one command,[24] turned their backs on the towns and marched to the hills, seeking the un-

[20] Edv. Bull, *et al., Det norske folks Liv og Historie,* vol. viii, p. 90.

[21] M. Deutschbein, *Das Wesen des Romantischen* (Cöthen, 1921), pp. 55-6.

[22] *N. Tids. f. Vid. og Litt.,* vol. ii, p. 126.

[23] J. Moe, *Samlede Skrifter* (2 vols., Chra., 1877), vol. ii, p. 13.

[24] H. Jæger, *Literaturhistoriske Pennetegninger* (Copenhagen, 1878), p. 219.

corrupted peasant and the charming chalet girl, hoping to pursue the fairy *Huldre,* or visit the subterranean dwarf folk. Like buzzing bees they swarmed among the valleys and up the hill sides [25] looking for every vestige of peasant life and custom that might reveal the qualities of the Norwegian nationality, while an artist like Adolph Tidemand depicted this attractive peasant life on his broad brown-toned canvases. Collectors underwent both discomfort and personal sacrifice in order to assemble folk tales and folk songs, fairy tales and ballads, proverbs and nursery riddles, and most significant of all, perhaps, to copy samples of the numerous dialects. Convinced that such activity belonged to their " time's great performance " these romanticists pressed on, supremely confident that, because it was national, the task of drawing forth anything belonging to the people was its own justification.[26]

* * * * *

The expectation that a closer acquaintance with the peasant and his ways would net a clearer picture of the nation in its historical as well as its contemporary aspect [27] was part of the romanticist veneration for what was old and traditional. Somewhat in the manner in which their eighteenth-century predecessors had waxed enthusiastic over life in a state of nature, the romanticists felt that individual peoples once had their day of innocence and purity [28] before they became contaminated by foreign contacts. The tangible remains of this golden age of national perfection were the customs and traditions still flourishing among the peasants. If some

---

[25] H. Jæger, *Illustreret norsk Literaturhistorie,* vol. ii, p. 309.

[26] P. C. Asbjørnsen and J. Moe, *Norske Folke-eventyr* (Chra., 1841-44), p. vi; *cf. Alm. n. Maanedskr.,* vol. ii, p. 477.

[27] *Cf. " Studenter Samfundets Nordiske Fest til Fædrenes Minde,"* *Den Const.,* 1847, no. 15.

[28] *Cf.* H. Jæger, *Literaturhistoriske Pennetegninger,* pp. 158-9.

practices had in time been reduced to mere vestiges of their former sway, they seemed therefore only the more precious. The romanticists were truly disturbed by the extent to which the Norwegian nationality had been contaminated by long centuries of alien rule and influence. After the Reformation, a foreign clergy and bureaucracy, and also a foreign burgher element, had introduced and established in Norway a culture, which was quite " foreign " to the folk spirit; [29] one that kept the Norwegian branch of the human spirit from " coming into its own." [30]   Naturally this influence in time had been absorbed by the urban element of domestic origin as well.   To make a bad situation worse this influence more recently was spreading from the towns to the neighboring rural areas, [31] a circumstance that on occasion made the romanticists pessimistic. Some countrysides, said Munch, were now so denationalized that their people had become less Norwegian than the distant inhabitants of the Faroe Islands. [32]   Vinje spoke of the bureaucracy as " colonists," [33] and an editor of Moe's ballad collection observed that it was very difficult to sustain any " Norwegian life " in the Danish part of the population. [34]

Mindful of the danger to which the Norwegian nationality had been exposed by the official, urban and intellectual classes, the romanticists turned eagerly to the peasant to find that in all essentials he had preserved his national identity intact; [35] he had maintained the folk uniqueness with

[29] *Den norske Folkeskole*, vol. iii, pp. 106-7 ; *cf. Krydseren*, 1852, no. 142.

[30] *Dølen*, 1859, no. 20.

[31] I. Aasen, *Skrifter i Samling* (3 vols., Chra. and Copenhagen, 1912), vol. iii, p. 96.

[32] Munch, *Saml. Afh.*, vol. iii, p. 400.

[33] *Syn og Segn*, vol. xxiv, p. 237.

[34] J. Moe, *Norske Viser og Stev* (Chra., 1870), *Forord*.

[35] H. Wergeland, *Digterværker og prosaiske Skrifter*, vol. v, p. 169-70; *cf. Alm. n. Maanedskr.*, vol. ii, p. 480; *Maal og Minne*, 1924, p. 147.

least corruption.[36] The romanticists were fascinated to think that when face to face with him they were in the immediate presence of their true nationality. What struck them most, it would seem, was the sense of this immediacy ("*umiddel-barhed*").[37] Hence they sought to get closer to the "people," closer to that life " which so marvelously brought one back to the immediateness of a bygone age." [38]

The romanticists liked to think that the nationality of the peasant was still close to its primeval purity. In his presence, it was said, one might feel again the pulse beat of northern antiquity.[39] He had kept the old national character and the old traditions almost unaltered for a thousand years, down to the very threshold of the present.[40] His literature was a direct continuation of the old mythology,[41] and his ballads, as they spirited one away across the centuries, brought one face to face with saga days.[42] The peasant embodied the sum of Norwegian freedom; [43] never having bent the knee to feudalism, he took naturally to the new independence in 1814.[44] Just as he had been the real kernel of the nation in antiquity, so around him must be built the political society of modern Norway.[45]

Their eagerness to identify the peasant's modern nation-

[36] *Cf. Krydseren*, 1852, Aug. 28.

[37] *Cf. Bergenske Blade*, 1848, no. 5.

[38] *Maal og Minne*, 1909, p. 58. S. Bugge to Sv. Grundtvig, May 29, 1857. *Cf.* the interest in *Møllargutten*, *infra*, pp. 63-4.

[39] *Cf.* Welhaven, *Saml. Skr.*, vol. vi, pp. 289-90.

[40] J. Aall, *Nutid og Fortid*, vol. i, pt. iii, pp. 46-47; *Stort. Forh.*, 1830, vol. iv, p. 222; *Dølen*, 1859, no. 20; *Den Norske Folkeskole*, vol. iv, p. 345.

[41] *Den Const.*, 1847, nos. 25, 26.

[42] P. A. Munch, *Saml. Afh.*, vol. i, p. 114; vol. iii, p. 395.

[43] R. Keyser, *Efterladte Skrifter* (2 vols. Chra., 1866-1867), vol. ii, pt. ii, p. 75.

[44] Henrik Krohn, *Skrifter* (Bergen, 1909), p. 524.

[45] *Morgbl.*, 1849, no. 26.

ality with that of Norse antiquity led the romanticists to point out links or connectives between the two. P. A. Munch thought of the dialects salvaged by Aasen, and of the ballads made known by Landstad as just such connectives, and on one occasion he spoke expressively of Landstad's collection as a " bridge " from the ancient to the modern age.[46] Jørgen Moe saw a similar connective in the diction of the folk tales.[47]

*   *   *   *   *

The romanticists esteemed the peasant very highly for his faithful preservation of their nationality, but the time had come, they had to admit, when he was beginning to fail his trust. He had been influenced by the spirit of modern progress and had begun to regard his traditions as outworn and backward, as something to be discarded. After having guarded the national heritage for so many centuries, he was squandering and dissipating it. The situation was poignantly tragic. He was deserting his rôle just as the cultured awoke to appreciate it.[48] In another generation his heritage would probably be gone and with it would pass the last opportunity to gaze upon the unadulterated nationality. On every hand, the corroding influences of general European civilization were making headway against the local traditions. Intellectual and material progress, increased contact with the outside world, political agitation and lay religious fanaticism—all were doing their share to push back into the recesses the venerable old customs and traditions. Year by

[46] Munch, *Saml. Afh.*, vol. iii, pp. 376-7. *Cf.* p. 358. He wanted to build the proposed jury system on the vestigial usages of the *Lagrettes-mænd*, thus preserving " an historical connection " and imparting to the new reform " a national tone." *Ibid.*, vol. i, pp. 578-9; *cf.* vol. iii, p. 15.

[47] P. C. Asbjørnsen and J. Moe, *Norske Folke-eventyr* (Chra., 1851-2), p. vii.

[48] *Cf. Nor*, vol. iii, pt. iii, p. 120.

year these lost more of their unique characteristics.[49] The handicrafts were discontinued, and in some instances even the venerable old churches were torn down,[50] sometimes for the very good reason that as population increased, they proved too small. The desire to get away from the old took on in extreme cases the nature of persecution. In the Christianssand region in the late 'fifties, a copy of Ole Vig's *Sange og Rim* was burned lest it foster superstitious ideas.[51]

There seemed to the romanticists a real danger that the tide of progress might entirely efface the characteristics of nationality, and the prospect aroused apprehension, especially among the folklorists.[52] Might the current be reversed? Perhaps, if the peasant could be imbued in time with a new respect for his own traditions; if, as Aasen was so anxious to point out, he could be made to realize that those traditions really had been kept in honor by his own forefathers.[53] Within a generation the peasant did begin to reverse the current, but this is part of the early history of the *landsmaal* movement to which we shall refer later.[54]

Meanwhile we may look to one interesting mid-century manifestation of the paternal solicitude of the cultured for the preservation of the rural traditions. It was associated with the undertaking called *Selskabet til Folkeoplysningens Fremme* (" The Society for the Promotion of Popular Enlightenment "). This organization was founded on the initiative of Hartvig Nissen and its sponsors had in mind

[49] Chr. Tønsberg, *Norske Nationaldragter* (Chra., 1852), *Forord*.

[50] H. Koht, " *Bonde mot Borgar i nynorsk Historie*," (*norsk*) *Historisk Tidsskrift*, vol. v, pt. i, p. 81.

[51] *Folkevennen*, 1859, p. 457.

[52] *Infra*, pp. 254-5.

[53] I. Aasen, *Skr. i Saml.*, vol. iii, pp. 87, 91 ; Aasen, *Norske Ordsprog* (Chra., 1856), pp. iii, xxiii.

[54] *Infra*, chapters xix and xx.

diverse purposes. The more democratic intended it primarily to help banish the peasant's traditional ignorance and to encourage him to take a more active rôle in public life. Others feared the effects of just such participation; frightened by the subversive tendencies of 1848-9 and a democratic movement,[55] they hoped through education to counteract these tendencies. Still others, and they concern us here, were primarily interested in teaching the peasant to respect his nationality and his traditions.

The prospectus of the venture was signed by twenty-six persons of prominence, including several who are mentioned from time to time in this study, e.g., M. J. Monrad, Martin Nissen, Eilert Sundt, J. C. Berg, Rudolf Keyser and P. A. Munch.[56] The announcement urged the need of wider adult schooling and of more familiarity with newer political viewpoints (to combat liberalism?). That some of the motivating impulses were national is evident, for the undertaking intended to develop the people's self-consciousness by directing its gaze to the past and making better known those centuries when it had been an independent folk.

The venture turned out to be effective chiefly through its organ, *Folkevennen* (" The People's Friend "), a long-lived periodical (1850-1899). In the policy of this organ was reflected much of the spirit of the first editor, Ole Vig (1824-1857). Something of a leader among the elementary school teachers, Vig had been strongly influenced by the Dane, Grundtvig, to think of recapturing the heroic spirit of the ancient north and applying it to a popular renewal of Christian and national vigor.[57] Vig's activity had a semi-

[55] *Cf.* T. Knudsen, *P. A. Munch og samtidens norske sprogstrev* (Chra., 1923), p. 85.

[56] *Morgbl.*, 1850, no. 118. The *Indbydelse* is dated April 23, 1850.

[57] O. Vig, *Sange og Rim for det norske Folk* (Chra., 1854), p. viii; L. Eskeland, " *Ole Vig*," *Syn og Segn*, vol. xxx, p. 56.

pietistic bent, and even the prospectus noted above promised, in a tone reminiscent of Grundtvig, that much reliance would be placed upon the " living word." While *Folkevennen* announced in the first issue that it aimed to be instructive in a broad way, its program was also definitely national. It sought, among other things, to give the scattered hamlets a stronger sense of national consciousness and a sense of their common interest, by awakening a love of home, fatherland and mother tongue, and by instilling respect for the ways of the forefathers.

In terminating this discussion of the interest in the peasant, we may observe that when romanticism beckoned the cultured from their academic groves and led them out to the lowly cottage of the peasant, there to learn of life's deep wisdom from his homely tradition, it reversed a natural order. It asked them to abdicate,[58] to commit " spiritual suicide." [59] It led some to wonder whether certain disciplines of culture were not a positive danger to nationality.[60]

* * * * *

Romanticism in Norway rose to high intensity on two different occasions, once in the second half of the 'forties and again in the later 'fifties. On each occasion the peasant naturally was in high favor and there was also a certain correlation between the flow and ebb of romanticism and the intensity of the historical interest, if one may judge from the rise and fall of membership in such an organization as the archæological society, *Foreningen til norske Fortidsmindersmærkers Bevaring* ("The Association for the Preservation of Norwegian Antiquities"). Its roll of members rose sharply

[58] *Cf.* A. Burgun, *Le Développement linguistique en Norvége depuis 1814*, vol. ii, p. 7.

[59] *Cf. Chra.-Post.*, 1858, no. 310.

[60] M. J. Monrad, " *Om Philosophiens Betydning for Nationaliteten,*" *Nor*, vol. iii, pt. iii, pp. 106-7.

from the beginnings in 1844 to 1848, then fell off considerably until 1857 only to rise perceptibly again by 1859.[61]

During the first period of its ascendancy, romanticism overwhelmingly dominated the work of scholars and collectors, as we shall have ample opportunity to see later, and at the same time it also evoked the enthusiasm of the general public. Perhaps it was more than a chance happening that an order of merit—the Order of St. Olaf—was founded in 1847,[62] while a gratifying event the next year was the completion of the new royal palace giving the country once again, as of old, its own royal residence.

By 1849 the enthusiasm rose to flood tide. There was mutual felicitation because Norway, thanks to her stolid peasant, had remained " free and happy " in the face of general European upheaval.[63] Due to the disturbances elsewhere a number of Norway's renowned sons, chiefly artists and musicians, returned home, and during that winter the social and cultural life of the little capital assumed unwonted brilliance. The high point was perhaps the grand program arranged by the art association, *Kunstforeningen,*[64] featuring the country's more illustrious talents. A part of the vocal and instrumental music was distinctly national; Lindeman was represented, and Ole Bull, now famed abroad, played several selections. Welhaven wrote a prologue for the occasion. A poem by Jørgen Moe was recited as well as a selection from the romantic littérateur, Andreas Munch. Tableaux were arranged for several so-called national scenes, some of them flanked by canvases from those masters of peasant portraiture, Gude and Tidemand. There were ex-

---

[61] *Foreningen til norske Fortidsmindersmærkers Bevaring. Aarsberetning,* 1859, p. 4.

[62] *Cf.* P. A. Munch, *Lærde Brev,* vol. i, p. 232. Aug. 25, 1847 to Rafn.

[63] " *Festmaaltid paa Klingenberg,*" *Morgenbladet,* 1849, no. 26.

[64] On March 28, 29, 30, 1849.

hibitions of peasant diversions—a " belt dueling " number had to be repeated no less than three times. The entire program was repeated twice, and still there were regrets at the failure to present it once again.[65] A part of the fervor carried over to the next autumn when a private director, Klingenberg, gave a *" National-divertissement "* of melodies and folk dances in national costume, with selections upon bagpipe and chalet horn.[66] This program too was popular enough to be rendered several times.[67] Just after New Year in 1850 Ole Bull launched the " Norwegian Theater " in Bergen to promote a native dramatic art.

That the circles of refinement might go far in their un-natural infatuation for the peasant's rusticity was strikingly shown in the case of Thorgeir Audunsson, better known as *Møllargutten* (" The Miller Boy ").[68] Audunsson, an itin-erant country fiddler and a somewhat shiftless family pro-vider, had mastered a very sizable *repertoire* of popular tunes. Th. Kjerulf (1825-1888), a young scientist, on a tour over Haukalidfjeldet in company with Jørgen Moe, who was gathering folklore, " discovered " him.[69] But the person who raised him from his lowly estate to the concert stage, there to be flattered and patronized by the most fastidi-ous circles of the capital, was none other—and this is the most revealing aspect of the matter—than the world re-nowned Ole Bull. From his very first appearance early in 1849 *Møllargutten* was accepted as a sensation.[70] Admirers

[65] *Morgenbladet*, 1849, nos. 89, 91. See also the advertisements in nos. 86, 87, 88.

[66] *Ibid.*, 1849, nos. 281, 287.

[67] On Oct. 9, 11, and apparently also on Oct. 14 and 15.

[68] The father had been a miller. See *Norsk Biografisk Leksikon* and Idar Handagard, *" Vinje om Ole Bull og Myllargutten,"* *Nordmands-forbundet*, 1926, pp. 405-9, 455-60.

[69] Halvorsen, *Norsk Forf.-Lex.*, vol. iii, p. 273.

[70] *Morgbl.*, 1849, no. 17.

pronounced his execution untrammeled by any artificial systems of musicianship, and in his presentation they could experience direct "the true national folk spirit with all its singularities." [71] Such uncritical enthusiasm over the peasant was well-nigh universal among the cultured and only a few tempered their praise with moderation.

With the arrival of the 'fifties, romanticist enthusiasm abated for a time, due mainly to the disturbing tendencies of 1848-50. Markus Thrane (1817-1890) had begun to organize the urban laborers and the poorer *husmænd* [72] for political action. The propertied took alarm; and in the reaction that followed, Thrane's movement was scattered. But the prevailing admiration for the peasant also lagged. He did not seem so appealing now that some elements in his estate had made efforts to exchange an apparent docility for a larger measure of political control. It became the fashion again to find fault with his ways. Religious fanaticism, it was pointed out, still flourished in the more backward valleys and there was a high percentage of insanity in rural areas. Some of the peasant's morals were also a bit questionable. [73]

The center of interest shifted from the romantic concerns of the 'forties to economic subjects. It was a matter of pride that railway construction was begun and the telegraph adopted, while roads and canals were likewise being improved. After England repealed her Navigation Acts in 1849, the carrying trade also prospered, especially during the Crimean War. In these years the interest in national concerns was best sustained by scholars and collectors, most of whom continued to work on under the momentum of the romantic 'forties. Landstad finished his ballads in 1853

[71] *Chra.-Post.*, 1849, no. 207.

[72] Somewhat akin to the English cotters.

[73] Chr. Tønsberg, *Norske Nationaldragter*, pp. 5-6.

and P. A. Munch began his massive history of the Norwegian people, while Aasen continued his studies of the dialects. But there were also defections in the ranks. After the scholarly edition of folk tales (1851-2), Moe devoted himself to pastoral work and Asbjørnsen became absorbed in science and technology.

Ere the decade was over, however, the atmosphere changed again and romanticism had a revival. Possibly the economic dislocation following the financial panic of 1857, scattered some of the attention lately concentrated on matters economic and industrial, and favored the reaction. A fresh interest in the peasant was aroused by Bjørnson and Ibsen. In the late 'fifties there was a striking case of linguistic nationalism involving the use of the Old Norse,[74] while there were indications that history was becoming the concern of a broader public. P. A. Munch finally issued the royal sagas in his long-projected popular edition (1857-9) and the government of the day broke with the traditions of its prosaic predecessors to urge a generous public support for the cultivation of national history.[75] Of the general quickening in nationalist sentiment at the close of the decade, we have spoken above in chapter one.

But whatever strength these manifestations of national feeling drew from the renewal of romanticism, was weakened when the latter waned in the 'sixties. Equally temporary was the revived veneration for the *bonde*. Vinje, fully aware of the peasant's sharp realistic sense, showed that Bjørnson had quite idealized him; in fact Bjørnson himself recoiled somewhat. The charming idyl of rural life so recently pictured by the intellectuals was now discredited as a phantasy that never had existed in reality.[76] The studies

[74] *Infra*, p. 313.
[75] *Infra*, pp. 85, 163-4.
[76] *Ill. Nyhbl.*, 1866, p. 220.

of Sundt and Dahl indicated that the *bonde* was living in ignorance and filth, in ugliness and immorality.[77] The peasant helped to discredit himself in the eyes of the upper classes, with his growing participation in political affairs. By 1865 Jaabæk was forming his *Bondevenforeninger* ("Societies of Friends of the Peasant") and four years later Johan Sverdrup fused certain peasant, labor and liberal elements into a definite political organization, the new party of the Left.

[77] *Cf. Morgbl.*, 1860, no. 277.

CHAPTER III

THE ROMANTICIST INTEREST IN NATIONALITY AND CULTURE

THAT Norway under her liberal constitution might soon devote herself to the proper cultivation of learning and the arts, was a hope shared by all patriots, including those who were not romanticists. However, the matter seemed particularly urgent to the romanticist scholars and publicists, no doubt because in a special way they related culture to nationality. Their understanding of this relationship rested in turn upon their concept of nationality; what views they had on these matters we may learn from incidental references in their writings and from occasional longer passages.

In treating the phenomenon of nationality, these writers usually took for granted that its chief determinants lay in natural influences and in the abstraction of the Idea. The less philosophical among them laid some stress upon climate and geography,[1] holding that in a very early period these factors fashioned basic differences in national customs [2] and stamped themselves upon the national character of the populations they affected. In Norway, for instance, the wild majestic mountain landscapes accounted pretty well for the courage, the strength and the firmness of the people,[3] just

---

[1] In this connection there were infrequent references to the soil. *Cf. Alm. n. Maanedskr.*, vol. ii, p. 468; "*Jordbundens Indflydelse paa National-charakteren,*" *Ill. Nyhbl.*, 1858, p. 182.

[2] P. A. Munch, *Verdenshistoriens vigtigste Begivenheder* (Chra., 1840), p. 2.

[3] *Morgenbladet*, 1849, no. 14.

as the hardships of the climate bred in them a receptive intellect and a sharpened moral sense.[4]   The Norwegian national soul imbibed " from the waste of the plateau, from the quiet charm of birchwood and mountain valley, and from the deep stillness of the primeval forest," a strain of melancholy.[5]   On the other hand, nature's brighter side (and she had it: " the forest is not always dark and silent.   Sometimes the sunbeams dance among the trees ") communicated to the folk character a strain of optimism that could see the humor in adversity, and imparted to it a sense of drollery that was quite unexpected among a people in so stern a clime.[6]

The romanticist felt that these qualities of the Norwegian national character were best reflected in the current folklore and in the ancient mythology.   Employing the interpretative approach called nature-symbolism—the idea that the traditions reproduced the phenomena of nature under hidden figures of speech—the romanticists held that nature's various attributes, impressed first on the popular phantasy, were in turn reflected in the oral traditions.   Rightly understood, then, the stories revealed the nation's topography, flora and climate.[7]   In line with this reasoning Asbjørnsen spoke of the fairy tales as " nature poems." [8]   The historians for a time had a tendency to apply the same interpretation to the old myths.[9]   Keyser predicated an involved interaction be-

[4] Jacob Aall, "Indledning om Sagaskriftens Oprindelse," Samlinger til det Norske Folks Sprog og Historie vol. iv, p. 188.

[5] Den Const., 1842, no. 81.

[6] Ibid.

[7] Norsk Tidsskrift for Videnskab og Litteratur, vol. ii, p. 125.

[8] P. C. Asbjørnsen, Norske Huldre-eventyr og Folkesagn (Chra., 1845), p. iii.   Cf. his notations in Chr. Tønsberg, Norge Fremstillet i Tegninger (Chra., 1846-48), pp. 101-2.

[9] P. A. Munch, Forn-Swenskans och Forn-Norskans Språkbygnad (Stockholm, 1849), p. xviii; cf. Morgbl., 1841, no. 124.

tween nature and life in the Old Norse period, wherein outward circumstances bred a striking physical prowess and this
feeling of strength in turn evoked a warlike spirit that was
perpetuated in the old mythology.[10]   Nature-symbolism
strongly influenced the historians and folklorists in the later
'forties, but they soon deserted it, and after the mid-century
it remained only with the littérateurs.[11]

*   *   *   *   *

Those of a more philosophic turn among the romanticists
related nationality to that mysterious inner principle, the
Idea. In Norway this relationship was explained very sonor-
ously by the philosopher, Monrad, a simon-pure exponent of
German Idealism.[12]   The nation, droned Monrad, was something ideal, something " spiritual," [13] it had " a significance,
a call."   The Idea and not outward circumstance (that is,
chance) was the ultimate determinant in fashioning national
character.   Monrad objected to Keyser's implication that the
ancient folk character and the Old Norse mythology had
been fashioned by nature, and repeated his conviction that
these had been determined by historical necessity, by " the
wise plan of Fate."[14]

The romanticists spoke much of nationality's being re-

[10] R. Keyser, *Nordmændenes Religionsforfatning i Hedendommen*
(Chra., 1847), pp. 168-9; *cf.* also pp. 18-19.

[11] Moltke Moe, "*Det nationale Gjennembrud og dets Mænd*," Gran,
Nordmænd i det 19de Aarhundrede, vol. ii, pp. 253-4.

[12] Marcus Jacob Monrad (1816-1897) abroad at Berlin, imbibed
both pro- and anti-Hegelian points of view, and completely accepted
the former. After visits to Italy and Paris he returned in 1845 and
taught philosophy at the university until the year of his death. *Cf.* J. B.
Halvorsen, *Norsk Forfatter-Lexikon*, vol. iv, pp. 88-91; A. Aall,
"*Hegelianismens Enevælde, M. J. Monrad,*" *Det Kongelige Fredriks
Universitet 1811-1911* (2 vols. Chra., 1911), vol. ii, pp. 399-405.

[13] "*Om Philosophiens Betydning for Nationaliteten,*" *Nor*, vol. iii,
pt. iii, p. 108.

[14] *Den norske Rigstidende*, 1847, no. 55.

born,[15] and again we may let Monrad explain what they meant. Every nation, he said, had a "mysterious connection" with its Idea—a dim feeling of its own unique character and destiny.[16] In primitive life, he thought, that feeling might be very keen; it had often been well expressed in tribal literature. When the complexities of modern life were reached, however, these obscured all sense of the nation's connection with the Idea. Until that sense reawakened, nationality was "dormant" and the process of awakening constituted that nationality's rebirth. From such a point of view, and with an eye to the salvaging of the popular traditions, the romanticists spoke of recovering or reviving nationality,[17] and of resuscitating those parts of national character that had been lost.[18]

Because they so closely identified nationality with the Idea, the romanticists felt in a special way that every nationality had been assigned a part to play in the unfolding drama of history—a part determined by the Idea.[19] Life was a grand orchestra of peoples in which each nationality played its own unique instrument.[20] Nationality was not to be assumed or discarded at will; its maintenance was a serious obligation.[21] Each people must play its rôle within the framework of the cosmic plan in order to promote the great common aim.

[15] *Den Const.*, 1847, nos. 25, 26.

[16] *Morgbl.*, 1842, no. 39.

[17] *Moss Tilskuer*, 1840, nos. 66, 67. Reprinted in *Maal og Minne*, 1924, p. 145.

[18] *Alm. n. Maanedskr.*, vol. ii, pp. 445, 486.

[19] J. Lieblein, "*Norsk Sprog og Nationalitet,*" *Ill. Nyhbl.*, 1859, no. 5, pp. 22-24. What Lieblein thought of nationality may be gathered from his article, "*Die weltgeschichtliche Bedeutung der Nationalitäten,*" in *Der Gedanke*, vol. iii (Berlin, 1862), pp. 251-66.

[20] A. O. Vinje, *Om vaart nationale Stræv* (Bergen, 1869), p. 25; *cf.* p. 5.

[21] *Chra.-Post.*, 1858, no. 320.

valid for many other nationalist movements

What might that aim be? And what the specific rôle of each? This would indeed be interesting to know, but we are not told.[22] It was enough, however, to recognize that instead of being confused or capricious the aim was orderly and purposeful, and simultaneously so vast that it could not be attained unless each nationality did its part. Hence it was that each might bring forward its unique " offering," and lay it on the " altar of nationality." [23] Uniformity among nationalities would produce merely one-sidedness; diversity was indispensable.[24]

But since the unfolding world panorama was orderly, there must be a directive and intelligent force behind it. That force was Fate. Fate moved the nationalities about at will like chessmen on the gaming board of history.[25] Fate, that is, " historical necessity," and not human will or human ingenuity, dictated world development; a nation must obey its " history." [26] Against the judgment of Fate there was no appeal.[27] In the great plan of things there was no place for chance, that " ogre of history;" Monrad especially would give it no peace, and demanded that it be treated as " excommunicate." [28]

Nationality was thus justified supernally, and this, to patriots, was a comforting reflection. In Fate's sagacious plan, national character was no accident but an indispensable manifestation of the Idea. History, not chance, had willed

[22] J. Lieblein, *op. cit.*, 1859, no. 5.

[23] *Dølen*, 1858, no. 1.

[24] *Ibid.*, 1859, no. 20; *Aftenbladet*, 1876, no. 11.

[25] *Cf.* P. A. Munch, *Det Norske Folks Historie* (6 vols. Chra., 1852-59), vol. i, p. 794.

[26] *Chra.-Post.*, 1858, no. 335.

[27] *Aftenbl.*, 1876, no. 11.

[28] *Den norske Rigstidende*, 1847, no. 55.

that there be nationalities,[29] and hence national uniquenesses bore the sanction of the eternal.

But in the light of this teleology, what was expected of the Norwegian nationality? For a long time after the Kalmar Union it appeared to have been removed from Fate's "checkerboard."[30] Yet it had not been lost, and in 1814 it had again been entered to play its national rôle.[31] And what was that rôle? Nothing less than the preservation and dissemination of the pristine Germanic attribute of equality.[32] For that equality had disappeared elsewhere and had been preserved only in medieval Norway where the population had never divided into two classes of noble and serf.

There were frequent references in the later 'fifties to the rôle of Fate and historical necessity. It was a time when the interest in larger political consolidations[33] readily led to discussions of the part that the individual nationality should play in the larger sweep of world development. Those younger patriots of 1859[34] who made a new stand against foreign influences in Norway, warned the nation not to desert the rôle assigned to it but to take a "hint" from Fate and prepare for the service it owed to others by consolidating itself as a nation truly independent in politics, language and art.[35] Of course, cosmopolitan tendencies could not be ignored, but a nation had its own categorical nature, an imperative that it must follow.[36] Submission to

---

[29] *Ibid.*

[30] J. Lieblein, *op. cit.*

[31] *Chra.-Post.*, 1858, no. 320; *Aftenbl.*, 1876, no. 11.

[32] Christianity also had this mission, said Lieblein, but Fate might be using more than one means to attain the same end. J. Lieblein, *op. cit.*

[33] Abroad, the Austro-Sardinian War was in progress.

[34] *Supra*, p. 42.

[35] *Det Unge Norge, 17de Mai 1859*, p. 1.

[36] J. Lieblein, *op. cit.*

the foreign was betrayal,[37] a sin against humanity in leaving unfulfilled the assigned historic world task.[38]

But the teleological argument of the patriots was a double-edged weapon.   It could, on occasion, be used on the other side to defend the cosmopolitan trends (i.e. unionism and Scandinavianism) or to harmonize the cosmopolitan with the national.   Monrad used the argument as a means to justify the broader concerns of his own cultured class and to harmonize them with the interests of nationality.   In doing so he developed an emaciated synthesis that might be termed cosmopolitan nationalism.   He pointed out that nationality had two phases, one negative and limited, setting bounds that marked it off from every other; and a second that was positive, limitless, universal.[39]   A nation, he contended, was able to see its specific significance only in terms of the larger world process.   But it could see that significance only by breaking the barrier of its negative nationality.   So he urged acceptance of the cosmopolitan, not so much to wipe away all boundaries of the national as to gain a clearer consciousness of the nationality's purpose and thereby a sharper perception of its limitations.[40]   From the opposite view, it was admitted that there could be a danger of one-sidedness in guarding nationality too exclusively against foreign influences; but the time was not come, said Lieblein, when any appreciable part of the population could raise itself to the required level of universality and cosmopolitanism, and what was more, that was perhaps not yet intended by the " divine will." [41]

[37] *Ibid.*

[38] *Det Unge Norge, 17de Mai 1859,* p. 1.

[39] M. J. Monrad, " *Om Philosophiens Betydning for Nationaliteten,*" *Nor,* vol. iii, pt. iii, pp. 118-9.

[40] *Ibid.,* vol. iii, pt. iii, p. 121.

[41] J. Lieblein, *op. cit.*

The generation of the mid-century was quite whole-heartedly committed to the cause of nationality.[42]   The special task of the age was to promote the national strivings progressing on every hand.[43]   Nations, it was said, had come to regard it as their " holiest duty " to develop what was in them of the " national element; " awakened from their " slumber," they were determined, not only to be, but to be " themselves." [44]   A new " world struggle " was on in which the peoples edged forward, one past the other, to " clear and firm self-consciousness." [45]   Writers held it incumbent on a nationality, particularly on one so outstanding as the Nor-wegian, to develop what was unique in its folk life.[46] Norway, it was asserted, possessed a " real uniqueness," a " soul " that fitted her well for separate statehood and independence.[47]

*   *   *   *   *

The romanticists predicated a close connection between nationality and culture,[48] but any effort to explain this tie more carefully was apt to be a bit philosophical.   In order to understand the connection, one must, according to Monrad, appreciate the rôle of national consciousness. Nationality, he explained, manifested itself in two stages, one the unconscious, in which the reactions were in-stinctive, unreflective, traditionalist, and the second, in which the nationality was conscious, alert, assertive of

---

[42] *Nor*, vol. iii, pt. iii, pp. 114-5.

[43] Munch, *Saml. Afh.*, vol. ii, pp. 8, 81.

[44] *Nor*, vol. iii, pt. iii, p. 106.

[45] J. Moe, " *Tale ved Bragebægeret*," *Saml. Skr.* (1877), vol. ii, p. 285.

[46] A. O. Vinje, *Om vaart nationale Stræv*, p. 25.

[47] *N. Tids. f. Vid. og Litt.*, vol. vii, pp. 18-19.

[48] *Cf.* M. J. Monrad, " *Om Theater og Nationalitet*," *N. Tids. f. Vid. og Litt.*, vol. vii, pp. 4-5, 7-8; *Dølen*, 1859, no. 20; " *Om den norrøne Litteraturs Forhold til Norge og norsk Kultur*," *Norden*, 1868, p. 161.

its individuality, and in possession of a clarified image of its Idea. If it were to maintain itself, or to resist foreign influence successfully, a nationality must pass from the first stage to the second,[49] and that transition was to be accomplished through the mediation of culture. It was in the circles of culture that the scattered elements of nationality were brought to a focus, and through them only could a nation truly attain to self-consciousness.[50]

The most vitalizing among the disciplines of culture were history, art and philosophy. History drew attention to the intangible realm of national tradition. It helped to emphasize that nationality was " a treasure of memories," " a holy ancestral heritage." [51] But as a scholarly discipline history had one serious drawback; it gave its rewards only to long and patient labor. It was only for the few and it could never operate directly upon the masses.[52]

This shortcoming of history was offset by art. Poets and other artists with their vital imaginations captured " the true eternal spirit," [53] and revealed the basic Idea, free of trivialities.[54] Hence it was that the uniqueness of a nationality, " that entire store of emotions, inclinations and powers," [55] remained chaotic until embodied in definite form by art; only then emerged that transfigured image of the fatherland on which the simplest citizen could bestow his patriotism.[56]

[49] Monrad, "*Om Philosophiens Betydning for Nationaliteten*," *Nor*, vol. iii, pt. iii, p. 109.

[50] *Morgbl.*, 1858, no. 287.

[51] *Nor*, vol. iii, pt. iii, p. 111.

[52] *N. Tids. f. Vid. og Litt.*, vol. vii, p. 4.

[53] *Ibid.*, vol. vii, pp. 4-5.

[54] *Cf.* J. S. Welhaven, *Saml. Skr.*, vol. i, p. 102; A. Krogvig, *Fra det nationale gjennembruds Tid*, pp. 176-7. Moe to Asbjørnsen in the autumn of 1839.

[55] *Nor*, vol. iii, pt. iii, p. 110.

[56] *N. Tids. f. Vid. og Litt.*, vol. vii, pp. 4-5.

Among the arts, it was especially the stage, reflecting the customs, morals and popular traditions, which enabled the nation to see itself most lucidly,[57] thereby clarifying the folk consciousness and bringing the nation closer to the realization of its Idea.[58]   But in Norway the interpretation of the Idea was in a bad way.   After half a century both the literary medium and the actors on the stage were still Danish, and the results were apparent.   Danish hegemony in the art of the theater was a " dark spot," [59] indicating an incompleteness in the nationality.   It displaced and counteracted the national customs and the language, and kept nationality itself in restraint and immaturity, unable to enjoy its " full uniqueness." [60]   The tendrils of the dramatic art were so entwined about nationality [61] that the theater could develop its potentialities only if the stage were Norwegian; there was no justification for a Danish theater in Christiania.[62]

But as a medium for revealing nationality to itself, art, like history, had its shortcomings.   Both lacked comprehensiveness.   History, said Monrad, apprehended the nationality only in its past, and art only in its present, while neither was able to encompass the Idea in its entirety.[63] Only philosophy, he was proud to announce, was able to reveal a nation's eternal Idea as both a conditioning principle and a result of development, " as the eternal in the temporal."   Philosophy alone could penetrate the Idea clearly

---

[57] *Det Unge Norge, 17de Mai 1859*, pp. 6-7.

[58] *N. Tids. f. Vid. og Litt.*, vol. vii, pp. 6-7.

[59] *Ibid.*, vol. vii, pp. 23-24.

[60] *Ibid.*, vol. vii, p. 20.

[61] *Morgbl.*, 1858, no. 102.

[62] *Ibid.*, 1858, nos. 93, 102.

[63] *Nor*, vol. iii, pt. iii, pp. 112-113.

and give a nation self-consciousness and self-knowledge, and make it realize its destiny among other peoples.[64]

*   *   *   *   *

It seemed logical enough, that since Norway had recovered her political independence, that is, since her nationality was being reborn, she was bound to develop a culture of her own. Her new freedom, it was felt, must automatically bring a release of energies and a creative outburst in the arts, particularly, it was expected, in literature. Conversely, too, many were convinced that a creative literature was equally indispensable to the future of national independence. Wergeland was apprehensive lest the lack of a national literature, in the face of Danish cultural hegemony, might demoralize the faith in Norway's newly-won freedom.[65] An independent art and literature could be a very important means to strengthen and develop the nationality.[66] Superior intellectual ability alone, it was stated considerably later, could assure Norway's independent existence.[67] So long as a nation had no literature to reflect its character, the measure of its existence was but " half." [68]

During the first generation of independence, Norwegian patriots had reason to be full of anxiety and misgiving. Only in the field of historical investigation were there signs of " an awakening national striving." [69] But in literature proper the outlook was not encouraging, as years lengthened into decades. Wergeland begged in verse for the anticipated

---

[64] *Ibid.*, p. 114 *et seq.*

[65] Wergeland outlined a systematic effort to counteract this lack of faith. *Cf. Samtiden*, vol. xix, p. 352. Letter in Sept., 1832, from Wergeland to Bjerregaard.

[66] *N. Tids. f. Vid. og Litt.*, vol. vii, p. 5; *cf. Krydseren*, 1853, no. 208.

[67] *Morgbl.*, 1868, no. 40.

[68] *Den Const.*, 1842, no. 81.

[69] *Maanedskrift for Literatur*, vol. xvii, pp. 282, 285.

literature.[70]   Welhaven complained privately that during all
these years of freedom there had not appeared "a single
pithy cultural product," [71] and Jørgen Moe later called for
poets who might voice again, like scalds of old, the people's
deepest sentiments.[72]

Some, in extenuation, pointed out that since 1814 the new
Norway had expended so much of its energy on politics
and economics,[73] that little was left for cultural concerns.[74]
It must be remembered too that Norway was not a rich
country, and had very few citizens who might serve as
patrons of the arts.   As late as the mid-century it was pronounced difficult for an artist to make a livelihood in
Norway.[75]

The lack of a national literature seemed much more
awkward when the delinquency began to be noticed by
foreigners.   Many had wondered, said F. C. Petersen, a
Dane, who did not spare the sensitiveness of his Norwegian
readers, why the new constitution with its freedom of the
press and every other kind of freedom had not produced
more vigorous literary results; perhaps, he added tauntingly,
those who expected the free constitution to " awaken the
sense for the sublime " must conclude instead that " Norway
had come by its constitution too easily." [76]

[70] *"For den Norske Literatur, 1840," Digterværker og Prosaiske
Skrifter*, vol. i, pp. 299-300.

[71] O. Skavlan, *Henrik Wergeland*, p. 276.   Welhaven to Michael Sars,
Aug. 20, 1835.

[72] J. Moe, *Saml. Skr.* (1877), vol. ii, p. 285 *et seq.*

[73] Munch, *Norges, Sveriges og Danmarks Historie til Skolebrug*
(Chra., 1838), p. 488.

[74] *Saml. t. d. N. F. Spr. og Hist.*, vol. iv, pp. 279-80; *cf. (norsk) Historisk Tidsskrift*, vol. i, pt. i, p. 424.

[75] *N. Tids. f. Vid. og Litt.*, vol. vi, p. 309; *cf.* also vol. i, p. 124.

[76] *Tidsskrift for Litteratur og Kritik*, vol. v, p. 414.   There was at
this time considerable argument about the Norwegian constitution.   *Cf.*
infra, pp. 101-4.

This was no pleasant thought, and yet to those who observed critically the facts were unescapable. A few names — Keilhau, Abel, Hansteen — had brought Norway some renown in the natural sciences, but in belles-lettres proper there was little more to point to than Mauritz Hansen's historical novels, hastily composed in the manner of German romanticism, and some verse, which might have lasting value, by the principals in the Wergeland-Welhaven controversy. Both Wergeland and Welhaven, by the way, like many of their compatriots were thinking in terms of the *anticipated* national culture.[77]

The Danish hegemony, to which Wergeland was so much opposed, was perhaps most strikingly dominant in the publishing field. In 1841 an aggressive writer appealed in *Morgenbladet*[78] for the organization of a *Norsk Literær Forening* (" Norwegian Literary Society ") to combat the Danish influence. Dependence on a foreign state, he asserted, was as dangerous in the field of the spiritual as it was in the realm of the political. " If we are not to be swallowed up by Denmark we must take serious steps to initiate a literary activity." " Have none of you sufficient ability and patriotic zeal to make a serious attempt? " Anxious to stimulate pride in what had been done already, Chr. C. A. Lange[79] at the time of *Norskheds-bevægelsen* issued a list of books published in Norway during the first decade and a half of independence; the list showed something accomplished.[80] Fifteen years later, when Nissen brought the list down to 1847, Lange pleaded for an independent Norwegian literature, gradually emancipated from " the Danish sister-litera-

---

[77] *Cf.* Wergeland, *Digterværker og Prosaiske Skrifter*, vol. i, pp. 299-300.

[78] No. 62.

[79] *Infra*, pp. 152-54.

[80] C. C. A. Lange, *Fortegnelse over de i Norge udkomne Bøger i aarene 1814 til 1831* (Chra., 1832).

ture." [81]   The year following he took an important step
toward that end when he replaced Dahl's short-lived *Literaturtidende* ("News of Literature," 1845-46) with his own
learned periodical, *Norsk Tidsskrift for Videnskab og Litteratur* ("Norwegian Review of Science and Literature").[82]
By the mid-century Danish influence in this field was in
retreat.   According to one writer there had not been a single
native book-dealer in the country prior to 1814, but by 1848
there were no less than twenty-two such dealers in Christiania alone.[83]

The independent cultural development so eagerly anticipated arrived in the second half of the 'forties.   Stir and
commotion were everywhere and in the face of this exuber-
ance the anxiety of earlier decades gave way to a tone of
bouyancy and self-congratulation.   "Our" literature, wrote
one, was coming of age, choosing domestic themes from the
popular traditions and getting over the idea that it should
imitate other national literatures.[84]   Welhaven, who had
been so caustic a few years earlier, could proclaim that
Norwegians were now united in promoting "the fatherland's
powerful and versatile regeneration."[85]   In the closing
'forties, the public was showered with literary and scholarly
works, especially with writings on Norwegian history.[86]
Apropos of this P. A. Munch wrote to Stephens: "I think

---

[81] Mart. Nissen, "*Statistisk Udsigt over den norske Litteratur fra
1814 til 1847.*" *N. Tids. f. Vid. og Litt.*, vol. iii, pp. 177-8.

[82] Vols. i-vii, 1847-55.

[83] Mart. Nissen, *op. cit.*, p. 204.

[84] *Den Const.*, 1847, nos. 25, 26.

[85] "*I Studenter Samfundet,*" *Saml. Skr.*, vol. vi, p. 273.

[86] In the winter of 1846-7 alone there appeared, among other things, a
volume of the ancient laws, an edition of the *Edda*, the first number of
Lange's periodical, Keyser's essay on the religion of the Northmen,
Munch's narratives of national history, and his grammar of the *norrøn*
tongue.

it is very much for our poor country—but the spirit, the true Norwegian spirit, is awakened. You cannot imagine the fervour with which our young generation embraces the study of their old language, manners and institutions. . . ."[87]

A great deal of this enthusiasm was concentrated on the literature and the antiquities of the Old Norse period, a matter of particular satisfaction to Munch, who years before had claimed that such an interest, once aroused, would stimulate independence in literature.[88] Classes in Old Norse, which Keyser and he conducted, were well attended. The language was becoming really " a national concern," [89] even among "ladies;" [90] Prince Gustav, then visiting Christiania, studied it with Keyser two hours daily.[91] Munch anticipated the time when Old Norse would be read fluently by " every cultured man or woman," [92] and some years later he happily remarked that the desire for investigating patriotic history was perhaps not as strong in any other country as in Norway.[93]

The enthusiasm for Norse antiquity threatened at times to displace a part of the traditional cultural heritage. Portions of both the Greek and the Hebrew inheritance were called in question. An administrative ruling, effective in 1848, regarding the teachers' examinations (*philologiske Embeds- eller Skolelærer-Examen*), permitted the substitution of the Old Norse language and literature for the custom-

[87] Munch, *Lærde Brev*, vol. i, p. 167. Nov. 8, 1846 to Stephens.

[88] Munch, *Saml. Afh.*, vol. i, p. 25.

[89] Munch, *Lærde Brev*, vol. i, p. 210. June 25, 1847 to Grimm. The latter's congratulatory reply is in *ibid.*, pp. 246-7.

[90] *Ibid.*, p. 384. Aug. 25, 1849 to Stephens.

[91] *Ibid.*, p. 229. Aug. 11, 1847 to C. C. Rafn.

[92] *Ibid.*, p. 385. Aug. 25, 1849 to Stephens.

[93] *Ill. Nyhbl.*, 1856, pp. 118-9.

ary requirement in Hebrew.[94]   Next to the Hymnal and the
Bible, wrote Munch, every Norwegian ought to treasure
Snorre's great work.[95]   It was hoped that the study of
Greek would give way to that of English and Old Norse.[96]
The mythology of the Greeks, so long hallowed in western
culture, had been challenged in Denmark in the early part of
the century, when admirable qualities were perceived in the
vigorous mythology of the Norsemen.[97]

We have here spoken more of scholarship than of belles-
lettres.   But in literature, too, promise was nearing ful-
fillment.   In the 'fifties Bjørnstjerne Bjørnson and Henrik
Ibsen began their epoch-making work.   Since then, Norway has contributed more than her proportional share to the
world of letters.   It may not be too far-fetched to credit
her achievement in part to the momentum of this mid-century
tradition that an independent people must produce a national
literature.

*   *   *   *   *

We should note that developing a national culture had
also its financial aspect.   Some of the scholarly ventures
were costly affairs and their support was quite beyond the
resources of the individual investigator, who found it
necessary to appeal for financial aid.

Private Mæcenases were rare.   During the first generation of independence, Jacob Aall essayed the rôle of patron.
He had a deep interest in national history and he possessed
the wealth to make his interest effective, but he died in 1844
just on the threshold of national romanticism and its creative outburst.

[94] Magnus Olsen, "*Filologi*" in *Det Kongelige Fredriks Universitet*,
vol. ii, pp. 310-11; *cf.* Munch, *Lærde Brev*, vol. i, p. 143.   Dec. 8, 1845
to C. C. Rafn.

[95] Munch, *Lærde Brev*, vol. i, p. 1.

[96] *N. Tids. f. Vid. og Litt.*, vol. vii, p. 414.

[97] J. S. C. Welhaven, *Saml. Skr.*, vol. vi, p. 229.

A successor, in a limited sense, was Chr. Tønsberg, a publisher. Though not exactly a man of wealth he undertook a series of patriotic, but financially somewhat dubious, publishing ventures. Thus, he published a book of very large plates, to make better known " our fatherland so rich in scenic grandeur," [98] and followed it up with a work of similar format to illustrate the national costumes of various country districts.[99] He issued several series of Tidemand's scenes from peasant life [100] and published a collection of national biography.[101] With prospects none too promising he published Landstad's ballads. His most ambitious undertaking was the printing of P. A. Munch's massive work, *Det Norske Folks Historie*. The risks on this venture were considerable; another publisher had already refused it and Tønsberg's loss finally amounted to 2500 *Spd.*[102] A present-day admirer says he was a model of national publishing,[103] but his patriotism certainly proved expensive; as Tønsberg himself said, he " had gone to ruin " by his encouragement of national literature and art.[104]

The public agencies of which scholars and collectors sought financial aid were mainly three: the *Storting,* the University and *Det kongelige norske Videnskabers Selskab* (" The Royal Norwegian Society of Science "). The latter, founded in the 'sixties of the previous century, had to its

[98] Chr. Tønsberg, *Norge fremstillet i Tegninger* (Chra., 1846-48), *Forord.*

[99] *Norske Nationaldragter* (Chra., 1852). P. A. Munch had a part in preparing the seals on the title page.

[100] *Norske Folkelivsbilleder* (Chra., vol. i, 1854; vol. ii, 1858; vol. iii, 1861).

[101] *Berømte Nordmænd* (nos. 1-12, Chra., 1853-56).

[102] *Stort. Forh.*, 1872, vol. vii, no. 84, p. 390.

[103] Chr. Brinchmann, *National-Forskeren P. A. Munch* (Chra., 1910), p. 97.

[104] *Stort. Forh.*, 1872, vol. vii, no. 84, p. 388.

credit a distinguished list of benefactions in support of a
developing national culture.   Aside from its promotion of
the natural sciences, it had, for instance, helped to make
better known various Norwegian antiquities, had aided
publications like *Nor* and *Norske Universitets- og Skole-
Annaler;* and had appropriated a substantial sum to help
publish Norway's ancient laws.[105]   Among its benefactions
to individuals were its grants to C. C. A. Lange and Ivar
Aasen.

In the 'forties the University came to be very helpful with
its fellowships and grants-in-aid.   It gave timely assistance
to Asbjørnsen and Moe, it sent Lindeman out in 1848 to
gather folk melodies,[106] and the next year, it dispatched P.
A. Munch abroad to look for remnants of Norse nationality and language in the "older colonies," that is, in the
Western Isles, the Orkneys and Normandy.   It arranged a
substantial accommodation in 1845, in connection with the
printing of sources, which had no attraction for private
publishers, when it permitted the scholars to substitute
medieval Norwegian texts in the University semester programs which traditionally were printed in Latin.[107]   A wider
interest in Norway's glorious past was thereby fostered
among all ranks of university life.

What the *Storting* did to publish historical sources will be
spoken of later; here it is enough to note that in the closing
'fifties the national government took itself seriously as the
patron of national culture.   Not that it had been particularly delinquent heretofore.   It had taken steps to get the
ancient laws printed and had provided the means with which

---

[105] C. N. Schwach, "*Kort Udsigt over det kongelige norske Videns-
kabs-Selskabs Historie fra dets Oprindelse til Udgangen af 1844,*" *Det
kgl. n. Vid.-Selsk. Skr.,* vol. iv, pt. i, pp. 20-22.

[106] *Norske Univ. og Sk. Annaler,* series 2, vol. v, pp. 281-311.

[107] *Cf. infra,* pp. 161-2.

to begin printing the huge collection of sources, the *Diplomatarium Norvegicum.* It had likewise helped to subsidize the learned and semi-patriotic societies at Trondhjem and Bergen. But in the later 'fifties it broadened its patronage. A report to the *Storting* of 1856-7 by the government of the day was distinguished for its patriotic argumentation.[108] It was in substance a lecture to the *Storting* on the obligation of a state to foster its national culture. The state, it was said, must nourish the prevailing desire to know something of the history of the fatherland. Far more of the sources must be made available, and as the printing of them was unprofitable to private enterprise, the government must step in. Norway had already done something, but not so much as befitted the dignity of an independent state. The government's recommendation that 1050 *Spd.* be spent to make more historical sources available was accepted by the *Storting,* which in the same year began its generous support of P. A. Munch's work in the archives at Rome. At the next session it granted Lindeman the annual sum of 300 *Spd.* to continue collecting and publishing folk melodies, and it began also to support a national archæologist.[109]

* * * * *

Behind the public and private solicitude for a national culture was the compelling urge of patriotism. Among the scholars and publicists, patriotism sometimes merged with professional interest.[110] P. A. Munch, we shall see, pleaded that if placed in a history-teaching position at the University his talents would most benefit his fatherland.[111]

[108] *Stort. Forh.,* 1857, vol. i, no. 3, pp. 121-2.

[109] *Ibid.,* 1859-60, vol. vii, no. 126, p. 562; vol. ix, p. 84.

[110] *Cf.* Wergeland's picture of the self-denying archivist wallowing in dust and documents, uncomplaining and content thus to serve the honor of his country, in *Digterværker og Prosaiske Skrifter,* vol. i, pp. 417-18.

[111] Munch, *Lærde Brev,* vol. i, p. 9.

Likewise, young Monrad, when preparing for his teaching position at the University, declared that it was his " warmest desire " to be placed in a field of labor where his knowledge and his faculties could be made " productive for his fatherland." [112]   Like knights of old, the intellectuals of this period were entered upon " scholarship's resolute Crusade " to recover the " glorious Holy Land " [113] of their nation's past and vindicate for their people a faith in its unique character and culture.

*   *   *   *   *

As the 'sixties drew to a close a new age was advancing. Abroad *Realpolitik* in 1864, and at home the consolidation of the political opposition in Sverdrup's new party of the Left, helped to dispel the hazy mists of romanticism and Scandinavianism.   After 1870 the intellectual circles were attracted to Comtean views and to Darwinian naturalism. They became devoted to realism, and regarded as outmoded many of the premises most characteristic of the mid-century. The teleology of the Idea was put away as superfluous and the concept of development was given a new application. Heretofore thought of as having taken place within the matrix of the Idea, it henceforth was emancipated from all supernal control and confined only by the moulding influences of " natural " causes.   The laws governing the development of social groups, including nationalities, were to be sought within the groups themselves and within their physical environment.   Realism no less than romanticism viewed human life as organic, but organic in a mundane and biological sense; the teleology which it recognized was less personal and less inscrutable, more mechanical and rational.

The concept of nationality also changed.   While romanticism tended to think of nationality in terms of fixity and

---

[112] A. Aall, "*Filosofien*," *Det kgl. Fred. Univ.*, vol. ii, p. 400, note 1.
[113] *Cf. Frey*, 1848, p. 168.

rigidity, realism conceived it more as something dynamic and as a product of natural development. No longer could it be maintained, for instance, that nationalities had arrived from Asia long ago, finished and complete, and had since remained unchanged.[114] A folk, said Vinje, was a growth [115] — both spiritual and organic — in any case a growth. The realist point of view interpreted nationality largely as a resultant of cultural forces. Sars once defined it as " a sum of unique cultural impulses, historical memories, and impressions of nature, gathered into the focus of a self-conscious soul." [116] Patriotism, wrote Hartvig Lassen, was not a matter of instinct but of culture and must be taught before one could appreciate the significance of one's own people as an organic unity.[117]

To sum up briefly and broadly the trend of three general culture epochs: rationalism with its gaze on humanity at large was apt to consider nationality a means to realize its ideal of cosmopolitanism; national differences due to physical environment, it tended to regard as a bit superficial. Romanticism broadened the concept of nationality by thinking of it as organic, by giving it historical depth through the inclusion of past as well as present members, and by binding it in a mystic covenant with the Idea. But realism made superfluous this teleology and pronounced nationality a product of development evolved in conformity with tangible and palpable forces in history and society.

[114] J. E. Sars, *Udsigt over den norske Historie* (4 vols. Chra., 1873-91), vol. i, p. 49.

[115] A. O. Vinje, *Om vaart nationale Stræv*, p. 5.

[116] Berner and Sars, *To Foredrag om Norskhed og Skandinavisme* (Chra., 1867), p. 44.

[117] " *Norskheden för og nu,*" *For Ide og Virkelighed*, 1871, p. 514; H. Lassen, *Afhandlinger til Literaturhistorien* (Chra., 1877), p. 154.

PART II

THE HISTORIANS

CHAPTER IV

A Generation of Non-professional Historians

During the first generation of Norway's independence national history was cultivated almost exclusively by amateurs — persons for whom history was only an avocation. Several of these were clergymen and educators and two were men of practical affairs. At the recently established University, L. S. Platou (1788-1833), professor of history and statistics, was much absorbed in administrative duties, while C. E. Steenbloch (1773-1836), devoted himself chiefly to general history although he did occasionally lecture on the history of his own country. Neither teacher inspired any great interest in Norwegian history; as late as 1818 no university student had yet chosen history as a specialty.[1]

At this time the interest in national history was concentrated on two special periods, the saga age and the recent Napoleonic years. The historical articles in the first serious periodical to be launched after the events of 1814, a quarterly called *Saga,* were confined mainly to the two periods mentioned. There was a good reason for this—the sources for these periods were more readily available—but we need not overlook the fact that the saga period had been Norway's day of medieval glory and the Napoleonic years had brought the dawning of a new independence. It was entirely fitting that after 1814, the first connected account of the older period should come from Chr. Magnus Falsen, the " father " of the constitution at Eidsvold.[2] His four-volume

---

[1] *Budstikken,* Feb. 2, 1818, column 600, quoted by A. Bugge, "*Historie,*" *Det kgl. Fred. Univ.,* 1811-1911, vol. ii, p. 216.

[2] Falsen's family came of Danish stock and he had a tinge of that ultrapatriotism which may accompany a naturalized citizenship.

work, appearing in 1823-4,[3] well written but not too critical, was mainly a popular reworking of the sagas and of the accounts by Torfæus, Schøning and Suhm. Falsen's intent, according to his foreword, was to make known the deeds and accomplishments of the forefathers and to reveal how ancient Norway had long prospered under a constitution "substantially like the one now reborn among us." His foreword closed with the hope that the venerable saga examples of northern power and freedom, of fidelity to king and love of fatherland, might sear themselves indelibly on each Norwegian's heart and spread abroad that sense of patriotism which alone would raise the nation to its former honor and respect.[4] The lengthy work closed with the events of 1319, thus making it unnecessary for Falsen to enter upon that more ambiguous period when independence was lost in a union with neighboring states.

Falsen's work might serve for general reading but there was serious need of an elementary school text in the history of the fatherland. Andreas Faye, a pastor and pedagogue who had long waited in vain for such a text from some more "competent" hand,[5] finally wrote one himself in the 'thirties.[6] While he did not limit his survey to the saga period, he gave it considerable emphasis. Dedicating his

---

[3] C. M. Falsen, *Norges Historie under Kong Harald Haarfager og hans mandlige Descendenter* (4 vols. Chra., 1823-4).

[4] *Ibid.*, vol. i, p. x.

[5] A. Faye, *Norges Historie til Brug ved Ungdommens Underviisning* (Chra., 1831), p. v.

[6] Andreas Faye (1802-1869) studied theology, but in 1829 began teaching in the secondary school at Arendal. As pastor at Holt in 1833 he became closely acquainted with Jacob Aall who lived in the vicinity. Faye was rector of the new normal school at Holt from 1839 to 1860. His background had been rationalist but he was somewhat influenced by romanticism when in 1831 he visited the continent to study certain elementary school systems, especially those in Saxony and Prussia. *Cf. Norsk. Biog. Leks.*, vol. iv, pp. 85-87.

book to Jacob Aall, in whose library he had gathered much material, Faye hoped the text would increase the love of fatherland and awaken a desire to understand and emulate the manly achievements of the forefathers.[7] The government became interested in his text and distributed 500 copies among libraries and public school teachers.[8] The Department of Ecclesiastical Affairs later paid him 100 *Spd.* to prepare an abridged edition for elementary pupils and arranged to distribute it to studious-minded youth of the more remote countryside.[9]

* * * * *

We may digress from history for a moment to note that patriotism motivated also some interest in historical geography. When the printing of his history was delayed for financial reasons,[10] Falsen prepared as an introduction to it, a geographical survey of Norway. This he began with a reminder that Norway once had included much more territory than now; Wærmeland, Dalsund, Bahuus-Lehn, Jæmtland, Herjedalen, Helsingland, and Lapland had been among its provinces, and Norwegian kings had once ruled over the Faroes, the Shetlands, the Orkneys, the Hebrides, the Isle of Man, parts of Scotland and Ireland, and the far-off territory of Greenland.[11]

Falsen's book was merely a sketch, but a definitive work in national historical geography was undertaken by Gerhard Munthe.[12] Munthe prepared himself thoroughly for this

[7] Faye, *op. cit.*, p. viii.

[8] *Departements-Tidende*, 1832, p. 340.

[9] *Ibid.*, 1833, pp. 714-15. A fourth edition of the larger work appeared in 1856, and a sixth of the abridgment in 1858.

[10] Falsen, *Geographisk Beskrivelse over Kongeriget Norge* (Chra., 1821), *Forerindring*.

[11] *Ibid.*, p. 2.

[12] Munthe (1795-1876) taught drawing at the military academy until

task. Since no one in Norway could give him the knowledge he needed of diplomatics and Old Norse, he sought aid of Rask in Copenhagen. Much of the information for his study he had to glean from medieval parchment deeds and rent-rolls, many of them widely scattered around the country. After a dozen years of intermittent labor in reading some ten thousand documents, he published his geography of ancient Norway,[13] desirous that this guide might facilitate instruction in the " history of the fatherland." [14]

*   *   *   *   *

Any work in Norwegian history at this time was handicapped by the fact that relatively few historical sources were known or available. Certain important nuclei of materials were in possession of *Det kongelige norske Videnskabers Selskab* and the University Library, and of course there were some records in the royal archives at Akershus although the materials here were deplorably meagre as public record offices go, since the seat of authority during 400 years had been not at Christiania but at Copenhagen. Historians looked to the south, rightly assuming that in the Danish capital there must be much material pertaining to Norway. Norwegians stopping in Copenhagen were from time to time taking copies or abstracts of individual documents.

The first large body of sources to be repatriated was brought not from Copenhagen, but from Bavaria. After the Napoleonic Wars two sets of documents had come to light at Amberg in the northern part of that kingdom. It was correctly surmised that they were from the Danish and

1841 when he retired, broken in health, to his former home at Kroken in Sogn. Halvorsen, *Norsk Forf.-Lex.*, vol. iv, pp. 204-5; *Ill. Nyhbl.*, 1859, nos. 1, 6.

[13] G. Munthe, *Noregr. Kart over det gamle Norge før Aar 1500* (Chra., 1840).

[14] *Ill. Nyhbl.*, 1859, p. 29.

Norwegian archives; some were records which the fugitive King Christian II had taken with him in 1523 and others were those which the last Catholic archbishop of Trondhjem had brought away as he fled to join Christian. It was recognized that this collection would be of importance for Norway's history [15] and late in 1829 Gregers Fougner Lundh (1786-1836) with an appropriation of 800 *Spd.* from the University treasury, set off for Munich. At first he planned to transcribe the documents, but shortly the Bavarian govern-ment generously donated the entire set, and by March, 1830, Lundh was back in Christiania with the collection of five or six thousand manuscripts intact.[16]

Lundh's specialty was economics [17] and not history, but he took a lively interest in the latter and made the first serious attempts to carry out the historian's rather prosaic tasks of collecting and editing sources. For some time he had been assembling diverse materials on the history, the language, the customs and the institutions of the Norwegian people to the close of the sixteenth century, and by 1828 he wished to begin publishing them as a sort of Norwegian *Monumenta*. In order to enlist public interest he issued in that year a sample,[18] inviting compatriots to support his larger project. The latter would, he assured, provide the apparatus which " future historians of our country ought to have at hand . . . before they begin their great and long-delayed work " of rearing the structure of national history. He wanted to help make better known the honorable past of

[15] *Dept. Tid.*, 1829, pp. 761-2.

[16] *Ibid.*, 1830, p. 416.

[17] At the University he first lectured on technology but some years later he was made professor also of economics. He spent much time investigating improvements in the mining industry. Halvorsen, *Norsk Forf.-Lex.*, vol. iii, pp. 577-79.

[18] G. F. Lundh, *Specimen Diplomatarii Norvagici*, etc. (Copenhagen, 1828), p. iv.

a country which had experienced a high cultural development at a time when the rest of Europe bent under the yoke of the church and of feudalism. In a note of tremulous patriotism he dedicated the project " To You, Beloved Land of my Birth." [19]

It was partly his pure love of the fatherland, remarked one reviewer, that had taken Lundh completely out of his own field to assume this arduous task at private expense.[20] The same motive led him to stir up interest in the editing of the country's ancient laws. Again he published a sample (the medieval municipal law of Bergen) to show what he had in mind.[21] These medieval laws, he insisted, deserved the admiration of every thoughtful person; authorities had pronounced them models in their day for the rest of Europe. With an eye to the future, he dedicated his sample to *Det kongelige norske Videnskabers Selskab,* " from whose patriotic activity Norway hopes for the publication of its glorious . . . . ancient laws." That society, as we shall see, was largely to justify his hope.

In the winter of 1829-30, as we have seen, he went to Bavaria. Hardly had he returned before he was importuning the *Storting* committee on ecclesiastical affairs for a three-year appropriation to publish either the *diplomatarium* of medieval sources, or the ancient laws.[22] On the floor of the *Storting* there was a full debate during which Jacob Aall eulogized at length the saga fathers and their model institutions. The *Storting* appropriated a sum and *Det kongelige norske Videnskabers Selskab* made an additional contribution.[23] Lundh soon received a royal license to print, but

[19] *Ibid.,* p. viii.

[20] *Maanedskr. f. Litt.,* vol. i, p. 151.

[21] G. F. Lundh, *Bergens Gamle Bylov* (Copenhagen, 1829).

[22] *Storthings-Efterretninger,* 1814-1833, vol. iii, p. 126.

[23] *Ibid.,* p. 127; *Dept. Tid.,* 1832, p. 836.

took no further steps for the time being and a few years later he died an accidental death. He had, however, outlined the broad program which younger and more competent talents were to place well on the way to realization in the next generation.

* * * * *

During the first generation of independence there were two ventures—one at Christiania and the other at Bergen—to promote the historical interest through organized effort. The Christiania group was interested in history proper; more specifically, it desired an organ in which to publish some of the material Lundh had recently recovered from Bavaria.[24] Perhaps Lundh took the initiative; at any rate a small group late in January, 1832, banded together as *Samfundet for det Norske Folks og Sprogs Historie* ("Association for the History of the Norwegian People and Language"), and issued a prospectus inviting interested countrymen to join in their plan to edit materials on the history of "our precious fatherland."[25] J. C. Berg, R. Keyser, G. F. Lundh and G. Munthe signed the invitation and named Jens Kraft as a fellow supporter of their project. Of these five, only Keyser and Lundh were university men and only Keyser was an historian. "We may say almost joyfully," wrote P. A. Munch, "that the nation and not the University initiated the *Samlinger* ('Collections')."[26] The prospectus announced that Norwegians were tired of seeing their sources in Copenhagen used by Danish scholars, and made known on foreign soil. Every free and independent people, it went on, must regard it as a matter of honor to

[24] *Maanedskr. f. Litt.*, vol. xvii, p. 285.

[25] Printed later in *Morgbl.*, 1832, no. 91; reprinted in *Saml. t. d. N. F. Spr. og Hist.*, vol. i, pp. i-iv.

[26] *Maanedskr. f. Litt.*, vol. xvii, p. 285.

make certain that its history should be presented in an unbiased manner. This was a matter of importance also for the country's political future. Norway had once drifted into national decline, and with history as a guide, the danger of another relapse must be avoided. No people in Europe so much as the Norwegians, save possibly the Greeks and the Poles, needed to know the great works of their forefathers—as an example and a warning![27]

The responses to the invitation were generous but unevenly distributed; there were 157 subscribers from Christiania, but only two from Bergen.[28] It was definitely a middle-class undertaking; clergymen, intellectuals, administrative officials and the military were well represented, but in the list there was not a single yeoman or *bonde*.[29]

The society's periodical, the *Samlinger til det Norske Folks Sprog og Historie* ("Collections for the Language and the History of the Norwegian People"), which first appeared in February 1833,[30] dealt much with the period of Norway's medieval greatness and with the days of her recent national recovery. A frequent contributor of material on the older period was Jacob Aall who prefaced several saga translations with lengthy introductions in which he exalted such qualities of the forefathers as he thought might insure the new-won independence. However, the Danish period was not overlooked and some use was made of the material brought back by Lundh. The editor of the periodical, as far as it had one, and certainly its sustaining spirit, was J. C. Berg,[31] and some mention should be made of his numer-

---

[27] *Saml. t. d. N. F. Spr. og Hist.*, vol. i, pp. ii-iii.

[28] *Morgbl.*, 1833, Mar. 1.

[29] *Cf. Saml. t. d. N. F. Spr. og Hist.*, vol. i, p. xi *et seq.*

[30] *Morgbl.*, 1833, Feb. 28 (advertisement).

[31] Jens Christian Berg (1775-1852), chief justice at Christiania from

ous introductory notes and critical comments. Berg was a bitter critic of Denmark's rule under the union, and of her action in 1814. Even patriots who had no love for Denmark felt it necessary to object at times when his acerbities became too caustic, as when he charged that Danish encroachments were planned deliberately [32] and were based on the worst possible motives.[33]

The sixth volume of the *Samlinger,* which appeared in 1839, proved to be the last. Most of the active members in the society were busy with other things.[34] A later plan to revive the *Samlinger* came to naught.[35] Nevertheless the first venture did have a sequel; out of the chrysalis of the *Samfund* there emerged shortly the multicolored butterfly of the Norwegian Historical School.

The organized activity at Bergen was more concerned with national archæology. The prime mover here was Christie, one of the most distinguished figures in public life during the first years of independence.[36] Having an interest in natural curiosities and in historical inscriptions, Christie came to think it desirable to form a society of "enlightened" men, zealous for the arts and sciences, and

1814 to 1844, was unusually well read and had assembled a large private collection of documents on Norwegian history. His copious learning was most often tucked away in notes and comments on articles written by others. *Norsk Biog. Leks.,* vol. i, pp. 444-49; Halvorsen, *Norsk Forf.-Lex.,* vol. i, pp. 209-11.

[32] *Maanedskr. f. Litt.,* vol. xvii, p. 288.

[33] Munch, *Lærde Brev.,* vol. i, p. 35. Feb. 13, 1840 to Molbech.

[34] *Norske Samlinger,* vol. ii, *Forord*; P. A. Munch, *Lærde Brev,* vol. i, p. 61. Feb. 5, 1843 to Rafn.

[35] Munch, *op. cit.,* p. 144. Jan. 21, 1846 to Rafn.

[36] Wilhelm F. K. Christie (1778-1849), in 1814 and the years immediately following, exerted a decisive influence on the new political order in Norway. But when his health gave way early, he retired to Bergen and henceforth held only a local office. *Cf. Norsk Biog. Leks.,* vol. iii, pp. 13-22.

for "Norway's honor and nationality." When he publicly invited those interested to join him in such a society,[37] there was a generous response; many donated specimens and exhibits, the *Realskole* of Bergen volunteered housing space,[38] and by June, 1825, there was effected a regular organization.[39] It was a non-professional venture; the administrative board included no trained archæologist or historian. From these beginnings developed the institution still flourishing as *Bergens Museum.*

In October, 1829, Christie joined with two friends, Bishop Neumann and Schoolmaster Sagen, and formed a little discussion group to meet every three weeks when papers were read and comments made on materials in the growing collection.[40] As manuscripts accumulated they hoped to start a periodical, and when they issued a prospectus [41] in 1833 to determine whether the public was interested, the response, for those times, was overwhelming. Among the 500 subscribers, some 300 were theologians, office-holders and military men, and more than sixty were merchants and shopkeepers. There were three landed proprietors in the list but no ordinary yeoman or peasant. The new periodical began to appear late in 1834 and was appropriately called *Urda,* after the Norn of the past. Three volumes had appeared before it was discontinued in 1847.

*   *   *   *   *

In its concern for national history the generation after

[37] W. F. K. Christie, "*Om det Bergenske Museum,*" *Urda,* vol. i, pp. 3-4.

[38] A separate building was bought in 1832.

[39] With the grandiose title; "*Museum for Oldsager og Konstsager, og et Naturaliekabinet af indenlanske Naturalier.*"

[40] *Urda,* vol. i, p. iii.

[41] *Ibid.,* vol. i, pp. iv-v.

1814, as we have observed, gave no little attention to events in Norway during the Napoleonic period. We have now to note that in the early 'forties there developed an unusual interest in the Eidsvold Constitution and the history of its origins. The occasion for this interest was the accession in 1839 of Prince Christian Frederick as Christian VIII of Denmark, giving new point to an old question. Had the Prince, as king of Norway for a few months in 1814, taken a part in forming the progressive Norwegian document? If so, liberal circles in Denmark had reason to feel encouraged, and Norway's basic law became of interest to the Danish public.[42] The Prince himself, when he ascended his absolute throne, disclaimed any part in the Norwegian venture and pronounced it a work of haste.[43]

With the lapse of years Norwegian patriots had come to regard their constitution in its "noble Roman drapery"[44] as something well-nigh inspired. The gloom of the Metter-nichian reaction had passed in 1830 and the Norwegians found themselves among the people most politically advanced in Europe. Their constitution, now the "cynosure of foreign eyes,"[45] was admired by many in Sweden and in Denmark where it might prove disturbing to the older order,[46] and farther afield its example might influence even France and England.[47] In boasting of its virtues Norwegian publicists became actively propagandist. Brømel

[42] *Cf. Morgbl.*, 1841, no. 136.

[43] He had therefore no cause to promote constitutionalism in Denmark, wrote Munch. *Cf. Lærde Brev*, vol. i, p. 72. June 9, 1843 to Molbech.

[44] *Christianssands Posten*, vol. iv, no. 72.

[45] H. Wergeland, *Norges Konstitutions Historie* (Chra., 1841-43), p. iv.

[46] O. M. Ræder, *Den norske Statsforfatnings Historie og Væsen* (Copenhagen, 1844), p. 229.

[47] *Den Const.*, 1841, no. 129.

made it known to a German public.[48]   Wergeland in writing
of its beginnings kept one eye on Europe.[49]   A part of the
press in Norway as well as in Denmark suggested that the
Danes change their absolutism in conformity with Norwegian example.[50]   In his descriptive treatise on the Norwegian government,[51] O. M. Ræder pointed out that
economically, Denmark, under her absolutism, seemed less
prosperous than Norway with her free constitution.[52]

While Ræder dealt with the constitution descriptively,
Henrik Wergeland set about to write the history of its
origins.   He wrote his *Norges Konstitutions Historie*
(1841-43) partly to remind his countrymen that their price-
less treasure, the constitution, demanded eternal vigilance,[53]
and partly to capture the current Danish interest.   Wergeland brusquely denied the Prince any part in the shaping of
the Norwegian constitution.   This document, he affirmed,
was due neither to God, nor the Prince, nor to general good
fortune.   According to his interpretation, it had sprung
from the people's own strength and power; it was something
organic and well rooted in the past.   The thread of continuity had been supplied by Norwegian patriotism, which,
he thought, was well prepared for the overthrow of Danish

[48] A. Brømel, *Die Freie Verfassungs Norwegens* (Bergen, 1842).
I am indebted to Harold Larson, then a Traveling Fellow to Oslo, for
verifying an inquiry in 1930 about Brømel's work.

[49] Wergeland, *op. cit.*, p. iv.

[50] Munch, *Lærde Brev*, vol. i, p. 72.   June 9, 1843 to Molbech.

[51] Published, it is worth noting, in Copenhagen.   Ole Munch Ræder
(1815-95), who served in the administrative and consular services, is of
some interest to Americans, for as a young man he was sent abroad to
study the jury system and from 1846 to 1849 visited the United States
and Canada.

[52] O. M. Ræder, *op. cit.*, pp. 228-29.

[53] *Norges Konst. Hist.*, p. iv.

NON-PROFESSIONAL HISTORIANS

absolutism. In fact, several delegates, in anticipation of events, had drafted constitutions before they came to Eidsvold.[54]

Among the amateur historians perhaps none knew as well as Jacob Aall (1773-1844) how the constitution had come into being for he had taken part in the decisive events of 1814. " This Bayard in the realm of the spirit," as Jørgen Moe called him,[55] furnished a life-long example of noble patriotism and public spirit, as the eighteenth century had used the terms. After preparing for the ministry he turned to mining, and while studying some of its processes abroad he came in touch with romanticist circles at Leipzig, Göttingen and Copenhagen. He returned to amass a moderate fortune from the iron foundry at Næss and was frequently called upon to give his services to public affairs, while his patronage of national scholarship was distinguished.[56]

Aall at this time proffered his memoirs covering the first fifteen years of the century, modestly hoping that his observations might deserve a place on the " saga tablets " of the fatherland.[57] He admitted that the constitution as it came from the unpracticed hands of the Assembly was an unusual document; witness particularly how peaceful had been the transition from absolutism to an order of such political wisdom.[58] Many wondered what he who had been so obediently loyal to Denmark in 1814, might have to say of

[54] Wergeland, *Udvalgte Skrifter* (7 vols. Chra., 1896-7), vol. vi, p. 39; C. C. A. Lange also thought the Norwegians "ripe" for freedom in 1814. *Udtog af Norges, Sveriges og Danmarks Historie* (Chra., 1841), pp. 229-30.

[55] Krogvig, *op. cit.*, p. 195.

[56] *Portræter af Mærkelige Nordmænd*, vol. ii, pp. 57-64; *Norsk Biog. Leks.*, vol. i, pp. 13-20; Halvorsen, *Norsk Forf.-Lex.*, vol. i, pp. 9-13.

[57] J. Aall, *Erindringer, som Bidrag til Norges Historie fra 1800 til 1815* (3 vols. Chra., 1844-45), vol. i, pp. 2, 6, 12.

[58] *Ibid.*, pp. 4-5.

Christian VIII. Aall substantiated, in the main, the unflattering judgment of Wergeland, and thought that the
influence of the Prince had no decisive bearing on the
development of constitutional government.[59]

* * * * *

No one among the amateurs was so diligent as Aall in
cultivating the interest in saga history. We have noted that
he contributed faithfully to J. St. Munch's periodical, *Saga.*
He had previously offered Finn Magnusen an annuity to
make copies of the Icelandic documents for *Selskabet for
Norges Vel,* and defrayed the expenses of Werlauff's edition
of the *Vatsdælasaga* (1812) and Rask's edition (1814) of
Haldorsson's *Islandske Lexikon* (" Icelandic Dictionary ").
With some difficulty he learned to read the Old Norse and
translated several sagas, and with the aid of Faye, Munthe,
Keyser and Flintoe,[60] he arranged an edition of Snorre's
Kongesagaer (" Royal Sagas "), in part to replace the
Clausen translation which long had fed " the flame of
patriotism " [61] but was then out of print. It should be
observed that among Aall's outstanding qualities were
moderation and fairness; deeply as he respected the forefathers, he tempered his admiration with criticism when he
thought their actions backward and unenlightened.[62]

The amateur historians of this generation lived in an age
of transition; rationalism languished and romanticism had
not yet assumed full sway. But their general point of view
remained chiefly rationalist. When they dealt with the saga
period, they saw in it many noble examples of the public
spirit which they would have liked to foster among their con-

[59] *Ibid.,* vol. ii, pp. 397-99; *cf. Den Const.,* 1844, no. 210.

[60] J. Aall, *op. cit.,* vol. i, pp. xi, xii.

[61] *Cf. Saml. t. d. N. F. Spr. og Hist.,* vol. iv, p. 203.

[62] *Ibid.,* vol. iv, pp. 214-16; J. Aall, *Snorre Sturlesons norske Kongers
Sagaer* (3 vols. Chra., 1838-39), vol. i, p. x.

temporaries. They felt inadequately the deeper changes that take place over the stretch of centuries and found it easy, figuratively, to drop a period of time in order to place the past next to the present. Thus the saga period seemed only a step from their own day, which had resumed where the former left off, the ancient freedom and political order.

CHAPTER V

THE NORWEGIAN HISTORICAL SCHOOL: KEYSER AND MUNCH

THE cultivation of national history shifted in the later 'thirties from the amateurs to a small group of professional historians. These applied a set of new and distinctive interpretations to their country's history — interpretations sufficiently at variance with the prevailing ideas on Scandinavian antiquity to fill the world of northern scholarship with the din of controversy for the next three decades. The group became known, especially among its opponents in neighboring countries, as the Norwegian Historical School.[1] Its conspicuous champion was P. A. Munch, disciple of Rudolf Keyser, who, as we have observed, did his first work in collaboration with the amateurs. Our analysis of the Norwegian School's premises and teachings will rest mainly upon the writings of these two scholars. Also to be considered as members of the School are C. C. A. Lange and C. R. Unger, apt pupils of Keyser and Munch, but they were important primarily as collectors and editors of the sources and their work will be discussed in one of the following chapters.

JAKOB RUDOLF KEYSER (1803-1864)

In the group which so ambitiously had started the *Samlinger* in 1833, Rudolf Keyser had been the only historian. His early training, since his father, a bishop of Christians-

---

[1] Molbech coined the term. *Cf. (dansk) Historisk Tidsskrift*, vol. i, pt. i, p. 493.

sand, died when Rudolf was only seven, was much influenced by his mother who was well read in history. At the University he chose the theological course but soon he was devoting himself " exclusively " to history, especially northern history. In 1825 he entered upon a decisive experience; he was sent abroad to learn to read the Old Norse. This medium was then almost a sealed tongue to Norwegians. Steenbloch and Aall read it after a fashion; Adler at Gimsø was able to give a little instruction in it to P. A. Munch; [2] Munthe had sought aid in learning it from the "half-mummified" Rev. Mørch in Hursem but after two trials gave this up since Mørch labored through the old documents "as the Devil reads Scripture." [3] Lundh had found guidance in Copenhagen. It was deplorable that no one really knew the country's own venerable tongue. Now Keyser, with a two-year stipend, was sent abroad specifically to master it, and that too, at the source. For by way of Copenhagen he proceeded to Iceland, where at the country's only Latin school he learned it of Egilssón, a venerable interpreter of ancient scaldic poetry.

Keyser returned in August, 1827,[4] to be made lecturer in history and statistics at the University. He did no work in statistics but in 1829 he was authorized to lecture especially " on the history, the antiquities and the language of the fatherland." [5] In a few years he was designated to go abroad and copy the ancient laws and when that task was completed (1838) he settled down at the University as professor of history, a place he held until his retirement in 1862.

[2] Chr. Brinchmann, *National-Forskeren P. A. Munch*, p. 9.

[3] *Ill. Nyhbl.*, 1859, p. 29.

[4] A later date is given in G. Gran, *Nordmænd i det 19de Aarrundrede*, vol. i, p. 355.

[5] *Dept. Tid.*, 1829, p. 334.

As a teacher of history Keyser was to the manner born. His lectures were presented in very good form.   They might well have gone direct to the printer, but as Keyser was reticent and cautious, too often they did not, with the result that much of his work was printed posthumously.   The range of his instruction was restricted.   Save for some lectures in 1859 on the Germanic migrations, he confined himself almost exclusively to Norway's history in the medieval period.   He lectured and wrote on Norwegian constitutional development, on the medieval church in Norway, on Old Norse literature and culture, on the private and religious life of the old northmen.[6]   He once participated in a current discussion, namely, in the flag controversy. In this he sought to make Norway's independent status unmistakably clear and wanted to avoid a union sign that might hark back to the Kalmar Union;[7] his arguments influenced the royal decree on the subject in 1844.[8]

Just as his range of study was narrow, so was his point of view restricted. , As Sars put it, he saw things mainly through the lenses of the national awakening which had gone out from Germany at the opening of the century.[9]   A bit independent in his ways, he had little desire to coöperate with foreign scholars, because, as Munch explained, his " creed " was " so exclusively Norwegian." [10]   But in Norwegian historiography his achievement was decisive.   He cut across that bombastic eulogy of the saga forefathers which, among the amateurs, had passed as patriotic history,

[6] For titles of his works see bibliography, p. 375.

[7] Keyser, *Historisk heraldisk Undersøgelse angaaende Norges Rigsvaaben og Flag* (Chra., 1842), pp. 25-6.

[8] Keyser, *Samlede Afhandlinger* (Chra., 1858), p. iv.

[9] *Cf.* J. E. Sars, *Udsigt over den norske Historie*, vol. i, p. 16.

[10] Munch, *Lærde Brev*, vol. i, p. 31.   Oct. 21, 1839 to Molbech.

with the blade of a sharper critical method, and inspired a respect for scholarly evidence.[11]

PEDER ANDREAS MUNCH (1810-1863)

The year that Keyser first taught, there sat at his feet an enraptured disciple who later became his most diligent coworker, Peder A. Munch. Munch's father was both tutor and pastor and his mother, a good conversationalist and story teller, shared with her son a strain of wit and prankishness. Other talented persons in the family tree were J. St. Munch, an uncle, who edited *Saga,* and his son, Andreas, who became one of the prominent romanticist littérateurs; Ole Bull, the internationally renowned violinist, was a third cousin.

Precocious young Peder readily learned several modern languages from his father. His curiosity about Old Norse was aroused by the cryptic forms in some books in his father's library, including Rask's *Grammatik,* Haldorsson's *Lexikon,* and a few sagas in the original. At the University, Keyser soon took him aside to do more advanced reading in the Old Norse, and naturally aroused his interest also in history. As a student Munch took active part in the Wergeland-Welhaven controversy, attacking *Norskhedspartiet* [12] and helping to edit *Vidar.*[13]

Soon after Munch finished his course in 1834, while prospects were none too bright, there came to him a decisive opportunity—the chance to go abroad with Keyser and

[11] There is no satisfying account of Keyser's life. But see *Ill. Nyhbl.,* 1857, pp. 28-30; 1864, p. 220; Halvorsen, *Norsk Forf.-Lex.,* vol. iii, pp. 217-18; A. Bugge, "*Historie,*" *Det kongelige Fredriks Universitet,* vol. ii, especially pp. 224-34; *Syn og Segn,* vol. ix, pp. 5-13. *Cf.* L. Daae's generous estimate of Keyser in his *Stortingserindringer,* p. 278.

[12] *Supra,* p. 32.

[13] The articles signed ...h are Munch's. Munch, *Lærde Brev,* vol. i, p. 17.

make copies of Norway's ancient laws in the archives in Sweden and Denmark. The pair stayed at the Danish capital for two years but they had been at Stockholm only a short while when Munch hurried home in May, 1837, to assume at the University an appointment in history, a position he coveted intensely. In his application he pleaded that the appointment meant to him " life's most cherished gift," " the most appropriate position among all the appointments of the fatherland." Failure to attain it, he wrote privately, would wreck his " whole scheme of life (*livsplan*)." [14] Partly through the influence of Count Wedel Jarlsberg,[15] Munch received the appointment and with it, the undying enmity of a rival, Ludvig Kr. Daa, who also sought the position [16] and had some claim to consideration, as he had been filling the position temporarily.

Though now a teacher of history, it was years before Munch could give formal instruction in the history of Norway. This was Keyser's field and Munch was left to lecture on medieval European history and occasionally on the French Revolution. In 1845 he dealt broadly with the saga literature, and soon after took up the ancient history of Sweden and Denmark. As he set about to write his massive Norwegian history he investigated racial and national origins and from 1855 he lectured on the ethnology of various European peoples.[17] No matter how national his theme, he

[14] Munch, *Lærde Brev,* vol. i, pp. 9-11.   Nov. 10, 1836 to the Academic Council; *ibid.,* vol. i, p. 15.   Nov. 10, 1836 to Steenbuch.

[15] A. Bugge, " *Historie*," *Det kgl. Fred. Univ.,* vol. ii, p. 237.

[16] L. Larsen-Naur, *P. A. Munchs Levnet og Breve,* p. 27.   Cf. also Fr. Ording, " *Små tillegg til L. K. Daas biografi,*" in (*norsk*) *Historisk Tidsskrift,* vol. xxvi, pt. vi, pp. 372-77; *Norsk Biog. Leks.,* vol. iii, p. 159.

[17] Munch, *Det Norske Folks Historie,* vol. viii, p. xxxvii, note. This work will be cited as *NFH.,* and the first and second volumes of the unfinished second series carrying the subtitle, *Unionsperioden,* will be cited as *NFH.,* vols. vii and viii.

was able at all times, in contrast with Keyser, to rest his scholarship on a broad European base.

Munch's forte was research (he was a poor class lecturer) [18] and he received numerous grants-in-aid. Several of these took him abroad, to Normandy and Paris (1846), to Great Britain and the Western Isles (1849-50), to Berlin and Munich (1854), to Rome and the great treasures of the Vatican (1857-61), to Stockholm for shorter stays (1861, 1862) and finally back to Rome (1863). It was even proposed to make him a sort of historian laureate (*Rigshistoriograf*).

Munch was at the height of his reputation and perhaps Norway's most popular man when his unexpected end came in May, 1863, after his return to Rome. He was buried in the Protestant cemetery there; at his grave Gregorovius, the historian, tendered the tribute of German and European scholarship. Personally, Munch was of a sociable disposition, and acquaintances came to look upon his home as a gathering place. His personal finances were uniformly in a wretched state and he very often supplemented his regular income by hack-writing and translating. Even in Rome, when he had a respectable allowance, he had to be helped along by friends while he kept on asking the *Storting* for more and more aid, complaining on one occasion that he must have been born entirely without " economic talent." [19]

*   *   *   *   *

Munch's intellectual orientation was complex, partly because, having a somewhat pliable personality, he responded readily to changing currents about him. As a romanticist and a middle-class liberal he had considerable faith in development and progress. Sars has maintained that in

[18] J. E. Sars, "*P. A. Munch,*" *Samlede Værker,* vol. iii, p. 203; *cf.* also *Stort. Forh.,* 1859-60, vol. i, p. 14.

[19] L. Daae, *Stortingserindringer,* p. 52.   *Cf.* also pp. 66, 103.

so far as he came to think of nationality and the Old Norse literature as subject to growth, he anticipated the evolutionary view.[20]   But it is for us to note that Munch's most characteristic contributions sprang from his unmistakable romantic outlook.   In terms of its phraseology he spoke of the nation knowing its " call," [21] and imputed to the royal sagas a " national aroma." [22]   He would safeguard nationality by distinguishing the " heterogeneous," the " immaterial," the " spurious," and the " unnational," from the " genuine " and the " primeval," [23] much as in the matter of language he would separate out " the mutual, the characteristic " attributes from " the special or the accidental." [24]

As a liberal Munch admired the results of the French Revolution.[25]   But he was not equally attached to each of the slogans of that great conflict.   Being a middle-class apologist, he held the watchword to be " liberty " and subordinated to it both " equality " and " nationality."   Between these two he was most apprehensive of equality which levelled everything " either under despotism's dizzy height, or upon communism's billowy sea." [26]   The equality preached in matters economic, he thought, was pure socialism.[27]   If the state raised the common man to a higher station, it really violated the principle of equality whose only true meaning,

[20] *Cf.* A. Bugge, *et al., Norges Historie fremstillet for det norske Folk*, vol. vi, pt. i, p. 501.

[21] Munch, *Saml. Afh.*, vol. i, p. 123.

[22] Munch, *Norges Konge-Sagaer* (Chra., 1859), dedicatory page.

[23] *Den Const.*, 1847, no. 15 ; Munch, *Saml. Afh.*, vol. i, p. 360.

[24] Munch, *Saml. Afh.*, vol. ii, p. 458.

[25] *Ibid.*, vol. i, p. 375 ; vol. ii, p. 298.

[26] *Ibid.*, vol. ii, pp. 54-5.

[27] He was amazed in Rome to see that the poorer element had only the haziest notions of the right of property and its " holiness." *Ibid.*, vol. iv, p. 313.

" aside from equality before the law, is equality of opportunity." [28] Munch would have the normal social structure
composed of two classes, the uncultured and the cultured.
Ability and intelligence, he argued, should have a chance to
rise, but something was needed, perhaps an aristocracy, to
balk the climb of brazen parvenus. He was particularly
annoyed at Yankee " equality " and ill-breeding.[29] This
hauteur made him ill-fitted temperamentally to participate in
the mid-century infatuation for the peasant; and it is a matter
of interest that Jørgen Moe thought that Munch, when he
reworked any of the popular traditions, needed the help of
someone who better understood the folk life.[30]

If Munch disparaged equality, he also felt (especially
after the disturbances of 1848-9) that no great leeway could
be given to the forces of nationality. In excess they stimulated war and conquest [31] and endangered liberty. Munch
was thus no doctrinaire nationalist ready to champion nationality in principle. True enough, he developed a vested
interest in some very nationalist historical theses; but he was
far from urging the rights of nationality everywhere. Of
course he felt as many others did that the special task of his
age was to develop nationality,[32] but as an intellectual, he
thought that nationality and even liberty might be subordinated to " culture's holy process." [33] Perhaps, he suggested,
the true rôle of culture, Christianity, and civilization was to
erase national differences.[34] He was not at all sure, on one

[28] *Ibid.*, vol. iii, pp. 543-4.

[29] *Ibid.*, vol. iii, pp. 359, 545.

[30] *Cf.* A. Krogvig, *Fra det nationale gjennembruds Tid*, p. 228. Letter
in the spring of 1843 to Asbjørnsen.

[31] Munch, *Saml. Afh.*, vol. ii, pp. 4-5, 302.

[32] *Ibid.*, vol. ii, pp. 8, 81.

[33] *Ill. Nyhbl.*, 1857, p. 226.

[34] Munch, *Saml. Afh.*, vol. ii, p. 11; vol. iii, pp. 613-14.

occasion, that the idea of nationality was justified; in its most extreme form it was certainly not justified—though he made it clear that he spoke here of an excessive doctrinaire nationalism, one both unhistorical and impractical.[35]

How Munch might subordinate the concerns of nationality to the considerations of culture may be seen in his appraisal of the Finnish nationalist movement.[36] Though a liberal and a patriot, he disapproved strongly of the "Fennomanians" and justified his disapproval in the name of culture. A nationalism merited approval only if it promoted the interests of culture, and that it could do only if the population were homogeneous. But in Finland there were two nationalities, one a cultured Swedish minority and the other a "mass" nationality of Turanian civilization, if it be worthy of that name. This broader nationality had no culture and was impotent to develop one; Kalevala, the national epic, so-called, was but an assemblage of fragments from everywhere, even from foreign sources.[37] Finland, he insisted, was getting its culture from the Swedish nationality; how shortsighted then to interrupt cultural development merely to satisfy a nationality of the masses.[38] Of course Finland might strive for homogeneity by getting rid of its non-national (i.e. its cultured Swedish) elements and going back a thousand years to a "raw state of nature." [39] But it might also be that the Finnish nationality was not in any case a vehicle of culture, and perhaps it was doomed to die. Giving aid to a disappearing nationality, he wrote in

[35] *Ibid.*, vol. ii, pp. 10-12.

[36] Munch, *"Om Finlands Nationalitet og dens Forhold til den Svenske,"* *Norsk Maanedsskrift*, vol. i, pp. 1-39. Reprinted in *Saml. Afh.*, vol. iii, pp. 401-37.

[37] Munch, *Saml. Afh.*, vol. iii, pp. 431-2.

[38] *Ibid.*, vol. iii, p. 414; *cf.* pp. 422-23.

[39] *Ibid.*, p. 433.

another connection, was barbarous and even unchristian.[40]
Better, he reasoned, to have the Finnish movement fade away
and let the population at large accept the Swedish nationality
with a modern level of culture.

How sensitive Munch could be to thought currents about
him is well shown in his readjustment to the democratic
movement, after the upheaval of 1848-50. Like others
in the circles he frequented, he quite reversed himself on
the French Revolution.[41] Now his admiration for it was
over; its fruit was not liberty but social upheaval. He saw
the value of tradition—the wise arrangement by Providence
through which older generations controlled the younger; the
Revolution had sought to break that control by a hurried
and artificial departure.[42] He ascribed the " eternal democratic jargon " current in Norway to the vogue enjoyed
by the eighteenth-century ideas of liberty and simplicity.
They encouraged the notion that in ancient days Norway
had been a democracy. But Munch pointed out that Norway
at that time, though homogeneous in population, had nevertheless possessed a complete aristocracy. It may have been
more a family than a class aristocracy; but in any case, contrary to the prevailing impression, the old society of yeomen
had been far from democratic or levelling in its tendencies.[43]
Munch was convinced that Norway still needed an aristocracy of talent if not of birth or wealth, and worded his
argument to help rationalize the continued hegemony of the
cultured classes and the bureaucracy.

* * * * *

Munch was an indefatigable worker and begrudged the

[40] *Ibid.*, vol. iii, p. 613.

[41] He came to see it more as a final victory of the Gallican over the
Germanic (or noble) element. *Ibid.,* vol. iii, p. 473.

[42] *Ibid.*, vol. iii, pp. 356-7, 359.

[43] *Ibid.*, vol. iii, p. 485.

few hours he devoted to sleep.[44]   Distractions bothered him
little and he could simultaneously perform more than one
task — draw a detailed map while carrying on a serious
conversation, or read proof while correcting a daughter's
practice of her music lesson.   His memory for detail was
phenomenal.   Without notes he worked in bustling waiting
rooms or noisy trains, citing his page and volume references,
and even writing quotations [45] from memory, leaving the
verifying of occasional passages to his proof reader, Lange.

Munch's literary production was stupendous.   In Halvorsen's *Norsk Forfatter-Lexikon,* the titles of his works
with bibliographical data fill sixteen pages.   This production
was equally striking in its diversity; it included school texts,
popular histories, travel accounts, biographies, polemics on
current literary, political and national questions, lengthy reviews, popular as well as scholarly translations of national
historical sources, and learned monographs in not one but a
half-dozen specialized fields.   At times he was a newspaper
editor and on three different occasions he founded or helped
to found periodicals of general interest.

We may observe briefly the patriotic bent of some of his
writings.   For a time he planned an undertaking on the
order of Fryxell's narratives of Swedish history or Walter
Scott's *Tales of a Grandfather* [46] and began a series of
accounts mainly on Norway's earlier history.   His intention
was that these should reveal the " features of the Norwegian
nationality " and awaken, among those with little time to
read, an appreciation of the fatherland's historical memories.
He was interested in Norway's physical and historical
geography, doing some map-sketching and preparing several

---

[44] *Cf.* his *Lærde Brev,* vol. i, pp. 349-50.   March 22, 1849 to Stephens.

[45] Munch, *The Chronicle of Man and the Sudreys* (Chra., 1860),
p. xxxiv.

[46] *Den norske Rigstidende,* 1847, no. 62.

careful studies. As one admirer says, he felt a desire to give his nation a bird's-eye-view of that terrain which was the object of its patriotism.[47] He came to realize that the Scandinavian peninsula was the slope of a single ridge with the sharp high altitudes rising abruptly out of the Atlantic and easing off to the gradual decline in the east and south,[48] a circumstance which fitted in well with his thesis of a migration from north to south and southeast. In the field of historical geography he gave students what they had long been lacking, " a complete handbook in the older geography of our fatherland," [49] in which he centered his attention on the period from the twelfth to the fourteenth century when Norway's dominion had been most extensive. He could thus place her eastern boundary far over in Sweden, and include the one-time tributary lands in the west. These, he explained, were then always included in the phrase, Norway's dominion (*Noregsveldi*), and he thought people would find it reasonable that he did not confine his work to the country's present-day limits.

What seemed most astonishing to Munch's contemporaries was the amount of his detailed research. He scattered learned reviews and contributions about him with seeming abandon. When not yet twenty-one he reviewed Faye's *Norges Historie* in the dignified columns of the Danish *Maanedskrift for Litteratur*,[50] and revealed at the outset certain qualities that were to be characteristic of his later works—an overwhelming knowledge of detail, an interest in the migration of northern peoples, a pronounced anti-Danish attitude, and a concern for the patriotic history of the fatherland.

[47] Chr. Brinchmann, *National-Forskeren P. A. Munch*, p. 53.

[48] Munch, *Lærde Brev*, vol. i, p. 75.

[49] *Historisk-geographisk beskrivelse over Kongeriget Norge* (Chra., 1849), p. i.

[50] Vol. viii, pp. 78-100. Reprinted in his *Saml. Afh.*, vol. i, pp. 1-16.

We may note briefly that his more serious scholarship also had its patriotic emphasis. In his first independent study,[51] on the ancient office of the *lendirmand,* he concluded that Norway's constitutional development had been quite different from that of her neighbors. A pronounced Norwegian attitude in several of his school texts on Scandinavian history brought objections from a Danish reviewer, C. Paludan-Müller,[52] to Munch's treatment of Queen Margaret's rôle in the Kalmar Union, his tendency to carve apart the common Dano-Norwegian history and literature of the union period, and in general, his inclination to carry over the vindictive one-sidedness of J. C. Berg. Some years later, he made a vigorous attack on Danish scholarship,[53] denying its moral right to many of the documents in its possession and complaining of its one-sided interpretations. The Danes preferred to conciliate him and shortly invited him to membership in *Det kgl. nordiske Oldskriftselskab* ("The Royal Northern Ancient Text Society") thus admitting Munch to the respected columns of the *Annaler for Nordisk Oldkyndighed* ("Annals of Northern Archæology"). During the next few years he contributed to it several weighty articles, a part of whose scholarly evidence further substantiated the challenging theses of the Norwegian Historical School; he drew the same conclusions in a study,[54] occasioned by the Schleswig-Holstein problem, on the ethnography of early Denmark. Again, he discussed [55] ancient linguistic conditions in the north and sought to show that Old Norse

[51] *Saml. t. d. N. F. Spr. og. Hist.,* vol. v, pp. 72-94. Reprinted in *Saml. Afh.,* vol. i, pp. 77-101.

[52] *Tidsskrift for Litteratur og Kritik,* vol. iii, p. 193.

[53] *Literaturtidende,* 1845, nos. 1-4, reprinted in *Saml. Afh.,* vol. i, pp. 102-148.

[54] Reprinted in *Saml. Afh.,* vol. i, pp. 417-505.

[55] Reprinted in *ibid.,* vol. i, pp. 223-273.

—the language of the Eddas and the sagas—was not the parent of Old Danish and Old Swedish but a sister, co-ordinate with them; with better reason he could then claim that these venerable literary products were distinctively Norwegian.

* * * * *

Munch's most ambitious project was his plan to write a detailed history of Norway. His decision to undertake this task seems to have been quite impromptu. One day in 1851 he returned home from work in a good humor, exclaiming to his wife: " Nathalie, now I am going to write Norway's history." [56] The casualness of his announcement belied both the magnitude and the significance of the undertaking.

A prospectus [57] announcing his plan made clear that he set to work in a spirit of patriotism. Since the coming of independence, he explained, much specialized work had been done on the national history of Norway and this material ought to be gathered into a running account. " Warm-hearted " for his subject and his fatherland, Munch now would " try his powers " on a complete history of the nation and thus fill " a long-felt want in our young literature." Tønsberg, his printer, invited " every friend of the father-land " to subscribe for this " national work."

The history began to appear serially in October, 1851.[58] It was imperative, reiterated Munch, that a national history should appear as soon as possible,[59] and he assured his readers that he had spared neither time nor effort to contribute all he was able " for the honor and benefit

[56] L. Larsen-Naur, *P. A. Munchs Levnet og Breve*, p. 68.

[57] *Morgbl.*, 1851, no. 218.

[58] J. and W. K. Grimm, *Briefwechsel der Gebrüder Grimm mit nordischen Gelehrten* (Berlin, 1885), p. 263. Letter of Oct. 30, 1851 from Asbjørnsen to J. Grimm.

[59] Munch, *NFH.*, vol. i, pp. iii-iv.

of the fatherland." [60]   He pointed to a certain simplicity
in the early history of Norway; nothing definite was known
of the present Norwegian people before they arrived in
Norway, and conversely the country had no history of an
earlier people apart from the present Norwegian stock—an
identification of country and people that was flattering to
national feeling.[61]

Working with feverish haste, Munch added number to
number and volume to volume until he approached the year
1319, the close of the period of ancient independence. Before
him lay the centuries of foreign entanglement, the 400 years
of lethargy when Norway was well-nigh eliminated from the
list of states. From this point on, many of the sources
must be sought outside of the country. Munch decided to
investigate the records at Rome and applied for public aid
so that he might copy sources in the Vatican Library.

In his application to the *Storting* he made a pronounced
national appeal.[62]   He stood now, he said, on the threshold
of " the large and barren room " where he could no longer
rely on saga accounts, while the chronicles and records that
should take their place had been lost to Norway " through
carelessness or deliberate barbarism." Their recovery
wherever possible, he urged, was of great national importance. Like every other enlightened nation, the Norwegian,
which more than many others had experienced a " corruption " of its historical memories and an eclipse of its earlier
prestige and independence, should naturally desire to see its
history presented as plainly as possible. Even the more
obscure periods of Norway's existence should be lit up, for
in them the basis was laid for its modern constitution. In
the same vein, the government committee which approved

[60] *Ibid.*, vol. i, p. xii.
[61] *Ibid.*, vol. i, p. 1.
[62] *Stort. Forh.*, 1857, vol. vii, pp. 141-45.

his application argued that the diffusion of an appreciation for the nation's history " must be accepted as an effective means to promote a collective life based on love of fatherland." [63]

Munch's sixth and concluding volume brought the first series of the history to a close with the year 1319, and he planned a second series to go to 1536. Its first volume was out in October 1862 [64] but the second was not finished when death overtook him.[65] He had just reached 1387 and the Kalmar Union. Fate in a sense had been kind; it had given him full time to finish the glorious epoch of national independence but had spared him the uninspiring and " desolate " centuries of subjection to foreign rule. As it was, he had completed nearly eight volumes, or 6600 tightly-packed pages (including prefaces).

The work had its technical faults—it went into lengthy digressions on obscure points, for instance—but there was no denying its national significance. What Munch had really done, and that too in the face of considerable national pessimism, was to show his countrymen that Norway did possess a history of her own; and thus he justified, in the eyes of his countrymen, Norway's claim to an independent existence. As each succeeding volume took its place, the very size of the undertaking was convincing. The work would be read through by relatively few, but many could surmise from a superficial glance that Norway must have counted among the peoples of the past when she could have so bulky a history; it seemed to give her modern independence an added validity.

To define Munch's position in Norwegian historiography

---

[63] *Ibid.*, 1857, vol. viii, pp. 524-25.

[64] Larsen-Naur, *op. cit.*, p. 186.

[65] O. K. K. C. G. Lundh edited the volume after his death and P. Botten-Hansen wrote a biographical sketch for it.

is both easy and difficult—easy because it is so towering
and unmistakable, difficult because its influence ramifies so
deeply and widely that the limits of it are lost to view.   He
was central to the whole national renaissance; its " standard
bearer," he has been called in one figure, its " central power
station," in another.   While his impulses were imparted to
many branches of public life and national scholarship, his
energies were best concentrated in the patriotic efforts of the
Norwegian Historical School.[66]

[66] A definitive biography of Munch must await the publication of his
letters (projected in three volumes as *Lærde Brev fraa og til P. A.
Munch* of which the first appeared in 1924).   But see P. Botten-Hansen,
"*Udsigt over P. A. Munchs Levnet og Forfatter-Virksomhed*," in
Munch, *NFH.*, vol. viii, pp. iii-xxxviii; Chr. Brinchmann, *National-
Forskeren P. A. Munch,* a sketch emphasizing the importance of Munch's
scholarship for Norwegian nationalism; J. E. Sars, "*Peder Andreas
Munch*" in Gran, *Nordm. i d. nit. Aarh.*, vol. i, pp. 353-377; J. B.
Halvorsen, *Norsk Forf.-Lex.*, vol. iv, pp. 168-180.   L. Larsen-Naur,
P. A. Munchs Levnet og Breve i Familiekredsen provides glimpses of
Munch's home life.

CHAPTER VI

A Distinctive National Origin

THE first startling thesis of the Norwegian Historical
School was its claim that the Germanic stock had migrated
into Norway by way of the north.   This was a direct challenge to the traditional view well established by eighteenth-
century scholarship, which accepted the ancient north pretty
much as a unit with little sense of any early differentiation
into separate peoples of Danes, Swedes, Norwegians and
Icelanders. Characteristically enough, the eighteenth-century
writers related the Scandinavian ancestors to the Trojans,
and explained that from the original home near Tyrkland
(Turkey? Troy?) or the Don regions, they had made their
way, perhaps shortly before the Christian era, through south
Russia, Hungary, Germany and Denmark, and thence into
Sweden and Norway, thus peopling the peninsula from the
south and southeast.[1]

When romanticism after the turn of the century intensified
the interest in northern antiquity, it fortified this point of
view, especially in Sweden and Denmark.   Romanticism
glorified life in the ancient north, as such; it accepted the
great deeds of the Vikings as northern accomplishments;
northern power, northern daring and northern resourcefulness had ravaged and partially colonized the British Isles,
terrorized and stabilized northern France and Slavic Russia,
lent their services almost condescendingly to the great

[1] Munch, *Saml. Afh.*, vol. iii, p. 228 *et seq.* See also Keyser, *Saml.
Afh.*, p. 20 *et seq.*

imperium at Constantinople, and on the other side, had explored and colonized the stepping stones of the North Atlantic to America. Since these achievements were accepted as northern in the most general sense, the honors might be shared jointly by all the modern descendants, by Swedes and Danes as well as by Norwegians and Icelanders.

Against this seemingly gratuitous assumption of honors, the Norwegian Historical School made its protest, insisting that some performances were distinctively Norwegian and Icelandic. It protested against that " philological anti-quarian dilettantism " [2] which, especially in Denmark and Sweden had juggled the facts of northern history to fit them on the " procrustean bed " of national and political consider-ations,[3] and it hurled a major challenge at the accepted view on early settlement by propounding the idea of a migration from the north.

The issue involved more than mere historical accuracy; behind this migration question lay considerations of deep national pride. The part of Scandinavia first to be settled by north-Germanic peoples, it would seem, might claim to be the true center of gravity in their cultural affairs. Thus if settlement had proceeded via Germany and Denmark then cultural influences must have radiated from south to north; the modern tongues, as the older theory claimed, must be heirs of the extinct Gothic, and Denmark with the region about, must have been the natural center of culture and affairs.[4] Conversely, if the first settlement had been made by way of the White Sea or some other arctic route, then north-central Norway might be considered the earliest center of medieval Scandinavian culture.

The newer theory was first clearly enunciated and fortified

[2] Munch, *NFH.*, vol. i, p. vi.

[3] *Ibid.*, vol. ii, p. iii.

[4] Munch, *Saml. Afh.*, vol. ii, pp. 47, 51; *cf.* also p. 32.

with a long train of reasoning, in an article contributed by Keyser to the last volume of the *Samlinger*.[5]   It is possible that he did not originate the theory.   An epitome of Norwegian history by J. C. Berg, perhaps written before Keyser's article, and left among Berg's unpublished papers, touched on the possibility of a migration from the north,[6] and P. A. Munch, in his second published article, had implied that the chief north-Germanic center had been in Norway.[7] Despite this however, it is to be noted that Munch considered the theory to have been Keyser's.[8]

Such a theory was in actual fact, much older. /Gerhard Schøning (1722-1780) had published a treatise in 1769 partly to refute the statements of a German ~~scholar, Eccard~~ ~~(1674-1730)~~, who explained [9] that the ancestors of the Scandinavians had branched off from the German stock on the continent and thus came to Scandinavia from the south. Schøning took exception and maintained that they had come by a migration north of the Gulf of Bothnia and as proof he deduced from classical writers an elaborate scheme of early folk relationships.[10] The similarity between this theory and that of Keyser is striking, but even more striking is the fact that concerning it Keyser and Munch were completely silent.

[5] " *Om Nordmændenes Herkomst og Folkeslegtskab,*" *Saml. t. d. N. F. Spr. og Hist.*, vol. vi, pp. 263-462. Reprinted in Keyser, *Saml. Afh.*, pp. 3-246.

[6] A. Bugge, " *Historie,*" *Det kgl. Fred. Univ.*, vol. ii, p. 228, note 3.

[7] Munch, *Saml. Afh.*, vol. i, p. 18.

[8] Munch, *Lærde Brev*, vol. i, p. 35, Feb. 13, 1840 to Molbech.

[9] In a work he entitled *De Origine Germanorum eorumque vetustissimus migrationibus ac rebus gestis* (Göttingen, 1750).

[10] G. Schøning, *Afhandling om de Norskes og endel andre nordiske Folks Oprindelse* (Soroe, 1769). Schøning's line of thought was anticipated in a general way in some unprinted notations by Árni Magnússon (1663-1730). Cf. *Árni Magnússons levned og skrifter* (2 vols., Copenhagen, 1930), vol. i, p. 106; vol. ii, pp. 111-113.

Daae, Schøning's biographer, has suggested that they ignored previous studies on principle, and that in their desire to get to the sources they overlooked a seventy-year old formulation of the theory.[11]   At any rate, their formulation was not as original as it seemed at the time.

As expounded by Keyser and Munch the theory rested on the hypothesis of an Aryan people. From an original habitat somewhere in " high " Asia,[12] the first human stock had separated into two branches — an Iranian division living south of the Amu or Oxus river and a Turanian on the lowlands of the north.[13]   Between the two there early developed a disparity in culture.[14]   The Turanian rose above the " rawness of nomad life" only with difficulty and where he did so, as in the Far East, his culture settled down to something static.   The Iranian, on the other hand, having in him the germ of later European culture,[15] displayed a strength which marked him for future mastery.[16]

A series of migrations radiated from Central Asia.[17] Westward to Europe came two Turanian peoples, ancestors of the Finn and the Basque; next some Iranians, first the Celts, then the Greeks and the Latins.   Then certain Scythians about 700 B. C. moved near the Black Sea, to be followed a century later by the Slavic Sarmatians. Finally came the Germanic stock which at first was limited to the stretches of the upper Volga.[18]   Moving west by way

---

[11] L. Daae, *Gerhard Schøning* (Chra., 1880), p. 83.

[12] *Almeenlæsning*, p. 192.   Keyser put it in the mountainous region of the Pamirs.   Keyser, *Saml. Afh.*, p. 221.

[13] Munch, *Verdenshistoriens vigtigste Begivenheder*, p. 3.

[14] Munch, *Saml. Afh.*, vol. iii, p. 422.

[15] Keyser, *Saml. Afh.*, p. 222.

[16] Munch, *Verdenshistoriens vigtigste Begivenheder*, p. 4.

[17] Keyser, *Saml. Afh.*, p. 222 et seq.

[18] Munch, *NFH*, vol. i, p. 10.

of the Baltic and the Åland Islands it settled in its later
home and differentiated into low, high and middle (or
east) Germanic.[19] It early made advances in its cultural,
social and religious life,[20] developed a keen sense of personal
freedom and national pride, and displayed a warlike and
conquering spirit.[21] The mark of its disdain for those it
subjected was deeply imprinted on European history.
Wherever it made a conquest there developed the two classes,
noble and unfree,[22] but where there was no conquest, as
along the North Sea or in the Alps, a noble class failed to
develop and all classes remained free and equal. From this
it followed that the nobility in Europe was essentially of
Germanic origin.[23]

The differentiation of the Germanic stock into a northern
and a southern branch may have begun even in the ancestral
home.[24] The tribes of the northern branch—ancestors of
the Scandinavians—on the way west, stopped in the Volga
region where they might be identified as early as the sixth
century B. C.[25] Avoiding Sarmatian and Chudic (Finnish)
peoples east of the Baltic, they worked their way northwest
in the next three centuries through modern Karelia and
Finland between the White Sea and the Gulf of Bothnia
and ultimately along the Arctic Ocean into north-central
Norway.

Somewhere along this trail, possibly in the Ladoga and
upper Dnieper regions,[26] certain north-Germanic elements,

[19] *Ibid.*, vol. viii, p. xv; Munch, *Saml. Afh.*, vol. ii, pp. 17-18.
[20] Keyser, *Efterl. Skr.*, vol. i, p. 9.
[21] *Ibid.*, vol. ii, p. 3.
[22] Keyser, *Saml. Afh.*, p. 404.
[23] Munch, *Saml. Afh.*, vol. iii, pp. 454, 457.
[24] *Ibid.*, vol. ii, p. 155.
[25] Keyser, *Saml. Afh.*, p. 221; *cf.* Munch, *Saml. Afh.*, vol. i, pp. 7-8.
[26] Munch, *Saml. Afh.*, vol. ii, p. 193; vol. iii, pp. 415-6.

the Roxolans, were left behind.[27] Beyond a doubt these were to be identified with the Russ of a later day.[28] Crowded on various sides, now by south Germans, now by Slavs, or again by Turanians, they remained quite inconspicuous, though in close touch with their north-Germanic kinsmen in Sweden. The Russ were not of Slavic but of north-Germanic blood and their kingdom later was to be the *Gardarige* of saga days where the Old Norse language and customs held sway long before the days of Ruric.[29] By the ninth century these Russ had established a sort of supremacy over neighboring peoples, and it was in order to maintain this superiority that they invited Ruric and his followers—their own kinsmen—to come and help them.[30]

Before the main north-Germanic groups arrived in Scandinavia there had branched off two groups known as Sviar and Gøtar.[31] These had probably been cut off from the main body by Chudic tribes,[32] and some among them may have tried to settle along the eastern shore of the Gulf of Bothnia, leaving a Germanic substratum in what was to be later Finland, centuries before the Swedish reconquest of the twelfth century.[33] But others made their way across the Gulf of Bothnia, the Sviar establishing their ancient center at Uppsala, and the Gøtar settling to the southwest in the vicinity of modern Göteborg.[34]

[27] *Ibid.*, vol. ii, p. 202.

[28] Keyser, *Saml. Afh.*, p. 181 *et seq.*

[29] Munch, *Saml. Afh.*, vol. ii, pp. 247-250.

[30] Munch, *Lærde Brev*, vol. i, p. 430. May 23, 1850 from Rafn to Munch.

[31] Keyser, *Saml. Afh.*, p. 151; *cf.* Munch, *Norges Historie i kort Udtog*, 4 ed., 1858, p. 4. See also the reference to the linguistic differentiation, in Keyser, *Efterl. Skr.*, vol. i, pp. 28-9.

[32] Keyser, *Saml. Afh.*, p. 206.

[33] Munch, *Saml. Afh.*, vol. iii, pp. 416-422.

[34] *Ibid.*, vol. i, p. 199.

The main part of the north-Germanic stock, now the *norrøn* (or Norse) folk, coming through the White Sea region must have reached the Kiølen Mountains of Scandinavia by 300 B. C.[35] Finding the country uninhabited, or at best peopled by scattering nomads, the *norrøn* people passed on to establish a center of settlement in the protected Trondhjem district.[36] The suggestion was made that a locality like Vefsen in Inner Helgeland might well be considered the " cradle " of the Norwegian people.[37] From this area, *norrøn* settlements spread along the coast and over the mountains, the general direction of dispersal being from north to south and southeast.[38] Great distances and impenetrable forests long separated the *norrøn* outposts from the Sviar and Gøtar in Sweden.[39]

As the *norrøn* stock spread to the southeast, it came in contact with the *Goter,* a people living in northern Germany, Denmark and southern Sweden,[40] who must under no circumstance be confused with the north-German *Gøtar* along the *Göta* River.[41] The *Goter* were south-Germanic; they were the later Goths of the migration period.[42] When the Norse stock was advancing southeastward, the *Goter* were expanding up to southern Scandinavia, and the two

[35] Keyser, *Saml. Afh.,* p. 206.

[36] Certain cantonal divisions in the northwestern part of the country suggested that the earliest settlements had been in these areas. Munch, *NFH,* vol. i, p. 94.

[37] (*norsk*) *Historisk Tidsskrift,* vol. v, pt. iii, pp. 560-61. Letter of Aug. 16, 1846 from *Videnskabs Selskabet* in Trondhjem to Ivar Aasen.

[38] Munch, *Saml. Afh.,* vol. i, pp. 184, 426, note; vol. ii, p. 88.

[39] *Ibid.,* vol. iii, p. 246.

[40] Keyser, *Saml. Afh.,* p. 70 *et seq.*; Munch, *Saml. Afh.,* vol. ii, pp. 17-18, 167; Munch, *NFH.,* vol. i, p. 38.

[41] Munch, *Saml. Afh.,* vol. ii, pp. 18, 46.

[42] *Ibid.,* vol. ii, pp. 97, 108-9; Munch, *Lærde Brev,* vol. i, p. 252. Jan. 19, 1848 to Stephens.

must have met and clashed perhaps in the vicinity of the Göta River.[43]   The victorious *norrøn* element expelled or repressed the *Goter* or Goths, and established their control over southern Sweden and began to spread over the Danish Isles by the middle of the third century.[44]   Eventually the area of the western Baltic with its complicated racial relationships of *Gøter, Gauter,* Danes and Goths was subjected to the north-Germanic influence.

It was the disturbing activities of the Norse stock in these areas which occasioned the great Germanic migrations of declining Roman days. Feeling the increasing pressure, some of the Goths moved southeast to Dacia and the Black Sea region, and other south-Germanic tribes flung themselves more directly against the Roman frontier. When Slavic Wends in the fifth and sixth centuries interposed and broke the connection with the south, such tribes as the Angles, Saxons and Jutes were diverted to England.[45]

According to this migration hypothesis, the Danish nationality was a mixture of north- and south-Germanic elements, although the Danes protested that they were north-Germanic. The matter really hinged on the nationality of the ancient Goths, for it seemed evident that Denmark and south Sweden had had a prehistoric Gothic population unknown elsewhere in Scandinavia. Had these Goths been north- or south-Germanic? Norwegian scholars held that they had been south-Germanic and cited evidence from both history and philology. They pointed to differences in linguistic development. While linguistic unity had long prevailed within the Norwegian and Icelandic stock, in Sweden and Denmark there had early appeared a marked differenti-

[43] Keyser, *Saml. Afh.*, p. 154.

[44] *Ibid.*, p. 148.

[45] *Ibid.*, pp. 137-149, *passim*; Munch, *Saml. Afh.*, vol. ii, p. 161; Munch, *NFH.*, vol. i, p. 62.

ation into dialects suggesting an admixture of the south-Germanic.[46] Similarly, the village, a south-Germanic institution, was universal in Denmark but unknown in Norway.[47] In like manner the archæology of the bronze and iron cultures and the distribution of the two runic systems[48] pointed to a similar duality in the early population of Denmark. In fact, the very name, Dane, most likely was south-Germanic in origin.[49]

Having shut the Danes out from the sanctuary of national purity, the Norwegian scholars were free to claim that their nationality was in full possession of it. They could point to Norway as the focus and center of the *norrøn* (or Norse) nationality.[50] Here that nationality had been most homogeneous, here was the norm, the archetype, not alone for Scandinavia but for all Teutonic peoples. The whole German race, having so little of what was characteristic, needed renewal in that " primeval stuff " which was retained fresh and unwilted only in the Norwegian nationality.[51] Munch envisaged a pan-Germanism that should promote a sense of kinship among all the branches of the Germanic race, and it stirred his patriotism to think that in any such aggregation, Norway, which so faithfully had retained the pristine Germanic, would exercise a spiritual hegemony;[52] neighboring peoples would have to come to her to find their deeper selves. The teachings of the Norwegian School seemed to sub-

---

[46] Keyser, *Efterl. Skr.*, vol. i, p. 37.

[47] Munch, *Saml. Afh.*, vol. ii, p. 52; Munch, *NFH.*, vol. i, pp. 115-16.

[48] Munch, *Saml. Afh.*, vol. ii, p. 102.

[49] Keyser, *Saml. Afh.*, p. 76.

[50] Munch had difficulty with the word *norrøn*. In English the adjective " Scandinavian " was unsatisfying and he preferred the terms " northern " or " northmannish " as more adequate and national. Munch, *Lærde Brev*, vol. i, p. 115. Letter in the summer of 1845 to Stephens.

[51] *Den Const.*, 1847, no. 15; Munch, *Saml. Afh.*, vol. i, p. 559.

[52] *Den Const.*, 1847, no. 15; *cf.* Welhaven, *Saml. Skr.*, vol. vi, pp. 288-90.

stantiate fully the aims of the Schleswig-Holstein movement
and the program of the German nationalists.   If Denmark's
population had been formed by the imposition of a north-
Germanic layer upon a broad stratum of Gothic,[53] then her
nationality was largely south-Germanic.   That being the
case, why should not she—or at least the Duchies—be made
German in conformity with the principle of nationality.
With such conclusions, however, Munch had no sympathy,
and he pointed out that while the Danes historically were
largely south-Germanic because of their Gothic strain, that
warranted no modern claim.   The Goths and their language
and culture of ancient time had long ceased to be extant and
did not concern the Germans of today.[54]   In reality the old
Gothic element had been very close to the north-Germanic,
much closer than either the low or the high German.[55]   Moreover, the population of the country had come to be mainly
Germanic through the long amalgamation with the conquering Danes, and much the same was true of the language.[56]
This amalgamation, insisted Munch, had been uniform
throughout the country and no locality was more German
than another.[57]   There was nothing, therefore, in the migration theory to support the German claims to Schleswig-
Holstein.

While Denmark was unceremoniously excluded from the
place of honor among northern states, Munch pointed out
that she had occasion to be proud for other reasons.   Fate
had assigned to her people a specific rôle; that was to serve
in modern times as a link between descendants of the north-

[53] Munch, *Saml. Afh.*, vol. iii, p. 276.

[54] Munch, *Lærde Brev*, vol. i, p. 291.   July 25, 1848 to Rafn.

[55] Munch, *Saml. Afh.*, vol. i, p. 503.

[56] Munch, *Lærde Brev*, vol. i, p. 291; *cf.* p. 257; Munch, *Saml. Afh.*,
vol. i, p. 502; vol. ii, p. 52.

[57] Munch, *Saml. Afh.*, vol. i, pp. 497, 503.

and the south-Germanic peoples. Denmark was called to disseminate the true constitutional freedom of the Germanic race to the "innermost core" of Europe and set Germany the example of true national liberty. Denmark would find her salvation in being neither northern nor German but individually Danish.[58] Her people must not ignore the German (south-Germanic) element in their nationality and disregard the development intended for them by Fate.[59] Neither should they lament their rôle, for it was not necessarily a blessing to have "a pure and unmixed nationality." [60]

* * * * *

The theory of the northern migration in the long run proved untenable. Abroad it made little headway and the evidence against it accumulated. While the Norwegian scholars did not abandon it, Munch after the middle of the century began to introduce modifications [61] but these pertained to details; they did not unsettle for him the basic premise of a distinctive national origin.

What finally undermined the theory was the developing auxiliary science of archæology. Keyser, who had some interest in the subject (shortly after his return from Iceland he had been placed in charge of the University's collection of antiquities) had looked to archæology for additional proof of a northern migration.[62] But in the 'sixties this science became established on a firm basis and the work of men like Worsaae, Grundtvig, and Rygh led to the view that from very early times the whole north, including Denmark, had been peopled by a single folk, most likely from the south.

[58] *Ibid.,* vol. ii, p. 53.

[59] *Ibid.,* vol. ii, p. 31; vol. iii, pp. 601-2, 627, 629.

[60] *Ibid.,* vol. ii, p. 87.

[61] These are noted by P. Botten-Hansen in Munch, *NFH.,* vol. viii, pp. xv-xvi; *cf.* also *ibid.,* vol. i, pp. 88-89.

[62] *Cf.* Keyser, *Saml. Afh.,* p. 233 *et seq.*

In other fields, E. Sundt, and L. Daa, Munch's old rival, cited against the theory the conditions of primitive agriculture and certain deductions from the physical geography of northern Scandinavia.[63] The theory hardly survived the 'sixties.

[63] "*Helgeland den ældste norske Bygd,*" *Folkevennen,* 1864, *cf.* especially p. 136; L. K. Daa, "*Have Germanerne invandret til Skandinavien fra nord eller fra syd?*" *Forhandlinger ved de skandinaviske Naturforskeres 10de Møde i Christiania* (1868), pp. 16-53; *cf.* L. Daae, *Stortingserindringer,* p. 123.

CHAPTER VII

THE *Norrøn* LITERATURE

THE second challenging contention of the Norwegian Historical School—the second major dogma in its "confession of faith"[1]—was its claim that the Old Norse literature was exclusively *norrøn*, i. e., Norwegian-Icelandic. This idea met a stubborn hostility from Swedish, and especially from Danish, scholars[2] who had here a sort of vested interest to defend. According to the traditional view the venerable Old Norse literature was a common possession of the Scandinavian peoples which by the accident of history had been best preserved in Iceland. Romanticism, particularly in Sweden and Denmark, thought in terms of a single northern folk spirit and ascribed the old literature to an undifferentiated northern genius. This older view, according to Munch, had first been formulated to meet a German contention that the themes of the Eddas were Teutonic,[3] and in refuting this, Scandinavian scholars had established that they were "northern." Now a somewhat similar situation had arisen on a smaller scale, in that Norwegian scholars sought to restrict a possession hitherto regarded as broadly northern to Norwegian-Icelandic limits. That literature, they insisted, was not "northern" but *norrøn*, and therefore a

[1] *Cf.* Keyser, *Saml. Afh.,* vol. i, p. 30; Munch, *Lærde Brev,* vol. i, p. 237. Sept. 18, 1847 to Stephens.

[2] For a survey of the relations between the Norwegian and the Danish scholars see G. Indrebø, "*Den norske historiske skulen og Danmark,*" *Syn og Segn,* vol. xxxi, pp. 337-51, 369-83, 437-46.

[3] Munch, *Saml. Afh.,* vol. ii, p. 27.

135

product of the Norse stock in the narrower sense. It was "exclusively Norwegian,"[4] and Danes and Swedes had no share in it.

In challenging Danish claims the Norwegian historians objected strenuously to what they insisted was a misleading use of the word *norrøn*. This term, often met with in the sources, had been translated by the Danes as "northern"[5] and they had been particularly fond of applying it to the old literature.[6] When Munch in 1832 referred to the ancient tongue as "Old Norwegian," his Danish editors reminded him that the proper designation was "old northern."[7] Munch insisted that *norrøn* had never meant anything but Norse or Norwegian[8] and when used to distinguish cultural matters, he maintained that it applied only to Norway and her colonies.[9] The *norrøn* had been the language used in Norway until the fourteenth century, when it declined, and persisted only in Iceland.[10] Even the Icelanders continued to know it as the *norrøn* or Norwegian,[11] and as late as 1747 an Icelandic Bible translation was spoken of as made "*á norraenu.*"[12] The confusion of *norrøn* and northern had

[4] P. A. Munch and C. R. Unger, *Oldnorsk Læsebog* (Chra., 1847), p. iii.

[5] *Cf. Syn og Segn*, vol. xxxi, p. 375, note. Letter of Feb. 2, 1852 from Rafn to Wegener.

[6] Munch, *Saml. Afh.*, vol. ii, p. 179; *cf.* vol. i, p. 132.

[7] *Maanedskr. f. Litt.*, vol. viii, p. 81, note.

[8] Munch, *Saml. Afh.*, vol. ii, p. 25.

[9] *Ibid.*, vol. ii, p. 126; vol. iv, p. 503; *cf.* his request that Grimm change the abbreviation, "*altn.*," in his *Wörterbuch* to "*altnorwegisch.*" Jakob and W. K. Grimm, *Briefwechsel der Gebrüder Grimm mit nordischen Gelehrten*, p. 240. April 2, 1853 to J. Grimm. *Cf.* also Munch, *Lærde Brev*, vol. i, pp. 214-15.

[10] P. A. Munch og C. R. Unger, *Det oldnorske Sprogs eller Norrøna-sprogets Grammatik* (Chra., 1847), p. iv.

[11] Munch, *Saml. Afh.*, vol. ii, p. 116.

[12] *Ibid.*, vol. ii, p. 123; Munch, *Lærde Brev*, vol. i, p. 194. Apr. 28, 1847 to Grimm.

been facilitated in a measure by the Norwegian scholars themselves,[13] for in speaking of the migrations which had radiated from Norway to Denmark and Sweden, Keyser especially, had sometimes used *norrøn* when he meant north-Germanic.

Equally aggravating and difficult to explain away was the term, *donsk tunga,* a phrase early applied to the language of the north in general. Rafn claimed that *donsk tunga* was an older term than *norrøn* and that both were encompassed in the designation, *oldnordisk* [14] or old northern. But such use of *donsk tunga* and *norrøn* was annoying to the Norwegians for it seemed to carry the inference that the north had had one common tongue and that the literature engendered in it was also common, or, as many romanticists would have it, a product of the northern folk spirit.

The Norwegian School protested vigorously against these implications. When laying claim to the old literature, Keyser pointed out, they must insist that *norrøn* meant only Norwegian and Icelandic.[15] No such cultural Scandinavian unity as the Danes assumed ever existed, said Munch, save possibly among the north-Germanic people in very ancient days before they arrived in the Scandinavian peninsula.[16] In the later 'forties, Munch investigated at length the ancient linguistic relationships in the north, and incorporated his findings, as he went along, in a series of articles and handbooks. Whereas Keyser had thought that Old Swedish and Old Danish [17] were offshoots from the *norrøn,* Munch concluded that the two former were not derivatives of Old

---

[13] *Cf. Fædrelandet,* 1856, p. 737; *Ill. Nyhbl.,* 1857, pp. 29-30, note.

[14] *Syn og Segn,* vol. xxxi, p. 375, note.

[15] Keyser, *Efterl. Skr.,* vol. i, pp. 29-30.

[16] Munch, *Forn-Swenskans ... Språkbygnad,* pp. xii-xiii; *cf.* Munch, *Saml. Afh.,* vol. ii, p. 27.

[17] Keyser, *Saml. Afh.,* p. 9.

Norse, but parallel with it as branches of a primeval northern (*ur-nordisk*) parent stem,[18] and he worked out a genealogical table to show how this prehistoric tongue had divided into a west-northern (the *norrøn* or Norse, extant in Norway, Iceland and the colonies) and an east-northern branch (later bifurcated into Old Swedish and Old Danish).[19]

If it could be shown that the differentiation had taken place very early, this would help to establish the Eddic literature as *norrøn*. Norwegian scholars were convinced that the great literary development had begun after the linguistic homogeneity was past, at a time when Danish and Swedish were quite distinct from the Norse.[20] The differentiation, according to Munch, began about 1050,[21] and the lingering use of a common term like *donsk tunga* no longer corresponded with fact. Old Swedish and Old Danish had diverged from the parent stem of the north-Germanic very early,[22] and for them might be claimed the most distinguished primitiveness. Munch conceded this honor to them since he then found it easier to shut them out from a share in the Norwegian-Icelandic literature.[23] The *norrøn* alone was the language of the sagas and Eddas; [24] what was written in

---

[18] Munch, *Lærde Brev*, p. 214. July 2, 1847 to Grimm.

[19] Munch, *Saml. Afh.*, vol. i, p. 227; Munch, *Forn-Swenskans . . . Språkbygnad*, p. xiv *et seq.*

[20] Keyser, *Efterl. Skr.*, vol. i, p. 29.

[21] *Cf.* his opinion in one passage that the Norwegian was distinct as early as the discovery of Iceland. *Saml. Afh.*, vol. ii, p. 26.

[22] Munch, *Saml. Afh.*, vol. i, p. 227.

[23] *Ibid.*, vol. i, p. 268.

[24] *Ibid.*, vol. i, p. 363; vol. iii, p. 264; vol. iv, p. 508; Munch, *NFH.*, vol. iv, p. 1056; Munch, *Forn-Swenskans . . . Språkbygnad*, p. xiii; J. and W. K. Grimm, *Briefwechsel der Gebrüder Grimm mit nordischen Gelehrten*, p. 240. Letter of Apr. 2, 1853 from Munch to Grimm; *cf.* Aasen, *Skr. i Saml.*, vol. iii, p. 186.

the *norrøn* tongue must surely belong to the *norrøn* literature, which meant in this case that it was Norwegian.[25]

Neither the Old Danish nor the Old Swedish had developed a literature,[26] or, if it be conceded that the latter had
left something, compared with that in the Old Norse, it was
less national.[27]   Even some of the Swedish chronicles had
come originally from Norway.[28]   In Sweden, where denser
settlement hampered individuality, there had developed no
popular lore.[29]   The old mythology could not be considered
" northern " as Munch had entitled it in 1840; it must be
termed Norwegian, for the mythology of the Eddas was
neither Swedish nor Danish.[30]   And was there not a striking corroboration of these facts in modern life?   Neither in
Sweden nor in Denmark [31] but only in Norway could the
study of Old Norse be really popular; there was its " right
home " and true fountain head.[32]   The Dane did not naturally appreciate the sagas, while the Norwegian responded to
them as " flesh of his flesh and blood of his blood." [33]

Not only were Swedes and Danes without a share in the
norrøn literature, but at the time they hardly knew about it!
It was practically unknown outside of Norway and Iceland.[34]
Even so distinguished a man of Danish letters as Saxo was
ignorant of much of the better saga material,[35] while the

[25] Munch, *Forn-Swenskans . . . Språkbygnad*, p. xxxiii.

[26] *Den Const.*, 1847, no. 15.

[27] Munch, *Forn-Swenskans . . . Språkbygnad*, p. xxiii.

[28] Munch, *Saml. Afh.*, vol. ii, p. 490.

[29] Munch, *Forn-Swenskans . . . Språkbygnad*, p. xxx.

[30] *Ibid.*, p. xvi; Munch, *Saml. Afh.*, vol. ii, p. 26, note 1; vol. iii,
p. 248 *et seq.*

[31] Munch, *Lærde Brev*, vol. i, p. 210.   June 25, 1847 to J. Grimm.

[32] *Ibid.*, vol. i, p. 215.   July 2, 1847 to J. Grimm.

[33] Munch, *Saml. Afh.*, vol. i, p. 114.

[34] *Ibid.*, vol. iii, p. 270; *cf.* vol. ii, pp. 527-28.

[35] Munch, *Forn-Swenskans . . . Språkbygnad*, p. xxxi; *cf.* Munch,
Saml. Afh., vol. i, p. 440.

Swedes were but imperfectly familiar with *Ynglingasaga*.[36]
Yet Munch could offer the sister nations some consolation.
There stirred a " national element " in the Old Swedish and
Old Danish, and modern descendants might study the speech
of their forefathers direct without a tempting detour by
way of the Icelandic.[37]

Through an accident of history a good share of the
coveted literature had been copied down and preserved in
the restricted locality of Iceland. If it was correct to exclude both Sweden and Denmark from any honors in that
literature, what about leaving out also Norway?   That
would never do!   It must be shown that Norway and Iceland had shared that culture.[38]   When the old literature
flourished, Iceland had been an integral part of the Norse
community, sharing with it a single folk character and a
single language.[39]   Take the Eddic lays, for example; they
had been composed long before Iceland was discovered.[40]
True enough, they were written down centuries later by
Icelanders, but these considered themselves Norwegian,[41]
just as the themes they sang were Norwegian [42] and the
language they employed was that used in Norway.[43]   Instead
of calling the old literature Icelandic it would be better to
term it *norrøn*.[44]   One ordinarily did not name the language

[36] Munch, *Lærde Brev*, vol. i, p. 434.   June 13, 1850 to Grimm.

[37] Munch, *Forn-Swenskans* . . . *Språkbygnad*, pp. xxiv-xxv.

[38] Munch, *Saml. Afh.*, vol. i, p. 330.

[39] Munch, *NFH.*, vol. i, p. v; vol. iv, p. 1056.

[40] Munch, *Lærde Brev*, vol. i, p. 181.   Feb. 20, 1847 to Stephens.
Ibid., p. 194.   April 28, 1847 to Grimm.   *Cf.* Munch, *Saml. Afh.*, vol. i,
p. 206, note i; *ibid.*, vol. ii, p. 26.

[41] Keyser, *Efterl. Skr.*, vol. i, p. 21.

[42] *Ibid.*, p. 24; Munch, *Saml. Afh.*, vol. iii, p. 269.

[43] Keyser, *Efterl. Skr.*, vol. i, p. 34.

[44] As applied to the literature, the word " Icelandic " came into use only

of a people after its colony but after the mother country; Swedish books printed on the island of St. Barthelemy would hardly be spoken of as Barthelemyan.[45] It should be remembered too that the cultural center at the time was in Norway; hither the Icelander came to get his finishing,[46] and here he had privileges which he could not enjoy in Denmark or Sweden.[47] Everywhere men of the *norrøn* race looked to the royal court of Norway [48] and quite possibly the literature that was composed in Iceland as well as in Norway was calculated primarily for this court and its Norwegian aristocracy.[49] Iceland may have had more writers, but then Norway had more readers and the literary activity had really been a unit.[50]

In the Norse literature Norway not only had a share, but her part was the largest. In fact just a few things such as the lawbooks and the Icelandic sagas were indisputably Icelandic.[51] The brightest gem in *norrøn* literature, *The King's Mirror,* was quite likely written in Norway,[52] and such venerable records as Norway's ancient laws were obviously native.[53] Certain original documents found in 1846 in the

after the Reformation when little was left of the *norrøn* in Norway proper. Munch, *Saml. Afh.*, vol. ii, p. 26; vol. iii, pp. 272-3; Munch, *Forn-Swenskans . . . Språkbygnad*, p. xxxviii.

[45] P. A. Munch and C. R. Unger, *Det oldnorske Sprogs eller Norrønasprogets Grammatik*, p. iv; Munch, *Lærde Brev*, vol. i, p. 296. Aug. 3, 1848 to G. E. Klemming.

[46] Keyser, *Efterl. Skr.*, vol. i, p. 22.

[47] Munch, *Saml. Afh.*, vol. ii, p. 120; vol. iii, p. 253.

[48] *Cf.* Keyser, *Efterl. Skr.*, vol. i, p. 404.

[49] Munch, *Forn-Swenskans . . . Språkbygnad*, p. xxxiv.

[50] Keyser, *Efterl. Skr.*, vol. i, pp. 23-24; Munch, *Saml. Afh.*, vol. iii, p. 270.

[51] Munch, *Saml. Afh.*, vol. ii, p. 121.

[52] Keyser, Munch and Unger, *Konungs Skuggsjá* (Chra., 1848), p. v.

[53] Munch, *Lærde Brev*, vol. i, p. 296. Aug. 3, 1848 to G. E. Klemming.

public archives [54] had had very little, if anything, to do with
Iceland; their handwriting was Icelandic, but that proved
neither the one thing nor the other, for the writers may have
been merely copyists. In fact the discovery raised the
larger question whether the honors so often ascribed to
Icelanders for preserving the Norse literature should not
be shared with the Norwegians.[55] In fine: within the unit
of the *norrøn* culture, Norway had the leading rôle; the
language was hers and the old literature took its rise " from,
in, by and for," her.[56]

But to displace the Icelanders from their widely recognized
literary priority was a dangerous matter; so much evidence
was in their favor. Even Munch wavered in his convictions.
At one time he found it difficult to distinguish between the
contributions of the two.[57] More, perhaps, than any other
European colony, Iceland could justly refer to part of the
joint literature as her own.[58] Norwegian scholars, he wrote
again, had no desire to deny any honors to the Icelanders,[59]
and at another time he assigned to them the " preponderating
share " in the old literature.[60]

[54] *Infra*, p. 154.

[55] Munch, *Saml. Afh.*, vol. i, pp. 291-2.

[56] *Ibid.*, vol. i, pp. 103-4; Munch, *Lærde Brev*, vol. i, p. 215. July 2,
1847 to Grimm.

[57] P. A. Munch and C. R. Unger, *Oldnorsk Læsebog*, p. iii.

[58] P. A. Munch and C. R. Unger, *Det oldnorske Sprogs eller Norrønasprogets Grammatik*, p. iv.

[59] *Cf.* Munch, *Saml. Afh.*, vol. iii, p. 270.

[60] *Syn og Segn*, vol. xxxi, p. 383. Letter of May 8, 1857 from Munch
to Molbech; *cf.* Munch, *NFH.*, vol. iv, pp. 1032-3.

CHAPTER VIII

The Antipathy against Denmark and the Danes

In some respects the Norwegian scholars found their Danish colleagues well-nigh incorrigible. The Danes balked at the migration theory even when their investigations corroborated it,[1] and they continued to claim a share in the old literature. But some day they would have to recognize that " our obvious right " to that literature was " plain as noonday," and then would be silenced " the last croak " about its being northern or Icelandic.[2] Their reluctance to accept newer points of view must be due to unyielding national pride.[3] Munch, on the opening page of his first published article, wrote that patriotism often blinded the Danes in their treatment of Norway's history;[4] when facts were lacking they supplemented them with phantasy.[5] Most of the " patriotic exclusive ultras," he thought, were concentrated in the *Oldskriftselskab* [6] and sometimes he singled them out. Rask's animosity toward Norway, he thought, was well-nigh instinctive,[7] though the chief offender in this regard, he decided, was Registrar Petersen.[8] Even Rafn,

[1] Munch, *Lærde Brev*, vol. i, p. 41. Oct. 4, 1841 to Munthe; *cf.* Munch, *Saml. Afh.*, vol. ii, pp. 88, 113.

[2] Munch, *Lærde Brev*, vol. i, p. 376. July 11, 1849 to Lange; *ibid.*, vol. i, p. 385. Aug. 25, 1849 to Stephens.

[3] *Cf.* Munch, *Forn-Swenskans . . . Språkbygnad*, p. xl.

[4] Munch, *Saml. Afh.*, vol. i, p. 1.

[5] *Ibid.*, vol. i, p. 136.

[6] *Ibid.*, vol. i, p. 143; *cf. infra*, pp. 158-9.

[7] *Ibid.*, vol. ii, pp. 45, 76.

[8] Munch, *Lærde Brev*, vol. i, p. 98. Apr. 20, 1845 to Finn Magnusen.

whom Munch regarded more highly, once aroused his ire
by crediting an article in *Antiquités Russes,* which Munch
considered mainly his, to Finn Magnusen; Munch wondered
whether he should expose this affair with " *der Würm
Rafns.*" [9]   His distrust at times led him to suspicions that
were quite far-fetched; when an English survey of the
literature [10] of the northern countries gave very scant notice
to recent developments in Norway, he blamed the skimpy
treatment to the jealous suggestions of Danish advisers.[11]

Danish scholars showed their perversity in the way they
edited the old records, frequently to Norway's disadvantage.
In omitting matter uninteresting to themselves they could
pass over valuable Norwegian material,[12] and sometimes they
quite ignored the work of Norwegian scholarship.[13]   As
we have seen, Munch in 1845 directed a very heavy attack
on their editing of medieval texts [14] and their one-sidedness
drew the attention also of foreigners.[15]

In their eagerness to secure a full share in the honors for
northern achievement, the Danes laid claims to " memories "
belonging to another nationality—an action almost as unjust
as depriving a nation of territory; they did not need these
" memories " which Norway was too poor to lose.[16]   For

[9] Munch's point of view and to some extent Rafn's excuses may be
followed in *ibid.*, vol. i, pp. 433, 437, 441-43, 447-49, 469.

[10] W. and M. Howitt, *The Literature and Romance of Northern Europe*
(London, 1852).

[11] Munch, *Saml. Afh.*, vol. iii, pp. 194-6.

[12] *Ibid.*, vol. i, pp. 2-3; *cf. N. Tids. f. Vid. og Litt.*, vol. vii, p. 408.

[13] Munch, *Lærde Brev*, vol. i, p. 175.   Jan. 1, 1847 to Rafn.

[14] *Supra*, p. 118.

[15] Munch, *Saml. Afh.*, vol. i, p. 128.   The Anglo-Saxon scholar, J. M.
Kemble, also expressed a poor opinion of *Oldskriftselskabet's* "rapid
generalizations and unwarranted hypotheses." Munch, *Lærde Brev*,
vol. i, p. 261.   Feb. 10, 1848 from Kemble to Munch.

[16] Munch, *Saml. Afh.*, vol. i, pp. 122-3.

instance, they treated the great Viking achievements as the accomplishments of an undifferentiated northern nationality, and did nothing to dispel the traditional notion that the Vikings in Scotland, Ireland, and along the channel coasts were Danes, when in reality they were Norwegians. It was a pleasure, then, for Munch to greet [17] the first attempt, and that by a Dane in whom he had not too much confidence,[18] to place on a scholarly basis Norwegian accomplishments in these regions.[19] Such undertakings as the colonization of Iceland, Greenland and America had not been " northern," and certainly not Danish. Iceland had been colonized mostly by Norwegians with a sprinkling of Swedes and Irish and a few Danes, and while descendants of the latter claimed the honor for that event,[20] the colonization of the west had been a Norwegian national undertaking and the Danes might well keep their hands off of this " crowning feature of our history." [21] On the continent, Normandy had been settled chiefly by Danes, yet here too the Norwegian contribution had been considerable; witness the similarity between the *odel* practice and the Norman feudal tie,[22] and the evidence in Norman speech.[23] The Viking leader, Rollo, son of Earl Ragnvald, was no Dane but a Norwegian.[24]

* * * * *

The Norwegian writers had historic grievances also against the Danish people and their government in general,

[17] *Ibid.*, vol. iii, pp. 1-26.

[18] *Cf.* Munch, *Lærde Brev*, vol. i, p. 376. July 11, 1849 to Lange.

[19] J. A. A. Worsaae, *Minder om de Danske og Nordmændene i England, Skotland og Irland* (Copenhagen, 1851).

[20] *Morgbl.*, 1841, no. 62.

[21] Munch, *Saml. Afh.*, vol. i, p. 131.

[22] Munch, *NFH.*, vol. i, pp. 677-8.

[23] Thus the " *bø* " in *boeuf* or *Elboeuf*, said Munch, was more akin to the Norwegian " *bø* " than to the Danish " *by* ". *Ibid.*, vol. i, pp. 680-1.

[24] Munch, *The Chronicle of Man*, pp. vii-viii.

"wrongs" growing out of the 400 years of Dano-Norwegian union. They could cite encroachments of the Danish nobility and broken promises of the kings. Munch would not blame the people at large and he disbelieved in any far-reaching plans to subjugate the Norwegians.[25] Lange, however, was more disparaging; Denmark, he thought, had over-ridden and suppressed Norway deliberately.[26] The charges against Denmark were many. She had tried by various means to enfeeble Norway's national character; she had sought to thin out her language; in denying her a university, she had made it difficult for Norwegians to keep up with European culture.[27] Munch may also have had Denmark in mind when he complained that many of Norway's archival treasures had been destroyed through carelessness or "deliberate barbarism."[28] Danish rule had left a legacy of disrespect for things Norwegian; the Dane, once having held the Norwegian in subjection, continued to think himself somewhat superior, and pictured the Norwegian as boorish and rustic, and as usually lacking in learning and good manners.[29]

During the union period Denmark had deleted 400 years from Norway's national and cultural development. In that stretch of time—years of lethargy and torpor—Norway had been missing from the list of European states.[30] Well might she paraphrase the complaint of the English at the

[25] *Maanedskr. f. Litt.*, vol. xvii, pp. 288-9.

[26] C. C. A. Lange, "*Bidrag til Norges Historie under Unionen*," N. *Tids. f. Vid. og Litt.*, vol. i, pp. 264-5.

[27] *Alm. n. Maanedskr.*, vol. ii, pp. 470-1.

[28] *Stort. Forh.*, 1857, vol. vii, p. 141.

[29] Munch, *Saml. Afh.*, vol. ii, pp. 6, 28 *et seq.*

[30] Munch, *Forn-Swenskans . . . Språkbygnad*, p. xl; Munch, *NFH.*, vol. vii, p. 934; N. *Tids. f. Vid. og Litt.*, vol. vi, p. 309; *Cf. Ill. Nyhbl.*, 1858, pp. 191-2.

time of the calendar reform and say: give me my 400 years.[31]
Denmark had also helped to obscure the glorious history of
Norway's earlier period; Danish writers inferred that Norway before 1814 always had been a Danish province without any history or literature of her own.[32]

Naturally the Norwegian School shied at the Danish
period. Munch spoke of it as that " huge and barren
room," [33] and Wergeland in the figure that became so well
known called it the " false soldering " between the ancient
and the modern Norway.[34] Lange found little to interest
him in Norway's history after 1537; the story of her miser-
able submission to the dictatorial tone of the Danish Royal
Council was not an account to inspire the imagination or
stimulate national pride.[35] " We feel sorely enough," wrote
Munch in 1853, " the gap in our history from 1537 to 1814,
and since we cannot close it, we seek . . . . to preserve and
cultivate the older part of our history. . . ." [36]

*　*　*　*　*

The Norwegian historians, with their general antipathy
to all things Danish, naturally viewed Scandinavianism,
which flourished most at Copenhagen, with caution and misgiving. Keyser took a stiff unyielding position against
any " collusion " with the Danes, fearing that it might
endanger Norway's still feebly-developed nationality.[37]
Munch, however, here as elsewhere sensitive to currents
about him, entered, with much rationalizing, upon a some-

---

[31] Munch, *Saml. Afh.*, vol. i, p. 123.

[32] *Ibid.*, vol. ii, p. 530 *et seq.*

[33] *Stort. Forh.*, 1857, vol. vii, p. 141.

[34] *Digterværker og Prosaiske Skrifter*, vol. v, p. 165.

[35] *N. Tids. f. Vid. og Litt.*, vol. i, p. 243.

[36] Quoted in Brinchmann, *National-Forskeren P. A. Munch*, p. 17.

[37] *Det kgl. Fred. Univ.*, vol. ii, pp. 247-48.

what tortuous path.[38]   He had difficulty in harmonizing his antipathy to German encroachment on Denmark with his determination to concede nothing to the proponents of Scandinavianism at Copenhagen, who were now capitalizing those traditional views of northern history so resolutely opposed by the Norwegian School.   Munch really favored a form of pan-Germanism; "*Ich schwärme für den Pangermanismus, Scandinavien und Deutschland in einem engen Staatenbunde,*" he wrote to Grimm.[39]   He thought panracial agglomerations quite natural if they encompassed all the branches of a race.[40]   His pan-Germanism looked to a federation of five or six German republics built on old tribal nationalities like the Suabian or Bavarian, plus the three Scandinavian states, and possibly Holland and England.[41] This aggregation would be sufficiently decentralized to permit a varied cultural life and simultaneously it would retain sufficient strength and unity to oppose the "barbarizing" influence of panslavism and Russia.[42]   Whatever chance this grandiose conception had of becoming a reality was ruined, according to Munch, by the zealous little band agitating at Copenhagen for Scandinavianism.   Among the members of the Germanic race their agitation was the Pandora's box that let loose a national frenzy in the Germanies and ignored a chance to placate the Holsteiners.[43] However, when matters reached a crisis Munch considered

[38] Made even more tortuous no doubt, because his old rival, L. K. Daa, vigorously espoused Scandinavianism, especially in the columns of *Christiania-Posten.*

[39] Munch, *Lærde Brev,* vol. i, p. 361.   Letter of May 1, 1849.

[40] *Den Const.,* 1847, no. 15.

[41] Munch, *Saml. Afh.,* vol. ii, pp. 78-81; Munch, *Lærde Brev,* vol. i, p. 275.   Apr. 27, 1848 to Stephens.

[42] Munch, *Saml. Afh.,* vol. iii, p. 610.

[43] *Ibid.,* vol. iii, pp. 614-15; *cf.* vol. ii, p. 15.

the German expansionists a similar menace to his pan-German scheme.[44]

While Munch had no sympathy with political Scandinavianism as it was preached in Copenhagen, the moving events of 1848 made him its champion temporarily.[45] Seeing in these events a threat to what he now thought of as the common nationality of the north,[46] he rushed into the realm of political action, rejoicing, for the moment that he was no " *stubengelehrter.*" [47] With the aid of a merchant named Frølich, he organized a demonstration on May 1, 1848, and could report a " stupendous," almost " fanatical," popular enthusiasm.[48] Turning propagandist he employed his knowledge of history to show that in Charlemagne's day the Eider had been made the boundary in perpetuity.[49] He urged Norway's entry into the war in order that she might share the economic advantages of victory; the city of Hamburg could be made to pay war contributions and its trade might be diverted.[50] Furthermore, Norway's warriors needed practice, and her people would have a chance to vindicate their national honor, since war—that is, a just war—could have also its good qualities. Like any overwhelming national event which submerged petty egoism, argued Munch, war silenced " the baser passions and conjured forth all that was great and noble." Not that he was anxious to have his country

[44] Munch, *Lærde Brev*, vol. i, p. 275. Apr. 27, 1848 to Stephens.

[45] Yet the Scandinavianism he espoused was military rather than political; he favored intervention without promoting closer union. *Cf.* Munch, *Saml. Afh.*, vol. ii, p. 7.

[46] *Ibid.*, vol. i, pp. 377, 386.

[47] Munch, *Lærde Brev*, vol. i, p. 275. Apr. 27, 1848 to Stephens.

[48] *Ibid.*, vol. i, pp. 278-9.

[49] Munch, *Kort Fremstilling af Aarsagerne til Krigen mellem Danmark og Tyskland* (Chra., 1848), p. 3.

[50] Munch, *Saml. Afh.*, vol. i, pp. 378-9; Munch, *Lærde Brev*, vol. i, p. 284. May 27, 1848 to Krieger.

experience the horrors of warfare, but he reasoned that hostilities were already on, and they ought to be shortened to best advantage. Besides, the risks were comparatively small in this instance, for Germany without seapower would be unable to reach Norway![51]

As the crisis eventuated in an unfavorable outcome, Munch returned to his study. He regretted that an armistice had doomed the Norwegian troops to play so inactive a rôle. He disapproved of Denmark's cautious policy and lost confidence in England. His enthusiasm had waned by the opening of the new year, and by June of 1849 he had quite deserted the ungrateful pursuit of politics. It was hardly to be expected that members of the Norwegian Historical School would take readily to Scandinavianism. The movement revived too many memories of the old Kalmar Union; a new combination might have the same fatal consequences for Norway. Certain practical exigencies would again give the hegemony to Copenhagen and place the "focus" of the northern nationality once more in Denmark.[52]

But according to the hypothesis of a northern migration, that focus belonged in Norway where the northern nationality had been least Germanized. Throughout the long polemic on Scandinavianism (especially with Ludvig Kr. Daa) Munch lost no opportunity to widen and deepen the historical argument for the migration theory. If the Danes would only recognize a migration from the north, he had written a bit earlier, they would see that the aid they most needed in combating the German influence was to be found, as several times in the past, in looking more closely to the northern nationality.[53]

---

[51] Munch, *Saml. Afh.*, vol. i, pp. 382, 387.

[52] *Cf. ibid.*, vol. ii, pp. 63-64; vol. iii, pp. 617-19.

[53] *Ibid.*, vol. i, p. 121.

CHAPTER IX

ASSEMBLING AND PRESERVING THE RECORDS

IN seeking to present a more adequate picture of the history of their fatherland the Norwegian historians labored under special difficulties with regard to sources. A great deal of the material " so precious for our national history," [1] was lodged in foreign archives, especially in Copenhagen, a circumstance that tended to feed the anti-Danish temper of the Norwegian School. Norwegian scholars devoted considerable effort to the repatriation of these records and thus began a venture which, as it happens, is not yet entirely finished.

The first to be recovered were certain records returned in the readjustments with Denmark following upon the events of 1814, and the notable collection which Lundh in 1830 recovered from Bavaria.[2] It was Lundh also who sought to arouse an interest in what proved to be the major effort of the 'thirties in this field, namely, the plan to copy Norway's ancient laws. A committee of the academic council of the University was authorized to look into the matter,[3] and its members recommended that one of their own countrymen [4] be sent abroad to copy these laws. It was specified that he be a native, in spite of the widespread opinion that no Norwegian had the necessary qualifications, on the ground that what he might lack in technical com-

---

[1] *Morgbl.*, 1830, no. 201.

[2] *Supra*, pp. 94-5.

[3] *Cf. Dept. Tid.*, 1832, pp. 811-26, 833-48.

[4] A critic urged that the matter be dropped if they could not send a competent foreigner, perhaps an Icelander. *Morgbl.*, 1832, no. 339.

petence he would make up for with a " more intense solicitude for the cause." [5]   The *Storting* provided somewhat
inadequate appropriations and when *Det kgl. norske Videnskabers Selskab* ("The Royal Norwegian Society of
Science") added a contribution, the project took concrete
form.   A committee composed of Steenbuch, Hersleb and
Lundh, was established to supervise the work from Christiania when Keyser offered to go abroad for two years with
an assistant.   For this purpose, as we have said above, he
chose his brilliant pupil, P. A. Munch, who was a practiced
copyist by that time and a master of Norway's ancient
language. [6]

In May, 1835, Keyser and Munch set out for Copenhagen
where they remained nearly two years and then went to
Stockholm.   Munch soon departed for home [7] but Keyser
continued the work, going also to Uppsala, Lund, and back
to Copenhagen, where he concluded his task in December,
1837. [8]   With a pious solicitude, the two men copied a total
of four thousand large pages *in quarto,* [9] and during spare
time at Copenhagen Munch had also copied many Norwegian parchment deeds and rent-rolls, in order, as he later
explained, in some degree "to vindicate them for the
fatherland." [10]

In the repatriation of the records abroad, of which the
ancient laws were only the lesser portion, a leading part was
taken by the archivist, Lange.   Christian C. A. Lange (1810-
1861), born near Christiania, received some of his early

[5] *Dept. Tid.,* 1832, pp. 820-21.

[6] *Ibid.,* 1834, pp. 661-71; *Norges Gamle Love,* vol. i, p. iv.

[7] *Supra,* p. 110.

[8] *Norges Gamle Love,* vol. i, p. iv.

[9] Now preserved at *Universitetsbibliotheket.*

[10] Munch, *Lærde Brev,* vol. i, p. 151.   June 6, 1846 to the Academic
Council.

instruction from his cousins, Christian and Rudolf Keyser, and found his interest in history quickened at the Cathedral School in Christiania under the instruction of Albert Lassen. That interest became centered on saga history and Old Norse during Lange's second year at the University when Keyser returned from Iceland, aglow with new enthusiasm. On the completion of his theological course, Lange shortly (1834) arranged to teach Norwegian, geography, history and religion in the Naval Academy at Fredriksværn. Some years later, when he planned to enter the ministry, it was pointed out that he might succeed Wergeland in charge of the royal archives. Wergeland, whose health was failing,[11] soon came to his untimely end, and shortly afterwards Lange succeeded to the office (1845). By his effective administration and his assiduity as a collector both at home and abroad he became the real organizer of the Norwegian royal archives.

On his appointment, Lange was no novice in handling sources. He had written a school text,[12] and had become interested in the influence exerted on Norway's cultural life by her medieval monastic orders. When *Det kgl. norske Videnskabers Selskab* offered to reward the best essay on this subject, Lange in 1843 employed a stipend from the society to copy manuscripts in the museums and archives of towns along the coast. From this material he wrote his history of Norwegian monasteries.[13] Meanwhile he had been sent on a wider quest. The government in April, 1843, dispatched him on a three-months trip to the cities of northern Germany to seek materials on "the older history of the

[11] In one quarter there was what may seem an unbecoming eagerness to see his end. Munch wrote that Wergeland could hardly last long but he was "tough as the devil." Munch, *Lærde Brev*, vol. i, p. 103. May 8, 1845 to Lange.

[12] *Udtog af Norges, Sveriges og Danmarks Historie* (Chra., 1841).

[13] The society awarded no prize as it could get no one to judge this work but with a subvention the study was later printed (18[45-]47).

fatherland." [14]   The next summer he visited Copenhagen, Hamburg, Lübeck (where he made his richest finds), Wismar, Rostock, Stralsund, and Greifswald.   Thereafter he went abroad often, going to Copenhagen in the summers of 1845, 1849, 1850 and 1851, and to Stockholm and Uppsala in 1853, while four years later he went to Belgium, Holland, and again through northern Germany.[15]

Shortly after Lange took charge of the public archives, an unexpected find was made.   When dusting off some seventeenth century account books it was observed that they had been tied up and bound with old parchments.   These proved to be manuscripts from the thirteenth century, the classic period of Norse culture!   Evidently tax collectors in the first half of the seventeenth century had used them to bind up reports to the Danish exchequer.   More than sixty fragmentary codices were found, and the number was augmented by further search.[16]   What a treatment, indeed, to give to sources that now were worth "their weight in gold."[17] Munch reported the discovery in the opening number of Lange's new journal[18] and hailed the find as proof conclusive that thirteenth-century Norway had been "a very well-read nation," and enjoyed a higher state of literary culture than was commonly supposed.

At the very outset of his career Lange hit upon a trail whose end, in a sense, has not yet been reached.   He found evidence which convinced him that the Danes were in possession of a number of Norwegian manuscripts to which they were not exactly entitled.[19]   While he was working in

[14] His report is in *Nor*, vol. iii, pt. iii, pp. 1-16.

[15] For sketches of his life see Halvorsen, *Norsk Forf.-Lex.*, vol. iii, pp. 432-3; *Ill. Nyhbl.*, 1857, pp. 101-2, 121-2.

[16] Munch, *Lærde Brev*, vol. i, p. 205.   June 6, 1847 to Werlauff.

[17] *Ibid.*, vol. i, p. 171.   Dec. 13, 1846 to Stephens.

[18] *N. Tids. f. Vid. og Litt.*, vol. i, pp. 25-52.

[19] *Nor*, vol. iii, pt. iii, p. 3.

the episcopal archives at Christianssand in 1843, there had
been called to his attention certain vouchers purporting to be
from Árni Magnússon, the Copenhagen librarian and archivist of the early eighteenth century. The vouchers acknowledged as a loan the receipt of certain records from those
archives.[20] But if they were a loan, how did it come about
that they were still in Copenhagen? Quite likely they had
gotten into Danish possession when Árni Magnússon's
private collection was willed to the University at Copenhagen. Lange confirmed his suspicion the next year while
at the Danish capital. If the records were but a loan it
would seem that they should sometime have been returned
and that Denmark had no legal or moral claim to them. It
was Lange's hope that the generosity shown toward Lundh
by the Bavarian king in 1830, would be imitated, as he put
it in general terms, by governments nearer home who had
little right to some of the documents in their possession.[21]
Norway should demand the return of these records, said
Munch; so long as they remained outside of the country
they were but " dead treasures." [22]

The effort to repatriate these sources was but partly
successful. Lange in 1850 began negotiations and late in
1851 reached a tentative agreement according to which many
documents in the Norwegian section of the Árni Magnússon
collection were to be exchanged for those records of
Christian II in Norway that were of major interest to the
Danes.[23] But the negotiations were only partly successful
and many important documents were still left in Denmark

[20] Munch, *Saml. Afh.*, vol. i, pp. 144-5, note 1; *cf.* Munch, *Forn-Swenskans . . . Språkbygnad*, p. xxxv, note.

[21] *Fædrelandet*, 1846, p. 676.

[22] Munch, *Saml. Afh.*, vol. i, pp. 102, 132.

[23] Munch, *Lærde Brev*, vol. i, p. 444. July 4, 1850 from Lange to Munch.

The question of their return developed into a chronic dispute.[24] More recently, in some quarters (especially among the assertive *landsmaal* groups) this has become a matter of national prestige. An international commission of two Danes and two Norwegians in 1930 tried to settle the vexed question.

*   *   *   *   *

No one did such spectacular work in disclosing the sources abroad as P. A. Munch. In 1849, for instance, he discovered a Latin chronicle, the *Historia Norvegica,* in Edinburgh.[25] But his most notable results were gained in the papal archives. He had long had his eye on this depository. When Pope Pius IX was in exile after the upheaval of 1848 and when the future of the Papacy looked precarious, Munch had thought it a good time for Denmark to purchase cheaply all the documents concerning the north, in the Vatican archives.[26] Eight years later, he set out in person to copy some of those records.

Getting access to the papal archives at that time was an extremely difficult matter, but in this Munch was very successful. He was helped by his facility for making friends. On his way south he came to know in Copenhagen a certain Mgr. Etienne Zwonkowski,[27] one time Prefect in Norway,

[24] A Danish retort to Norwegian imputations may be consulted in the very unflattering account of Lundh's procedure at Munich in 1829-30 by C. F. Allen, *Breve og Aktstykker til Oplysning af Christiern den Andens og Frederik den Førstes Historie* (Copenhagen, 1854), pp. vii-xxxviii. See further *Fædrelandet,* 1850, nos. 132, 133, 135, 159, 160 and Munch, *Saml. Afh.,* vol. ii, pp. 528-554.

[25] *Stort. Forh.,* 1857, vol. vii, p. 144; *cf.* Munch, *Lærde Brev,* vol. i, p. 434. June 13, 1850 to Grimm.

[26] Munch, *Lærde Brev,* vol. i, p. 368. June 27, 1849 to Rafn.

[27] This cleric, once Greek Orthodox, was now of the Roman Catholic faith; later he abjured that also and went over to Protestantism. *Cf.* Larsen-Naur, *P. A. Munchs Levnet og Breve,* pp. 84, 92, 125-6.

who did him several good turns after he arrived at Rome, and in Vienna he met the Prince-Archbishop, Cardinal Rauscher, who presented his cause to the Librarian of the Vatican, Father Theiner.[28] The latter knew something of Munch's work and received him very cordially, granting him unusual privileges at the outset—an indication of the esteem Munch now enjoyed among European scholars. He did his own copying, instead of paying an attendant to do it, and he was permitted to go directly into the repositories and select his own materials.[29] Working in this wealth of sources he enjoyed what were perhaps the happiest years of his life. He was importuned by neighboring countries to take along what he could on the history of the north in general and his activity became a kind of international concern.

*   *   *   *   *

It was not sufficient that the historical records be found; in many cases they ought also to be printed and on this task the Norwegian historians expended no little effort. We may look first to their work with the ancient laws, whose printing was of some practical as well as scholarly importance in so far as they might interest the legislator and the jurist. Nevertheless it was the scholars who took the initiative. Since not all of the moneys appropriated for the copying of those laws had been used, the surplus was applied to their editing. In the late 'thirties Keyser began this work

---

[28] Though P. F. Mengel, a Swedish newspaper man, years later explained the preliminaries differently. *Cf.* J. B. Halvorsen, *Norsk Forf.-Lex.*, vol. iv, p. 173.

[29] Larsen-Naur, *op. cit.*, pp. 132-3; *Det kgl. Fred. Univ.*, vol. ii, p. 253. A long account which Munch wrote of his discoveries was read before the Christiania *Videnskab-Selskab* on Oct. 5 and Nov. 16, 1860, and deposited in the royal archives. Years later, after both Munch and Father Theiner were dead the account was published in Munch, *Saml. Afh.*, vol. iv, pp. 423-500.

and after a time he was relieved by Munch.[30]   Then the
project lagged for some years until revived in 1844,[31] and
Keyser and Munch jointly resumed the editorial work.

Those interested in the project had to rely mainly upon
the *Storting* to bear the cost of printing.   Hoping to enlist
the serious attention of this body at its next session (1845),
Munch urged all haste in having a volume ready then for its
inspection.[32]   This was not accomplished but the *Storting*
made a triennial appropriation,[32] which, with further aid
from the *Videnskabers Selskab*, put the matter of printing
well under way.   The editors did their best, as they explained in the first installment (1846), to make the project
worthy of its sponsors, i.e., the society at Trondhjem and
"the nation." [34]   The foreign acclaim which greeted the
effort praised the generosity of a lean public treasury in pro-
viding for a " national monument " which so fittingly repaid
" the debt to the forefathers." [35]   For a time, progress was
rapid; a second volume came out in 1848 and a third in
1849.   But a fourth, to include various technical impedi-
menta, which after all were of less national significance, had
to wait a full generation.[36]

In the field of northern antiquities generally, a good many
things had been edited by the Danes.   For a generation
their activity had been centered in *Det kongelige nordiske
Oldskriftselskab* (" The Royal Northern Ancient Text

[30] *Dept. Tid.*, 1839, p. 325.

[31] The reader may note how this renewal of interest synchronized with
the advent of national romanticism.   *Cf. supra*, p. 53.

[32] Munch, *Lærde Brev*, vol. i, pp. 92-3.   Report of April 11, 1844 to
the Law Commission.

[33] *Stort. Forh.*, 1845, vol. ix, p. 52.

[34] *Norges Gamle Love*, vol. i, p. 12.

[35] *Nyt Historisk Tidsskrift*, vol. i, p. 674.

[36] Divided as volumes IV (1885) and V (1895).

Society "), which had been founded on January 28, 1825, by C. C. Rafn and three Icelanders,[37] to edit older texts and to help awaken a love of the " fathers and the fatherland." In the several formidable series of text editions put out under its auspices were printed many of the important texts on northern history but, of course, with no effort to distinguish those that might be considered Norwegian-Icelandic. Norwegian scholars felt that the Danes were left to exploit the field pretty much as they wished, and they came to see a strong national bias in the Danish editing.

There was no corresponding organization in Norway, but one result of Munch's attack in 1845 on the narrow Danish point of view of *Oldskriftselskabet* was the concilatory proposal to form a branch of the Danish society, in Christiania, an arrangement in which the parent society it seems, definitely bound itself to give no further offence by equating *norrøn*, that is, Norse, with northern, or by denying Norway the honor of having colonized Iceland.[38] The prospectus for the Christiania branch, signed by Lange, Munch and Unger, urged everyone with " an interest in the history of the fatherland " to grasp this offer of foreign coöperation. Here was an opportunity to make the *Oldskriftselskab* truly northern and rectify " the general opinion that Norway is a province of Denmark, in cultural respects as it once was in political affairs." [39]

This arrangement began with promise but proved short-lived. The Norwegian scholars soon questioned the good faith of the Danes, when a new organization called *Det Nordiske Literatursamfund* ("The Northern Literary

[37] F. Jonsson, *Utsigt over den norsk-islandske filologis Historie* (Copenhagen, 1918), p. 42; Munch, *Lærde Brev*, vol. i, p. 126.

[38] Munch, *Lærde Brev*, vol. i, p. 173. Dec. 13, 1846 to Stephens.

[39] *Program. Det kongelige nordiske Oldskrift-Selskab. Norsk Afdeling*, p. 6; reprinted in Munch, *Lærde Brev*, vol. i, pp. 125-128.

Society ") appeared in Copenhagen; in making broad claims
to the ancient literature this society seemed bent on mini-
mizing its Norwegian quality.[40]   More than ever Norwegian
scholars felt it "humiliating and unnatural" to depend on
Danish editing.[41]   In May of 1849 Keyser, Munch, Brandt,
Winter-Hjelm and Unger took steps to organize, independently of the Danes, a *Foreningen til norske Oldskrifters
Udgivelse* (" The Association for the Publication of Ancient
Norwegian Texts ").[42]   As a matter of fact the society was
little more than a group of guarantors to assure the printing
of Old Norse texts by Keyser, Munch, and the careful young
scholar, C. R. Unger.   Several texts prepared by Unger and
Keyser were printed, but then the undertaking lapsed for
lack of regular literary support.[43]   Unger's effort to rejuven-
ate the project a decade later led in 1861 to the formation of
Det norske Oldskrift Selskab (" The Norwegian Ancient
Text Society "), a venture that proved more permanent; but
as its emphasis was quite exclusively philological we need
follow it no further here.

Carl Richard Unger (1817-1897), the fourth member of
the Norwegian Historical School, specialized on text editing.
In the light of what was to be his lifework it is an interesting coincidence that he was born at Akershus, in whose
vicinity were some of the national archives.   During a stay
(1830-32) with the poet and pastor, S. O. Wolff,[44] his feeling
for language was sharpened by the piquant Telemark dialect

---

[40] Munch, *Lærde Brev*, vol. i, p. 467.   Oct. 10, 1850 to Stephens; *cf.*
also vol. i, p. 182.   Feb. 23, 1847 to Rafn.

[41] *N. Tids. f. Vid. og Litt.*, 1854-5, p. 408.

[42] *Aarsberetning om Foreningen til norske Oldskrifters Udgivelse
afgiven i general forsamling den 2den Mai 1850*, p. 2.   The prospectus
was published in *Morgbl.*, 1849, no. 124.   *Cf.* Munch, *Lærde Brev*, vol.
i, p. 384.   Aug. 25, 1849 to Stephens.

[43] *Indbydelse til et norsk Oldskrift Selskab* (1861) dated May 28.

[44] *Infra*, p. 269.

of the district. When Unger came to the University, Keyser confirmed his interest in Old Norse. Continuing his studies in Anglo-Saxon, Old German and Old Norse, Unger went abroad for a lengthy stay, first to Copenhagen, then to Paris in 1843, and then to London for Anglo-Saxon manuscripts in 1844. On his return he began a long career at the University as teacher of philology.[45] Unger was most at home in the minutiæ of text editing and Norse glossaries. Collaborating at first with his masters, Keyser and Munch, and later working alone, he prepared a large number of critical texts, and, with Lange, he undertook the preparation of the endless *Diplomatarium Norvegicum.* Alone or in collaboration he edited Norse texts totaling thousands of pages.

Before speaking further of the *Diplomatarium* just referred to, we may note how the University arranged to sponsor the printing of several Old Norse sources. There was an established academic tradition that the person giving instruction in Latin should issue twice a year on the occasions of the Reformation festival and the royal birthday, (and also in connection with promotions to the doctorate),[46] some learned document or treatise as a University " programme." These had to be in Latin, a linguistic straitjacket which prevented their use for Old Norse texts. But P. A. Munch ingeniously got around this obstacle. In January, 1843, he published in this manner " the first larger fruit " of his Copenhagen stay, *Bergens Kalvskind,* a medieval rent-roll of the chapter at Bergen,[47] meeting the requirements by keeping all his notes and addenda in Latin.

---

[45] *Cf.* Halvorsen, *Norsk Forf.-Lex.,* vol. vi, pp. 59-61; Magnus Olsen, " *Filologi,*" *Det kgl. Fred. Univ.,* vol. ii, p. 315 *et seq.*

[46] M. Olsen, " *Filologi,*" *Det kgl. Fred. Univ.,* vol. ii, p. 296.

[47] Munch, *Lærde Brev,* vol. i, p. 47. Nov. 8, 1842 to Munthe; vol. i, p. 59. Feb. 5, 1843 to Rafn.

" Better that than nothing at all," he commented,[48] and in 1845, within the same restrictions, he filled both of that year's " programmes " with the lengthy text of *Munkeliv Kloster Copibog.*[49]   The University relented and ruled that the "programmes " need not appear in Latin,[50] and the next year it sponsored no less than three important texts—*Den ældre Edda, Fagrskinna,* and *Konungs-Skuggsjá.*

Plans for printing a comprehensive *Diplomatarium* of medieval documents had first been sketched by Lundh in the 'thirties, only to be brought to partial realization by Lange and Unger.   As in the case of the ancient laws, this was a project which must depend on support from the public treasury.   In order to present the issue satisfactorily to the next *Storting,* Lange and Unger [51] in 1847, with the aid of 175 *Spd.* from the *Videnskabers Selskab* at Trondhjem, printed a sample installment.[52]   Applying to the *Storting* (1848) for an annual appropriation of 500 *Spd.* they supported their request with a pointed argumentation [53] in which they made a strong appeal to national pride.   Everywhere in northern Europe, as Lange had had occasion to note on his trip in 1844, historians were feverishly at work publishing the treasures of their archives.   In this matter, said the applicants, a special obligation rested on the Norwegian State—an obligation toward the whole Germanic people. Norway's records were of special interest to Germanic philologists because her people during the Middle Ages were

48 *Ibid.,* vol. i, p. 68.   June 9, 1843 to Molbech; vol. i, p. 111.   July 25, 1845 to Grimm.

49 *Ibid.,* vol. i, p. 101.   May 8, 1845 to Lange.

50 It also dissociated them from the traditional festivals and placed them with the semester course announcements.   M. Olsen, " Filologi," *Det kgl. Fred. Univ.,* vol. ii, p. 314, note 3.

51 *Cf. Skilling Magasin,* 1888, p. 131, note.

52 *Stort. Forh.,* 1848, no. 30, p. 64.

53 *Ibid.,* p. 65.

among the very few to continue using the mother tongue. The nation ought not to ignore this " request " of the Germanic race, for the sake of its own honor as well as the honor of the forefathers. Lange and Unger presented their request through the committee for the publication of the ancient laws, whose work was now nearing completion, and this body heartily recommended the project for reasons both scientific and patriotic. The *Storting* gave its approval and subsequently often renewed its support. The first volume appeared in 1849,[54] and four more were ready before Lange died in 1861; each contained more than a thousand documents and letters dating chiefly from 1100 to 1550.

The *Storting* of 1857, which very seriously undertook to patronize national history,[55] gave considerable support to the printing of texts. With a portion of the authorized annual outlay of 1050 *Spd.*[56] to promote historical research, it was possible to give more attention also to sources of the union period, and steps were taken to begin printing a set of records from the Danish Chancery, pertaining to Norwegian affairs,[57] and a collection of post-Reformation writings.[58]

Though it was not primarily a matter of text editing, we may mention one other venture which was to share in the annual appropriations begun in 1857, namely, the new attempt to give Norway a historical periodical. The old *Samlinger til det norske Folks Sprog og Historie,* it will be

[54] *Diplomatarium Norvegicum. Oldbreve til Kundskab om Norges indre og ydre Forhold, Sprog, Slægter, Sæder, Lovgivning og Rettergang i Middelalderen* (Chra., 1849 ——). The volumes now number a score.

[55] *Supra,* pp. 84-5.

[56] These sums, managed first by Lange, were known as *Det norske historiske Kildeskriftfond.*

[57] *Norske Rigs-Registranter,* 1523-1660 (12 vols. Chra., 1861-1891).

[58] *Norske Magasin* (3 vols. Chra., 1858-70). The Department of Ecclesiastical Affairs aided the printing of old deeds and foundation charters in *Norske Stiftelser* (5 vols. Chra., 1854-1894).

recalled, was defunct in 1839. A decade later Lange had
assembled several " friends of the fatherland's history " [59]
and in 1849 had launched the *Norske Samlinger* whose first
volume was brought to a close in 1852. But this venture
proved unprofitable and also lapsed. Meanwhile, the need
for a medium was still felt and in 1857, with a share in the
Storting appropriation of that year, Lange renewed the
attempt. The second volume of the *Norske Samlinger*
(1858-60) was a still greater fiasco; it hardly repaid the cost
of print and paper. [60]

Editing the medieval texts might in some respects seem a
dreary task, but we should recall that in part it was cheered
on by a fervent patriotism. It was, of course, a special
pleasure to edit records pertaining to the two great kings—
Olaf Tryggvason, who was associated with some of the
" happiest events " in Norway's history (i.e., the coming of
Christianity and the consolidation of national independence), [61] and Saint Olaf, " the true founder and organizer of
our fatherland's political and religious life." [62] From the
linguistic standpoint as well, text editing had its compensa-
tions. The saga of St. Olaf, for instance, had previously
been edited by the Danes from a later and somewhat blem-
ished text, but there was a certain satisfaction in making this
king's career known among " the country's children " in a
" worthy form." [63] The literary qualities of some of the
texts were proof that Norway's medieval language had been

[59] *Norske Samlinger*, vol. ii, *Forord*. The ' friends ' were T. H. Aschehoug, D. Bech, J. C. Berg, Fr. Brandt, H. Helliesen, Chr. Lange, P. A.
Munch, N. Nicolaysen, A. Schweigaard, M. B. Tvethe and C. R. Unger.

[60] *Ibid.*

[61] P. A. Munch, editor, *Saga Olafs konungs Tryggvasunar* (Chra.,
1853), p. iii.

[62] Munch and Unger, editors, *Saga Olafs konungs ens Helga* (Chra.,
1853), p. iii.

[63] *Ibid.*, pp. iii, xliv.

distinguished. A manuscript like *Fagrskinna* was of special interest in that it apparently had been committed to writing in Norway rather than in Iceland.[64]

* * * * *

Contemporary with the arrival of romanticism appeared a new and sustained interest in the country's antiquities and ruins. A preliminary aspect of that interest was the concern shown since the 'twenties by J. C. Dahl (1788-1857), a painter, over the tendency in many localities to replace the old church buildings with new ones. Many of these edifices were of the characteristic stave or mast construction and, though built of wood, were centuries old. But Dahl's early efforts were ineffective. It was he likewise who first urged the restoration of the Valkendorf tower and *Haakonshallen* in Bergen and of the Cathedral in Trondhjem.[65]

The first effort to organize the archæological interest came also from Dahl. It was on his initiative (he was then living in Germany) that Keyser, Frich, Nebelong, Holst and Tidemand in December of 1844 took steps to form an organization known as *Foreningen til norske Fortidsmindersmærkers Bevaring* ("The Association for the Preservation of Norwegian Antiquities"), to work for the preservation of the country's archæological remains.[66] Its intention was to make these remains better known to the public and it meant to concentrate on those which best illustrated the nation's early skill and artistry.[67] The organization grew rapidly, proving very popular with students and the bureaucracy,[68] and in four years it came to number nearly 900 members.

[64] Munch and Unger, *Fagrskinna*, p. v.

[65] *Bergens Stiftstidende*, 1841, Dec. 26; *ibid.*, 1843, no. 31; *cf.* Munch, *Lærde Brev*, vol. i, p. 318. Undated letter in 1848 from M. Dahl to Munch.

[66] *Cf.* its *Aarsberetning*, 1859, p. 4.

[67] *Ibid.*, 1845, p. 13.

[68] *Ibid.*, p. 15 *et seq.*

Those in charge lost no time in getting to work. With the coöperation of the ecclesiastical department, the clergy of the country were circularized for reports of any remains in the local parishes. Officials of the society visited a number of ruins in the vicinity of Christiania—the fortress of Akershus, Akers church, the episcopal palace in Oslo, and the cloister ruins on Hovedø, where they began excavations. A bit later they took steps to preserve the few ruins that were left of Hamar Cathedral.[69]

The *Forening* after a time sought to be brought directly under the patronage of the state, pleading that its functions were really of national concern. A country's material remains, it was argued, were important, now that nations were developing their self-consciousness and coming to realize that they possessed " a history." The society requested that an " Inspectorate " be created whose occupant should have charge of the collection and the preservation of the country's antiquities. In substance this was done in 1859 (without establishing the Inspectorate as such) when N. Nicolaysen, who had succeeded Keyser as chairman of the *Forening* in 1851-2 was promised 500 *Spd.* annually to take charge of this sort of work.[70]

* * * * *

The country's most distinguished ruin was the Cathedral at Trondhjem. This reminder of the nation's past glory had once been a splendid example of the Gothic, perhaps the finest in the north; it still arrested the attention of travelers and foreigners. But now it was little more than a shell,

---

[69] *Ibid.*, 1847, p. 4.

[70] *Ibid.*, 1856, p. 10; *ibid.*, 1859, p. 3; Nicolay Nicolaysen (1817-1911) headed the important excavations of *Munkeliv Kloster* in Bergen (1860), *Maria Kirken* in Oslo (1865), and beyond the limits of our period, of the *Gokstad* ship in 1880. The restoration labors on *Haakonshallen* and the Trondhjem Cathedral also benefited from his advice. Halvorsen, *Norsk Forf.-Lex.*, vol. iv, pp. 255-6.

due to neglect and to successive fires since the fourteenth century. The nave was gone and the transept walls were crumbling; only the choir was still usable. The process of ruin had synchronized with, and was likewise symbolic of, the gradual loss of national independence. Small wonder that the restoration of the Cathedral came to impress some as an important step in the task of national regeneration.

But a restoration would have to wait on broad national support, for the costs would amount to thousands, perhaps hundreds of thousands, of *kroner*. Any such support seemed most remote, for only a handful of persons had any interest in it. To most people the ruin was a ruin and nothing more. What remained of the choir was kept from disintegration only because a local congregation was using it for services, and now that it was becoming too expensive, the parish was planning to build a church of its own.[71]   But here and there a few were loath to have it deserted altogether. According to the Constitution of 1814, royal coronations, as in medieval days, were to take place there and in 1818 Karl Johan had been the first Norwegian king crowned in the country since Christian II in 1514. The government came to feel that the remains ought to be kept fit for coronations and when the local congregation hesitated to carry out the recommendation of an episcopal commission that it spend twice the capital value for repairs, the government tried unsuccessfully in 1836-37 to get from the *Storting* a three-year annual appropriation of several thousand *Spd*.[72]

The early 'forties brought the first interest in a larger restoration. A report in 1841 to the ecclesiastical department recommended the expenditure of moneys not only to preserve what was still standing, but also to get an expert estimate on the probable costs of a complete restoration.

[71] *Stort. Forh.*, 1842, vol. ix, p. 203.

[72] *Ibid.*, 1836-7, pp. 164-7, 199.

Such costs, it was said, should be borne by the public
treasury, partly because of the coronations and partly because the project would have antiquarian (and national)
importance.[73]   A government committee in 1842 estimated
the total costs at 300,000 *Spd.;* it recommended that the
amount be expended over a twenty-five year period, and proposed to commission a young German architect, H. E.
Schirmer, to make drawings and descriptions " in order to
show the Cathedral as it once was—a task which the nation
thinks it owes to its own honor." [74]   The money spent for
this purpose would be worth while, without any commitment
to an actual restoration, for Schirmer's prints would, at any
rate, preserve for posterity the memory of this great
memorial, this " sanctuary of the fathers," and do it in a
manner worthy of " its former glory and the nation's
honor." [75]   The Budget Committee of the *Storting* thought
that while a new structure might be built, the older one
would have " far more interest for the nation." [76]   This
body would not approve the expenditures for a full restoration, but it recommended, and the *Storting* passed, the appropriation of moneys for several preliminary purposes: to get
drawings of the Cathedral, to determine whether the state
should take over the building from the local parish, and to
estimate the costs of fitting the church for coronations.

Schirmer made his drawings and wrote reports.   In 1845
he announced that a full restoration would be far more
difficult than he had thought at first.   In 1851 he urged
either a complete abandonment of the remains to the local
congregation or an effective restoration of the portions that
were used, estimating this cost at more than 200,000 *Spd.*

[73] *Ibid.*, 1842, vol. ix, p. 200.
[74] *Ibid.*, p. 207.
[75] *Ibid.*, pp. 199, 209.
[76] *Ibid.*, p. 214.

He favored the latter course, and supported it with a moving appeal. Great historical accomplishments, he said, reminded peoples that they must be worthy of their past; a nation showed its self-respect by preserving its historical monuments. While other European nations preserved as " holy treasures " a number of archæological remains, Norway had largely forgotten hers during the four hundred years when she " forgot herself," save for this one " whose sunken ruins from an old memorable past gazed into the present." The Constitution of 1814, argued Schirmer, in a way anticipated a restoration, by requiring that the Cathedral be the scene of coronations under the new order. Let the state take the initiative, he urged, and private endeavor would respond.[77]

Others too agreed that restoration was a matter of national significance. The ecclesiastical department regarded it as an effective means to stimulate respect for the nation's independence; the neglect of such a task exposed an independent nation to misjudgment.[78] But while the *Storting* of 1845 made a triennial appropriation for preliminary activities, that in 1851 failed by one vote to make further provision.[79] On the legislative front the matter then rested for a time.

After this reverse, those interested began to appeal direct to the public.[80] At Trondhjem steps were taken to interest *Foreningen til norske Fortidsmindersmærkers Bevaring*[81] and there was started a popular subscription which in two years raised over 5000 *Spd.*[82] In 1855 P. A. Munch spent the summer about the ruins of the Cathedral gathering data which were incorporated in a book of large plates. For this,

[77] *Ibid.*, 1851, vol. iii, pp. 13-15.
[78] *Ibid.*, p. 16.
[79] *Ibid.*, p. 17; *ibid.*, 1854, vol. i, p. 294.
[80] *Cf. Morgbl.*, 1851, no. 268.
[81] See its *Aarsberetning*, 1851, pp. 19-24.
[82] *Stort. Forh.*, 1854, vol. i, p. 294.

Schirmer made the drawings and Munch wrote the descriptive historical texts in Norwegian and English. The format of this work was pretentious—it may have helped to fan the interest in an eventual restoration—and the notes bespoke a fervent patriotism. It was but natural, said Munch, that reborn Norway should wish to save what it could of the eloquent reminder of its great past; for this Cathedral, bound to the nation by the ties of closest intimacy, mirrored that nation's one-time power and grandeur and housed in its crypt the body of the national patron and protector, St. Olaf, the lodestone which had first drawn all Norwegian hearts together as a nation.[83]

The actual work of restoration was the concern of the generation beyond the limits of our period. It was begun in 1869 and has since become a great national enterprise.[84] Nevertheless it was the age of romanticism and of the Gothic revival which first perceived the deeper national significance of a restoration and undertook the necessary preliminary agitation.

[83] P. A. Munch and H. E. Schirmer, *Trondhjems Domkirke* (Chra., 1859), pp. 4-5.

[84] On July 29, 1930, the 900th anniversary of Saint Olaf's fall at Stiklestad, the nation could dedicate the restored nave of the Cathedral.

CHAPTER X

The Evidence of a Great Medieval Culture

WHILE history was cultivated in mid-century Norway in various special fields, these endeavors had in common a desire to portray especially what the nation had accomplished in the Middle Ages. The relatively large expenditures of public and private moneys, the painstaking investigations of archæologists, the patient concern with the minutiæ of text editing, the zealous efforts to redeem the literary tradition as distinctively northern, even the proof of a northern origin— all sprang in part from a desire to show the world what Norway once had done in the way of cultural achievement. Although located out on Europe's very fringe, she had, in the age of barbarism, so-called, taken a distinguished place among the nations.[1] This was apparent from the extent of her medieval dominion, for instance, or from the advanced state of her culture.

*   *   *   *   *

In the field of colonization, a striking accomplishment had been the establishment of a far-flung Norse Empire across the north Atlantic. A restless expansion in the ninth and tenth centuries had established Norwegian settlements in the Shetlands, in the Faroes and in various parts of the British Isles, and set up larger societies in Iceland and Greenland; in the west it had touched the American coast, perhaps even Florida and the West Indies.[2] In various parts of

---

[1] *Cf.* Keyser, Munch and Unger, *Konungs Skuggsjá,* p. xii; Munch, *Saml. Afh.,* vol. i, p. 325.

[2] Munch, *Verdenshistoriens Vigtigste Begivenheder,* p. 552.

western Europe the northerners had left the imprint of their
racial heritage and their institutions.   In the Orkney and
perhaps on the Shetland Islands they absorbed the Gaelic
population; in the Western Isles, though in a minority, their
influence predominated.[3] Their expansion attained its
greatest extent in the thirteenth century under Haakon
Haakonssøn, when the north Atlantic was truly a *mare
nostrum* for the Norwegians; Norway then commanded the
respect of Europe.   At one time or another the Norwegian
dominion included Finmark, the Hebrides, Anglesey and the
Isle of Man;[4] Norse kingdoms held sway in Ireland and
northern England, and Thorfinn Jarl of the Orkneys, lord
of the notorious Macbeth, had subjected most of Scotland.[5]

Munch believed that what now was best in the culture of
these western lands they owed to these medieval invaders
from the north.   On the Isle of Man the picturesque annual
assembly (the ceremony at Tynwald Hill) was but a vestige
of older Norse practice;[6] in Ireland commercial relations
had been fostered with most zeal not by native but by Norse
kings.[7] The Vikings were reputed to have spread destruc-
tion and barbarism in England, but instead they quickened
her peaceful arts and imparted to her that spirit of enterprise
and perseverance on which rested her later greatness.   To
judge from the names of persons many clerics and statesmen of the Anglo-Saxon period must have been of northern
origin.[8] In Normandy the Northmen had developed their

[3] Munch, *Chronicle of Man*, p. xviii; *cf.* Munch, *Saml. Afh.*, vol. iii,
p. 20.

[4] Keyser, *Efterl. Skr.*, vol. ii, p. 19; Munch, *Historisk-geographisk
Beskrivelse over Kongeriget Norge (Noregsveldi) i Middelalderen*, p. 1.

[5] Munch, *Saml. Afh.*, vol. iii, pp. 16-7.

[6] *Ibid.*, vol. iii, p. 21; Munch, *Chronicle of Man*, p. xxv.

[7] Munch, *Saml. Afh.*, vol. iii, p. 22.

[8] *Ibid.*, vol. iii, pp. 10-13.

own refined, "though genuine Norwegian," nationality, which set the tone, Munch believed, for western and southern Europe.[9]   Here, he said, they laid the basis for feudalism and chivalry, for French literature and French culture.

It was satisfying to point out that in these western lands, traces of the old connection with Norway were long preserved.   The case of Iceland was obvious.   Judicial and commercial ties with the Shetland Islands had been maintained until the sixteenth century, while the Norwegian language held its place there as a spoken tongue until a century ago.[10]   The Faroes, though now under Danish rule, had remained Norwegian, nationally as well as linguistically.[11]

For P. A. Munch the opportunity in 1849-50 to visit these Western Isles and look for "vestiges" of the Norwegian language and nationality in Norway's ancient colonies, where the forefathers had ruled so mightily, proved the experience of a lifetime.   Years before he had tried to visualize the restless Northmen abroad in distant lands when he prepared a detailed exposition of the Viking wars in these regions.[12]   Now it warmed the cockles of his heart to pay them a visit in person.[13]   The Orkneys, he mused, had once been as Norwegian as Norway itself.   They harbored so many memories of the great deeds of "our forefathers"; the scattered nature of their settlements seemed palpable proof that they had been settled in the Norwegian manner. He was gratified to find so many vestiges of Norse influence and to learn that the islanders still had enough national feel-

[9] *Ibid.*, vol. ii, p. 23.

[10] *Ibid.*, vol. iii, p. 82.

[11] *Ibid.*, vol. iii, pp. 386, 400.

[12] Munch, *Lærde Brev*, vol. i, p. 17.   Dec. 4, 1836 to the Academic Council.   Four years earlier he had upbraided Faye for being too brief on Viking accomplishments in these parts.   *Maanedskr. f. Litt.*, vol. viii, p. 89.

[13] Munch, *Saml. Afh.*, vol. iii, p. 33.

ing to glorify the Old Norse period.[14]   On Iona he watched
a sunset from the island eminence and found it " marvelous
to think that all these massive isles as far as the eye can
see and much beyond have been a part of Norway's realm." [15]
But the prospect had also a touch of sadness; the vistas were
after all but reminders of Norway's one-time greatness.[16]

*   *   *   *   *

At the time when Norse political influence enjoyed its
greatest extent, Norse culture, it was likewise asserted, had
undergone a striking development.   Early Norse political
organization, described by Keyser as " patriarchal democratic," had evolved a complex system of public and private
law by the ninth century.[17]   Whether there had or had not
been scattering nomads who roamed the country when the
Germanic element first arrived, feudalism had in any case
made no headway and there had been no development of
estates.[18]   The population had remained politically homogeneous; no exception need be made in the case of thralls and
bond servants, for as the lord's possessions they were never
counted with the folk proper! [19]

In treating of Norse culture there was a tendency to distinguish two periods.   The first, when the heathen culture
was at its best, had been well established by the ninth

[14] *Ibid.*, vol. iii, pp. 53, 57, 62, 64, 82.

[15] *Ibid.*, vol. iii, pp. 45-6.

[16] *Ibid.*, vol. iii, p. 59. The feeling was perhaps akin to the " sad
pleasure " he felt at times in working with the documents of that same
period. *Cf.* Munch, *Lærde Brev*, vol. i, p. 104.   May 16, 1845 to Finn
Magnusen.

[17] Keyser, *Efterl. Skr.*, vol. i, p. 52; vol. ii, pp. 6-7.

[18] *Stort. Forh.*, 1830, vol. iv, p. 223; Keyser, *Efterl. Skr.*, vol. i, p. 26;
Keyser, *Saml. Afh.*, pp. 405-6; Munch, *Saml. Afh.*, vol. i, p. 78; vol. ii,
p. 306; vol. iii, pp. 462-3.

[19] Keyser, *Efterl. Skr.*, vol. ii, pp. 146-7.

century.[20] The most distinguished product of this period was no doubt the virile Norse mythology, bred of the military spirit and the love of the sea.[21] The second period, in the day of Christian influence, had reached its apogee in the thirteenth century at a time when, according to Keyser, most of Europe was lost in theology and scholasticism.[22] This had been something of a golden age in architecture, for instance, as we noted briefly in the preceding chapter, and likewise in literature, in which were produced some of the finest fruits of the Norwegian spirit.[23] Take, for example, the *King's Mirror,* reflecting a life of culture and refinement almost unequaled elsewhere in Europe during the age very commonly called one of barbarism. Just as the distinguished Edda, the old literature's " finest adornment," " our oldest and most noble national work," enshrined, in the lay of *Hávamál,* a dignified heathen interpretation of life, so the *King's Mirror* embodied a noble philosophy touched by Christian influence.[24] In the thirteenth century the language had been developed to classic perfection. Quite without equal in Sweden or in Denmark,[25] it had been effectively fashioned as in the *King's Mirror* to express even abstract philosophical thought; in this regard it was perhaps superior to any vernacular in Europe.[26] With a remarkable virility the Norse tongue had withstood the encroachments of the alien Latin and had developed a style marked by hard,

[20] *Ibid.,* vol. i, pp. 11-12.

[21] Keyser, *Nordmændenes Religionsforfatning i Hedendommen,* pp. 168-9.

[22] Keyser, *Norges Historie* (2 vols. Chra., 1866-1870), vol. i, p. 568.

[23] Munch, *NFH,* vol. iv, p. 1056.

[24] Keyser, Munch and Unger, *Konungs Skuggsjá,* p. xii; Munch and Unger, *Den Ældre Edda* (Chra., 1847), p. xviii.

[25] Munch, *NFH.,* vol. iv, p. 420.

[26] Keyser, Munch and Unger, *Konungs Skuggsjá,* p. xii.

abrupt, naïve and forceful qualities,[27] a style really distinguished when compared with that in the dry chronicles
of the Anglo-Saxons or in the equally arid German, Danish
and Swedish annals.[28]

In the possession of native records Norway took a high
rank. Next to the Anglo-Saxons, her people had the distinction of possessing the oldest public documents in the
vernacular.[29]   While Sweden's history was almost "barren"
from 1050 to 1250 and Denmark had but few parchments
even from the fourteenth century, and those, too, in Latin,
Norway could boast of very distinguished records from the
early part of the thirteenth century,[30] records so unique as
"testimonials" of the Norwegian nationality, that they
ought to attract the attention also of scholars abroad.

The historians thought of medieval literature in terms
that were characteristically romanticist, particularly in two
respects.   First, like their contemporaries in the fields of
folklore and folk music [31] they regarded that literature not
as an individual but as a group possession; it was a creation
of the folk spirit and thus anonymous.[32]   Its qualities—a
lively composition, a discriminating taste, and a tone of
veracity — were not the qualities of an individual person
so much as they were those of the whole people.[33]   When
the literature was committed to writing the rôle of the

[27] Keyser and Unger, *Strengleikar eða Lioðabok* (Chra., 1850), p. iv;
Keyser, *Efterl. Skr.*, vol. i, p. 27.

[28] *Ill. Nyhbl.*, 1857, p. 37.

[29] Munch, *Saml. Afh.*, vol. i, p. 559.

[30] *Ibid.*; *Stort. Forh.*, 1857, vol. vii, p. 143.

[31] L. M. Lindeman, *Halvhundrede Norske Fjeldmelodier* (Chra., 1862),
p. v.

[32] Keyser, *Efterl. Skr.*, vol. i, pp. 15-16, 118; Munch and Unger,
Oldnorsk Læsebog, p. iii.

[33] Keyser, *Efterl. Skr.*, vol. i, pp. 3, 7; Keyser, *Norges Historie*, vol.
ii, pp. 236-7; *cf.* Keyser and Unger, *Strengleikar eða Lioðabok*, p. iii.

copyist was very subordinate; he merely "moved the pen" as tradition dictated [34] (although Munch later conceded that the copyist had played a more independent rôle). In the process of copying, a scrupulous fidelity was observed, making it justifiable to place a good deal of reliance upon the historical accuracy of the traditions.[35]

Equally romanticist was the notion that this literature in its earlier oral form possessed a measure of rigidity. Once the traditions had been worked into fixed and polished forms they were henceforth varied little by successive repetitions.[36] The historical sagas had taken form three centuries before they were committed to writing,[37] and Munch sought to date the Eddic poems as early as the sixth century.[38] The oral Norse literature, in the final period from 1050 to 1150, almost outdid itself striving to perfect its form, as if preparing for the copying to come.[39] A factor making for rigidity, in the case of the sagas particularly, was the institution of the wise-men. These custodians of legal and religious knowledge maintained something like schools where successors were trained. They taught the art of the scald, so highly prized among the north-Germanic people, and they passed on the historical tradition. At the royal court it was their duty to remember events, and their fidelity to what had been recounted helped to fix the saga tradition.[40]

*   *   *   *   *

[34] Keyser, *Efterl. Skr.*, vol. i, pp. 15, 408-9, 417-18; Munch and Unger, *Oldnorsk Læsebog*, p. iv.

[35] Keyser, *Efterl. Skr.*, vol. i, pp. 399, 401, 415-16; Munch and Unger, *Oldnorsk Læsebog*, p. iii; Munch, *Saml. Afh.*, vol. ii, p. 527.

[36] Keyser, *Efterl. Skr.*, vol. i, p. 407; Munch and Unger, *Oldnorsk Læsebog*, p. iii.

[37] Keyser, *Efterl. Skr.*, vol. i, p. 409.

[38] Munch and Unger, *Det oldnorske Sprogs eller Norrønasprogets Grammatik*, p. 2.

[39] Keyser, *Efterl. Skr.*, vol. i, p. 15.

[40] *Ibid.*, vol. i, pp. 53 *et seq.*, 401-2.

The historians, like others critical of the " Latin " tradition, distrusted medieval Christianity.   They made a distinction between the spread of Christianity in the eleventh century and the establishment of the hierarchy in the century following.   While the first seemed largely beneficial, they saw much in the second which they condemned.

In several respects the arrival of Christianity had benefited the Norwegian nationality.   Christianity had minimized the trend toward despotism on the one hand and toward feudalism on the other.[41]   The kings who espoused the new doctrine were native to the country, a circumstance which from the outset gave the new faith a national imprint.[42] By spreading the glory of sainthood over the dynasty (in the tradition of Saint Olaf) Christianity had facilitated national consolidation.[43]   As it turned out, the Norwegian clergy was less set apart by privileges than others, and hence Christianity here was more intimately identified with the mass of the people.[44]   The Catholic clergy in Norway had been patriotic.[45]   The fact that Christianity had come via England [46] had minimized the danger of alien influence, for the first English preceptors bore no hostility to the Norwegian nationality; many of them, no doubt, were themselves descendants of Norsemen and Danes.   The Anglo-Saxon clergy, less disdainful of the vernaculars than other clerics, had imparted some of the respect for the popular tongue to their Norwegian colleagues.[47]   The prejudice in

[41] Munch, NFH., vol. i, p. 794.

[42] Keyser, Den norske Kirkes Historie under Katholicismen (2 vols. Chra., 1856-57), vol. i, p. 120.

[43] Munch, Saga Olafs konungs Tryggvasunar, pp. iii, iv.

[44] Keyser, Efterl. Skr., vol. ii, p. 183.

[45] Maanedskr. f. Litt., vol. xvii, p. 297.

[46] Munch, Saml. Afh., vol. ii, p. 23.

[47] Keyser, Efterl. Skr., vol. i, p. 14; Keyser, Den norske Kirkes Historie under Katholicismen, vol. i, p. 34.

Norway against clerics who could not speak the native tongue had impressed itself even on the curia at Rome, and among the Vatican records the paucity of provisions for benefices in Norway suggested that most of the appointees had been natives.[48]   Norway had been fortunate too in that her clergy had not shared the usual repugnance toward the heathen mythology, but had committed it to writing with some fidelity.[49]

Factors of this sort served to mitigate in Norway the deleterious effects of Christianity on native culture.[50]   Here the Latin made little headway because those who read it were few, and this refusal to take up an alien tongue left the Norwegian literature with a strong national imprint; the " fatherlandic element " in it emerged unmistakably clearer than if it had been strapped in " the corset of Latinity." How refreshing in the highly latinized Middle Ages to find so pronounced an assertion of nationality![51]   At no time did the " sickly Roman establishment " repress entirely the interest in the language and the history of the fatherland.[52] Although there began to take shape a literature in Latin, it remained small in comparison with the native tradition.[53] In public affairs the power of the clergy grew but slowly, for the spirit of freedom was strong; King Sverre had vigorously fought off the political pretensions of the hierarchy.[54]

[48] Munch, *Saml. Afh.*, vol. iv, p. 499; Munch, *NFH.*, vol. vii, pp. 347-8, 934.

[49] Munch, *Saml. Afh.*, vol. i, p. 559; vol. ii, p. 207.

[50] Keyser, *Den norske Kirkes Historie*, under Katholicismen, vol. i, p. 121; Keyser, *Norges Historie*, vol. i, p. 568.

[51] Munch, *Saml. Afh.*, vol. i, p. 558.

[52] *Ibid.*, vol. i, p. 325.

[53] Keyser, *Efterl. Skr.*, vol. i, p. 27.

[54] Keyser, *Norges Historie*, vol. ii, p. 139 *et seq.*; Keyser, *Den norske Kirkes Historie under Katholicismen*, vol. i, pp. 289-318.

Yet in the long run the influence of the clergy had been unfortunate even in Norway. "Already then," wrote Keyser, "the Roman curia was absorbed in selfishness and little interested in a poor country like Norway."[55] "The half Roman, half barbarian, half theologico-philosophical, half juridico-ecclesiastical training"[56] of the medieval Church was fatal to much in the old native culture. When the clergy committed the venerable traditions to writing they had to do so in a manner to give no offense to "fanatical" Christian teachers.[57] They could hardly help but frown upon the old mythology and, under the shadow of this ecclesiastical disapproval, the popular mind evolved from the older traditions the supernatural characters of the folk tales and legends.[58] Among the higher classes, at this time, the interest in the deeds of the forefathers gave way to a concern for the alien themes of west-European chivalry and medieval romances.[59] The informal arrangement of the wise-men was supplanted and no provision was made to carry on their traditional instruction in law, fatherlandic history and the scaldic craft. Untended, these arts withered away in the fourteenth century.[60] Once the popular traditions were copied down, they languished among the people. In the later fourteenth century even the sagas, once so much an object of pride, were read less and less. The learned clergy who might have cultivated them studied abroad and read instead pandects, decretals and theology.[61] The corruption which in the thirteenth and fourteenth centuries was

[55] Keyser, *Norges Historie*, vol. i, p. 568.

[56] Keyser, *Efterl. Skr.*, vol. i, p. 19.

[57] Keyser, *Saml. Afh.*, p. 22.

[58] Keyser, *Efterl. Skr.*, vol. i, pp. 63, 510 *et seq.*

[59] Munch, *NFH.*, vol. vii, p. 362.

[60] Keyser, *Efterl. Skr.*, vol. i, pp. 56-59.

[61] Munch, *NFH.*, vol. vii, p. 933.

allowed to eat its way into the venerable ancient language proved the worst affliction for Norse culture.[62] Decline became inevitable as Norway was gradually drawn into the Romano-Germanic cultural vortex and the complexities of political union with Sweden and Denmark.   Around the old national culture closed the shadows of a 400-year night of alien influence.

[62] Keyser, *Efterl. Skr.*, vol. i, p. 20.

CHAPTER XI

The Romanticism of the Norwegian Historical School

THAT the orientation of the Norwegian Historical School was strongly romanticist may best be seen in its conception of nationality. But we can get at this matter only indirectly, for the members of the School never supplied a crisp definition of the word nationality, and they often used it in contexts that were oblique and ambiguous, as when they referred to the " Germanic" nationality,[1] the " northern " nationality,[2] " the nationality of the northern peoples," [3] the " literary and social nationality " of the Icelanders,[4] or to Norway's want, for centuries, of " any political or literary nationality." [5] Nor is it any more enlightening to learn that nationality was " not a chimera, but a reality, a life element." [6] The members of the Norwegian School, as good nationalists, were apt to take nationality for granted, and remained somewhat indifferent to a formal definition of nationality.

More philosophically, the historians shared with contemporaries [7] the idea that nationality was a manifestation of the ubiquitous Idea. They conceived of a national "soul" or a national " spirit " endowed with the qualities of personality. To the Old Norse nationality they ascribed attributes

[1] Munch, *Saml. Afh.*, vol. ii, p. 27.

[2] *Ibid.*, vol. iii, p. 13.

[3] Munch, *Lærde Brev*, vol. i, p. 114. Letter in August, 1845 to Stephens.

[4] Munch, *Saml. Afh.*, vol. ii, p. 77.

[5] Munch, *Lærde Brev*, vol. i, p. 104. May 6, 1845 to Finn Magnusen.

[6] Munch, *Saml. Afh.*, vol. i, p. 378.

[7] *Supra*, pp. 69-74.

of fidelity, attachment to the fatherland, chivalrous love, scaldic ability, and a " manly " feeling of independence, and likewise shrewdness, combativeness, cunning, violence and a spirit of revenge.[8] This nationality, according to Keyser, possessed a courage that sometimes became a military " fever," a prudence that occasionally turned to dissimulation, a sense of independence that sometimes culminated in personal wilfulness. Exalted self-control, hospitality, sacrificing fidelity, and a sense for law and order were matched by severity, grim revenge, arrogance, egotism and a scrupulosity in observing legal forms. Over the old folk character, he wrote, there had rested a crust of stiffness and self-satisfaction; but it had been external and more the fruit of prudence, than of any meanness of disposition.[9] The Northmen had been accused—by sources that were alien, it should be observed—of cruelty and barbarism. Yet judged by the standards of their own time, the Vikings, it was contended, conducted themselves with unusual uprightness and humaneness. There had been among them no such blood-thirstiness as that which had been characteristic of the Merovingians. Some northern customs had been cited as undeniably cruel, in particular the play with infants on spear tips ("at hænde Smaabørn") or the practice of the "blood-eagle," but it was explained that these had at bottom a ceremonial and religious import and were in no wise associated with any gruesomeness in the national character.[10]

*   *   *   *   *

Nationality to the mid-century historians had about it something well-defined and unitary—something that helped to keep each nationality distinct from all others and hindered the penetration of outside influences. It is significant that

[8] *Den Const.*, 1847, no. 60.

[9] Keyser, *Saml. Afh.*, pp. 396-7.

[10] Munch, *NFH.*, vol. i, pp. 451-2.

in a number of instances the Norwegian scholars visualized
the nationalities of an earlier day as separated by deep
impenetrable forests, a circumstance, we note, which made
more graphic the sharpness of the national boundaries.[11]
How each nation remained exclusive, was best seen in its
earlier and more primitive periods.[12]   The Russ, a Germanic
people, long insignificant politically and surrounded by other
races, had still retained their national character.[13]   Perhaps
the best example was that of the Normans in France.   The
" externals " of their nationality, such as language and
customs, had slowly disappeared in the days of Duke
Richard I, yet the Normans retained their Norwegian character and Norwegian national spirit.[14]   They appropriated
the French language but they did not assume the French
nationality,[15] and wherever they went (England, Sicily)
they remained true to their heritage and revealed their Norwegian origin.[16]

A people might lay aside its traditional nationality and
appropriate another but the process took place in units, ex-
cluding any idea that nationalities might fuse or mix.
Peoples changed nationality much as an individual changed
garments.   For example, the Gothic Jutes on Jutland at
some time " went over " to the nationality of the Danes,[17]
while the medieval Russ in eastern Europe first lost their
north-Germanic nationality and then appropriated in its place
the Slavic.[18]   In the same way Munch expected the Finnish

[11] *Cf. ibid.*, vol. i, pp. 49-50.

[12] Munch, *Saml. Afh.*, vol. ii, p. 617.

[13] Keyser, *Saml. Afh.*, p. 187.

[14] Munch, *NFH.*, vol. i, pp. 680-81 ; vol. ii, p. 219.

[15] Munch, *Saml. Afh.*, vol. ii, p. 23.

[16] Munch, *NFH.*, vol. i, p. 682.

[17] Munch, *Saml. Afh.*, vol. i, p. 499.

[18] *Ibid.*, vol. i, p. 425, note.

people, at present low in the scale of culture, to lay aside their nationality and take on Swedish culture and nationality.[19]

Nationality, to these writers, was also something inherently static. Nationalities had entered on the stage of history full-grown and had come on down through the centuries with a certain fixity and rigidity. The *norrøn* stock, for instance, had arrived in Scandinavia with every feature of a nation's self-contained existence.[20] Usages that were firmly rooted in the national character, might persist (unnoticed) for centuries only to find a later expression. The use of " swearers " among the Franks was actually but a modification of something very old that " from primeval days had lain in the Germanic conciousness." [21] So too the Normans had not appropriated the French nationality.[22] William the Conqueror embodied a modification of the " northern " nationality. Accounts of chroniclers like Dudo were " genuinely northern, one might say Norwegian," for they had some of the qualities of the sagas [23] whose art thus lived again in the Norman-French trouvères. In the realm of government, the old Norwegian arrangement of the *len* had been accepted generally, with some adaptation, as a means to hold medieval society together in the face of feudal anarchy.[24] So too, the English jury seemed, in large part, derived from the legal practices of the northern peoples.[25]

The static quality ascribed to nationality was implied in the favored use of the word " treasure " in a way to connote unchangeability. In the terminology of the day, the medieval

---

[19] *Supra*, pp. 114-5.

[20] Munch, *Saml. Afh.*, vol. i, p. 199.

[21] *Ibid.*, vol. i, p. 590.

[22] *Ibid.*, vol. iii, p. 13.

[23] Munch, *NFH.*, vol. i, p. x.

[24] *Ibid.*, vol. i, p. 683.

[25] Munch, *Saml. Afh.*, vol. iii, p. 15.

historical records and letters were a rich or hidden
" treasure," [26] or, if still outside of the country, they remained " dead treasures," [27] while the ancient laws were
reckoned among the most " precious national treasures " [28]
of the fatherland. The medieval ruins likewise were " holy
and venerable treasures," [29] while the Norwegian ballads
were part of a " treasure the most precious the people
possessed." [30]

Though nationality was thought of as something static,
it did not always remain unimpaired. In the course of time
it might be corroded and worn away, as in modern days, by
too much cosmopolitanism, too much contact with foreign
influences. In this regard, those most guilty of offense were
the cultured, as they took up with things European and lost
much of what was national.[31] In the past, many nationalities had suffered from too much contact with alien cultures,
though all had not been equally affected. To begin with
at any rate, Norway's situation in this regard seemed quite
encouraging to some of the romanticists. Her out-of-the-
way position, as well as her climate and her geography, had
helped to preserve the nationality and retard the effects of
cosmopolitanism.[32] Some of the south-Germanic peoples
however, had been involved in the " incongruous " and
" unfortunate " systems of Roman and feudal law, and had
become entangled with dynastic unions and with the

[26] *Stort. Forh.*, 1830, vol. iv, p. 224; *ibid.*, 1848, no. 30, p. 65; *Nor*,
vol. iii, pt. iii, p. 16.

[27] Munch, *Saml. Afh.*, vol. i, p. 102.

[28] *Stort. Forh.*, 1830, vol. iv, p. 204.

[29] *Ibid.*, 1851, vol. iii, pp. 13-14.

[30] Munch, *Saml. Afh.*, vol. iii, p. 376; *cf.* Munch, *Norges, Sveriges
og Danmarks Historie til Skolebrug*, p. 465; *Maal og Minne*, 1909, p. 58.
S. Bugge to Sv. Grundtvig, May 29, 1857.

[31] *Cf.* Munch, *Saml. Afh.*, vol. iv, p. 309.

[32] Welhaven, *Saml. Skr.*, vol. vi, p. 291; *Den Const.*, 1845, no. 215.

machinations of a universal clergy, all of which had sullied
their pure Germanism.[33]   The groups which settled on the
plains and conquered and mixed with other peoples lost more
of their national purity than did those who settled less
accessible regions.   In the Alps and along the North Sea
marshes the German stocks more successfully warded off
the unnational and retained much more of the " *ur*-Germanic
nationality." [34]

With the writers of the mid-century, the prefix *ur-,* meaning primordial, was a strong favorite.   The term was used
often to describe the attributes of nationality in its earlier
(and therefore better) state.   Nationality in its more primitive days had been least contaminated and closest to perfection.   Hence the prevailing enthusiasm for the early
Germanic period when national qualities had been most pure.
Writers postulated, for the Germanic race, an *ur*-type, or
an *ur*-tribe coming from the *ur*-home in Central Asia,[35] and
spoke or thought in terms of *ur*-alphabets, or *ur*-old legal
customs; [36] there had been a Germanic *ur*-language, and
there had flourished an *ur*-literature.[37]

The Norwegian School, and Norwegian romanticists
generally, found it gratifying to point out that the primeval
Germanic had been best preserved in the north-Germanic
branch [38] and hence true Germanism was still to be found
only in the northern language and the northern mythology,

---

[33] *Den Const.*, 1847, no. 15.

[34] Munch, *Saml. Afh.*, vol. i, p. 504.

[35] *Den Const.*, 1847, no. 15; Munch, *Saml. Afh.*, vol. i, pp. 423-24.

[36] Keyser, *Efterl. Skr.*, vol. i, pp. 46, 509-10; Munch, *Saml. Afh.*, vol.
i, pp. 459, 591; vol. iii, pp. 400-1.

[37] Munch, *NFH.*, vol. i, p. 7; *N. Tids. f. Vid. og Litt.*, vol. ii, p. 97;
cf. Morgbl., 1852, no. 41.

[38] Munch, *Saml Afh.*, vol. i, p. 505; *cf.* Munch, *Nordens Gamle Gude
og Helte-Sagn* (Chra., 1840), pp. 1-2.

and in northern institutions.[39]   So too, in turn, within the
north-Germanic group certain qualities had distinguished
the *norrøn* branch; it had best revealed the old north-Germanic military spirit while in cultural matters the *norrøn*
tongue had possessed its own sharp individuality suggesting
that it had been no party to any fusion of languages, but
harked back even to Iranian antecedents.[40]   The genuine
elements of this tongue were best preserved in the Old
Norse,[41] which was preëminent with its phonetic system and
its vowel mutation, being superior in these respects to the
Swedish and Danish and approached only by the German.[42]

In connection with his studies of the Old Norse, Munch
was fascinated by the peculiarities of the Gothic, the oldest
Germanic tongue to leave any record,[43] whose forms and
constructions gave him a peep into what he called " the
older linguistic machinery " [44] or the " secret workshop " [45]
of early linguistic development and transition.   The Gothic
was most important " for us," he remarked, because above
every other language it stood closest to the Germanic *ur*-
tongue; [46] it was the " oldest " and it had been the last to
diverge from the Germanic *ur*-stem, and thus it had kept
most of the artificial constructions of the earlier medium.[47]
In the sense that linguistic age depended on the longest

[39] Munch, *Saml. Afh.*, vol. i, pp. 418, 424; vol. ii, p. 42; *Den Const.*,
1847, no. 15; Keyser, *Nordmændenes Religionsforfatning i Hedendommen*,
p. 2; cf. *Morgbl.*, 1841, no. 124.

[40] Keyser, *Saml. Afh.*, pp. 7-8.

[41] Munch, *Saml. Afh.*, vol. iii, p. 292; Aasen, *Det norske Folkesprogs
Grammatik*, pp. iii-iv.

[42] Aasen, *Skr. i Saml.*, vol. iii, p. 127; *Maal og Minne*, 1917, pp. 10, 20.

[43] Keyser, *Efterl. Skr.*, vol. i, p. 28.

[44] Munch, *NFH.*, vol. viii, p. xviii.

[45] Munch, *Det gothiske Sprogs Formlære* (Chra., 1848), Forord.

[46] Munch, *Saml. Afh.*, vol. i, p. 227; vol. ii, p. 458.

[47] *Ibid.*, vol. i, p. 423.

retention of primeval forms, the oldest tongue, next to the extinct Gothic, was the north-Germanic; [48] and between these two there was the closest " internal relationship." [49] Hence a knowledge of the Gothic helped to show that among the tongues to leave any extensive literary remains, the *norrøn* was closest to the primeval Germanic.

But in spite of its priority in some important respects, such as the matter of language, the Norwegian nationality had been much impaired. It had been sorely tried in the later medieval period when exposed to an aggressive outside European culture, feudal and Latin in its tradition. Much that was unique in the everyday life of the north had been modified by, or forced to give way to, borrowed customs. [50] In the upper layers of society, where the French romances gained increasing popularity, the contamination had been most marked, and it was discernible in such a work as the *King's Mirror,* which, compared with *Hávamál,* the great poem of the heathen period, revealed the Norwegian folk character with duller outlines, worn down by contact with Christianity and the general European tradition. [51] Under foreign influence, the native works may have acquired a more florid and polished style, but they lacked the power, the abruptness and the naïveté of earlier native productions, which, as Keyser confessed, with their rougher effects, attracted " us " more than the things produced under foreign influence. [52]

In its decline, the Norwegian nationality was exposed to the debilitating influence of a political and cultural union

[48] *Ibid.,* vol. i, p. 227; vol. ii, p. 153.

[49] Keyser, *Saml. Afh.,* p. 10.

[50] Keyser, *Efterl. Skr.,* vol. ii, pt. ii, p. 3.

[51] Keyser, Munch and Unger, *Konungs Skuggsjá,* p. xii.

[52] Keyser and Unger, *Strengleïkar eða Lioðabok,* pp. iii-iv.

with another country, and was so impaired that after several
centuries Danish influence had made itself supreme in language and literature, in social life and administration.   But the
nationality survived even this overwhelming contamination.
Something of a boundary between the Danish and Norwegian nationalities had held for the entire period; if one
looked to the essentials of each, one would see how in habits
of thought and language, in customs and national character
they had remained quite different.[53]

*   *   *   *   *

The Norwegian Historical School had a very high regard
for the discipline of comparative philology.   Believing that
relationship in language betokened relationship in nationality,[54] its members regarded this discipline as a most reliable
means, when history " deserted " them, of tracing early
tribal and national genealogies.[55]   Today we find it difficult
to realize the fervor with which romanticist scholars em-
braced this " exhilarating " study.   They felt it to be the
" pride of their century," the " thread of Ariadne " which
led them through the labyrinths of tribal relationships and
migrations,[56] and disclosed what they were most anxious to
know about early national affinities.   They expected comparative philology to prove as important for historical research as the perfecting of the steam engine had been in
the industrial field.[57]   They considered it significant for all
the social disciplines; applied to folklore, for instance, it
might serve very well to distinguish the characteristic in one

[53] Munch, *Saml. Afh.*, vol. ii, p. 25; *cf. Ill. Nyhbl.*, 1857, pp. 225-6.

[54] Keyser, *Saml. Afh.*, p. 4.

[55] H. Nissen, " *Om den sammenlignende Sprogvidenskab,*" *Nor*, vol.
ii, pp. 177-78; *Chra.-Post.*, 1858, no. 313; Munch, *Saml. Afh.*, vol. ii,
pp. 95, 144, 147; vol. iii, pp. 222-23.

[56] Munch, *Saml. Afh.*, vol. ii, p. 159; vol. iii, p. 222.

[57] *Ibid.*, vol. ii, p. 93.

folk spirit from that in another and thus play an important
part in the current " national strivings." [58]

With the use of the comparative method the Norwegian
School often combined a liberal quota of hypothesizing.
From what the historian knew of a later situation, complained Keyser, he often had to guess at an earlier one.[59]
In this art of scholarly guessing (and often he proved to be
correct), none was so adept as Munch, and he amazed his
learned contemporaries with his faculty for seizing upon a
point or formula outside of the available evidence and then
working his way back to the documents. At times he had
no hesitancy in jumping to conclusions though the evidence
was scarce. For instance, Munch had no records to shed
any light on the language of the early Karelians, but he
thought that these people must have borrowed from the
Russians, remarking, of this " we can be pretty sure." [60]
Some of the reasoning of the Norwegian School was artless
and naïve. Keyser argued that since it took possession of a
much larger stretch of territory and gave the name to the
whole north-Germanic branch, the *norrøn* stock must have
been larger than the Sviar group.[61] Likewise he maintained
that the north-Germanic branch must have come from the
east and not the south, because the lands south of the Göta
River were occupied; south-Germanic peoples had lived
there a long time and the Celts had been there before them.[62]

With the aid of comparative philology it was possible,
when necessary, to " invent " a tribe or a language. Munch
deliberately set about to " reconstruct " the " approximate

[58] Jakob and W. K. Grimm, *Briefwechsel der Gebrüder Grimm mit
nordischen Gelehrten*, p. 270. J. Moe to J. Grimm, Oct. 12, 1849.

[59] Keyser, *Saml. Afh.*, pp. 412-13.

[60] Munch, *Saml. Afh.*, vol. iii, pp. 426-27.

[61] Keyser, *Saml. Afh.*, p. 151.

[62] *Ibid.*, p. 177.

appearance " of the oldest northern tongue.[63]   Relying much on the linguistic evidence in the Chudic (Finnish) word, *ruotsi,* and the forms *ruotzolaine, ruotzolane, (ruotsalainen)*, Keyser and he built up a case for the supposed existence of a north-Germanic people, the Russ, in early Russia.[64]   Munch hoped to work out a chronicle for the pre-Ruric period with the aid of comparative philology but " without leaning too much on guesses." [65]

*   *   *   *   *

When some of the foregoing considerations are applied to the Norwegian School's least tenable hypothesis, the migration theory, we observe how the latter was colored by romanticist thinking and nationalist considerations.   For the historians it was desirable to show that the *norrøn* nationality, kept free of miscegenation [66] and in possession of its primeval perfection, had reached the Scandinavian peninsula as a folk " apart " and the explanation that would best satisfy this consideration was that of a separate migration from the north.

While foreign colleagues thought them moved by an " irritable sympathy for the fatherland," [67] the Norwegian scholars, in their championship of the migration theory, professed to be disinterested and disclaimed any patriotic motive.   " Politics and national pride," wrote Munch, " have had not the least to do with our investigations "; the historian, he insisted, must follow the facts even when they did little to flatter national vanity.[68]   " High " above all

---

[63] Munch, *Saml. Afh.,* vol. i, p. 224.

[64] *Ibid.,* vol. ii, p. 197, especially; Keyser, *Saml. Afh.,* p. 185 *et seq.*

[65] Munch, *Lærde Brev,* vol. i, p. 212.   June 30, 1847 to Rafn.

[66] Keyser, *Efterl. Skr.,* vol. i, p. 12.

[67] Cf. *Tidsskrift for Litteratur og Kritik,* vol. i, p. 273.

[68] Munch, *NFH.,* vol. ii, p. v, note; Munch, *Saml. Afh.,* vol. ii, p. 68; vol. iii, p. 271.

national pride,. "looking neither to right nor left," Munch had sought only the truth.[69] He had not been anti-Danish in treating of Denmark's encroachments on Norway for he had dealt with them as he would have treated those of any other country. He protested that his studies were done *sine ira et studio.*[70]

That Munch was sincere in his protestations of objectivity there is little reason to doubt. He could on occasion cite facts that were quite unflattering to Norwegian national pride.[71] But he, as well as his colleagues, seemed unable to appreciate that others might disagree with them on the migration theory for valid reasons. The Norwegian scholars placed the theory beyond the pale of legitimate doubt; the submission of contrary evidence must be ascribed to intellectual dishonesty. There was something just a bit naïve in Munch's charge that exaggerated patriotism kept the Danes from accepting the migration hypothesis,[72] when the same sort of patriotism, as a matter of fact, sustained his own labors for the " vindication of our old literature," [73] and once led him to admit, somewhat incautiously, that he did not much care whether the north-Germanic element had come from the north or from some other direction; the migration theory in itself was not so important, if his opponents would but concede that there had lived two separate peoples in ancient Scandinavia, one in the north and one farther south, each with its characteristic nationality.[74]

[69] Munch, *Forn-Swenskans . . . Språkbygnad*, p. xxiii *et seq.*

[70] Munch, *Lærde Brev*, vol. i, p. 35. Feb. 13, 1840 to Molbech. *Ibid.*, vol. i, p. 97. April 20, 1845 to F. Magnusen; *ibid.*, vol. i, p. 349. Mar. 22, 1849 to Stephens.

[71] Munch, *Saml. Afh.*, vol. i, pp. 41, 58, 123.

[72] *Cf. supra*, pp. 143, 150.

[73] To borrow a phrase which he used in a different context; *cf.* Munch, *Lærde Brev*, vol. i, p. 208. June 19, 1847 to the Academic Council.

[74] Munch, *Saml. Afh.*, vol. ii, p. 159.

That history might be employed in the service of patriotism was not a romanticist idea particularly; in a way it was
as much a characteristic of the preceding enlightenment and
of the succeeding age of realism.   But distinctively romanticist perhaps was the special importance ascribed to the nation's
" memories," that is, the reminders of national greatness, as
if some peculiar virtue were involved in the mere act of
preserving these memories.   The great deeds of the past,
in no sense detached and external, were manifestations of
the nation's intrinsic and imperishable strength.[75]   Only
through its memories did a nation learn to know itself and
its " call." [76]   As a later writer, firmly rooted in the romanticist heritage, put it: a people without respect for its great
historical memories was " nationally sick " and " certain of
death." [77]   There could be no better example of this than
Norway.   Perhaps more than any other nation she had
suffered the fate of having her glorious ancient memories
blighted.[78]   They had been allowed to lapse in the period
of decline [79] and they had also suffered much from positive
influences—from the unfortunate union with Denmark and
the fanaticism of the Protestant Reformation.[80]   To cap it
all there was the well-nigh fabulous circumstance that some
of the great accomplishments recorded in her memories were
credited to others.[81]   But now things were to be different:
" Norway's name shall not be forgotten if we vindicate its
right."

The orientation of the Norwegian School, we may con-

[75] Welhaven, *Saml. Skr.*, vol. v, pp. 229-30.

[76] Munch, *Saml. Afh.*, vol. i, pp. 122-3.

[77] Henrik Krohn, *Skrifter* (Bergen, 1909), p. 519.

[78] *Stort. Forh.*, 1857, vol. vii, p. 142.

[79] Keyser, *Efterl. Skr.*, vol. i, p. 416.

[80] *Vidar*, 1833, p. 44.

[81] Munch, *Saml. Afh.*, vol. iii, pp. 19-20.

clude, was unmistakably nationalist. Its glowing patriotism
made it easier to champion the hypotheses of a distinctive
national origin and an illustrious national culture. At a
time when many traditions of subserviency inherited from
the Danish period threatened, with their enervating influence,
to counteract the patriotic efforts, the work of the School
gave the nation more confidence in its new-won independence. The primary importance of the School, as a Swedish
historian has remarked, may well have been not academic,
but political; it imparted to its countrymen the self-confidence
necessary to play the rôle of a free people.[82]

The members of the Norwegian School failed to make
the most of one matter that would have lent additional
weight to their case. While they exploited the glories of
the older period of national history—the age that had given
fullest expression to what was " characteristic " of their
nationality—they overlooked the possibilities of the Danish
period. Against the latter, they were prejudiced of course,
for it seemed to present mainly a succession of Danish
encroachments. Nevertheless, through that period as well,
the nationality had lived on, then best represented by the
peasant. It is a bit odd that in the midst of the prevailing
enthusiasm for the peasant, and the tendency to see in his
ways connectives between the old and the new Norway,
more was not made of the history of the peasant class during
the Danish centuries, especially after Wergeland in his history
of the constitution had pointed out the peasant as the true
link between the old and the new.[83] It should be remembered,
however, that the mid-century historians were rooted in the
urban tradition, and furthermore, that being romanticists

[82] N. Höjer, *" Norsk National Historieskrivning,"* (*svensk*) *Historisk
Tidskrift*, vol. vi, p. 131.

[83] See the introductory part of his history, upon which there is a critical
essay by G. Vislie, *" Historisk Gransking hjaa Henrik Wergeland "* in
Avhandlinger fra Universitetets historiske Seminar, vol. ii, pp. 1-36.

they thought of nationality as something static, something which the peasant had *preserved*. They were hardly prepared to appreciate the sense in which within the Danish period a *growth* had taken place, anticipating the developments in 1814. Growth, in this sense of the term, was a concept more familiar to realism with its sociological orientation, than it was to romanticism. Among the younger Norwegian scholars, Sars took up the earlier suggestion of Wergeland and in the next generation made it clear that the " barren " Danish centuries had been very significant for national development.

PART III
THE FOLKLORISTS

CHAPTER XII

THE FIRST FOLKLORE COLLECTIONS

SINCE much national importance was ascribed to the traditions of the peasant, the task of collecting and editing folklore in mid-century Norway was an enterprise of interest, not alone to scholars, but to a wider public. The leading figures in this undertaking were P. C. Asbjørnsen, Jørgen Moe and M. B. Landstad. Andreas Faye, largely in the spirit of rationalism, made a preliminary effort, and some of the earlier work of Sophus Bugge presaged the close of this romanticist enterprise. The titles of the collections arranged, and frequently reëdited, constitute a bewildering array, but something will be gained in clarity by remembering that the collectors were concerned mainly with three *genre* of folklore, namely, folk tales, fairy tales and ballads. Together Asbjørnsen and Moe began work on the folk tales; then after a time Moe withdrew and left the reëditing to Asbjørnsen, while from the outset the latter edited the fairy tales alone. The ballads were first taken up by Moe and then treated definitively by Landstad.[1]

* * * * *

Although the yield of Norwegian folklore proved to be

[1] For general discussions of the subject see: Moltke Moe, "*Det nationale Gjennembrud og dets Mænd*" in Gran, *Nordm. i. d. nit. Aarh.*, vol. ii, pp. 144-268, reprinted in M. Moe, *Samlede Skrifter* (Oslo, 1925-27), vol. iii, pp. 1-196; A. Krogvig, "*Jørgen Moe's Ungdom*" in his *Fra det nationale gjennembruds Tid.*, pp. 3-74. Hans Hansen's *P. Chr. Asbjørnsen: Biografi og Karakteristikk* (Oslo, 1932) became available to me while my work was in the press.

a very rich one, the work of assembling it got under way rather late.   True, there were those who early showed a passing interest in the popular lore.   Lyder Sagen and C. E. Steenbloch by 1810, apparently, had made inquiries about ballads in the western part of the country.   They found some, but only those more recently composed were Norwegian; the older ones all seemed to be Danish.[2]   In the years following the separation from Denmark, while neighboring peoples were bringing to light treasures of popular lore, some Norwegians also felt a sense of obligation in this respect, and a no less distinguished person than Jakob Grimm was interested in seeing the supposed Norwegian folklore investigated.[3]   A Swedish observer in 1830 referred to the striking paucity of Norwegian ballad material,[4] and Wergeland who in years past had made inquires locally about popular traditions, as late as 1840, in an oft-cited passage, stated his belief that a folk balladry did exist in the country though he was not too sure about it, or as he put it, he would not " swear " to it.[5]   Wergeland was among the minority who appreciated that some folklore did exist, but any general understanding of its nature and extent had to wait upon more consistent investigation.

The first serious effort to assemble and publish Norwegian folklore was made by Andreas Faye [6] who in 1833 published his *Norske Sagn* (" Norwegian Legends "), a collection of tales of various types.   As a pastor, Faye had copied down

[2] So reported the Danish ballad editor, R. Nyerup, to J. C. Berg. *Illustreret Nyhedsblad*, 1865, p. 24, quoted by R. Berge, *M. B. Landstad* (Risør, 1920), p. 45.

[3] *Cf.* Gran, *Nordm. i det nit. Aarh.*, vol. ii, p. 187.

[4] *Maal og Minne*, 1918, pp. 46-7.

[5] H. Wergeland, *Udvalgte Skrifter*, vol. vii, p. 397. Letter of Feb. 4-5, 1840 to Fredrika Bremer.

[6] *Supra*, pp. 92-3.

some of the traditions current among his parishioners, with
the expectation of turning them over to some "more competent hand" for use, but later he decided to edit them himself.
His model was Jacob Grimm, to whom he wrote: "you may
justly consider these legends an echo of your own." [7]

There was, however, some dissonance in the echo. While
Grimm's stories were conceived in the spirit of romanticism,
Faye's were treated mainly in the spirit of rationalism. With
an attitude [8] characteristic of a pastor of the enlightenment,
he viewed the stories chiefly as manifestations of credulity,
as superstitions holding the mind in ignorance and darkness.
He had no fear that making these "untruths" better known
would help to consolidate the hold of the superstitions; he
was inclined to feel that when their origins were accounted
for rationally they would die of their own accord. Superstitions, he thought, were like weeds to be torn up by the root
and left to wither: they throve well in darkness,[9] but once
pulled up "into the hot sun" they would crack "like gnomes
and goblins." [10] Faye kept in mind the didactic qualities of
his accounts. Children might find his stories entertaining
and moralists would discover in them heroic characters
whom they might cite as models of private and public virtue.
Beyond this, his intention was also patriotic. Poets would
have a convenient handbook from which to chose more
"domestic," i.e., more national, themes.

The later influence of Faye's collection was slight. There
was the external reason that the moment of its appearance
was inauspicious; Norway's talents were then absorbed in

[7] Without a knowledge of the Grimm stories, he wrote, he would
hardly have thought of making such a collection. J. Grimm and W. K.
Grimm, *Briefwechsel der Gebrüder Grimm mit nordischen Gelehrten,*
p. 308. Letter of May 17, 1834.

[8] *Cf.* A. Faye, *Norske Sagn,* pp. ix-xix.

[9] *Ibid.,* p. iv.

[10] *Cf.* Gran, *op. cit.,* vol. ii, p. 188.

the Wergeland-Welhaven controversy.   It is necessary to take into account also Faye's rationalist treatment of the folklore, which we have analyzed in order to contrast it later with the romanticist approach.   What impulses were imparted to the future came not so much from Faye's collection as from a review by the young P. A. Munch.[11]   It is possible that Munch's notice gave the initial impulse to Landstad's ballad-collecting and perhaps prompted both Moe and Asbjørnsen to take an interest in the folk tales.[12]   Munch brought romanticist (as well as nationalist) canons of criticism to bear on Faye's rationalist treatment.   He objected to the editorial style; Faye's subdued and even tone made the stories dull.   Then in line with the romanticist urge to enhance the " unique," he criticized Faye for the failure to appreciate and exalt what was " characteristic "; Faye had missed one of the main purposes of such a collection.

But in spite of the imperfections, Munch was enthusiastic over one thing.   The legends of the collection proved that the popular mind had not entirely forgotten the memories of Norway's one-time glorious past.   It displeased him to see that Faye had chosen stories indiscriminately from both the glorious saga age and the gloomy Danish period, even from so recent a date as the early eighteenth century.   However, there was enough from the medieval period to show that the people had not forgotten all its brilliance, and this too in spite of the ravages of time and circumstance.   Those memories had been nearly blotted out by the Reformation and the union with Denmark, but Faye's collection proved that some of them were still intact in modern times.

Faye, who grumbled at Munch's strictures on his style,[13] in 1844 issued a second edition which seems to have been

[11] *Vidar*, 1833, no. 58; reprinted in his *Saml. Afh.*, vol. i, pp. 26-34.

[12] Gran, *op. cit.*, vol. ii, p. 193.

[13] *Vidar*, nos. 67, 68.

quite without significance. Munch had been right: another style would be necessary—necessary because the fancy of the age was unmistakably turning toward romanticism. Those who were competent to give the folklore a treatment in conformity with the new tastes were already at work, and felt none too sympathetic toward Faye's book; we know that Asbjørnsen, Welhaven and P. A. Munch in 1842 wondered if it would be feasible to frustrate Faye's plan for a second edition.[14]

It should be noted that Faye was not unaffected by the newer current of romanticism. His second edition was entitled, not *Norske Sagn* but *Norske Folke-Sagn,* introducing the adjective *folke*—which was to be so popular with the romanticists. The first time he had spoken readily enough of the " superstitions "; in the second printing, as well as in a review of the booklet *Nor* to be mentioned shortly, he was more concerned over the rapid disappearance of these " national tones " from the people, and spoke of saving them from the advance of modern progress. In conformity with the romanticist phraseology, he identified nationality largely with the residue of song and story passed on from one generation to the next, and spoke of the homely tales that had been droned about the cradle, or of the legend which on many a dusky evening had kept in suspense the fireside circle of his childhood. Faye was, in short, a transitionary figure, rooted in the old but influenced by the new.

* * * * *

A little picture book entitled *Nor: en Billedbog for den norske Ungdom* (" Nor: A Picture Book for Norwegian Youth ") which appeared during the Christmas season of 1837-8 gave Norwegian readers their first sample of a

[14] Anders Krogvig, *Fra det nationale gjennembruds Tid.,* p. 206; Gran, *Nordm. i. d. nit. Aarh.,* vol. ii, p. 193, note.

romanticist folklore treatment.   The publishers intended the
booklet to serve patriotic as well as holiday purposes.   For
older children, they explained, there was a dearth of " real "
Norwegian stories, meaning " such as are patriotic," or
present " so much genuine nationality " that the reader may
feel that " these flowers have grown on Norwegian soil." [15]
Heretofore the country's juvenile literature had been supplied from Denmark, and the publishers wanted to issue a
children's book arranged entirely by domestic talent.

The stories of the first part of the book, printed under the
pompous title, *Store og Gode Handlinger af Nordmænd*
("Great and Good Deeds of Norwegians"), had been
assembled by the young archivist, Bernt Moe, cousin of the
more renowned Jørgen Moe.   These stories of various outstanding personalities in Norwegian history were edited in
the spirit of rationalism.   Whether a figure was a saga hero
or a distinguished citizen of the eighteenth century made
little difference; he was endowed with the traditional Norwegian virtues—courage, outspokenness, loyalty—and was
presented as a very worthy example to juvenile readers.

The dry didacticism of these accounts by Bernt Moe was
in sharp contrast with the brisk and racy style of the stories
in the second part of the book, whose several folk and fairy
tales were arranged ostensibly by P. C. Asbjørnsen alone.
Jørgen Moe wrote an anonymous introductory poem for the
whole volume in which he half apologetically commended the
popular tales for their simplicity.   He might have spared
himself the effort; for the stories in the second part of the
book caught the fancy of many readers, anticipating the
coming enthusiasm for the popular folklore.

The book was something of a literary curiosity, for within
its covers were typified in sharp contrast the tempers of
rationalism and romanticism.   The transition from one

[15] *Nor: en Billedbog for den norske Ungdom* (Chra., 1838), p. v.

epoch to the next was but a matter of pages. But in actual life the transition was not quite so rapid; rationalist influences were not dissipated by the first breezes of romanticism, a fact brought home to Jørgen Moe when the book was reviewed by Faye, " the corrupter of history," [16] in whom Moe had little confidence. Moe had desired a capable, even though it be a caustic, notice from P. A. Munch.[17]

Faye commended the book because its stories, compared with those in the books from Denmark, were more national; [18] *Nor* would be a better book for the youth of Norway. As a rationalist he was impressed by the didactic stories of Bernt Moe in whose heroes he saw many models of virtue and public spirit. But in his judgment on the stories of the second part he wavered, granting however, that these folk and fairy tales might perhaps be " refined " by literary talents so that they too would yield inspiring examples of heroism and virtue.

JØRGEN MOE

At this point we may stop to say something of Jørgen Moe, whose work as a folklorist was to be so important. Jørgen Engebretsen Moe (1813-1882) grew up in the hilly interior district of Ringerike, a picturesque region of light green hillocks and dark pine-crested ridges. The section still had its gnarled and individualistic types, a bit queer at times, but frequently well-informed about the folklore of the region. They might tell a phenomenal number of tales and stories, once their confidence was gained, and they seemed to belong to the entire locale. Jørgen's impressionable mind stowed away, in memories that proved of incomparable

[16] *Cf.* Krogvig, *op. cit.*, p. 152.

[17] In fact, he privately expressed his disapproval of Faye's review just *because* it was too much of a panegyric. Krogvig, *op. cit.*, p. 150.

[18] In *Morgbl.*, 1838, no. 52.

value to him later as a folklorist, the whole ensemble of brownie, fairy, vale and hill, and narrator.

As a younger son of a locally-prominent freeholder, Jørgen had no prospects at home and he was pushed off to school and a possible career. In his second year at Norderhov, he met a Christiania boy, P. C. Asbjørnsen, who had been sent there by his father in the hope that he might develop more studious habits. Though Asbjørnsen was soon ordered home, the brief contact had been long enough to forge a link in that friendship which later was to be so significant for the collecting of Norwegian folklore.

At the University, where Moe took but a moderate part in student affairs, he matured the friendship with Asbjørnsen. Ill health in 1834 forced Moe to leave for his home. But he continued to read Danish and German works, including those of Jean Paul Richter and some of the collections of the Grimms. In 1837 he returned to Christiania for intermittent stays until 1842, dividing his time between his professional study, theology, and his new interest in folklore.

Again seeking relief for his health, Moe in 1842 took a tutorial position in the family of Nicolai Aall at Næss in the southern part of the country. This locality was a haven of lingering eighteenth-century rationalism; on the manor itself—the " principality," as Moe called it [19]—lived the national patriarch, Jacob Aall, father of Nicolai, while not far away at Holt was Andreas Faye. The intellectual atmosphere was not to Moe's liking but his contacts with Jacob Aall, who had recently issued a translation of Snorre, further developed Moe's new interest in saga history.[20]

After two years Moe returned to the capital to teach for some time, meanwhile becoming absorbed in his work with

[19] *Cf.* Krogvig, *op. cit.*, p. 231.
[20] *Ibid.*, p. 182.

the folk tales.   We can touch briefly on the circumstances of
his later career.   In 1853 he withdrew to devote himself to
pastoral work.   After serving the parishes of Sigdal and
Vestre Aker he was honored in 1870 by appointment as
bishop of the diocese of Christianssand from which position
he retired five years later.

In his earlier years Moe felt personally maladjusted.
Given to introspection and without a satisfying philosophy
of life, he felt deeply the need for a steadying influence.
Almost despairingly he wrote to Asbjørnsen: "Often I
know neither in nor out.   In a double measure I lack any
clear conception of life and of art."   "I need what you in
your unobstructed perception of life's phenomena do not
need—a system."[21]   At various times he spoke of the
effort to maintain his individuality.[22]   With so restless a
character he longed for a sense of peace and unity, and he
sought it in retrospection, which took him back to his childhood home[23] with its world of gnome and fairy folk.   That
Moe should find his true metier in reworking the popular
folklore was thus in harmony with deep personal needs.
It is to be noted too that his personal development had
reached maturity by the time he completely dissociated himself from further concern with the popular traditions.

Moe had a lively sense of patriotism, but no sympathy for
political democracy.   For a time in the early 'forties, he, as
well as Asbjørnsen, had flirted with a tendency looking a
bit vaguely, in imitation of the Danish movement led by
Steen St. Blicher, to a wider political and social democracy
for the peasant.[24]   There was here a certain synchronism;
just at this time the two folklorists were busy gathering

21 *Ibid.*, p. 233.   May 24, 1843 to Asbjørnsen.
22 *Ibid.*, p. 141; *cf.* pp. 175, 229.
23 *Cf.* Gran, *Nordm. i. d. nit. Aarh.*, vol. ii, p. 267.
24 Krogvig, *op. cit.*, pp. 66-69.

popular traditions and hence they were in intimate contact with peasant life. But before the mid-century, Moe's democratic interest had waned, and ere long he was back safe in the conservative fold, where with the rest of the romanticists he could admire the peasant's traditions without encouraging his political demands.

That, after all, was where Moe belonged, for he was by temperament no democrat. In 1835 he wrote of the nation as "that ignorant, stupid and timid mass, which, true enough, constitutes the plurality"[25] (a thrust, perhaps at *Norskheds-bevægelsen*). In the explosive year, 1848, he shared the general apprehension of his circle about the rising tide of democracy and quite distrusted the relatively moderate movement in Christiania for a new and more responsive ministry. On the panel of members proposed he found only "two decent names."[26]

As a patriot Moe exalted the saga period. At first his expressions seemed still to have something in common with the pompous phrases of the rationalists, as when in a moment of youthful pique and disgust he privately castigated his fellow countrymen for meekly obeying the king's authorities in 1829 during the "Battle of the Market Place."[27] How unlike their forbears were the Norwegians of the present! Norway's ancient freedom and honor were now but a legend;[28] he wished that it too had been effaced, for then posterity would at least not be able to point out the

[25] *Ibid.*, p. 138.

[26] He thought the authorities might "go way down" to select men like Stabell, Ueland, and Dahl, whom he regarded as leaders of the "raw opposition." Krogvig, *op. cit.*, pp. 269-70.

[27] *Cf. supra*, p. 26. Moe believed the people were first at fault because they dispersed so slowly when the hour grew late, but he thought that the manner in which the royal officials scattered them should have aroused more protest.

[28] Krogvig, *op. cit.*, p. 83. Letter of June 1, 1829.

Norwegians as the " horrible " example of how " degenerate
the descendants of an illustrious ancestry could become."
In time his attitude toward the older period came to be
typically romanticist. In 1846, speaking at a student celebration, he stated his conviction that " our national memories," the sagas, ought to imbue the present with " holy
enthusiasm " for the importance of " our people," [29] and in
closing he pitched his appeal in an exalted key : might the
beckoning figures of the saga forefathers steel the wills of
his listeners and fill them with a premonition of coming
victory in that " noblest of all struggles, the battle to secure
the full, free and true development of our folk character."

* * * * *

The *Samling af Sange, Folkeviser og Stev i norske
Almuedialekter* (" Collection of Songs, Folk Ballads and Re-
frains in Norwegian Popular Dialects ") which Moe in the
summer of 1840 arranged for the publisher Malling was the
first collection of Norwegian folklore to be edited out and
out in the spirit of romanticism. But it was still a faltering
beginning. Almost two-thirds of the rhymes were from
known authors, especially from Rousseauean poets of the
eighteenth century. Two of the poems were from Wergeland who in his versatility had tried to redeem the apparent
absence of a folk balladry in Norway by composing rhymes
of his own. But Moe's collection helped to settle the uncer-
tainty regarding the existence of Norwegian ballads. Welhaven for example had expressed his belief in their existence
four years earlier [30] and now Moe's collection gave a definitive answer. No less than sixteen of the forty-six ballads
were genuine folk creations—enough to establish beyond
much doubt that Norway too had a true folk balladry.

[29] Jørgen Moe, *Saml. Skr.* (1877), vol. ii, p. 286.

[30] Welhaven, *Samlede Digterverker* (4 vols. Chra., and Copenhagen,
1906-1907), vol. ii, p. 116.

Moe had a specific national purpose in arranging his collection—he wanted to hurry forward the development of a national literature. This could best be done, he thought, by placing before poets and littérateurs a selection of the country's popular traditions. These embodied that true folk spirit which would be needed to vitalize the talents of the formal writers if they were to compose in a national vein. A literature was fundamentally sound so long as it mirrored the basic features of the popular traditions, but once out of touch with them it became barren.[31]

Moe, like many of his contemporaries, felt that the coming of political independence enjoined cultural maturity in literature and the arts. He deeply regretted the fact that as yet there was little sign of such a maturity in Norway; so far only one prose writer, Mauritz Hansen, had "lost" himself in the domestic life of the people, and no poet had yet succeeded in releasing the country's natural scenery from "the petrification in which it lies bewitched."[32] He appreciated that it would take some time to develop a national literature in Norway, partly because of the general concern with politics and partly because of the lingering Danish influence from the deplorable union period, when the Norwegian "Pegasus" had moved down to the Danish plains, "there to be mistreated in French and German" while he forgot his wonted flight from "mountain top to mountain top." But now there was to be a change. Moe had among his ballads several selected from the genuine folk poetry. Henceforth the cultured reading public would more readily feel "a love of the national element in our developing literature" and the young littérateurs would have direct ac-

[31] J. Moe, *Samling af Sange, Folkeviser og Stev i norske Almuedialekter* (Chra., 1840), pp. v-vi.

[32] *Ibid.*, p. vi.

cess to the inspiration of the popular traditions; soon there must appear a national literature.

Moe made one proposal that seemed disturbing to some, when he pointed a way to make the language more national. His suggestion was that writers should borrow terms from the popular speech in whose " gold mines " might be found many " ores " to help a Norwegian to express just what he wished to say.[33] By taking up more and more words of dialect origin, writers would gradually make the language more Norwegian.

While Moe's collection elicited no Norwegian notice, this inattention at home was more than offset in Copenhagen where F. C. Petersen devoted a long article to it.[34] What moved the Dane to discursiveness was not so much Moe's literary theories as his assertive patriotism. Two contentions aroused the reviewer: one, that Denmark " had tamed the Norwegian lion "; the other, that there should be fashioned a "more national" Norwegian language. Petersen hurried by the first point, remarking that it was a demagogic phrase to use at a time when Norwegian circles were sensitive about their patriotism, adding that one hardly knew what to think of a people which for centuries had " permitted itself " to be tamed as " a poodle dog." [35] But he tarried longer with the second point, that Norwegian writers should enlarge their vocabularies by employing words from the vernacular. Did this, he asked, imply a desire to elevate the Norwegian dialects to the dignity of a literary medium? [36] Norway should not give up her present literary language (Danish) for through it she had attained her culture. In addition the new suggestion involved a practical

[33] *Ibid.*, p. vii.
[34] *Tidsskrift for Litteratur og Kritik*, 1841, vol. v, pp. 405-23.
[35] *Ibid.*, p. 407.
[36] *Ibid.*, p. 408.

difficulty. It would be necessary to decide which among the many dialects should be used as a standard or base. Moe's proposal, thought Petersen, was motivated not by a wise solicitude for the best interests of Norway but by a mistaken patriotism. For that very reason he was sure it would be welcomed in the circle of younger Norwegian poets who, since 1814, had been trying " forcibly " to arouse [37] " something new and characteristic, something very different from Danish poetry—an effort which he thought would result only in wordy rhymes and empty bombast. He suggested, a bit caustically, that since no literature was yet appearing, Norway had perhaps come too " easily " by her new freedom and her constitution. Paying his respects to the capital city, he remarked that Christiania was possibly too small to sustain a national literature; at least it seemed to have appropriated " a good portion of American vulgarity." [38]

Moe's collection was only a beginning. In 1842 he became seriously interested in the ballads and three years later laid plans with P. A. Munch to issue a more ambitious collection. He kept on assembling new material and drafted a discourse on balladry. But the plans for a larger edition came to naught. Moe was busy otherwise, and after a time he shrank from the responsibilities of a ballad editor; perhaps Danish critical demands made him hesitant.[39] He would willingly have handed his additional materials over to the one person in whom he had confidence, namely Munch,[40] and it turned out that Munch arranged a second

[37] *Opjage* is the word used. In the language of the chase it means to " scare up."

[38] *Tidsskrift for Litteratur og Kritik*, 1841, vol. v, pp. 414-15.

[39] Krogvig, *op. cit.*, p. 209.

[40] *Ibid.*, p. 228. Letter to Asbjørnsen in the spring of 1843. Andreas Faye offered to use these materials but Moe would have none of him;

edition of Moe's little *Samling*. But the larger collection that Moe envisaged came a few years later from a person of whom Moe disapproved,[41] that is, from M. B. Landstad.

. "like an eel I have slipped him out of hand," he wrote. *Ibid.*, p. 209. Dec. 6, 1842 to Asbjørnsen.

[41] *Ibid.*, p. 276. Dec. 1, 1855 to Asbjørnsen.

CHAPTER XIII

The Folk and Fairy Tales

WHEN Asbjørnsen and Moe began in 1841 to publish their *Norske Folke-eventyr* ("Norwegian Folk Tales") which later attained such importance, they had been intermittently at work on the folk tales for several years. Which of the two had the prior interest in these stories has been a matter of argument among the historians of literature. It seems that, independently of each other, both became interested during the middle 'thirties; their new interest may have been matured by the prospect of helping Faye who was considering a new edition of his *Norske Sagn*. In 1837 Moe and Asbjørnsen laid plans to publish jointly some of the folk tales they had been collecting, and they agreed pretty well on the main principles that should guide their editing. There has been considerable discussion also concerning the question which of the two men had the largest influence in determining these principles, but Krogvig has gone over the whole subject rather carefully and ascribes the decisive influence to Moe.[1]

Moe's concern for the popular traditions was inspired in no small measure by the stimulus of patriotism. It is true that his first interest in them had been personal and literary; his earliest model as an editor had been Tieck, the German romanticist.[2] But soon he found that stories like those of Tieck and Oehlenschlæger were too general. Their style had no "Norwegianness"; none of them seemed of any

---

[1] Krogvig, *Fra det nationale gjennembruds Tid*, pp. 50-65. But regarding Asbjørnsen's early interest *cf.* also H. Hansen, *P. Chr. Asbjørnsen*, especially pp. 28, 58, 74, 159.

[2] Krogvig, *op. cit.*, p. 144. Oct. 23, 1836 to Asbjørnsen.

importance for his own nationality. Might not the Norwegian tales which he was learning to know acquire this importance if they were given the right treatment? From Ringerike he wrote in October, 1836, " If I ever get well again I am going to start telling folk tales. I have just read those edited by Adam.[3] By Jove! That's real business (" *Død og Plage, det er Greier* ") ! Yet his stories certainly are not Norwegian." " If ever I become entirely well again you shall hear about ' the seven foals,' and that shall be Norwegian ! "

The joint project of the two collectors took shape slowly, but in 1840 Moe prepared a prospectus,[4] in which he referred to the scientific importance of the stories. It was his belief that these accounts sprang from the innermost life of a people; hence they enshrined its traditional thought and phantasy and revealed its unique character. With the aid of the comparative method, he thought that the folk tale could be used to throw light upon the relationships of early peoples. " No cultivated person," he wrote,[5] " now doubts the scientific importance of the folk tales; . . . they help to determine a people's unique character and outlook." The editors announced that in retelling the stories they meant to follow carefully the phraseology of the peasant informants, with no embellishment and no changes save in passages that might offend the sense of decency.[6] " Our plan," closed the prospectus, " coincides with that of the Grimms in their excellent *Kinder und Haus-Märchen.*" [7]

---

[3] Adam Oehlenschlæger, *Eventyr af forskjellige Digtere.* The stories were chosen from Tieck, Musæus, Runge, Fouque and Grimm.

[4] *Den Const.*, no. 55. Reprinted in J. Moe, *Saml. Skr.* (1877), vol. ii, pp. 12-15.

[5] J. Moe, *op. cit.*, vol. ii, p. 12.

[6] *Ibid.*, p. 14.

[7] *Ibid.*, p. 15.

The outlook for a venture of this sort was not encouraging. Neither of the editors was publicly known, and a group of juvenile stories[8] would hardly be of interest to adults. Meanwhile the preparatory work went forward and in 1841 appeared the first installment of stories.[9] The public received them with some hesitation. Critics who should have led the way, were more or less puzzled, and while they faltered, the stories independently proved their popularity. As early as January of 1842 Moe could report from Christiania that they were making "a big success, almost a furore."[10]

The little collection elicited two enthusiastic and important reviews. Monrad lent the prestige of his newly-assumed position at the University to a favorable notice in *Morgenbladet*,[11] in which he lapsed immediately into an abstract, Hegelian reverie during the course of which he pointed out how the music and the poetry of a people helped to disclose the connection between its nationality and the Idea.[12] These *Folke-eventyr* were a wholesome sign, he thought, for an interest in popular folklore would facilitate the "rebirth" of the national Idea.

A less philosophical but equally flattering review was that by Rolf Olsen,[13] who liked the *Folke-eventyr* because they were so national. They had a "national ring," agreeably "free from all the dissonances" that usually accompanied

[8] They were announced as *Norske Folke- og Barne-eventyr*.

[9] The pamphlet appeared without any author's name, foreword, introduction or title.

[10] Krogvig, *op. cit.*, p. 191. Jan. 22, 1842 to Peter Brock.

[11] 1842, no. 39.

[12] *Cf. supra*, pp. 69-71.

[13] *Den Const.*, 1842, Mar. 22, no. 81. Olsen (1818-1864) was court attorney at Risør and the local *Storting* representative from 1854 to 1864. In his earlier years he composed several dramas (*Den Sidste Viking*, 1840) and wrote extensively as a journalist.

national productions in Norway. Their style was juvenile and naïve, indeed its very naïveté was " Norwegian." Like most of his contemporaries, Olsen felt that a national literature must be fashioned from the raw material of popular folklore for therein was enshrined the national " soul." In the future, littérateurs would find it easier to make the nation conscious of its soul—another way of saying that ere long there must appear a national literature.

The literary form of the collection was vulnerable, for in trying to capture the narrative style of the people the editors had made use of provincialisms and popular idioms. Olsen justified what had been done in this respect on national grounds! The editors, he explained, had undertaken to elicit what in each narrative was truly national, and to " translate " the rough idiom of each story in a manner to lose none of its uniqueness. In pursuit of the last aim it was inevitable that many provincialisms should be taken along, and in their task, he thought the editors had done well. But among the circles of literary taste, the purists were repelled by what they considered the barbarisms in the stories. When the accounts proved popular these circles wavered, nodding a reserved approval here, frowning a sincerer disapproval there. Their final capitulation was hastened by voices of appreciation from abroad. Jacob Grimm gave the stories unstinted praise and an anonymous review in the authoritative *Leipziger Allgemeine Zeitung* assigned the *Folke-eventyr* a place even above those of the Grimms because they mirrored better what was characteristically national.[14]

By 1844 Asbjørnsen and Moe had added three more installments to their *Folke-eventyr* and then further printing stopped; both editors were much occupied otherwise. Moe

[14] It was written by P. A. Munch who may have chosen anonymity to avoid the disapproval of his circle. Gran, *Nordm. i. d. nit. Aarh.*, vol. ii, p. 227.

moved back to the capital to begin his teaching career and Asbjørnsen was absorbed in the *Huldre-eventyr*. All further attempt to continue the series was finally given up and the four pamphlets became known collectively as the first edition.

PETER CHRISTEN ASBJØRNSEN

The next advance in the task of Norwegian folklore collecting was the publishing of the fairy tales, a venture undertaken by Asbjørnsen alone.[15]   Peter Christen Asbjørnsen (1812-1885), whose family's ancestral roots reached back to the provinces of Guldbrandsdalen and Søndmøre, was born in Christiania and, unlike Jørgen Moe, grew up in an urban environment. His father's glazier shop was a popular gathering place for apprentices and travelers from the country. Here were exchanged entertaining gossip and repertoires of folk and fairy tales. Among those who listened was young Peter; later in life he was to display his own brilliant gifts for story-telling. Peter did poorly in his studies and in 1827 he was sent to the secondary school at Norderhov, where, as we have seen, he met Jørgen Moe. As there was little improvement in his school work he was taken home and not until 1833 did he enter the University.

As a student Asbjørnsen scattered his energies. He devoted himself somewhat to journalism and dabbled in geology—enough to edit later in discontinuous fashion a *Natural History for Young People* (1838-48). Eventually he deserted his chosen course, medicine, for the natural sciences and in this field he later displayed a varied activity. He accompanied a scientific cruise to the Mediterranean in 1849-50, studied forestry in Germany (1856-58), and in

[15] There is now an adequate survey of his life by H. Hansen, *P. Chr. Asbjørnsen.* See also *Norsk Biog. Leks.*, vol. i, pp. 264-73; Halvorsen, *Norsk Forf-Lex.*, vol. i, pp. 104-6; Krogvig, *Fra det nationale gjennembruds Tid, passim.*

1860 became a government inspector of forests. At various times he was called into public service in technical capacities, on one occasion, for instance, to help investigate the peat-making industry.

It is something of a surprise to see a student of the natural sciences and a practical man of affairs make a notable contribution to the imaginative and " impractical " study of folklore. But Asbjørnsen combined a strong sense for the real and the concrete with a jovial interest in the art of story-telling. The one attracted him to the picturesque and the realistic in peasant life, the other easily directed his interest to the popular folklore. He could, of course, give only intermittently of his time to the popular traditions.

When first interested in the stories Asbjørnsen apparently had no very definite plan in mind for utilizing them. Some of his first tales served to accommodate Andreas Faye who was thinking of a new edition of his *Norske Sagn,* and at that time he referred to himself as Faye's " legend ambassador extraordinary." [16] After a bit he came to think of collecting and editing for himself; he was not entirely satisfied with Faye's didactic editing and we have noted how, with others, he considered the feasibility of thwarting Faye's second edition.[17] It turned out that Asbjørnsen's first collection of fairy tales was ready in 1845, the year after the appearance of Faye's revised *Norske Folke-Sagn.*

* * * * *

In preparing for publication his *Norske Huldre-eventyr og Folkesagn* (" Norwegian Fairy Tales and Folk Legends ") Asbjørnsen had adopted a literary stratagem which added much to their popularity. It was his idea that the stories should be presented as part of the locale from which they

[16] O. A. Øverland, *Hvorledes P. Chr. Asbjørnsen begyndte som Sagnfortæller* (Chra., 1902), p. 19. Letter of April 25, 1835 to Faye.

[17] *Supra,* p. 203.

had sprung.[18]   He " framed " the fairy tales, that is, placed
one or more stories within a portrayal of contemporary rural
life.[19]   In this way he was able to give them a true rustic
setting by having them told ostensibly by a peasant narrator
whose circle he described as part of his " frame."   In this
arrangement only the fairy tales proper were genuine, while
the " frames " or sketches by Asbjørnsen embodied his own
impressions of peasant life.   But he imparted such charm
to his sketches that his reading public admired them even
more than the fairy tales proper.

While the more fastidious, especially within the circles
which carried on the traditions of *Intelligentspartiet,* had
been very hesitant about the folk tales, they greeted the
Huldre-eventyr with surprising whole-heartedness, largely
because, in the interval, they had fully joined in the romantic
enthusiasm for the peasant traditions.   That their surrender
was quite complete is suggested by Collett's very favorable
review.[20]   Where three years earlier this coryphaeus of taste
had been most concerned over the barbarisms and the rawness in the folk tales, he now welcomed the folk literature
most enthusiastically as a " greeting " from " our wild,
fresh, yet ever youthful nature "—a greeting conveying all
the winsomeness of the Norwegian *Huldre*[21] to whose
" kingdom " he was attracted by the deep mysterious longing
which her charm engendered, meaning by her " kingdom "
" the magnificent nature of our fatherland."

[18] Asbjørnsen, *Norske Huldre-eventyr og Folkesagn* (Chra., 1845),
p. iv.

[19] He had the idea from Crofter Crocer's *Irish Fairy Tales,* published
in 1825. Jacob Grimm translated them as *Irische Elfenmärchen* (1826)
and a copy of this translation later fell into the hands of Asbjørnsen.
Gran, *Nordm. i. d. nit. Aarh.,* vol. ii, p. 245.

[20] *Den Const.,* 1845, no. 215.

[21] The word *Huldre* may possibly be derived from *hylja,* to hide—hence
hidden folk or *Huldre* folk.

Collett pointed out that the *Huldre-eventyr* had a deep
national significance, and rested his contention on the premise
that the stories were important for their nature symbolism.
According to this view, it will be recalled,[22] the phenomena
of nature were represented symbolically in the stories.
Thus, in Norway, the wild majestic terrain of the western
fjord country was personified in *Jutulen,* an ugly, proud,
malicious, imperious and demonic figure.   Likewise, nature's
dreamier aspects—the undulating hills of the south and
east with their leafy thickets of birch and their shady forests
of deep green pine—were symbolized in the wood-nymph,
Huldren.   She was a dainty sprite, refreshing and alluring, delicate and diaphanous, with golden hair set off by
eyes of deep blue, and frequently she wore a blue petticoat and
a white snood.   Her temperament was melancholy and
those who listened to her song and stringed music were
moved to sadness and tears.[23]   The most striking thing
about her (suggesting the gap between Man and nature, said
Collett) [24] was her lack of a soul and the circumstance that
she had grown a cowtail.   The romanticists became
thoroughly infatuated with her and she assumed a central
place in their nature symbolism.   More vividly than any
other figure she personified national traits (in nature symbolism there was postulated an intimate relationship between
folklore, natural phenomena and national character), and
Collett praised Asbjørnsen's collection because it pointed so
clearly to what was truly national in Norwegian character
and folk life.

[22] *Cf. supra*, pp. 68-9.

[23] Asbjørnsen, *Norske Huldre-eventyr og Folkesagn* (1845), p. iv.
Huldren took possession of forsaken hillside pasture clearings, and
passersby who submitted to her charms were invited into subterranean
halls to hear delightful music.

[24] *Den Const.*, 1845, no. 215.

Only one reviewer of the *Huldre-eventyr* spoke unfavorably of them and he too was judging according to the standard of national importance.[25]   He much preferred the *Folke-eventyr* where an " unmixed, harmonious naïve narration " revealed the genuine " national stuff " in its pristine clarity; no editor was needed here to rework the style of the original composer, that is, of the people.   The folk tales retained a freshness that was lacking in the *Huldre-eventyr* where the national element had been obscured; between the " original composer " and the modern reader there had intervened a cultivated personality—" a searching, ruminating, yes partly blasé, personality."

In his second collection of *Huldre-eventyr* (dated 1848 but apparently appearing late in 1847) Asbjørnsen placed even more emphasis on his sketches of contemporary folk life, and now that romanticism was at high tide, popular acclaim was proportional.   In a very eulogistic review, Andreas Munch pronounced Asbjørnsen exactly the right person to do this work and praised in highest terms his poetic temperament, his use of the " frames," and his unique ability as a narrator.[26]   It pleased him to see that Asbjørnsen had not treated the stories in " a comparative, analytical and scientific manner," that he had not stopped, for instance, to formulate abstract laws on the historical development of the fairy tales, or to make didactic comparisons with the old heathen mythology or with the traditions of neighboring peoples.   The pressing need had not been a scholarly edition —that could be taken care of at leisure—but a salvaging operation to save the remnants of folk-literature with what they contained of the " national element."

*   *   *   *   *

From the outset, Asbjørnsen and Moe believed that the

[25] *Morgbl.*, 1845, no. 258, *Tillæg.*
[26] *N. Tids. f. Vid. og Litt.*, vol. ii, pp. 125-32.

folk tales had a scholarly importance,[27] and as their first printing was discontinued they took up plans for a definitive edition. If this were to have the completeness they envisaged, its preparation would involve the expenditure of much time and money, for the distant parts of the country would also have to be exploited since, like pioneers who preëmpt first the richest and most convenient homesteads, leaving less fertile areas to be taken up later, the two collectors had first gathered up what they had easiest access to in the nearby regions of Ringerike, Hallingdal and Christiania.

The editors cast about for financial aid ere the first printing came to an end. Moe thought the *Norske Videnskabers Selskab* in Trondhjem, which was liberal enough in its support of "crazy" projects, might well lend its aid to folklore collecting,[28] and he planned a trip in 1844 to the districts about Bergen and Trondhjem. This plan did not materialize but in the second half of the decade both collectors turned to the University. From this institution, Moe received grants-in-aid to the extent of fifty *Spd.* in 1846 and ninety *Spd.* the following year, when Asbjørnsen was given 110 *Spd.* for the same purpose. In 1849 Asbjørnsen received 160 *Spd.* to be divided between a zoölogical investigation in the Christianiafjord region and a folklore collecting trip to Østerdalen and the diocese of Trondhjem.

The University in a sense gave its formal benediction to this work in 1849 when, on Moe's application, it established a fellowship obligating him to collect, and lecture on, folklore. This action was taken in the face of considerable opposition. Some thought this collecting too intangible a project to be subsidized by the University and urged the technicality that it deserved no aid, for it could not be classi-

[27] *Supra*, p. 215.
[28] Krogvig, *op. cit.*, p. 238. August 18, 1843 from Moe to Peter Brock.

fied under any existing branch of learning [29] and thus the recipient would never be able to offer instruction in it. Moe's first application was successful mainly through the intercession of P. A. Munch,[30] but when a year later the fellowship had to be renewed, Munch was in England and Moe turned to Jacob Grimm, asking only for an opinion on the general importance of folklore collecting without any commitment on Moe's qualifications. Grimm's reply, in which he paid a brief tribute to the previous work of Asbjørnsen and Moe,[31] brought a half year's renewal of the fellowship, but there all public support ended.

Moe took up the work of collecting in a spirit of patriotism. Regarding his intention to visit the western part of the country in 1844, he wrote to his father that he entertained " with warmth the plan to exalt (fremhæve) the poetic treasures which our folk life possesses." [32] In one of the applications to the University he argued that the intended edition must have a long introduction to show two things: first, the relationship of the native folklore to corresponding stories among other peoples, and second, the Norwegian folk tale's uniqueness.[33]

With the public aid they had received the two collectors visited various parts of the country. Moe in 1846 set out for Hardanger through Telemarken in the south central part of the country. There the people had preserved an unusually large number of traditions and Moe added materially to his ballad collection. His enthusiasm for this province

[29] *Ibid.*, p. 292.

[30] Jacob and W. K. Grimm, *Briefwechsel der Gebrüder Grimm mit nordischen Gelehrten*, p. 270. Oct. 12, 1849 from Moe to Grimm.

[31] Krogvig, *op. cit.*, pp. 296-98; printed also in Jacob and W. K. Grimm, *op. cit.*, pp. 269-70.

[32] Krogvig, *op. cit.*, p. 250. Letter of Dec. 31, 1843.

[33] *Ibid.*, p. 291.

grew as he came to realize that in other areas he would find relatively little. The next year on his way to Setesdalen in the south he again loitered through Telemarken, once more struck by the tenacity and fidelity with which the people clung to their traditions.[34]

Asbjørnsen investigated areas more to the north and east, though on his first trip, like Moe, he started for Hardanger, where his returns were little better. In Læsø he found some traditions still flourishing, and made something of a discovery. He came upon two abnormal types of *Huldre* and the abnormality in both cases pertained to the tail! One type, a satyr-like creature, wantonly urged her love on huntsmen and fisher folk alike, but instead of the usual cowtail she brandished a horsetail. The other resembled the normal *Huldre* in form and dress but she quite lacked that which was considered "the absolutely necessary national[!] attribute, a cowtail."[35] It was not easy to say why this region should have run so strong to abnormalities. On his second trip, which he did not make before 1851, Asbjørnsen passed through the heart of the great lumber district along the middle and upper Glommen valley, visiting Østerdalen, Elverum, Trysil and the neighboring Swedish border; only the lateness of the season prevented him from crossing over into the Trondhjem area.[36] He had expected, with some reason, that in the shady ravines and woody hillsides mantling the eastern ranges he would find a well-preserved lore. But he was badly disappointed. Here and there he came upon vestiges but they were mere reminders of what once had been, and there were no capable narrators left. A bit farther north in Kvikne he found

[34] Cf. *Norske Universitets- og Skole-Annaler,* series ii, vol. v, p. 272 *et seq.*

[35] *Ibid.,* series ii, vol. v, p. 267.

[36] *Ibid.,* series ii, vol. vii, p. 103.

some stories in better condition, but there as in Lærdal on the west coast, "pietism" had blanched a once colorful lore.[37]

By and large the expeditions undertaken at public expense had not netted the anticipated results in new stories. But they had been worth while in giving the collectors—who had assembled additional versions and pendants from practically "every part of the country except Nordland and Finmarken" [38]—a sense of completeness and finality, and they could now proceed with confidence to the definitive edition.

* * * * *

The most important feature of the new edition was the long introduction by Moe on the scholarly importance of the folk tales. In fact, his essay proved something of a contribution to the literature on European folklore.[39] He had planned such a discourse for the first printing, but by 1841 had given up this idea, feeling that both editors had yet too limited an acquaintance with the folklore of the more distant parts of the country. When he finally wrote the treatise he also intended it partly as a requital for the aid given by the University.[40]

When first he began to consider such an introduction his purpose was in part patriotic. He wanted to set in relief what was "characteristic of our folk tales" and an essay that did not emphasize their unique traits might just as well be "missing." [41] But in the meantime he found it difficult

[37] *Ibid.*, series ii, vol. vii, p. 92.

[38] Jacob and W. K. Grimm, *Briefwechsel der Gebrüder Grimm mit nordischen Gelehrten*, p. 261. Asbjørnsen to Jacob Grimm, Feb. 15, 1851.

[39] *Cf.* G. W. Dasent, *Popular Tales from the Old Norse* (Edinburgh, 1859), p. lxxix. Jæger remarks that in his introductory essay Dasent gave himself credit for the material in Moe's treatise of 1851-2. *Cf.* his *Literaturhistoriske Pennetegninger*, p. 222, note.

[40] Asbjørnsen and Moe, *Norske Folke-eventyr* (Chra., 1851-52), p. vii.

[41] Krogvig, *op. cit.*, p. 167. Letter of Dec. 1838 to Asbjørnsen.

to live up to his original purpose. In common with the students of his day, Moe accepted the Aryan hypothesis, but its acceptance for a time left him in "doubt and perplexity" [42] since the comparative method which figured so prominently in the formulation of the hypothesis seemed to point to a common Aryan folklore. This in turn suggested that the rich traditions which Asbjørnsen and he had gathered really were part of a common Aryan possession so that the Norwegian folk tales were really not distinctive. In his dilemma Moe came to doubt if a folk tale could be peculiarly national; everything seemed to indicate that the stories he had helped to collect were common and not distinctive, European or even Eurasian, not national.

After some reflection he got over his difficulty. He harmonized the idea of a common Aryan tradition with his favorite notion of a folklore unique for Norway, by making a distinction between the general themes of the stories and their details in plot or narration. The former, he pointed out, were common to all Aryan peoples but the latter were distinctive with each. The contradiction with which he had wrestled thus proved to be only apparent and when it had been resolved in this way, his earlier conviction, now "strengthened and clarified," [43] made it seem obvious that the Norwegian stories were really distinctive.

Some had suggested that the stories may have spread from one branch of the Aryan family to another, especially in connection with disturbances like the Teutonic migrations or the Crusades. To meet this line of thought Moe found that he needed the Aryan hypothesis. The similarities in the stories among various peoples were due to no such migration but to an ancient dispersal from a common center. Somewhere back in " the deeper stretches of Central Asia,

[42] Asbjørnsen and Moe, *Norske Folke-eventyr* (1851-2), pp. xi-xii.
[43] *Ibid.* (1851-2), p. xii.

where belong the Indian and Zendian tongues," the Aryan people must have developed a stock of common traditions. In the later tribal dispersals, these must have been carried to very diversified regions, there to be developed in the folk-literature of each people in a way to preserve the "basic thought"; this accounted for the wide similarities.[44] Whatever dissimilarities there were—and they concerned merely details of plot and style—had developed after the dispersals. Since no two people had had the same experiences and each acquired its own national character, the differences had been gradually worked into the traditions as minor variations of plot and style. It was to be noted, however, that the variations were in harmony with the character and the history of each folk; they were not borrowed but had "grown organically and from within."[45] Another factor which ruled out the possibility of borrowing was their age. They must be very old, since they retained vestiges of the heathen mythology, and since they had developed appreciable variations, for they had been retold with scrupulous fidelity from one generation to the next.[46] With the various aspects of the disturbing Aryan hypothesis thus put in their appropriate places, Moe could reaffirm that the folk tales were truly national; the scenery which they mirrored and the folk character which they portrayed were indisputably Norwegian.[47]

Moe could turn next to the more inviting task of pointing out just what qualities of the Norwegian stories were unique. Compared with other Germanic folk tales, the Norwegian stories presented their comical figures with more "definiteness and assurance." Their humor was a thing apart; springing

[44] *Ibid.*, pp. xxxv-xxxviii.
[45] *Ibid.*, p. xxxv.
[46] *Ibid.*, pp. xli-xlii.
[47] *Ibid.*, pp. l-li.

from a people living in the shadow of a harsh, inclement nature, it was compounded of the comic and the tragic, with one balanced against the other, using the terrifying to support the humorous play of ideas.[48] Grimm might be right in claiming humor as an attribute of the Germanic folk tale generally, but, insisted Moe, its quality in the Norwegian stories was something characteristic.

What most distinguished the Norwegian story was its narrative style and tone. The oriental tale, Hindu as well as Arabian, might tempt one with its sensuous scenery, the Italian with its light hurrying style, the French with its prim naïveté, " smelling of eau de cologne," the Danish with its child-like humor, " rounder, lighter, milder." As for the Swedish, it was often lacking in humor, and had a stiff annalistic style. Only the German story resembled the Norwegian; both employed an epic diction and the German might be even more genial and hearty. Yet there was a thoroughgoing difference: the Norwegian story, as compared with the German, seemed told " by a masculine mouth." [49]

The uniqueness in the style of the Norwegian story was more understandable when one recalled that its diction had a continuity reaching back to the ancient saga. The true kinship between the old saga and the modern folk tale lay not in the preservation of archaic turns and annalistic phrases,[50] but in a characteristic diction developed and preserved for centuries by Norwegian narrators. The most distinctive quality of this diction was a direct and " reckless " choice of words.

[48] *Ibid.*, pp. xlix, li. *Askeladden*, said Moe, was typical of Norwegian confidence in a secret higher power; *Smeden man ikke turde slippe ind i Helvede* showed Norwegian resourcefulness, while *Vesle Per* revealed a gruesome, expressionless humor.

[49] *Ibid.*, pp. lxi-lxvi.

[50] *Ibid.*, p. lxvi.

Since their style was of national significance it was important that the folk tales be told in the proper literary medium. It might seem that their essential qualities would be best reproduced in pure dialect, a medium which Moe thought well adapted to the legends, whose scope was local.[51] But the folk tale was common to the whole country and it should be reproduced in the medium prevailing generally. On the other side, Moe paid his respects to the purists who had felt that the earlier edition had conceded too much to the popular idiom. These had quite missed the point that the barbarisms, so-called, were really manifestations of the continuity in style from ancient saga to modern folk tale. The editors had made no attempt to avoid the barbarisms; in fact, they had rather been attracted to them. The folk tales if they were to retain their national significance must be told in a folklike manner; their style, if lifted above the popular range of vision, might easily be deprived of " all that was Norwegian." [52]   An editor must stand " above the people " and simultaneously maintain " an intimate connection with it." [53]   If the style employed was not good art—then very well said Asbjørnsen and Moe—but they refused to sacrifice uniqueness [!] for the sake of art.[54]

We can, of course, understand the misgivings of the purists. From the line of thought just followed, it was not far to the inference that the language became more national when vulgarized, an assumption to which a writer in another connection had objected more than a dozen years earlier.[55]

*   *   *   *   *

[51] *Ibid.*, p. lxvii.
[52] *Ibid.*, p. lxvii.
[53] *Ibid.*, p. vi.
[54] *Ibid.*, p. lxvii.
[55] Nationality, said he, was not a matter of phraseology but of the unique and characteristic in the thought and action of a people. *Maal og Minne*, 1924, pp. 94-5.

The new edition of the folk tales appeared in 1851-2 and contained in addition to the stories and Moe's introduction, a learned appendix, 115 pages long, of critical notes, variant texts, and references to related traditions in neighboring countries. In his review [56] of this scholarly edition, P. A. Munch dwelt upon the scientific importance of the stories and warned that they were not " mere pleasure reading." The long introduction and the critical notes, he thought, made contributions to the studies of history, mythology and ethnography,[57] but he predicted that the chief merit of the stories would be not scientific but national, for they were clothed in a " superb, national . . . . style, a mode of expression that spoke direct to the childlike mind and heart."

*   *   *   *   *

Jørgen Moe took no active part in the editing of the folk-lore after the scholarly edition of folk tales was finished, but for another generation Asbjørnsen found time, in the midst of various pursuits, to reëdit and prepare new printings of the popular traditions. He brought out a new edition of the first volume of *Huldre-eventyr* in 1859, and of the second in 1866, and then both collections were combined in a third edition in 1870. Likewise he issued the jointly edited *Folke-eventyr* as a third edition in 1865-66, as a fourth in 1868, and as a fifth in 1873. In 1871 he edited a new set of folk tales [58] from materials that Moe and he had left over from the large edition of 1851-2, reëditing these in 1876 and supplementing them in 1879 and 1882.

Much of the general interest in these later printings was centered upon their editing, and of that Asbjørnsen spoke

---

[56] *Morgbl.*, 1852, no. 41; reprinted in *Maal og Minne*, 1912, pp. 127-41.

[57] Munch disagreed with some of Moe's conclusions. Folklore, he thought, did not appear after mythology, but preceded it. Where Moe distinguished a northern and a southern type, Munch would rather have the distinction between a masculine and feminine.

[58] Asbjørnsen, *Norske Folke-eventyr. Ny Samling* (Chra., 1871).

at length. In the *Huldre-eventyr* which he reprinted in
1859, he explained that although he knew that some changes
should have been made, he had made very few alterations,
pleading a long illness, the popularity of the stories in their
existing form, and a lack of time. His notion of literary
style had changed much since 1845 and an application of his
new ideas would necessitate innumerable changes.[59]

He recognized that there had been insinuations about the
editing of his stories—suggestions that he had treated his
texts "frivolously" or had embellished them. These insinuations he sought to meet by pointing out that, save in a few
instances, nothing had been added or deleted; the stories
were told as they still lived on the " lips of the people," a
statement as true then as it had been when first made in
1845.[60]

Yet Asbjørnsen's explanation was weakened somewhat by
the fact that he had to make a disclosure. It so happened
that a number of people had aided him in the preparation of
the first edition and of this he had said nothing because Mme.
Collett, who had given him most assistance, wanted her name
withheld and, as a consequence, Asbjørnsen had refrained
from mentioning any of the others.[61] He thought that this
omission helped to account for the aspersion cast upon his
editing; in any event he recognized the omission as an error
and printed a full acknowledgment,[62] protesting meanwhile
that his early neglect was not a reason for doubting the
authenticity of the stories, and reaffirming that he had
personally recorded all but five of them.[63]

[59] Asbjørnsen, *Norske Huldre-eventyr og Folkesagn* (1859), p. ix.

[60] *Ibid.* (1859), p. x; *cf.* the edition of 1845, p. v.

[61] *Ibid.* (1859), p. xxviii.

[62] The list included the names of Welhaven, Grötting, the Colletts,
Unger, Thaasen, P. Botten-Hansen, Schubeler and P. Schmidt.

[63] Asbjørnsen, *Norske Huldre-eventyr og Folkesagn* (1859), p. xxx.

In the printing of 1866, Asbjørnsen pointed out that he had reworked all the stories " painstakingly," [64] and he listed the names of those who had lent their aid in 1848.[65] When he reëdited both collections in 1870 he assured his critics that he had " painstakingly looked through anew, and occasionally improved " his stories,[66] adding, with an eye to the growing language controversy, that this had been done without making any sweeping changes in " linguistic form." Fortunately, in reëditing the folk tales, Asbjørnsen had been able to rest his judgments on the earlier joint work with Moe, and it is of interest to note that when he prepared a new collection of folk tales in 1871 he sought support in the sound linguistic advice of " another friend." [67]

* * * * *

The later printings of folklore did not meet the same unanimous acclaim as their predecessors in the 'forties, when romanticism was in the ascendant. They were thrust into the midst of the language controversy, and because the editors had modeled their style after the popular idiom they proved to be peculiarly vulnerable. It would seem that the new *landsmaal* might very appropriately have been applied to a material like the popular traditions, but Asbjørnsen showed little or no tendency to employ it, and the cultivated circles of the capital which, in the early 'forties, had objected to the style of the *Folke-eventyr,* warmly defended his medium and gratefully noted that he had not changed it merely to humor the *landsmaal* camp. By holding to the accepted Dano-Norwegian and " sanely " incorporating only rural words

[64] *Ibid.* (1866), *Forord,* p. v.

[65] *Ibid.*, pp. v-vi. In the list were Aasen, Gram, Grötting, Steensrud, Sundt and Thaasen.

[66] *Ibid.* (1870), *Forord,* p. iii.

[67] Asbjørnsen, *Norske Folke-eventyr* (1871), *Forord,* p. vi. Moltke Moe says this friend was Jakob Lökke. Gran, *Nordm. i. d. nit. Aarh.,* vol. ii, p. 263.

of general serviceability, he built a bridge between the literary medium and the popular speech, between European culture and the simple morals of the people.[68]   The cultured especially approved the fact that the folklore editors had caught the essence of what was national in the vernaculars, without endangering the hegemony of the Dano-Norwegian. They had elicited what was truly folklike, and given it form in a language acceptable to the cultured classes.[69]   These were glad to see that Asbjørnsen had deserted what in the 'sixties they chose to term his recent flirtation with the *landsmaal* movement;[70] they had earlier imputed to him a desire to effect " a cheap purification " of the language.   In the 'seventies the conservatives could not praise him enough for the care with which he weighed his words on " scales of gold," and he was pronounced " lord and master " of the language.[71]   Unlike many others, it was said, he had never adopted the affectation of writing in *landsmaal* to demonstrate that he had appropriated the form if not the essence of the " folklike." [72]   It had seemed at times very much as if he really favored the *landsmaal,* but this had been deceptive for he leaned toward it merely to bring out the Norwegian spirit of the stories.[73]   It was clear that he intended no concession to that movement, for he had returned to the moderate plan of nationalizing the established literary medium by gradually incorporating only the " suitable Norwegian words."

[68] *Ill. Nyhbl.,* 1859, no. 35, p. 156.   Asbjørnsen judged the *landsmaal* to be impractical.   *Cf.* J. and W. K. Grimm, *Briefwechsel der Gebrüder Grimm mit nordischen Gelehrten,* p. 264.

[69] *Ill. Nyhbl.,* 1865, no. 30, p. 137; *Morgbl.,* 1865, no. 351, Dec. 20.

[70] *Ill. Nyhbl.,* 1866, no. 47, p. 220.

[71] *Adressebladet.   Tillæg til Almuevennen,* 1872, no. 7.

[72] *Aftbl.,* 1870, no. 296, Dec. 20.

[73] *Ibid.,* 1871, no. 294.

To a modern reader, it seems almost as if the only thing about the stories that mattered to contemporaries was their style. Their themes, said one writer,[74] were common to many peoples but the mode of expression was distinctive with each, and an editor had it in his power to garble or ruin a collection. There had been no danger with Asbjørnsen, for he had understood and performed well the editor's proper function; he had conveyed all the essential folklike qualities, and done it in a language that some considered impotent to express what was genuinely Norwegian—in a medium " now patronizingly called Danish." It would be a long time, said this writer somewhat tauntingly, before the *landsmaal* literature produced a work in the " royal Norwegian language " which so effectively as the Asbjørnsen collection would express the folk spirit.

From the *landsmaal* elements, however, came only disapproval. It was, said Vinje, specifically in the medium he had employed that Asbjørnsen had so definitely failed.[75] In imitation of the broad descriptions of Walter Scott, he had used a romantic style, " full of emptiness," when he should have written in a " clean," that is, a colloquial Norwegian. It was possible, said another, to present the stories in their " full originality " only in the language of the peasant.[76] Asbjørnsen and Moe, said Henrik Krohn,[77] had really mutilated the folk tales; they had done no less than " translate " them from the *landsmaal* in which the people had originally composed them—simply done them into what he called Danish. But Krohn insisted that between the unique Norwegian folk-literature and the linguistic form in which it first had been couched, there was an intimate con-

[74] *Bergensposten*, 1868, no. 15, Jan. 17.
[75] *Dølen*, 1859, no. 45.
[76] *Aftbl.*, 1859, *Tillæg til* no. 234.
[77] *Bergensposten*, 1868, no. 18, Jan. 21.

nection, and any attempt to minimize that connection was " a vicious attack " on the idea of nationality. There could be no release for the people, in having their folk tales printed in " a foreign tongue " and there was need of an edition in the medium (*landsmaal*) in which they had first been composed. Yet he conceded that in their existing form, they might serve the useful purpose of helping to educate the town youth " in a national direction."

We must understand that behind the incessant disagreement over the style of the later folklore collections was the broader social antagonism between peasantry and upper classes. In the 'sixties the cultured again reacted against the peasant, and against the tendency to identify the popular and folklike with the national. People talked too glibly of patriotism, said one writer, and they too easily equated it with every concern for the folklike;[78] the two were not identical and much of the careless talk about things national and things folklike turned out to be mere frothing. Just as there were persons of doubtful piety who misused the name of the Lord, so there were among the patriots, self-styled, those who came near taking in vain the name of " the people "—having, in the meantime, a very poor conception of what was truly folklike. Much of what passed as popular and folklike, said Lassen, really was foreign; it had once come in with the upper classes and had then filtered down to the masses.[79] The day was now over, wrote another, when any passing attempt to " toot the national Alphorn moved the public to join in with tones of pompous praise." [80]

[78] *Morgbl.*, 1865, no. 351.

[79] H. Lassen, " *Norskheden för og nu,*" *For Ide og Virkelighed*, 1871, p. 524.

[80] *Morgbl.*, 1871, no. 351 A.

CHAPTER XIV

The Ballads

WHAT Asbjørnsen and Moe accomplished for the folk and fairy tales Landstad did for the ballads. Magnus Brostrup Landstad (1802-1880) was born within the Arctic circle, but spent his career as a clergyman in the southern part of the country. Starting as curate at Gausdal in 1828, he was pastor successively at Kviteseid from 1834, at Seljord from 1839, at Fredrikshald from 1848 and at Sandeherad from 1859. He was a hymnologist of note and prepared the Lutheran hymnal which in 1869 was authorized for general use; through this hymnal his name became a household word among several generations of Norwegians on both sides of the Atlantic.[1]

It is striking to see how many of the Norwegian folklorists were associated with pastoral work. Perhaps those who had the cure of souls in their charge, or stood near others who did, found it natural to take an interest in such beliefs and traditions of their parishioners as lay beyond the pale of established religious precept. Faye and Landstad were ministers of the gospel, and Jørgen Moe, during the years of his concern with the folk tales, was preparing for a theological career which he began as soon as the scholarly edition of *Norske Folke-eventyr* was finished. Olea Crøger (1801-1855) who collected a large store of ballads and folk melodies, was the daughter of a pastor in Telemarken.

---

[1] This religious work had also its patriotic aspect, since the hymnals hitherto in general use had been Danish. Various phases of Landstad's career are dealt with in sketches by H. Nilsen, O. T. Moe and C. L. Dahler, but he is treated primarily as a folklorist in Rikard Berge, *M. B. Landstad* (Risør, 1920).

Landstad and Olea Crøger began collecting ballads at about the same time, possibly stimulated by J. Moe's little *Samling* of 1840. But their beginnings were made independently, it seems, in spite of the previous association between them—the Crøger and Landstad families had long been acquaintances and on occasion in the later 'thirties Mlle. Crøger and Landstad coöperated in local church work (Mlle. Crøger was an apt instructress in choral singing). Landstad at Seljord in Telemarken in 1840 or 1841 began to collect only for " fun," [2] and that was just about the time that Olea Crøger began her collecting.[3]

Landstad later acquired many of Mlle. Crøger's ballads but obtained them only after the longest delay; since the circumstances connected therewith involved two of the familiar figures in this study we may notice them briefly. Anxious to have some of her materials printed, Mlle. Crøger in 1842 let the publisher, Malling, have them; through Malling they came into the hands of Jørgen Moe who took them with him when he went to Næss in 1842.[4] But he was not ready to use them, and Mlle. Crøger made other arrangements for their printing, first with a Pastor Tønnesen in Kviteseid and when he withdrew, with Landstad.[5] Meanwhile, Moe was reluctant to give up the lady's manuscripts and the matter dragged on for several years; perhaps the materials never were returned.[6] Landstad thought that Malling, Moe and Munch had decided to use the Crøger ballads with materials

[2] *Maal og Minne*, 1926, p. 34. Landstad to Chr. Lange, Dec. 16, 1848.
[3] *Cf.* K. Liestøl, " *M. B. Landstads Norske Folkeviser*," *Edda*, vol. xxvi, pp. 6-9. It has been contended that both collectors became interested somewhat earlier. *Cf.* H. G. Heggtveit and R. Berge, *Olea Crøger* (Risør, 1918), p. 34; R. Berge, *M. B. Landstad*, p. 26.

[4] *Maal og Minne*, 1926, p. 35; Landstad to Lange, Dec. 16, 1848; Krogvig, *op. cit.*, pp. 209, note, 227-28.

[5] *Maal og Minne*, 1926, pp. 35-36; *cf.* also p. 10.

[6] *Edda*, vol. xxvi, pp. 10-11.

of their own.[7]   At any rate, Moe, at the request of Munch
once asked Landstad to give up his plans for a ballad collection, and urged that Munch was more competent for this
work.[8] Landstad rightly suspected Munch of using a Crøger
manuscript for a ballad version which the latter contributed
to a learned Danish journal,[9] because in his rendition there
were corrections like those of Mlle. Crøger, and only one
other person knew the verses in that form.   Landstad
thought that Moe had a bad conscience in the whole matter,
although he assigned the larger blame to Munch.[10]   It was
a tortuous proceeding, but in the end Landstad did acquire
much ballad material from the lady and used it in his large
collection.

That collection did not begin to appear until 1852 although
a sample had previously been published in Lange's journal.[11]
The delay was due to various reasons.   There had been
difficulties about getting a publisher.   J. Skar has related [12]
an incident in connection with the appeal for a public subvention to help cover the costs of printing.   Riddervold, the
minister in charge of the appropriate department, conferred
with Aasen in regard to the request, inquiring, " Norwegian
folk ballads, what are they? "   " Some old songs which have
been transmitted by word of mouth and to which great
importance is ascribed," replied Aasen.   " Oh! Is that all! "
responded the cabinet minister, and nothing came of the

---

[7] *Maal og Minne*, 1926, p. 36; *cf.* also pp. 9-10.

[8] *Ibid.*, pp. 37-38.   Landstad to Chr. Lange, Dec. 16, 1848.   Moe and
Landstad were later on the point of being rivals also in the field of
hymnology.   *Cf.* L. Daae, *Stortingserindringer*, p. 256.

[9] " *Sagnet om Aasgaardsreien*," *Annaler for nordisk Oldkyndighed*,
1846, pp. 312-21.

[10] *Maal og Minne*, 1926, p. 41.

[11] Landstad, " *Pröver af Folkeviser samlede i Øvre Thelemarken*,"
N. Tids. f. Vid. og Litt., 1849, vol. iii, pp. 329-75.

[12] Retold by Liestøl in *Edda*, vol. xxvi, p. 17.

appeal. The risk of publishing was finally undertaken by Chr. Tønsberg.

There were other reasons for the delay, some personal [13] and others academic. Lange, who read the manuscript, wanted to have a comparison made with the Swedish ballads; another retarding factor was a difference of opinion regarding the orthography to be used. This dispute had nationalist implications. Landstad was early attracted to the Old Norse forms. He exchanged ideas with Aasen in 1845, when the latter on his travels stopped in the Telemark region [14] and he may then have acquired a keener sense of the unity among the dialects. He was much impressed with Munch's printing of the "Sigurd Svein" ballad in 1846 wherein the historian had pointed the way to the use of older forms. Landstad came to prefer these so far as possible. Referring to the popular speech on a later occasion, he pronounced it incorrect to speak of dialects, for the popular medium was the same as the Old Norse, maintained more or less intact.[15] Once committed to the use of the old forms, Landstad was reluctant to modify them [16] to satisfy Aasen, who kept urging that changes be made in favor of modern usage and the dialects.

The retention of the older forms, according to Landstad, made it easier to visualize the great age of the ballads. Like his contemporaries he was anxious to see as many bonds as possible between the old and the new Norway and he thought that he perceived in the ballads such connectives. He wanted his readers to be sure to see a relationship between the ancient literature and the modern ballad, and in foot-

[13] Maal og Minne, 1926, p. 43.   Landstad to Aasen, Dec. 3, 1851.

[14] Infra, pp. 291-2.

[15] Landstad, Norske Folkeviser, p. 711, note 1.

[16] Maal og Minne, 1926, pp. 17, 43.   Landstad to Aasen, Aug. 18, 1848 and Dec. 3, 1851.

notes he now and then pointed out that a particular ballad was very old, possibly it was a faint reëcho of, or directly traceable to, some ancient lay. As a general proof he pointed to a similarity between the qualities of the Eddic lay and the modern ballad. Rámund the Young he cited as "a good representative of the folk character," typifying that sense of righteousness and calm self-confidence which personal physical power had engendered in the heroic age; like responded to like, and the Telemark peasants still felt that the figure of Rámund was " flesh of their flesh and bone of their bone." [17] In this connection Landstad thought it interesting to see how the " folk spirit " had maintained its characteristic traits " for more than a millennium." [18] Even in the darkest centuries of Danish rule its continuity had remained unbroken as if to defy a foreign dominator and assert the persistence of a robust nationality. This folk spirit had been fastidious; when in the late eighteenth century a number of poets caught the Rousseauean infatuation for the countryside and set about to compose verses " for the people," these artificial creations had never been well received.[19]

Landstad found the clearest proof of the antiquity of the ballads in the pronunciation still maintained by the peasant narrators, which he thought revealingly close to Old Norse. But this put him in a dilemma regarding his orthography. How was he to convey that old pronunciation to the printed page? To employ the traditional Danish seemed inadequate, and to use several dialects was to court confusion. Another possibility—to select one dialect and bend all the others in its direction—seemed unjust, though he was tempted to try the Telemark vernacular as a standard—it seemed to be

[17] *N. Tids. f. Vid. og Litt.*, vol. iii, pp. 340-41.
[18] Landstad, *Norske Folkeviser*, p. v.
[19] *Ibid.*, pp. vi-vii.

the oldest, and it most closely approached the forms of the Old Norse. But he chose a plan more daring than any of these and decided to " jump across the centuries " to base his spelling upon what he called the " old Norwegian language." [20]   That procedure netted him two advantages: it gave him a uniform orthography and it offered him one more opportunity to emphasize the connection with the Old Norse. But this plan in turn entailed a new difficulty. Assuming that there had existed an Old Norse norm, uniform for the whole country, how was one to know its orthography. "Our good old mother tongue," conceded Landstad, was now so remote that it was impossible to return to it " with a single bound." [21]   But one might get back to it by degrees and his spelling would be a step in that direction; he hoped that it would be emulated and improved by later efforts. To those who objected that no one would be able to read the ballads in this archaic orthography, Landstad suggested that in the peasant's speech there was so much that resembled the tongue of the forefathers that rural folk would have little difficulty in reading the older forms.

Norway had a right to be proud of this collection, insisted Landstad. Among the nations of the North she had stood empty-handed, watching the rest contribute freely to a rich north-European cycle of balladry, but now the *Norske Folkeviser* (" Norwegian Folk Ballads ") showed that Norway might take her proper niche " without shame," knowing that her contribution better than those of the others could show a connection with the literature of old.[22]

*   *   *   *   *

[20] *Ibid.*, p. ix.

[21] *Ibid.*, p. x.

[22] *Ibid.*, p. xviii. A foreign reviewer quite agreed with this estimate. *Cf.* Chr. Molbech, *Blandede Skrifter* (4 vols., Copenhagen, 1853-56), vol. iv, pp. 441-2.

When the *Norske Folkeviser* appeared, P. A. Munch in a long review acclaimed [23] them in terms of the highest eulogy. He quite forgot the scholar's restraint and hurried forward to salute the *Folkeviser* as " a national treasure . . . . the most precious the people possess," [24] and he pronounced the ballad collection one of the most significant works published since the rebirth of Norway's political independence.[25] He liked the use of genuine Norwegian idioms and Old Norse forms and he commended Landstad for being the first to break with a tradition that had long " tortured " Norwegian spelling in the strait-jacket of Danish orthography.[26] If the established Dano-Norwegian would now follow the trail blazed by Landstad, then it too would reveal some of its real elegance and dignity. The editor, he thought, had been in every way competent for his task; with an interest in the cause he had combined " a proper poetic conception of the material." [27] What most delighted Munch was the evidence which he saw of another bond stretched across the dismal centuries from Norse antiquity to modern times, supplying palpable proof that, with less modification than might have been expected, the speech of the heathen period and some of its traditions had been preserved faithfully down to the present.[28] Munch emphasized that some of the ballads were very old, dating perhaps in certain instances back to antiquity. The most remarkable ballad " indisputably," was that of *Sigurd Svein* in which Munch detected reëchoes of the mythological figure, Sigurd Fafnesbane, the German

[23] *Morgbl.*, 1853, nos. 63, 66, 67, 241; reprinted in his *Saml. Afh.*, vol. iii, pp. 376-401.

[24] Munch, *Saml. Afh.*, vol. iii, p. 376.

[25] *Ibid.*, p. 401.

[26] *Ibid.*, p. 394.

[27] *Ibid.*, p. 381.

[28] *Ibid.*, pp. 376-77.

Siegfried.[29]   A number of ballads showed their age in their
poetic form; they resembled the Icelandic *Rimur* and since
these had flourished in the thirteenth and fourteenth centuries the ballads which resembled them must be equally
old.[30]

Munch's enthusiasm over the antiquity of the ballads
moved him to make a tenuous comparison between the
Folkeviser and the ruins of Pompeii in Italy.   Both ushered
one into antiquity at a single bound, but with what a difference!   The up-turned stones of Pompeii were now " dead
and silent," [31] but the antiquity one met in the Norwegian
ballads still flourished and was " our own."   How alluring
to think that the nursery rhymes once droned about the
cradle of a Haakon Jarl and an Einar Tambesjælver, or
hummed about the royal hall of Haakon Haakonssøn, had
been sung for all succeeding generations.   Listening to them
made antiquity seem real again and near at hand.[32]

Some of the ballads in the collection might not be indigenous; they were to be found also in Sweden and Denmark,
and their inclusion in a Norwegian collection could be
questioned.   But there seemed to be little danger of con-
fusing them with the true Norwegian ballads; those with
Swedish and Danish counterparts often had a definite
modern stamp suggesting a more recent origin.[33]   There
were also some verses of foreign origin that had come to
Norway very long ago, retaining their early forms better than
in Denmark.   Besides, not all the ballads with Swedish or
Danish duplicates were to be considered foreign; the nursery
ballad, in some cases, was descended from the early lays

29 *Ibid.*, p. 386.
30 *Ibid.*, pp. 381-85.
31 *Ibid.*, p. 395.
32 *Ibid.*, p. 398.
33 *Ibid.*, p. 393.

current among all the north-Germanic peoples; when these separated, the lays were retained by each so that there was no question of a transference from one people to another.[34] Such verses resembled foreign counterparts not because they had been borrowed, but because they were so old, antedating perhaps even the Eddic lays; in spirit and ancestry they were genuinely Norwegian.

Munch dealt less extensively [35] with the later sections of Landstad's collection, containing ballads of more recent origin. These ballads, he said, were " of less interest." [36] They seemed more foreign too; several of them imitated, or betrayed a derivation from, the Danish hero-ballad.

Landstad's *Norske Folkeviser* proved to be of decisive national importance. The moment of their appearance was opportune, for Norwegian liberals and patriots had been left somewhat dejected by the general reaction after 1848-50. The cumulative effect of two collections like the *Norske Folke-eventyr* (1851-2) and the ballads of Landstad (1852-3) was salutary and heartening. They helped to emphasize that the nationality which the patriots championed was not, as was so frequently insinuated, of recent origin, not a superficial creation of the year 1814, but a nationality whose continuity extended from the Norway of saga days to that of the present.

*   *   *   *   *

Sophus Bugge's concern with the ballads was early and brief, but it deserves to be noted here not only because it heralded the new age of realism in folklore editing but also because at the time of his concern with the ballads, Bugge

[34] *Ibid.*, p. 400.

[35] *Morgbl.*, 1853, no. 241. The Danish folklorist Grundtvig had criticised Landstad severely.

[36] Munch, *Saml. Afh.*, vol. iii, p. 397.

was still much of a romanticist.[37]   Like his contemporaries, he anticipated, with deep pathos, the impending disappearance of the ballads, and he felt drawn to that folk life which could put him in contact with the " immediacy " of a bygone age.   Stimulated by Landstad's work, Bugge was resolved to help save what might be left of the popular rhymes.   With aid from the University he visited Telemarken and neighboring provinces,[38] and he began to plan a definitive collection of ballad material.   At the moment, however, he thought it important to impress upon the public that Landstad had by no means completed the work of collecting and, urged by Keyser,[39] Bugge arranged a small preliminary collection of twenty-eight ballads.[40]   It turned out that this first installment of the larger plan proved to be also the last.

The little booklet was edited according to a standard new to romanticism.   From a scholarly point of view Landstad's large volume had several grievous faults (though later scholarship has judged it with more favor), the most mischievous being perhaps, his practice of fusing two or more versions of a ballad into one, without making a note of it.[41] Bugge dissociated himself from the looser editorial methods of his predecessors.   He took pains to point out that he had tried to be careful and exact; he had taken no liberties with the texts and had filled no lacunae with any additions of his own; he had not attempted to carry through any Old Norse or dialect orthography in order to establish a norm; he had painstakingly acknowledged in his notes every correction of

[37] Elseus Sophus Bugge (1833-1907) made his most upsetting claims and his most lasting contributions in the field of comparative Indo-Germanic, especially north-Germanic, philology. *Cf. Norsk Biog. Leks.,* vol. ii, pp. 356-68.

[38] *Maal og Minne,* 1923, p. 99.

[39] *Ibid.,* 1909, p. 57.   Sophus Bugge to Sv. Grundtvig, Dec. 9, 1856.

[40] *Gamle norske Folkeviser* (Chra., 1858).

[41] Gran, *Nordm. i. d. nit. Aarh.,* vol. ii, p. 210; *Edda,* vol. xxvi, p. 3.

supposed errors or corrupt idioms; he had noted every instance when several versions had been merged into one
composite ballad; he had sought the "correct" version, and
when there were several variants of the same ballad, he had
sometimes printed them all so that the reader might make
his own critical estimate; he had edited with no intention of
exalting the national qualities of the ballads; he had kept the
foreign expressions intact and had made no attempt to
nationalize them, but had rather welcomed them as valuable
clues to help trace the migration of the rhymes from one
people to another; finally, he had treated Danish and
Swedish versions as objectively as the Norwegian.[42]

These were unusual standards at the time, and the Norwegian public was hardly ready to appreciate them in 1858.
One reviewer was not fully in sympathy with Bugge's concern to have his edition "correct"; he had added so many
word variants to his ballads that they were positively forbidding! This writer conceded, however, that Bugge's
scholarship provided a solid foundation for future editing
of this sort.[43] Another notice ignored pretty much the
scientific aspect, in which Bugge took pride, and repeated
the traditional romanticist phrases, urging again the need
for haste in collecting the traditions and giving the assurance
that anyone who copied them down "did the nationality a
service."[44] The standards of Bugge's editing, somewhat
premature in their day, were to prove adequate to the demands of the age to come.

*   *   *   *   *

In connection with the ballads we should say a word
about folk music. The Norwegian folk-melodies were collected chiefly by Ludvig M. Lindeman (1812-1887), the

[42] Bugge, *Gamle norske Folkeviser, Forord*, pp. iv-v.
[43] *Ill. Nyhbl.*, 1858, Aug. 23, p. 144.
[44] *Aftbl.*, 1858, Oct. 2 (*Krydseren*, no. 2391).

son of a Trondhjem church organist. Lindeman studied
some theology but became a church organist in Christiania.
He began to collect folk songs about 1840, and acquired
many of the melodies collected by Olea Crøger. With
financial aid from the University he assembled during his
career more than a thousand melodies, mainly from the
wooded mountainous area of the eastern part of the country.
Lindeman found much the same difficulties that the folklorists had experienced; progress on every hand seemed on
the point of extinguishing the melodies, which were little
remembered save by occasional older folk who sometimes
sang them quite imperfectly. But Lindeman was well qualified for his work; he had a delicate musical ear and much-
needed patience and tact. The chief results of his collecting
were incorporated in three volumes of tunes arranged for
piano,[45] a valuable source for later composers in search of
Norwegian musical themes.

[45] *Ældre og nyere norske Fjeldmelodier* (3 vols., Chra., 1853-67).

CHAPTER XV

THE ROMANTICISM OF THE FOLKORISTS

As the transition from romanticism to realism was registered in some of the judgments on the later editions of the folk and fairy tales, it was clear that the popular traditions meant something different to the two periods. If one reviewer in 1870, in the terms of romanticism, still related the *Huldre-eventyr* to the innermost core of Norwegian folk life,[1] another sought to dissociate Asbjørnsen and his *Huldre-eventyr* altogether from romanticism and claim them for realism.[2] A Danish critic, Edvard Brandes, denied the much-vaunted national importance ascribed to the folklore, and praised Asbjørnsen for *omitting* to claim for his collection of 1876 a national significance. The popular traditions, said Brandes, became national only after modern poets had reworked them; in their native state nothing could be " more international." [3] That the basic points of view were changing is obvious, and the sharpness of the contrast between them makes it easier to perceive the characteristic romanticist attitudes toward the folklore.

* * * * *

Romanticism, with its subjective and emotional approach to the popular traditions, looked upon the country's folklore as an open-sesame to a fuller knowledge of the folk character.[4] Because the traditions had been best preserved

[1] *Morgbl.*, 1870, no. 348 B.

[2] *Aftbl.*, 1870, no. 296.

[3] *Det nittende Aarhundrede*, vol. v, p. 326.

[4] Cf. *Maal og Minne*, 1926, pp. 6-7. J. Moe's application of Jan. 30, 1846 to the Academic Council.

by the peasant it was but natural that the folklorists regarded
him as the foremost custodian of the nationality.   We have
already noted in Chapter II the tendency to identify the
nationality with the language and the traditions of the
peasant, as if these were the palpable expressions of the
national Idea.

No part of the peasant's heritage gave such adequate expression to nationality as his literary tradition; it was considered preëminent in this respect, partly because it was
related so intimately to the folk character.   The folk tales,
it was said, had " grown organically " from within the
peculiarity of each people; they were the clearest revelation
of the folk spirit.[5]   The folk-literature, having sprung from
the people's " innermost uniqueness," belonged " to us and
to no one else ";[6] in it was enshrined the " soul of the
nation." [7]   A Swedish writer referred to the traditions as
the " records," not of individuals but of a distant folk past,[8]
and much later they were spoken of as " living portraits of
the spirit which has coursed through the people from
earliest times." [9]

The folk traditions retained their national significance
only in so far as they remained essentially unimpaired by
foreign influence.   The more a folk had kept away from
the uniquenesses of others, observed a writer in the 'thirties,
the more it had retained its own nationality.[10]   In Norway,
the popular traditions were best preserved by the peasants
of the interior districts, and nowhere, it seemed to the
collectors, so well as in the less accessible district of Tele-

[5] Asbjørnsen and Moe, *Norske Folke-eventyr* (1851-2), pp. v, xxxv.

[6] *Bergenske Blade*, 1848, Jan. 18.

[7] *Den Const.*, 1842, no. 81.

[8] *Nordisk Tidsskrift för Politik, Ekonomi och Litteratur*, 1866, p. 511.

[9] *Kristianssands Stiftsavis*, 1879, Jan. 18.

[10] *Alm. n. Maanedskr.*, vol. ii, pp. 469, 487.

marken. In that region Moe and Landstad found many a
nugget of lore, and Aasen also observed that the people there
had an unusual sense for what was national in custom and
in speech.[11]   Of course, the inhabitants generally were quite
backward!   Moe found an entire settlement in Bygland
parish living in " political innocence "; even the son of an
Eidsvold representative knew " not the least about the 17th
of May or its significance." [12]   Yet the people were very
friendly and sweet-tempered, though somewhat raw, and
Moe noted that they nourished " a tenacious adherence to
everything antiquated."   Some persons might be repelled
by this backwardness but every friend of folk-literature and
nationality would find much of value here, and he would
be thankful that some district, at least, was still exempt from
the effects of progress.[13]

*   *   *   *   *

Speaking of the country at large, however, it was un-
deniable that progress had seriously impaired the nationality
by facilitating the penetration of foreign influences.   In the
course of time, whole elements of the population, particularly the cultured and urban populations and their neighboring peasantry, had been corrupted by cosmopolitanism.[14]
Dropping the time-honored customs and taking up the alien
habits, these elements had lost contact with the national
Idea; progress, which should have strengthened the nation-

[11] Aasen, *Skrifter i Samling,* vol. ii, p. 154. Telemarken was distinguished for its ballads, but it has since become evident that legends
and folk tales flourished in the region of Moe's home, Ringerike, and
its environs.

[12] Krogvig, *op. cit.,* p. 266. Letter from Jørgen Moe to his father,
Aug. 5, 1847.

[13] Landstad, *Norske Folkeviser,* p. iii.

[14] *Cf.* Munch, *Saml. Afh.,* vol. iii, p. 400; *Norske Folke-Kalender,*
1849, p. 83; *Stort. Forh.,* 1859-60, vol. vii, p. 562.

ality, really enfeebled and endangered it.[15] Of late the debilitating influence was spreading also to the remoter districts.

In certain areas, the traditions suffered much from progress on the material side. This was readily apparent in the vicinity of the larger towns, but it was marked also along the coasts. Even in an interior district like Hardanger, commercial contacts with the mouth of the fjord turned people's attention to externals, and precluded the introspection and peace that were so conducive to the preservation of a naïve folk-literature. On the other side of the country in the eastern lumbering district of Østerdalen, Asbjørnsen found similar influences effective. Here too, the people's attention had been given an " outward " bent, entailing the loss of that " naïve conception of nature " so indispensable to a flourishing folklore. Most unfortunate in these areas had been the atmosphere brought in by the " card-playing lumberjack " and the " town-clad timber marker." The *nouveau riche* peasant of this region (*Hedemarkskaxen*), who had sold his timber to the distant mills at the mouth of the river, brought in an influence equally hostile, for he had become sophisticated and blasé from these distant contacts and had grown unappreciative of the simple tales and legends.[16]

No less unfavorable was the pre-occupation with political affairs,[17] and the advance of intellectual progress generally. Faye had complained that the spread of a more rational spirit was undermining respect for the popular lore.[18] Book knowledge and Christian learning, regretted one writer, would

[15] *Maal og Minne*, 1917, p. 7.

[16] *Nor. Univ. og Sk. Annaler,* series ii, vol. v, pp. 263, 270; series ii, vol. vii, p. 83.

[17] *Ibid.,* series ii, vol. v, p. 270.

[18] Faye, *Norske Sagn*, p. vii.

soon expunge the "heathenism" still left in the fairy tale from "the living faith of the people."[19]   The attitude of lay religious movements was also deplorable; these were apt to regard the stories as "superstitions."   Asbjørnsen concluded that the paucity of lore in Hardanger and Øster-dalen was due partly to "pietism" and "head-hanging" (*læseri og hoved-hængeri*)[20] and Moe observed that in the districts of Bygland and Valle, the lay movement of Haugianism had condemned the popular accounts as the works of Satan.[21]   Even Landstad's ballad collection, it seemed, might be proscribed.[22]

It was not strange, as some admitted, that interest in the folk traditions should be rapidly disappearing.   Men could not be expected to feel the same regard for the supernatural characters of the popular stories when they roughly invaded their most secret haunts and destroyed their sanctuaries. When *Huldren* was disturbed by the cutting down of the forests, she "withdrew" to the mountain side, just as *Nøkken,* the watersprite, no longer throve within the swirl-ing rapids when the rivers had been tamed to run in "obedient canals" and the waterfalls had been mined and dammed.[23]   Asbjørnsen believed that a region's lore, when in decline, followed definite stages.   It lost first the unique qualities, the "pregnant" attributes, leaving the more gen-eral features—those common to the stories of neighboring countries—to eke out a lingering existence.[24]   He thought it easy to recognize the fairy tales in decline; the more they waned, the more they dealt with such characters as witches

---

[19] *Aftbl.,* 1859, *Tillæg til* no. 234.
[20] *Nor. Univ. og Sk. Annaler,* series ii, vol. v, p. 263; vol. vii, p. 92.
[21] Krogvig, *op. cit.,* p. 266.
[22] R. Berge, *M. B. Landstad,* p. 77.
[23] *Aftbl.,* 1859, *Tillæg til* no. 234.
[24] *Nor. Univ. og Sk. Annaler,* series ii, vol. vii, p. 85.

and the devil.   The lore which Asbjørnsen found in Solør
and Østerdalen was in this condition; its themes had much
in common with those of the lore in northern Germany and
the Netherlands.[25]   More than likely it was but the precipitate of a former rich tradition " whose freshness had been
washed away."   Its themes resembled also those of the
Swedish accounts, having the same flatness and lack of color.
The stories here gave the impression that they had been
imported from across the boundary and in contrast with
those from many other parts of Norway they were without
any unique or characteristic traits.[26]

*   *   *   *   *

Realizing that the folklore was fast disappearing, the
folklorists pleaded for haste in collecting the stories while
there was yet time.[27]   Change was in the air and not many
narrators were left.[28]   Few things were as impermanent as
the folk tales, urged Jørgen Moe, and to postpone their
collection was unsafe;[29] the lore was " overripe " (*drysse-
færdig*) and in danger of being blown to the ground by
the first " windpuff of a new culture."[30]   How regrettable
it would be if the stories were to die on " the lips of the
people."[31]   The work of salvaging them ought to become
the cherished task of the entire nation;[32] particularly students and pastors and all vacationists should be on the

[25] *Ibid.*, p. 89.

[26] *Ibid.*, pp. 85, 91-2.

[27] *Den Const.*, 1847, nos. 25, 26; *Alm. n. Maanedskr.*, vol. ii, p. 495;
cf. *Aftbl.*, 1859, *Tillæg til* no. 234.

[28] *Maal og Minne*, 1923, p. 106.

[29] Krogvig, *op. cit.*, pp. 292-3.   J. Moe's application for a Fellowship,
Nov. 28, 1848.

[30] *Ibid.*, pp. 292, 295; *Maal og Minne*, 1926, p. 7.   J. Moe's application
of Jan. 30, 1846 to the Academic Council.

[31] Jørgen Moe, *Saml. Skr.* (1877), vol. ii, pp. 13-14

[32] *Den Const.*, 1847, nos. 25, 26.

lookout. The generation of the day bore a responsibility to the future; if it permitted this " spiritual patrimony " to sink into the grave with the last oral custodians, then posterity would pass " a severe judgment " on its indifference to " this national concern." [33]

It is in the light of these sentiments that we are able to appreciate a somewhat plaintive note in the writings of the collectors and the romanticists—a note of reminiscence and of sorrowful leave-taking. They felt keenly that they were living in a period of transition and they realized that something they had just learned to regard very highly was irretrievably leaving them. They could feel the simple, static civilization of their childhood passing in favor of a more dynamic industrial order. Landstad spoke of the " burning house " of modern progress from which he had snatched just in time, what could be saved—namely, his ballads.[34] What pained the romanticists most was the inevitability of the process. So they lapsed easily into contemplation, reviving again in fancy the memories and impressions of the receding era, and embroidering it with some of the qualities of a golden age. In such a mood they lavished their attention on one of its vestiges, the dying folklore.

*   *   *   *   *

Since the folklore had such conspicuous importance, it seemed imperative that its salvaging should be done with the greatest possible accuracy. But the sources on which the collectors had to rely were frail and haphazard. The younger generation had little interest in the stories and took up with new and inferior songs.[35] If they remembered some of the older tales they were not so concerned about

---

[33] *Aftbl.*, 1858, Oct. 2.

[34] Landstad, *Norske Folkeviser*, p. iv.

[35] *Nor. Univ. og Sk. Annaler*, series ii, vol. v, p. 284.

their accuracy and might retell them quite arbitrarily.[36]
The few chance individuals on whom the collectors had to
rely were usually, though not always,[37] elderly folk and
sometimes a bit eccentric.[38] There was difficulty often in
getting them to recite; they were shy in the presence of
strangers and afraid that, with so much enlightenment
abroad, the neighbors would consider them old-fashioned and
superstitious.[39] Yet, somehow their silence must be broken
and something must be done to tear " the lock from their
mouths." [40] Success in this matter depended very much on
the proper approach. To ask the narrators outright for
their stories was as much a blunder as to offer to pay for
them. Tact was an indispensable quality; it must be combined with a genuine love for the traditions and with a
perspicacity able to see in them " the clearest and most
definite revelation of the folk spirit." When confidence
was finally won, the collector might find himself richly
rewarded, as was Moe on his trip in 1846 when he evoked a
full recital from the old narrator, Blind Anne.[41] Yet the
older informants could not always be relied upon. Moe got
in touch with a colorful narrator at Bandalsvand who
remembered a phenomenal number of ancient ballads, but
his memory seemed a bit treacherous, for after checking it

[36] Jørgen Moe, *Saml. Skr.* (1914), vol. ii, p. 154.

[37] An exception was one of Asbjørnsen's informants, Engebret Hougen.
Cf. Halvorsen, *Norsk Forf.-Lex.*, vol. ii, pp. 769-770. Regarding this
informant see further, Frik Hougen, " *Engebret Hougen og hans Bygde-
målsdiktning," Edda,* vol. xxxii, pp. 65-109, especially p. 71.

[38] *Nor. Univ. og Sk. Annaler,* series ii, vol. v, pp. 270-71; Jørgen Moe,
Saml. Skr. (1914), vol. ii, pp. 154-55; A. Faye, *Norske Sagn,* p. vii.

[39] Asbjørnsen, *Norske Huldre-eventyr og Folkesagn* (1845), p. 198.

[40] Asbjørnsen and Moe, *op. cit.* (1851-2), p. v; Aasen met a similar
reluctance on his travels. *Cf.* his *Reise-Erindringer og Reise-Indberetninger* (Trondhjem, 1917), pp. 80, 134.

[41] Jørgen Moe, *Saml. Skr.* (1914), vol. ii, pp. 148-53.

several times Moe found his narrative "less genuine." [42] Likewise an old tailor, though he possessed a very animated and compelling narration, had one serious defect; he lacked " that definiteness of expression " when he told his story a second time.[43]

The collectors were particularly anxious, in the case of the folk tales, to believe that the popular narrators had been scrupulously faithful to the diction of their stories and had transmitted them from one generation to the next without material alteration. Moe's faith in the word of his narrators was well-nigh absolute. He believed that the form of a story, once fashioned, had been faithfully preserved from one generation to the next.[44] Narrators, he thought, had been apprehensive about " adding to, subtracting from, or changing the slightest feature " of a story when retelling it, and this " conscientious accuracy " had guarded against " wilful perversion of the original." [45] If one could look back historically across the traditions of a people, said Moe, one would find that they had been " true to themselves " from age to age.[46] It should be recalled that Moe had in this matter something of a vested interest to defend, for he had based the national significance of the folk tales on their style and form, and this significance they could possess, from his point of view, only if the form had been fixed from time immemorial. But if the narrators had taken liberties, then the style of the stories might be more individual and personal than it was national.

Did the folklorists stretch a point in their admiration for the fidelity of their narrators? From modern psychology

[42] *Nor. Univ. og Sk. Annaler,* series ii, vol. v, p. 272.

[43] Krogvig, *op. cit.,* p. 155. Letter of Apr. 18, 1838 to Asbjørnsen.

[44] Jørgen Moe, *Saml. Skr.* (1877), vol. ii, p. 12.

[45] Asbjørnsen and Moe, *Norske Folke-eventyr* (1851-2), p. xlii.

[46] *Ibid.,* p. xxxix.

we know that even the best-intentioned person finds it diffi-
cut to report with scrupulous accuracy what he hears and
sees. Moreover the average peasant narrator must often
have been faced with the temptation to garnish his account.
As a story teller he was frequently the central figure of a
group—a performer, that is, and subject to the subtle seduc-
tions that may tempt the person in that position. It would
be natural enough if he should sometimes seek the favor of
his audience, by polishing a phrase here, by embellishing
another there, or by introducing even variations in theme.[47]

*   *   *   *   *

Since a deep national significance was ascribed to the
popular traditions it followed that the closest attention must
be given to their editing. As a general principle, the collectors spoke of reproducing the traditions " with fidelity,
exactly as we have received them from the narrator without
embellishment or change " [48]—particularly in the case of the
folk tales whose national significance was assumed to be in
their literary form. The fairy tales, however, in line with
the theories of nature symbolism, were thought of as more
plastic,[49] and an editor might have to vary the narrative in
order to catch the spirit of their locale and of the nature
supposedly symbolized in them. In editing them Asbjørnsen thought it " less necessary " than in the case of the folk
tales that the popular diction should be followed closely; he
was in no mood to be bound by the " reversed word order "
or the "groping expression" of "every blockhead's speech."
The fairy tales need not be edited with " diplomatic accur-

[47] Liestøl has been able to show that the oral tradition can be kept
accurate for a long, long time. *Norske Ættesogor* (Oslo, 1922). But
whether it actually is so kept very often, has been questioned by H.
Nordbø, *Ættesogor fraa Telemark* (Oslo, 1929), *cf.* especially pp. 7-8,
340-41.

[48] Jørgen Moe, *Saml. Skr.* (1877), vol. ii, p. 14.

[49] *Cf. Den Const.*, 1845, no. 231.

acy " as if they were a series of musty chronicles.[50] It is certain that in editorial work of this sort, where there was no literary medium to correspond with the vernacular, the editors, in their desire to capture the spirit of the peasant idiom, had to make countless editorial decisions in regard to questions of spelling, of syntax, even of the choice between variants. However much they might wish to do so, they could not reproduce the accounts of their narrators with absolute fidelity and they had to make many independent judgments.

It is permissible then to wonder whether the highly praised style of the stories owed more to the popular idiom or to the literary skill of Asbjørnsen and Moe. It seems that nearly all the field manuscripts of both editors, as well as their proof sheets, are lost; [51] but, it is possible to learn from chance references something of their editorial principles. One rule was simplicity. They were to avoid abstract words and involved grammatical constructions, as well as too frequent a use of relative clauses.[52] The word " so " should be employed sparingly if not accompanied by a dependent " that " clause.[53] Asbjørnsen advised against the redundant use of the personal pronoun.[54]

Another consideration with the editors—it can hardly be called a rule—was to exalt the most characteristic, that is, the most Norwegian. At the outset, Moe intended that the stories he would tell should be Norwegian,[55] and when his fancy was struck by a little sketch that he attributed to Asbjørnsen, he urged his coworker to go on writing with

[50] Asbjørnsen, *Norske Huldre-eventyr og Folkesagn* (1859), pp. xiii-xiv.

[51] Krogvig, *op. cit.,* p. 52; R. Berge, *M. B. Landstad,* p. 92.

[52] Krogvig, *op. cit.,* p. 186. J. Moe to A. Faye, June 15, 1840.

[53] *Ibid.,* p. 207. Nov. 9, 1842 to Asbjørnsen.

[54] *Ibid.,* p. 224. Letter to Moe in the winter of 1843.

[55] Krogvig, *op. cit.,* p. 144. Oct. 23, 1836 to Asbjørnsen.

" the same genuine Norwegianness." [56]   Asbjørnsen once
explained that he had modeled his style after that of the best
and "most unique" informants.[57]   One practice that was sometimes resorted to, called for considerable editorial discretion,
namely, that of fusing several versions of a tradition into
what became substantially a new account.   For example,
Asbjørnsen had two such versions in his first *Huldre-
eventyr*,[58] and he once reconstructed an entire story out of
several scattered fragments from the Christiania region.[59]
Moe thought it difficult to weave together several versions
of the important lay *Draumkvædi*.[60]   Landstad had sometimes followed the same practice in arranging his ballads.[61]

The Norwegian folk and fairy tales were edited with
sufficient excellence to arouse an interest in their style, and
this, in view of the national importance ascribed to that
style, particularly in the case of the folk tales, was at times
a bit annoying.   Foreign writers with their compliments
sometimes inadvertently called in question the style of the
Huldre-eventyr.   A Swedish reviewer referred to the
"graceful unities" which Asbjørnsen, from his own memory
or from field jottings, had " made " or " composed," [62] and
Thorp, an English writer, spoke of Asbjørnsen's version
of " *Die Katzenmühle*" as " probably embellished by the
author." [63]   A domestic admirer also later complimented
Asbjørnsen on his deftness in *altering* the popular narra-

[56] *Ibid.*, p. 232.   May 24, 1843 to Asbjørnsen.

[57] Asbjørnsen, *Norske Huldre-eventyr og Folkesagn* (1859), p. xiv.

[58] *Ibid.* (1859), p. x.

[59] *Ibid.* (1859), pp. xiv-xv.

[60] J. Moe, *Saml. Skr.* (1877), vol. ii, pp. 107-8.

[61] *Supra*, p. 246.

[62] Asbjørnsen, *Norske Huldre-eventyr og Folkesagn* (1859), p. x.

[63] Benj. Thorpe, *Northern Mythology* (3 vols., London, 1851-52), vol.
ii, p. 34; see Asbjørnsen's rejoinder in *Nor. Univ. og Sk. Annaler*, series
ii, vol. vii, pp. 88-89.

tives; he had not been content to repeat the stories " faith-fully," but had gone on to invest their uniqueness with his own entrancing embellishment.[64]

While Asbjørnsen and Moe insisted on their own good faith in the matter of editing, they sometimes wondered if their colleagues in neighboring countries had not taken occasional editorial liberties. Of Swedish editing, Asbjørnsen remarked that there crept into it a " chronicle style," [65] and even " the good Grimms " were not above suspicion; their stories seemed so well-rounded and complete that Moe wondered whether some of these qualities came from the pens of the editors! [66]

In short, between the rendition by the peasant narrator and the printed page of a folklore collection, there was a gap which the editors had to close by innumerable judg-ments of their own, based, it is true, upon a close familiarity with the spirit and the peculiarities of the peasant's speech. Nevertheless, there is reason to feel that the literary quali-ties of the traditions were not always popular and "national" in the full sense assumed during the mid-century, but that they owed something to the literary artistry of the editors.[67]

* * * * *

In appraising the romanticist folklore activities, it is necessary to bear in mind that the chief importance of these activities was national. The collections of *Folke-eventyr* and *Huldre-eventyr* respectively, turned out to be, as one writer aptly designated them, the " Old Testament " and

[64] A. Larsen, *P. C. Asbjørnsen. En literær-biografisk Skitse* (Chra., 1872), p. 8; *Ny Illustreret Tidende*, 1874, no. 45, pp. 353-4.

[65] Asbjørnsen, *Norske Huldre-eventyr og Folkesagn* (1859), p. xiv.

[66] Krogvig, *op. cit.*, p. 156. April 18, 1838 to Asbjørnsen.

[67] No matter how good the informants may be, says a modern scholar, something must be allowed for the rare literary tact of editors like Grimm, Asbjørnsen and Larminie. Krappe, *The Science of Folklore* (London, 1930), pp. 30-31.

the " New Testament " in the " Bible " of Norwegian folk life.[68]   The collections were of obvious importance in showing that Norway possessed a folklore as distinguished as that of other northern peoples.   They also served to emphasize the continuity of the nationality, in so far as the diction of the ancient saga could be distinguished in the modern folk tale.   Of outstanding importance was the fact that the *Folke-eventyr* imparted to the narrative style of the developing Norwegian literature, a " national direction," [69] for while the editors, instead of using the dialects, had employed a medium that could be generally understood, they had also managed to capture the spirit of the traditions.   Finally, we note that the folklore collections, as Moe had hoped three decades earlier,[70] gave definite impulses, in the late 'fifties, to the creation of a new literature.   Ibsen chose his character of Peer Gynt from one of Asbjørnsen's stories, and in his *Gildet paa Solhoug* (1856) drew upon themes from the folk ballads.[71]   Bjørnson memorized many of Landstad's ballads and often recited them.[72]   The *Folke-eventyr,* it has been said, turned out to be the " cornerstone " [73] in the structure of the long-awaited national literature.

[68] *Morgbl.,* 1870, no. 348 B.

[69] *Ill. Nyhbl.,* 1865, p. 137.

[70] *Cf. supra,* p. 210.

[71] *Cf.* H. Ibsen, *Samlede Verker* (20 (?) vols., Oslo, 1928—), vol. iii, p. 12; vol. vi, pt. i, p. 19 *et seq.*

[72] *Edda,* vol. xxvi, p. 1.

[73] *Hjemmet,* 1883, p. 59.

PART IV

THE PHILOLOGISTS AND THE LANGUAGE QUESTION

CHAPTER XVI

The Separation from Denmark and the Question of Linguistic Independence

The age of romanticism left Norway with a legacy of linguistic cleavage, whose final issue is not yet decided. For several generations, her public life has been disrupted by the agitations of opposing linguistic elements, which agree on the broader aim—that Norway shall have a national language—while they differ on the means. The one side known as that of the *landsmaal,* heavily indebted to national romanticism for much of its ideology, has sought to break abruptly with the established literary medium of recent centuries and to go to the speech of the peasant or even back to the Old Norse, in order to get a medium that will be indisputably Norwegian. The other side, which has become known as that of the *riksmaal,* is more urban in its orientation, and prefers to accept the literary tradition of recent centuries and gradually modify it with domestic usages until it is equally Norwegian.

After a survey of the early proposals to make the language more national, and a glance at the empirical program of Knudsen, we shall examine some of the romanticist premises in philology, and then take up Ivar Aasen's significant program and the controversy which attended it.

*　*　*　*　*

During the centuries of the Dano-Norwegian union, Danish became the established literary medium in Norway as well as in Denmark, and after the separation in 1814 it was inevitable that in Norway some question should arise in regard to the language.¹   The natural thing, of course, since it had been established in official use for so many generations, was to regard the prevailing medium as Norwegian. It should be remembered that during the long period of political union, the common medium, though Danish in origin, had absorbed occasional Norwegian elements, a tendency that seemed on the increase in the last century of the union especially among the writers of Norwegian background.   Their successors now called the language Norwegian, thus irritating the Danes,² and some made further claims.   A decade after the separation, it was argued by P. Peterson for instance, that the established medium common to the two countries was basically more Norwegian than Danish; its " northern linguistic stuff " had been taken more from Norwegian than from Danish sources.   Steenbuch made the most of this line of thought by suggesting that Denmark was probably the linguistic province of Norway.³   In the matter of linguistic terminology, others, like Mauritz Hansen,⁴ took the empirical stand that as Norwegians, their compatriots must call their " mother tongue " Norwegian.

Under the circumstances it was inevitable that those who gave serious thought to the language should remember the Old Norse which had lapsed as a literary medium in the latter part of the Middle Ages.   If words and phrases from it could be incorporated into the modern medium they would

¹ The standard work on the linguistic history of modern Norway is A. Burgun, *Le Développement linguistique en Norvége depuis 1814* (Chra., 1917-21).   D. A. Seip has recently published the first volume of a general linguistic history of Norway, *Norsk Sproghistorie* (Oslo, 1931).

² *Cf.* D. A. Seip, *Norskhet i Sproget hos Wergeland og hans Samtid*, p. 13 *et seq.*

³ *Ibid.*, pp. 32-33.

⁴ M. C. Hansen, *Grammatik i det norske og danske Sprog* (Chra., 1828), *Forerindring.*

make it additionally certain that the latter's nationality was Norwegian. J. St. Munch, editor of *Saga*,[5] reasoned thus, and so did his faithful contributor, Jacob Aall; both of them in translating parts of the old sagas into modern Norwegian used the opportunity to retain occasional Old Norse and dialect phrases. But there were other zealous patriots to whom the taking of such liberties with the language seemed a danger. Anders Bonnevie (1782-1833) from Kongsberg, professed to see in some of the new words used an approach to modern Swedish forms. He was among those who felt it supremely important to keep Sweden's influence in the union within limits, and who thought it necessary to prevent the Swedish language from attaining any unwarranted prec-- edence. He attacked Aall for having given Swedish words " civic rights in the Norwegian " in one of his saga trans- lations.[6] It was no justification whatever, said Bonnevie, for Aall to plead that the words were familiar to Nor- wegians;[7] he had deliberately and openly pointed the way to a corruption by, and an amalgamation with, the Swedish. Did he not realize, asked Bonnevie, the importance of langu- age—" the holiest flower a nation can foster? " Language was the lasting basis for the attainment and the preservation of a people's independence. What an obligation rested, therefore, on writers and littérateurs; if language was the nation's " sanctuary," then its priests, the writers, assuredly must do their utmost to guard its purity.[8] There were reëchoes in the press for a time of Bonnevie's vigilant con- cern; but we need not trace them here.

*   *   *   *   *

While it was pretty generally taken for granted during

[5] *Supra*, p. 91.

[6] The substance of the attack later appeared in pamphlet form as *Nogle Nødvendige Ord i Anledning af Tidsskriftet Saga* (Drammen, 1817).

[7] *Ibid.*, p. 6.

[8] *Ibid.*, p. 9.

268 NATIONAL ROMANTICISM IN NORWAY

the first years of independence, that the language was Norwegian, this assumption was frankly questioned in the
'thirties, and particularly in 1832 (*Norskheds-bevægelsen* was
then very active) by several publicists who suggested various
changes to make it more national.   It is difficult to say when
the idea of a separate Norwegian language first took form;
possibly the thought can be discerned from time to time even
during the period of the union.[9]   Certainly G. F. Lundh had
the idea almost a decade before the union ended.[10]   However, the priority in formally and publicly urging the desir-
ability as well as the feasibility of a separate language has,
been variously ascribed to three publicists who participated
in the discussion of the 'thirties—Munch, Wergeland and
Hielm.[11]

J. A. Hielm,[12] whose analysis of the linguistic situation
was unusually keen for his day, distinguished not only the
literary Danish and the rural dialects, but also a third
medium in the everyday speech of the townsman.   Hielm
proposed a definite program; he thought a national language
would have to be " created," and somewhat daringly he proposed that it be built on the urban medium; he would have
fellow patriots investigate the speech of the peasant, which,
it is important to note, he regarded as the real language of
the country, in order to " abstract " therefrom its real
grammar and apply this result to his proposed medium.   It
would be best, he thought, to build on the urban speech
because this had a certain unity still lacking in the dialects
and it also possessed sufficient uniqueness to defend its
" Norwegianness." [13]

[9] *Cf. Maal og Minne*, 1924, pp. 135-36.
[10] T. Knudsen, *P. A. Munch og samtidens norske Sprogstrev* (Chra.,
1923), p. 19.
[11] *Cf. Maal og Minne*, 1912, p. 123; 1918, pp. 46-7, 121-3.
[12] *Supra*, p. 34.
[13] *Alm. n. Maanedskr.*, vol. ii, pp. 463-67.

Another proposal was that of the poet and pastor, S. O. Wolff, who would arrive at a national language through a formal process.[14] He proposed that the littérateurs should begin immediately to write in the various dialects. Then a committee would select from these efforts the " best " words, using one criterion, the resemblance to the Old Norse; a large number of the words, he thought, would come from the local Telemark dialect. The list thus drawn up would be nationalized by a law of the *Storting*. There would surely be some objection, but final success would rest with a " calm strong patriotism," determined to be free of all " leading strings."

A third proposal, printed shortly before Wolff's article, was presented with the weight of considerable scholarship, by P. A. Munch. His view appeared in the course of an attack which he made in the opening issues of *Intelligents-partiets* organ, *Vidar*,[15] on the practices of those he termed the " reformers," that is, those who sought to reform the established medium by borrowing words from the popular speech. Taking his stand on the disagreeable premise that Norway did not have her own literary language, Munch explained how this had come about historically. During the centuries of union with Denmark, the true language of the country, the Old Norse, had gone out of official and literary use and had been replaced completely by the Danish. When the separation came in 1814 the Danish was left as the medium common to the two countries and Norway entered upon independence with an alien tongue. Munch

---

[14] *Den vestlandske Tidende*, 1832, pp. 46-7. It has recently been asserted that his contribution was written with ironic intent. *Cf.* J. U. Wolff, " *Omkring S. O. Wolffs Maalartikkel av 1832*," *Maal og Minne*, 1932, pp. 154-56.

[15] *Cf.* his *Saml. Afh.*, vol. i, pp. 16-26. Munch's part in the language controversy has been analyzed fully in Trygve Knudsen, *P. A. Munch og samtidens norske Sprogstrev*.

agreed that a distinctive language was prerequisite to a full-fledged nationality, and appreciated why some had cast about for a remedy—first in designating the established medium Norwegian, and then by trying to Norwegianize (*norvagisere*) it and patch it up with words and expressions from the dialects.

Munch rejected summarily every effort to tinker piecemeal with the Danish; the unrestricted introduction of plebeian terms was a violation of all rules of logic and esthetics. The essence of a language, he urged, lay not in vocabulary but in constructions, and no matter how many Norwegian words and expressions were incorporated they would not change the Danish character of the literary medium.[16] The procedure of the " reformers " was planless and tactless; they took up all sorts of words—rare Norwegian ones, as well as Swedish and German—and their efforts produced " a very disagreeable impression."

In suggesting how to develop a truly national language Munch proposed to drop all idea of reforming the Danish, and to take a fresh start by going back to the Old Norse, as the Hellenes had gone back to the old Greek.[17] The best way would probably be to select one (or several, as he would have it in the 'forties [18]) of the " purest " modern dialects and apply to this dialect the Old Norse orthography. When thus developed, this plan, he thought, would have certain advantages. The oral form of the literary medium might be adopted as the uniform spoken idiom for the whole country. More desirable still, in line with Munch's pronounced historical emphasis, was the prospect that when generally adopted, the new medium, if close enough to the Old Norse, would, without further interpretation, enable the

[16] Munch, *Saml. Afh.*, vol. i, p. 23.

[17] *Ibid.*, vol. i, p. 24.

[18] *Ibid.*, vol. i, p. 154; *cf.* p. 269, note 1.

common people to read the venerable classics in the ancient tongue; as a corollary, this familiarity would promote, what all patriots wished to see, " a purer striving for independence in literature."

Henrik Wergeland had not been specifically mentioned in Munch's article but he had a right to infer that the aspersions cast on the reformers were intended also for him, since he was trying to enrich his literary expression by drawing upon the popular idiom. He took the trouble to prepare a reply to Munch's article though it was not published immediately.[19] Without opposing Munch's plan for a new language he defended his own practice of incorporating dialect words, on two grounds. Since a writer ought to enrich his expression by every legitimate means, why then continue to employ foreign words in the literary Norwegian when domestic expressions would serve just as well. The other consideration was that the Danish influence ought to be reduced; the existing linguistic situation, which left the Danish well entrenched, remained a positive danger to national independence.

We discern in this agitation for a more national language, three clear plans. Wergeland wanted to incorporate more and more Norwegian words into the established Dano-Norwegian. Hielm would make a fresh beginning on the speech of the townsman, and Munch urged a complete break with the present by going back as far as possible to Old Norse.

* * * * *

A program such as Munch's, which contemplated some return to the Old Norse, seemed fanciful at first, but in the 'forties, in line with the romanticist concern for the peasant

[19] "*Om norsk Sprogreformation*," *Bondevennen*, 1835, pp. 132-67, reprinted in his *Udv. Skr.* (1896), vol. i, pp. 288-314. He had first written it in 1832, says Seip. *Norskhet i Sproget hos Wergeland og hans Samtid*, p. 57, note 2.

and his ways, there developed a broader interest in the rural dialects. While the Old Norse had early gone out of use as a literary medium, lingering longest in connection with the need for interpreting passages in the ancient laws, as a spoken medium it had remained in the country districts and mountain valleys to develop in its own way. From the time of the Renaissance an occasional interest was devoted to the popular dialects; one investigator has been able to enumerate a number of individuals of learning or position before the nineteenth century, who found it interesting to assemble lists of dialect words from various localities.[20] That some of these collectors realized that the dialects represented a continuity from the Old Norse is evident; and after the separation from Denmark there were more frequent and more definite references to the "vestiges" of the Old Norse tongue still to be found in the dialects.[21] The interest in these became marked in the 'forties. Jørgen Moe referred to the connection between the Old Norse and the dialects in his ballad collection of 1840,[22] which collection, by the way, did its part to broaden the interest in the rural speech. If the report of a private conversation can be credited, Wergeland was led to perceive from Moe's collection that his own earlier piecemeal efforts to improve the language were inadequate, and to realize more clearly that an approach to the Old Norse would be possible. He is supposed to have stated during a chance meeting with Moe that the language issue was a question of linguistic " restitution," involving not alone an enrichment of the language but a thorough reconstruction, utilizing ancient forms and endings, in fact

[20] T. Hannaas, " *Norske bygdemålsarbeid fyrr Ivar Aasen,*" in *Festskrift til Amund B. Larsen* (Chra., 1924), pp. 87-105.

[21] *Saga*, vol. i, pp. 5-6, 210, 300; *Alm. n. Maanedskr.*, vol. ii, p. 480; *Saml. t. d. N. F. Spr. og Hist.*, vol. iv, p. 198; H. Wergeland, *Digterværker og Prosaiske Skrifter*, vol. v, pp. 169-70.

[22] J. Moe, *Samling af Sange, Folkeviser og Stev*, p. vii.

"everything that does not sound too unpardonably wrong." [23]
The idea spread that, prerequisite to the work of fashioning
a more national language, there must be a fuller knowledge
of the dialects as well as of the Old Norse.[24] As one writer
phrased it, in seeking to nationalize the established language by substituting Old Norse for foreign terms, it
would be necessary to know the dialects better, and to that
end he urged the preparation of dictionaries of the speech of
the various localities.[25]

In the 'forties, one man set about to investigate the
dialects methodically, and he came to results that placed the
popular speech in a new light, but before speaking of linguistic romanticism and of Ivar Aasen's work, we should devote a word to the somewhat matter-of-fact program of
Knudsen.

* * * * *

Knud Knudsen (1812-1895) was born in the parish of
Holt which we have previously associated with Jacob Aall
and Andreas Faye. His father, a cotter, did some primary
teaching. Knudsen also became a teacher, but later he entered
the University (1832). He taught at the Latin School in
Drammen from 1840 to 1846 and then moved to the
Cathedral School in Christiania, where he remained for
many years. He was one of the founders, and long a
director, of *Selskabet til Folkeoplysningens Fremme.*[26] As
an educator, he sought to remove the Latin from its domin-
ating position in the secondary school curriculum, and from

[23] J. Moe, "*Dagbogsoptegnelser fra en reise over Hadeland, Toten,
opad Mjøsen til Froen,*" in O. Skavlan, *Henrik Wergeland* (Chra., 1892),
pp. 271-2.

[24] Cf. *Maal og Minne*, 1924, p. 149; *Den norske Rigstidende*, 1847, no. 27.

[25] Holmboe, "*Om en norsk Ordbog,*" *Nor*, vol. iii, pt. i, p. 148. C. A.
Holmboe (1796-1882) was professor of Oriental languages and a founder
of the *Norske Universitets- og Skole-Annaler.*

[26] *Supra*, pp. 59-60.

the outset he was interested in the matter of a national language. In the fall of 1849 he helped to form a literary group, in *Studentersamfundet* (" The Students' Union "), which in 1852 became a more definite organization called the *Sprogforening* ("Language Association"), and adopted mainly his views.[27]   These he continued to champion decade after decade with dogged persistence, and with little encouragement from any quarter.   But a later generation has come to appreciate that his program had considerable validity.[28]

Knudsen's point of view was decidedly empirical and realist.[29]   He would have nothing to do with the *a priori* notions of Munch and Aasen about the " spirit " of a language, or with their desire to reach its " ideality." [30]   Language, instead of being fixed and static, was to him, living and dynamic; [31] its basic element was the spoken word from which was derived the written medium.   Among the essentials of language, the most important was vocabulary.[32]   He viewed the language controversy largely from the standpoint of the teacher, observing how language would affect the ease or the difficulty of the learning process.   It was from a pedagogical, as well as a pragmatic, point of view, that he urged a simplified system of spelling [33] and a wider use of indigenous words.

[27] K. Knudsen, *Det norske maalstræv* (Chra., 1867), p. 47; *Edda*, 1914, p. 145.

[28] There are very brief sketches of his career in Halvorsen, *Norsk Forf.-Lex.*, vol. iii, pp. 307-9 and *Arkiv for Nordisk Filologi*, vol. xii, pp. 92-7.

[29] Though even he did not escape entirely the romanticist influence, *cf., infra*, p. 279, note 7.

[30] Knudsen, *Det norske maalstræv*, p. 182 *et seq.*

[31] *Nor*, vol. iii, pt. ii, p. 57.

[32] Knudsen, *Det norske maalstræv*, p. 13; *cf.* p. 218 *et seq.*

[33] He estimated that superfluous letters in the traditional spelling cost *Morgenbladet* alone an annual sum of 10,000 *Spd. Nor*, vol. iii, pt. ii, p. 121, note.

In his program for attaining a more national language [34] Knudsen proposed to take as a basis that urban speech to which Hielm tried to direct attention in the early 'thirties. While that speech without more ado was regarded generally as Danish, Knudsen refuted this assumption and accepted [35] the urban speech as the valid basis for a national language. He argued that if this urban speech, particularly that of the cultivated townsman, were committed to writing and allowed to take up additional words from the dialects, Norway would get a literary language of her own. This medium would have the virtue of being truly national because it would rest on a basis that was uniform and valid for the whole country.[36] Furthermore, in contrast with some of the rival programs, this procedure would build on something actually flourishing, while the romanticist opponents wanted to go back three or four hundred years [37] and build on norms that were no longer in use.

Knudsen's program was unmistakably nationalist. A proposal which he made in the *Sprogforening,* to bring about a "linguistic improvement" in "a Norwegian direction" by ridding the established medium of foreign words and adopting those more indigenous,[38] summed up the essentials of his later program. His agitation, he once explained, turned out to be more negative than positive; [39] he did less to adopt new words of unmistakably Norwegian lineage, and more to reject foreign words—especially Greek, Latin and many,

[34] Knudsen's ideas on the language issue at the mid-century may be followed, aside from the *Nor* article just quoted, in " *Om Norskhed i vor Tale og Skrift,*" *N. Tids. f. Vid. og Litt.,* vol. iv, pp. 205-273 and *Morgbl.,* 1853, nos. 3, 4, 9, 11, 147, 148, 149.

[35] *Cf.* Knudsen, *Det norske maalstræv,* p. 147 *et seq.*

[36] *Ibid.,* pp. 67, 236.

[37] *Nor,* vol. iii, pt. ii, p. 42.

[38] Knudsen, *Det norske maalstræv,* pp. 47-8.

[39] *Ibid.,* p. vii.

but not all, German terms—which he " set outside " " by
the thousand." [40]

Though he sought a language no less national than that
desired by Munch and Aasen, Knudsen felt that these broke
too sharply with the medium of the present. All were agreed
that the language was in a bad way because it had taken up
so much that was alien, but the proposals of Munch and
Aasen, Knudsen thought, would bring its extinction, while his
own program looked to an eventual, though gradual, restoration.[41]   They proposed a break that would be too sharp.
Knudsen argued that just as a people could not alter its history though it might consider it unfortunate, so it could not
in impromptu fashion fling aside its literary medium when
this was no longer considered good enough.[42]   The anticipated national language must be built on something existent
and this, Knudsen thought, should be the unified speech of
the townsman.

Nevertheless, Knudsen had a high respect for the speech
of the peasant,[43] and even conceived its usages as an ultimate objective for his own striving.[44]   He was willing to
recognize that both his own agitation and that which came
to be associated with the *landsmaal* sought the same end—a
language that would be more Norwegian.[45]   The two points
of view might well continue peacefully side by side toward
an ultimate rapprochement; [46] each had something to con-

[40] *Ibid.*; *cf.* also p. 155.

[41] *Ibid.*, pp. vii, 12-13, 145-6.

[42] *Ibid.*, pp. 53-4.

[43] Knudsen, *Haandbog i dansk-norsk sproglære* (Chra., 1856), p. 459
et seq.

[44] Knudsen, *Det norske maalstræv,* p. vi.

[45] *Ibid.*, p. 234. He was sufficiently interested in the program of the
radicals to contribute monetary aid to *Dølen. Cf. Maal og Minne,* 1918,
p. 55.

[46] Knudsen, *Det norske maalstræv,* pp. 240, 243.

tribute and something to sacrifice. The urban folk must relinquish part of their vocabulary, and the peasants must make concessions in matters of form and enunciation.[47] Although the parallel activity which he anticipated has been anything but peaceful, his view on this matter was somewhat prophetic; at present it seems evident that in this spirit of concession must lie the ultimate way out of the Norwegian language controversy.

[47] *Ibid.*, p. 83.

CHAPTER XVII

ROMANTICISM IN PHILOLOGY

BEFORE treating of the most romanticist of the language programs we may analyse some of the characteristic mid-century premises in philology. Much as the folklorists looked upon the popular traditions as fixed in form, the philologists held the nature of language to be essentially static; being linked to the ubiquitous Idea,[1] it seemed to take on some of the latter's immutability. Such a line of thought occasionally encouraged a vague phraseology. In speaking of language, there were references to its " nature," its " spirit " or its " genius," [2] or to a certain inner " harmony " [3] expressing the fundamental quality of its being, or again, to its " purity " or its "inner perfection." [4] Sometimes that purity had been impaired,[5] but such damage apparently could be made good again. Munch, at any rate, described his language program as an attempt to recover the form which the Old Norse would have had today [6] in

[1] H. Nissen, " *Om den sammenlignende Sprogvidenskab,*" *Nor*, vol. ii, pp. 164, 183. Comparative philology should investigate language in search of the Idea, said Nissen, who thought the Idea revealed most distinctly in the Indo-European family of languages.

[2] *Cf.* Munch, *Saml. Afh.*, vol. i, p. 36; vol. iii, pp. 294, 314; Keyser, *Efterl. Skr.*, vol. i, p. 37; J. Moe, *Norske Viser og Stev i Folkesproget* (Chra., 1848), p. ix; *Den Const.*, 1837, no. 72.

[3] Munch, *Saml. Afh.*, vol. iii, p. 331; *Maal og Minne*, 1917, pp. 13, 20.

[4] *Maal og Minne*, 1917, p. 6; *cf. Saml. t. d. N. F. Spr. og Hist.*, vol. iv, pp. 204-5.

[5] Munch, *NFH.*, vol. vii, pp. 362-3.

[6] Munch, *Saml. Afh.*, vol. iii, p. 292.

case its development had not been interfered with by the Danish.[7]

In like manner, a language was thought of as a self-contained system, cohesive within and sharply defined at the boundaries with no vague overlapping. In some mysterious way each tongue had within itself the laws of its own development; it might admit changes, but in contact with another medium it never lost the features of its own class or genus.[8] In conformity with this line of thought, a group of younger patriots in 1859 referred to the " laws " of the Danish as " foreign." [9] In Norway's linguistic situation this point of view had for some a practical application. It suggested how illogical were those reformers who tinkered " artificially " with the established Danish in the effort to Norwegianize it by incorporating individual Norwegian words.[10] What mattered, was not the individual word but the internal system of construction [11]—the substitution of single words would not change the " linguistic spirit." [12] The net result of tacking on a few Norwegian patches here and there would simply be to leave the language Danish.[13] Better, reasoned Munch, to retain the Danish in its purest state than to mar it in a manner not consonant with its character.[14] Danish and Norwegian would not mix, and one must supersede the other; [15] Munch was quite convinced

[7] Even the empirically-minded Knudsen was romanticist enough on this point to think of the Norwegian as possessing a past as well as a future " perfection." Knudsen, *Det norske maalstræv*, pp. 3, 7.

[8] Munch, *Saml. Afh.*, vol. ii, p. 148.

[9] *Det Unge Norge*, p. 5.

[10] Munch, *Saml. Afh.*, vol. i, p. 269, note 1; vol. iii, pp. 293-4, 394-5; Aasen, *Skr. i Saml.*, vol. iii, pp. 123-4; *Maal og Minne*, 1917, p. 7.

[11] Aasen, *Skr. i Saml.*, vol. iii, p. 172.

[12] Munch, *Saml. Afh.*, vol. iii, p. 294.

[13] *Ibid.*, vol. iii, p. 272; cf. *Maal og Minne*, 1917, p. 7.

[14] Munch, *Saml. Afh.*, vol. iii, p. 299.

[15] *Dølen*, 1859, no. 20.

that any attempt to fuse the Danish and the dialects would bring extinction for the rural speech.[16]

From the belief in an inner perfection of the language sprang the assumption that some dialects were " better " and more "perfect" than others.   But what was the criterion for determining excellence?   The touchstone agreed upon, naturally enough in romanticist thought, was age; the most perfect and most genuine dialects were the most archaic, the most like the Old Norse.[17]   Judged by this standard the best dialects were those of the west and the interior mountain valleys.   The areas about Bergen were very distinctive, for the language here at all times had been spoken " most neat and pure "; it was very regular in form and strikingly similar to the Old Norse.[18]   A person from Bergen normally used many more " national " words than one from Christiania or the south.[19]   Munch thought the speech in Hordaland and Sogn closest to the classic forms; [20] Aasen found the Hallingdal dialect " genuine," [21] and noticed in Setesdalen and Telemarken that the speech there had much similarity with the Old Norse and the Icelandic, especially in the matter of vocabulary.[22] Even the southern areas about Mandal and Stavanger, though they showed a marked Danish influence in vocabu-

[16] Munch, *Saml. Afh.*, vol. iii, p. 300.

[17] Aasen, *Det norske Folkesprogs Grammatik* (Chra., 1848), p. 4; *Maal og Minne*, 1917, p. 14. The idea that some and not all of the dialects had maintained their kinship with the Old Norse, existed before the separation from Denmark, according to Seip. *Maal og Minne*, 1924, pp. 138-40.

[18] *Det kgl. n. Vid.-Selsk. Skr.*, vol. iv, pt. i, p. 58; Aasen, *Det n. Folkespr. Gram.*, p. 4; Munch, *Saml. Afh.*, vol. iii, p. 269; Munch, *Lærde Brev*, vol. i, pp. 145-6.

[19] Munch, *Saml. Afh.*, vol. iii, p. 328; *cf.* also p. 342.

[20] *Ibid.*, vol. iii, p. 334.

[21] Aasen, *Reise-Erindringer og Reise-Indberetninger*, p. 138.

[22] *Ibid.*, p. 132; *Det kgl. n. Vid.-Selsk. Skr.*, vol. iv, pt. i, p. 58.

lary, had remained " quite national." [23] But the eastern
part of the country was much poorer in this respect; its
dialects seemed irregular,[24] and Aasen thought less of the
" broad " pronunciations of the Christiania, as well as of the
Trondhjem, areas.[25] Munch also regarded the eastern dialects as the least genuine; they had been seriously impaired
by Danish and Swedish.[26] It is of interest to note that
Aasen planned his travels as a collector so that he might give
greater attention to those districts which, as he put it, had
retained most of the national words and forms;[27] as a
result, his activities in the eastern part of the country, save
in isolated areas, were somewhat superficial.

Munch could explain historically how the dialects had
come to differ so markedly. There had been a correlation
between the political and cultural leadership of a region, and
the time when its language reached the fullest development.
The hegemony of Trondhjem was associated with the pre-
literary age, just as the eastern part of the country had taken
the lead in the day of linguistic denationalizing and decline.
But Bergen and the region thereabout had been in the ascendant just at the time when the language was in its most classic
period,[28] and some of the perfection then attained had been
carried down through the centuries by the dialects of the
west.

We are here touching upon an idea that played no small
part in the linguistic ideology of the romanticists — the
notion that the popular speech possessed the ability to retain
intact the perfection of the language. For centuries the

[23] Aasen, *Reise-Erindringer og Reise-Indberetninger*, p. 132.
[24] *Ibid.*, p. 138.
[25] *Maal og Minne*, 1917, p. 21.
[26] Munch, *Saml. Afh.*, vol. iii, pp. 385-6.
[27] Aasen, *Reise-Erindringer og Reise-Indberetninger*, pp. 131-33.
[28] Munch, *Saml. Afh.*, vol. iii, p. 339.

Norwegian dialects had been without the steadying influence
of a literary medium, but nevertheless they had kept many
essentials of the ancient tongue more or less intact.[29] Some
modification there had been in the lapse of time but mainly
in non-essentials; with surprising ease the peasants still
understood the ancient tongue when it was read to them.[30]
Munch accounted for this remarkable retentive ability by
claiming that the people possessed a sort of " etymological
consciousness," that is, a certain grammatical sense which
enabled them to keep in mind the correct forms of their
national language.[31] But in the long run it could not be
shown that the peasant of today had any knowledge of what
the old Norwegian phonetics had been; Munch himself had
to admit reluctantly that it had disappeared from the people's
consciousness.[32]

*   *   *   *   *

The romanticists felt that nationality and language were
very intimately associated; when they became separated some
violence or wrong was done. Language was pronounced
the sharpest and likewise the finest and most " soul-like "
expression of nationality and its uniqueness.[33] Hence,
language was not a thing to be assumed or discarded at
will,[34] being essential to a people's spiritual life.[35] The
demand (as in Norway) that a nationality should have a

---

[29] Munch, *Lærde Brev,* vol. i, pp. 194, 210; Munch, *Saml. Afh.,* vol. i,
pp. 19, 360-1 ; vol. ii, p. 434; vol. iii, p. 300; Aasen, *Norsk Grammatik*
(Chra., 1864), pp. 17-18, note.

[30] *Syn og Segn,* vol. xxx, pp. 23, 31 ; Munch, *Lærde Brev,* vol. i, p. 215;
Aasen, *Det norske Folkesprogs Grammatik,* p. ix.

[31] Munch, *Saml. Afh.,* vol. i, p. 155; *cf.* vol. ii, p. 437.

[32] *Ibid.,* vol. ii, p. 440.

[33] Keyser, *Saml. Afh.,* p. 4; *N. Tids. f. Vid. og Litt.,* 1854-5, p. 14.

[34] Kr. Janson, *Hvad vi Maalstrævere vil* (Chra., 1876), pp. 5-6.

[35] *Alm. n. Maanedskr.,* vol. ii, p. 468.

written medium of its own refused to be turned aside;[36] since the folk individuality was Norwegian, it followed as a "natural necessity" that the language also would insist on being Norwegian.[37]

It was maintained that nationality acquired its distinctiveness from the unique in thought and in language;[38] the latter, in fact, was the most distinctive mark of nationality.[39] In the qualities of the language might be discerned the spirit of a nation and the attributes of a people.[40] Language was the link binding together all the national generations from the past to the present.[41] To despise the mother tongue, this "costly treasure," [42] this gift of God, was to make light of the fatherland and the spirit of the national forbears.[43] If other insignia of nationality faded away, their language would identify the modern Norwegians as " true children of the old Northmen." But should it also lapse, there would then be no point in speaking further of any " Norwegianness." [44] One owed a special veneration to one's language precisely because it was one's own; no matter how poor it might be, it must never be renounced.[45] Even though the Danish were as good as the Norwegian ("which it is not"), the latter should still be preferred;[46] any Norwegian dialect

[36] *Nor*, vol. iii, pt. i, p. 142.

[37] E. Mohn, *Om Maalsagen og det Bergenske Maalstræv* (Bergen, 1868), p. 22.

[38] *Dølen*, 1858, no. 1; *cf.* no. 20.

[39] Aasen, *Skr. i Saml.*, vol. iii, pp. 94, 208, 324; *Chra.-Post.*, 1858, nos. 313, 320; Munch, *Saml. Afh.*, vol. i, p. 148.

[40] *Ill. Nyhbl.*, 1859, pp. 22-4; *cf.* Wergeland, *Udv. Skr.*, vol. i, p. 300.

[41] *Morgbl.*, 1858, no. 336.

[42] Aasen, *Skr. i Saml.*, vol. iii, p. 8.

[43] *Folkevennen*, vol. i, p. 74.

[44] Aasen, *Skr. i Saml.*, vol. iii, pp. 94, 107.

[45] *Ibid.*, vol. iii, pp. 99, 117.

[46] *Dølen*, 1858, no. 1.

would be better than that from Zealand.[47]   Because of
Norway's lack of a literary medium, a mixed Dano-
Norwegian language might possibly be developed, but it
would not be " what we seek "; " we want a Norwegian
language." [48]

Nationality and language were held to be related in such
a manner that the elements of one language, when introduced
into another, retained their identity as carriers of the original
nationality.   Take the case of the Danish: it was a medium
in which two languages, the Anglo-Gothic and the *norrøn,*
for centuries had competed for mastery,[49] and—this was the
important point—throughout the long tussle, each had kept
its identity.[50]   Following this line of thought, Munch held
it impossible to write in a foreign language; in order to
compose French, he said, it was necessary to divest oneself
of one's own nationality and appropriate that of the
French.[51]   From the same point of view it was pronounced
illogical to expect that in Norway, a unified language might
emerge from the two nationalities (or languages).[52]   Statesmen appreciated clearly enough the connection between the
two when they sometimes sought to wipe out a nationality
by striking at its language.[53]

In the light of some of the foregoing premises, Norway's
linguistic situation was deplorable.   The gravest violence
had been done to the bond between her nationality and her

[47] Berner and Bruun, *To Foredrag om Maalsagen* (Chra., 1866), p. 23.

[48] *Chra.-Post.,* 1858, p. 320.

[49] Munch, *Saml. Afh.,* vol. iii, p. 277.

[50] From this point of view we can better understand the references
to "nationality" or the "national element" in language. *Cf.* Aasen,
Ordbog over det norske Folkesprog (Chra., 1850), p. iv; *Chra.-Post.,*
1858, no. 313; Aasen, *Skr. i Saml.,* vol. iii, pp. 45, 47.

[51] Munch, *Saml. Afh.,* vol. iii, p. 314.

[52] *Chra.-Post.,* 1858, no. 313.

[53] *Ibid.,* 1858, no. 320.

language; where the latter should prevail in politics, business, and culture, its place had been preëmpted by a foreign tongue.[54] The Danish had no historical right in Norway and its position there was "impossible." It had undermined Norway's independence and it continued to separate the Norwegian people from "its true past."[55] This circumstance had occasioned no great concern in the first days of independence, for the established medium was felt to be as much Norwegian as Danish, and was arbitrarily called Norwegian.[56] But Munch and Aasen, in the next generation, were not to be swayed from their claim that the medium established in Norway's public life was exclusively Danish and alien, both in form and "nationality."[57]

The more clearly it was appreciated that the country's official language was alien, the more anomalous the situation seemed in connection with Norway's political independence. For it was generally assumed that political independence enjoined the acquisition of a national language. To develop the nation's unique language was pronounced the most significant guarantee of political independence and of "national individuality";[58] no one would in any spirit of equity deny the claim of an independent people that its literary medium should be national.[59] Wergeland considered the absence of a national language a menace to political independence. People were encouraged to think that Norway had not alone her language but also her culture

[54] Munch, *Saml. Afh.,* vol. i, pp. 16-17.

[55] *Det Unge Norge,* p. 5.

[56] *Supra,* p. 266; cf. Aasen, *Norsk Grammatik,* p. viii.

[57] Munch, *Saml. Afh.,* vol. iii, pp. 272-3; cf. Aasen, *Det n. Folkespr. Gram.,* p. vi.

[58] F. Bugge, *Det offentlige Skolevæsens Forfatning* (3 vols., Chra., 1839), vol. iii, p. 112; cf. *Ill. Nyhbl.,* 1859, p. 24; Kr. Janson, *Hvad vi Maalstrævere vil,* p. 5.

[59] *Nor,* vol. iii, pt. i, p. 142.

from Denmark, and the resulting lack of national self-confidence might shortly be transferred to the political realm.[60]   Daa thought that the urge within a people to express its uniqueness in a distinct language would surely produce in Norway a medium separate from the Danish.[61] Now that independence was rewon, reasoned Aasen, there was an opportunity to think also of " spiritual emancipation," and once the separate language was established it would strengthen the sense of independence and vitiate all feeling of servility toward foreign domination.[62]

*   *   *   *   *

Norway's very unfortunate linguistic situation was blamed upon Denmark and the Danish influence.   That situation had begun to develop with the Union of Kalmar,[63] and then, in a critical period, the ruling classes had taken up the foreign tongue, while the art of printing soon introduced served to consolidate and stereotype the hegemony of the Danish.[64] Perhaps those who employed it were only " a very small part " [65] of the whole population, admitted Aasen, but it was used in strategic places.   The older medium was forgotten for all higher intercourse, and its vestiges among the commonalty came to be regarded merely as corrupt variations of the official medium.   So it came about that the Danish was accepted as the language of Norway; it was adopted by all those who pretended to set the social tone, and it gradually became the language of culture.[66]

[60] Wergeland, *Udv. Skr.*, vol. i, p. 314.

[61] L. K. Daa, *Bør lærerne paa de høiere norske Skoler studere Oldnorsk eller Hebraisk?* (Chra., 1836), p. 15.

[62] *Maal og Minne*, 1917, pp. 15, 17.

[63] Munch, *Lærde Brev*, vol. i, p. 173.   Dec. 13, 1846 to Stephens.

[64] Aasen, *Det n. Folkespr. Gram.*, p. vi; *cf. Maal og Minne*, 1917, p. 6; 1924, p. 145.

[65] Aasen, *Skr. i Saml.*, vol. iii, p. 139.

[66] *Maal og Minne*, 1917, pp. 6-7.

This situation bred a growing resentment toward the foreign influence still entrenched in Norway. The " rich and perfect original Norwegian " [67] had been seriously impaired and kept from its full development by the Danish; [68] the latter continued to bewilder the people's " linguistic sense " so that they no longer were able to distinguish clearly between what was foreign and what was indigenous and national.[69] The presence of the Danish had the most deleterious effect on the peasant; it lessened his respect for his own speech and led him to imitate the foreign, while it perverted his standard of judgment, in encouraging him to give preference to the dialects that were most like the Danish.[70] Furthermore, it tempted him to practise outright deception. When he had anything to say he must learn to hate all that his forefathers had said or done, or else court ridicule. Why should he have to learn a tongue that was foreign, the moment he stepped into the *Storting,* and for what reason should he rise in esteem the instant he deserted the traditions of his rural background—or be called a fool if he retained them? [71] What a shame that a good share of the Norwegian nation must prostitute itself merely because a small people (the Danish) had chosen to impose its language on it, and in so doing had branded the nation on the " forehead," with the mark of the " slave," perhaps for " eternity." [72]

It was therefore imperative that the Norwegian language be rehabilitated. The prolonged borrowing of the Danish

---

[67] F. Bugge, *Det offentlige Skolevæsens Forfatning,* vol. iii, p. 112.

[68] Aasen, *Ordbog over det norske Folkesprog,* p. xv.

[69] Aasen, *Det n. Folkespr. Gram.,* p. iv; Aasen, *Skr. i Saml.,* vol. iii, p. 41.

[70] Aasen, *Norsk Grammatik,* p. ix.

[71] Aasen, *Skr. i Saml.,* vol. ii, p. 189; vol. iii, pp. 44-45.

[72] *Maal og Minne,* 1924, pp. 145, 147; *Dølen,* 1858, no. 1.

for literary purposes was a servile legacy from the period of national humiliation.[73]   Only when the nation had recovered its own medium and the last restriction of Danish tutelage was gone would the nationality develop freely and independently in conformity with "the wise determination of Fate."[74]   It was pointed out that the restoration of Norway's true language would be a service also to the Danish, on the assumption that the latter had long ago been overwhelmed by the south-Germanic influence when both German and Anglo-Saxon elements crowded into it.[75]   The Norwegian, which had retained what was truly northern, would, if brought into repute and general use once more, redress the balance and save the Danish from further Germanization.[76]

[73] Kr. Janson, *Hvad vi Maalstrævere vil,* p. 10.

[74] *Ill. Nyhbl.,* 1859, pp. 22-4.

[75] Aasen, *Skr. i Saml.,* vol. iii, p. 41 ; Munch, *Saml. Afh.,* vol. i, p. 19; vol. iii, pp. 283-4.

[76] Munch, *Saml. Afh.,* vol. iii, pp. 299, 317; *Det Unge Norge,* p. 2.

CHAPTER XVIII

Ivar Aasen and the *Landsmaal* Program

Ivar Aasen (1813-1896) was born on an isolated peasant holding in Søndmøre,[1] a wild fjord region in the west where nature is majestic and terrifying in appearance, and niggardly in her satisfying of human needs. Aasen had the impulse to study, but the ordinary paths of learning were not to be followed by one born in his station. However, after five " uncomfortable " years as a farmhand (he was orphaned when twelve), he became the local schoolmaster, and sought further instruction of a rural dean. Ultimately he decided against an academic career; partly for the reason, it is worth noting, that he might do more for the enlightenment of the common people if he did not become too far removed from them.

In the well-stocked library of Captain Daae at Solnør, where Aasen served as a tutor for several years after 1835, he was able to do much reading, being interested especially in natural history and in linguistics. Here he was in a position to get a survey of the language controversy of the 'thirties and he broadened his knowledge of Norwegian and other modern languages. Grammar interested him especially; he read Mauritz Hansen's *Grammatik* " many times," and pored over Rask's *Veiledning* (" Guide ") gaining therefrom a keener sense of the connection between the Old Norse

---

[1] For studies of his career see Garborg, Hovden and Koht, *Ivar Aasen, Granskaren, Maalreisaren, Digtaren* (Chra., 1913) ; *Norsk Biog. Leks.*, vol. i, pp. 45-62; Gran, *Nordm. i. d. nit. Aarh.*, vol. ii, pp. 277-326. For the early part of his life see the autobiographical sketch in Aasen, *Skr. i Saml.*, vol. i, pp. 3-8.

and the modern dialects. He became interested in the local
Søndmøre dialect, gathered data on it, and by 1839 had
prepared a grammatical survey of it. While at Daae's in
1836 he jotted down the long unpublished memorandum [2]
which subsequently turned out to be important in disclosing
his early ideas on language. It seems that he already had
a pretty clear conception of the path he would take in order
to give the country a literary medium. Considerations of
national honor, he wrote, demanded that there be reinstated
and restored the country's own language. This medium, it
was true, had gone out of literary use long ago, but it had
been hoarded and saved through the centuries by the peasant.
Since the country thus had a language of its own, there was
no need, as some implied, to make over the Danish, for one
might build on the broad basis of the dialects existing at
present. In his proposal, Aasen was thus more realistic
and empirical than Munch, who would use a single dialect as a
means to approach the Old Norse; on the other hand, he was
more daring than Wergeland or Hielm—for he took as his
starting point that rural speech of the present, which the
others hoped to approach gradually in some distant future.

Aasen's work was quite esoteric until the end of the
'thirties, but then he sought to interest others. In 1841,
after a vain effort in the previous year to impress the rural
dean at Molde, he sailed to Bergen, taking with him his study
of the Søndmøre dialect and a systematic nomenclature
which he had arranged of Søndmøre's fauna and flora. One
work was as carefully prepared as the other, but it was the
grammatical study which aroused most interest. Bishop
Neumann wrote an article about the young tutor in *Bergens
Stiftstidende* underscoring the plan for "a distinctive
national language," and incorporating an autobiographical

---

[2] It was entitled "*Om vort Skriftsprog*" and first printed in *Syn og
Segn*, 1909, pp. 1-5; reprinted in Aasen, *Skr. i Saml.*, vol. iii, pp. 7-11.

sketch by Aasen,[3] as well as a part of Aasen's introduction to his dialect study. In this Aasen had stated his conviction that the scattered dialects contained the core of a single independent language, one uniquely Norwegian, and pointed out that its displacement in literary use by a foreign dialect was "disagreeable" to national feeling. The Danish by this time was so well entrenched that there could be no question of supplanting it, but he thought it might be supplemented, when writing for the common people, with a form of the country's own language, based on a comparative study of the various dialects; such an arrangement, he reasoned, would facilitate popular enlightenment and simultaneously render justice to the nationality. Privately, Neumann called Aasen's work to the attention of Fr. Bugge, then at the head of the *Videnskabers Selskab* in Trondhjem. Bugge grew enthusiastic and consulted Holmboe and Keyser, who agreed that something must be done to help Aasen; the practical outcome was in 1842 an award from the society,[4] authorizing Aasen to collect the remnants of Norway's "displaced ancient language" in the western part of the country, and to work out a grammatical dissertation on the dialects.

Then began his great Odyssey. For five years (an expanded grant from the patron society after two years authorized him to extend his investigations also to other parts of the country) Aasen wandered in and out of the local parishes of western and central Norway gathering words and usages, and seeking to understand the grammatical principles of the living dialects.[5] In approaching a district he consulted the printed works available on its dialect, and with these as a guide, he assembled more data from " in-

[3] *Supra*, p. 289, note.

[4] Amounting to 120 *Spd.*, later raised to 150 *Spd.*, a year.

[5] His memoranda and reports have been edited by Koht as *Reise-Erindringer og Reise-Indberetninger* (Trondhjem, 1917).

telligent common folk," especially from those who spoke un-contaminated the "language of the fathers." He endeavored to get as much information as possible direct from the current speech.[6]   By December, 1846, he had visited all the important areas except Østerdalen, some stretches east of Christiania, and the northern part of Nordland.[7]   In September, 1847, he arrived in Christiania to arrange his data for publication.   Henceforth, Aasen's career was more prosaic; by the middle of the century it was evident that his work was of great national significance and the state took over the responsibility for his maintenance.   From 1851 it assured him a competence, which was continued until his death four and a half decades later.[8]   Nearly every summer until the later 'sixties, he was out collecting data, but he remained relatively inactive after his dictionary appeared in a second edition in 1873.

Upon analysis, the personality and temperament of Aasen prove a bit unexpected.   Everything about him, his lowly birth, his later orphanage, his contacts with a society still marked by the narrowness of pietism, his lack of academic training, his somewhat dyspeptic bachelorhood,[9] even his outward appearance, all lead one to expect a dour personality, but instead, his general outlook was broad and even indulgent.   He was religious but not pietistic, appreciative of good breeding and its refinement but deeply resentful of its superficialities.   Jealousy was alien to him and his sense of fairness was noteworthy.   He never forgot, in controversy, that some rights belonged to others.   One may con-

---

[6] *Ibid.*, p. 133; Aasen, *Ordbog over det norske Folkesprog*, p. v; "*Fyreskipnaden for arbeidet aat Ivar Aasen*," *Syn og Segn*, 1902, p. 465.

[7] Aasen, *Reise-Erindringer og Reise-Indberetninger*, p. 153.

[8] Set first at 300 *Spd.* a year but later increased gradually until it amounted to 3500 *Spd.* annually.

[9] *Cf.* L. Daae, *Stortingserindringer*, pp. 128, 220, 256, 367.

trast his polemics with those of P. A. Munch, and realize
at once that while the latter might dazzle with the flamboy-
ancy of his style and the profundity of his learning, Aasen's
contributions had a fair chance to impress reflecting minds
with their gentle reasonableness.   There was no trace of the
chauvinist in Aasen.   He was overly modest and once hesitated to suggest that his own linguistic proposal might give
Norway a language comparable to that of her neighbors,
lest it be interpreted in a personal manner, as an insult or as
boasting![10]   Those who declaimed on Norway's progress
were reminded that other countries had also progressed,[11]
and the vainglorious compatriot who thought his own
people the most diligent and the most courageous, right in
every argument and victorious in every battle, was urged to
read more foreign history.[12]   When a writer reproached the
Danes for their conduct toward Norway in the long centuries
of union, Aasen rather defended the Danes and laid much
of the blame for what happened on the Norwegians
themselves.[13]

Aasen retained the attitudes characteristic of the humbler
class from which he had sprung.   He had a passion for
equality of opportunity, and loathed distinctions of class.   Ill
at ease in the presence of refinement, he resented very much
any display of superior airs.   He felt bitter at the disparage-
ment cast upon common folk[14] and the sport made of the
popular idiom.   " It has always hurt me bitterly," he wrote
in 1836, " to hear our common speech made fun of, either

[10] Aasen, *Skr. i Saml.*, vol. iii, p. 118.

[11] *Ibid.*, vol. ii, p. 193.

[12] *Ibid.*, vol. iii, p. 34.

[13] *Syn og Segn*, vol. xxviii, pp. 3-4, citing from *Dølen*, June 19, 1859;
cf. Aasen, *Det norske Folkesprogs Grammatik*, p. vii; Aasen, *Norsk
Grammatik*, p. vii; Aasen, *Skr. i Saml.*, vol. iii, p. 205.

[14] Aasen, *Skr. i Saml.*, vol. iii, pp. 67, 98, 153.

by well-intended attempts to purify it or by well-dressed
ignorance." [15]   Aasen retained much of the peasant's deep-
seated conservatism; he would keep the old ways and customs
as long as possible, provided they did not obstruct mental
progress.   They should be honored and respected, for they
contained so many treasures handed down by the forefathers as a " holy inheritance." [16]   But in Aasen's day men
were losing respect for this legacy and developing a craving
for novelty which led them to discard traditional arrangements merely because they were old.   Change, insisted
Aasen, should be more than a thoughtless transition; it
should be a real improvement, closely correlated with the
old.[17]   General enlightenment, if it entailed the cashiering
of the traditional speech and ancient customs, would be too
dearly bought.[18]   Like the folklorists, Aasen was apprehensive about the changes then sweeping away so much of
peasant tradition,[19] yet with a difference; where the folklorists as townsmen had just discovered the rural tradition,
Aasen was born and bred in it, and his affection for it was
natural and wholehearted.   He was therefore well qualified
for the arduous and tedious labor of assembling the dialects.

The mainsprings of Aasen's labors were two in number,
one benevolent and one patriotic.   While P. A. Munch could
afford to play with a language now extinct, Aasen had to be
less academic and more pedagogic; he was pressed by circumstance to seek a medium which might be used to facilitate the
peasant's intellectual progress.[20]   He had early resolved to

[15] *Ibid.*, vol. iii, p. 8.

[16] *Ibid.*, vol. iii, p. 325.

[17] *Ibid.*, vol. iii, pp. 88-9.

[18] *Ibid.*, vol. iii, p. 80.

[19] *Cf. Det n. Folkespr. Gram.*, pp. x-xi.

[20] It is to be noted that he had an interest in simplifying the Dano-
Norwegian so as to make it more effective as a medium of communication.
Cf. Maal og Minne, 1922, pp. 1-19.

devote himself to the service of his own class, and to work for " alert and inquiring common folk." [21]   That class, reasoned Aasen, was seriously hampered in his day by the prevalence of a foreign tongue, and he meant to do what he could to bring the peasant's speech into the repute which he thought it deserved.[22]   It would be a prodigious task; but after all this speech was " our own," and its rehabilitation was a duty to " our land and our people." [23]   From the outset Aasen was thus moved also by the patriotic impulse. Among his earliest meditations on the language question, in the memorandum of 1836, that is, before [24] he had read Rask or begun to study the Søndmøre dialect, he pointed to the national significance of having an independent Norwegian language.   His patriotic interest was touched some years later when L. Kr. Daa proposed certain linguistic changes, looking toward an eventual merging of the Scandinavian tongues.[25]   Aasen recognized that Daa's plan seemed reasonable but the general idea made him " despondent "; it seemed to lessen respect for the peculiarly Norwegian.[26]

*   *   *   *   *

From time to time in the language discussions, it had been stated that the popular dialects were related to the Old Norse, but they were usually regarded as little more than vestiges.   Aasen had from the outset considered the relationship more pronounced and he regarded the dialects less as vestiges than as elements of a completed language.[27]   From

[21] Aasen, *Skr. i Saml.*, vol. i, p. 6; Aasen, *Det n. Folkespr. Gram.*, p. xiv.

[22] Aasen, *Det n. Folkespr. Gram.*, pp. v-vi; Aasen, *Ordbog over det norske Folkesprog*, p. iv.

[23] Aasen, *Skr. i Saml.*, vol. iii, p. 117.

[24] Garborg, Hovden and Koht, *Ivar Aasen, Granskaren Maalreisaren, Digtaren*, p. 52; *Norsk Biog. Leks.*, vol. i, pp. 56-7.

[25] *Cf.* L. K. Daa, *Svensk-Norsk Haand-Ordbog* (Chra., 1841).

[26] Aasen, *Skr. i Saml.*, vol. ii, p. 135.

[27] *Cf.* Aasen's memorandum of 1836; *Bergens Stiftstidende*, 1841, nos.

the materials which he had gathered on his wanderings in the 'forties, he prepared a grammar and a dictionary of the dialects in which he was able to establish conclusively that the dialects were independent of the established Danish, and in no wise an " offshoot " of it.[28] With equal finality, he demonstrated that the dialects were heirs of the Old Norse, the language which, after being crowded from the printed page and lost to official view, had lived on with the common people. Men had forgotten its lineage, but nevertheless, as an " indispensable possession " it had been indigenous since time immemorial.[29] However, we must not infer from the results of Aasen's conclusive studies, that the very common view, according to which the dialects were regarded as provincial forms of the Danish,[30] was dissipated at once. As late as the closing 'fifties one writer referred to the country speech as Danish.[31]

Convinced that the dialects constituted a true national language, Aasen, in proving them to be heirs of the Old Norse, was anxious to make clear that behind their diversity was a coherent unity.[32] Divergencies that might seem important were really subordinate and non-essential; [33] contrary to the suggestion from the administrative body of his patron society that he arrange a lexicon for each district,[34] a plan frequently discussed in the first half of the 'forties,

67, 68; and Aasen's proposed plan for a dictionary, " *Om en Ordbog over det norske Almuesprog*," *Det kgl. n. Vid.-Selsk. Skr.*, vol. iv, pp. 57, 61, 66.

[28] *Cf.* Aasen, *Skr. i Saml.*, vol. iii, p. 110.

[29] *Cf.* Aasen, *Det n. Folkespr. Gram.*, p. ix; *Maal og Minne*, 1917, p. 19.

[30] *Dansk Litteraturtidende*, 1829, p. 671.

[31] *Morgbl.*, 1859, no. 294; cf. *Syn og Segn*, vol. xxviii, pp. 4-5.

[32] Aasen, *Det n. Folkespr. Gram.*, p. viii; Aasen, *Ordbog over det norske Folkesprog*, p. v; *cf. Maal og Minne*, 1917, p. 9.

[33] *Det kgl. n. Vid-Selsk. Skr.*, vol. iv, p. 60.

[34] *Cf. Syn og Segn*, 1902, p. 466 *et seq.*

he chose to prepare one dictionary for all the dialects, treating them as variants of a single language.[35]

Aasen sought to arouse a broader interest in the popular speech. It would soon go out of use, he pleaded, unless a new concern for it was quickly developed.[36] An active interest in it would have both practical and patriotic implications. It would help to dispel the notion that a person was cultivated only when he forgot his mother tongue, and it would counteract the prevailing craving for the new and the strange.[37] Besides, in conjunction with a wider familiarity with the Old Norse, it would help to distinguish what really was Norwegian and aid in eliminating from the official language the foreign and " heterogeneous " elements.[38]

* * * * *

In his grammar and his dictionary Aasen was dealing with unfamiliar material, and hardly anyone in Norway could pass judgment on his work. Those acquainted with the Old Norse were the best qualified, and it was appropriate enough that both works were given substantial reviews by P. A. Munch.[39] Munch greeted the *Grammatik* profusely as a " comfort " and a " pride," as " an adornment for our literature," and " a national work of which we can be proud," and in the same vein he designated also the *Ordbog* (" Dictionary ") " a national work." In this connection he empha-

---

[35] *Det kgl. n. Vid.-Selsk. Skr.*, vol. iv, p. 61 ; Aasen, *Ordbog over det norske Folkesprog*, p. v.

[36] *Det n. Folkespr. Gram.*, pp. x-xi.

[37] *Ordbog over det norske Folkesprog*, p. xv.

[38] *Cf.* Aasen, *Det n. Folkespr. Gram.*, p. v ; Aasen, *Skr. i Saml.*, vol. iii, pp. 169-70 ; F. Bugge, *Det offentlige skolevæsens Forfatning*, vol. iii, p. 112.

[39] *N. Tids. f. Vid. og Litt.*, vol. ii, pp. 282-98 ; vol. iv, pp. 335-380. The latter was a review article, as it treated also several works of C. A. Holmboe. The two are reprinted in Munch, *Saml. Afh.*, vol. i, pp. 360-74 ; and vol. ii, pp. 433-76.

sized that Aasen was receiving aid from the *Videnskabers Selskab* for what was truly a " national cause." [40]   Munch pronounced Aasen, who was self-educated and a " born peasant," [41] unusually well qualified for this task for he had a first-hand knowledge of the popular speech.

In the case of both works Munch was anxious to call attention to their national significance.   They showed that the language of the existing dialects was the same as that of the old literature; [42] for a thousand years the *norrøn* tongue had persisted even more pure at home than in Iceland. The resemblance which had been disclosed was the more remarkable since Aasen had been working with the dialects alone; it was so marked that Munch thought it possible, if what remained of the Old Norse were lost, to reconstruct its forms again from the norms Aasen had found in the dialects (after borrowing inflectional forms from the Icelandic). It was now unmistakably clear that the dialects, with a constancy like that shown in the modern Greek,[43] had retained all the essentials of the Old Norse in its best period; the vocabulary had been kept almost complete.   In the course of time, many individual grammatical forms had been dropped, and little differences had developed, but these were mainly of a local character and the actual changes were less than those which the Latin in Italy, France and Spain had undergone, or the Anglo-Saxon in England.   The next Old Norse grammar to appear, Munch would call simply a " Norwegian " grammar.   It will be recalled that at this time he was busy in his own field, seeking to establish the saga literature as exclusively Norwegian-Icelandic and here

[40] Munch, *Saml. Afh.*, vol. i, pp. 373-74.

[41] *Cf.* also Munch, *Lærde Brev*, vol. i, p. 360. May 1, 1849 to J. Grimm.

[42] *Cf.* also Munch and Unger, *Det oldnorske Sprogs eller Norrønasprogets Grammatik*, pp. iii, vii.

[43] Munch, *Saml. Afh.*, vol. i, p. 361 ; vol. ii, p. 434.

in Aasen's work he found additional proof for his contention. The language of the sagas and the Eddas, he reiterated, was not old northern as the Danes would have it, but
narrowly Norwegian or Old Norse,[44] and since the old
northern folk spirit had been most pure in the *norrøn*
tongue, Aasen had therefore exposed the Norwegian people's
" pure and genuine nationality."[45]

Munch was an enthusiastic but also a dangerous critic—
dangerous because at the mid-century his influence was over-
powering in any field wherein he chose to express himself.
He spoke so definitely on the subject of a national language
that we may pause to explain his point of view more fully.
His approach to the language question was national, esthetic,
and aristocratic. He argued from the historical point of
view, and sometimes from that of the museum curator.
" If I establish a collection of antiquities," he wrote apropos
of the language situation, " I have no intention of putting
the old swords into use." [46] The national language which
he sought, was designed to satisfy the esthetic sense and
national pride. Save during his brief flirtation with democracy he was not so much concerned to attain a language for
general usage, as to get one that might be admired nationally
and culturally. To Munch the dialects were important
largely because they might facilitate a better understanding
of the Old Norse,[47] and it has been aptly pointed out that
when later studies showed the dialects to be less important
than he supposed in explaining the ancient tongue he lost
interest in the rural speech.[48]

Munch's pronounced Old Norse emphasis proved to be

[44] *Ibid.*, vol. i, p. 363.

[45] *Ibid.*, vol. i, p. 360.

[46] *Ibid.*, vol. iii, p. 316.

[47] *Cf. ibid.*, vol. i. p, 158.

[48] *Cf.* T. Knudsen, *P. A. Munch og samtidens norske Sprogstrev*, p. 132.

significant for much of Aasen's work.   In order to appreciate that influence it is necessary to note that while the two
agreed on many points pertaining to the linguistic situation
they differed on several matters of strategic importance.
They shared an enthusiasm for the peasant speech, yet what
was to Munch but a means to the attainment of a national
language was to Aasen that language itself.   Of the two,
Munch had the more definite ideas about the orthography
to use in committing the rural speech to writing.   He would
reproduce the peculiarities of dialect pronunciation so far as
possible with the aid of the archaic Old Norse orthography,
and thus emphasize the etymological connection between the
ancient and the modern mediums.[49]   Aasen, when planning
his dictionary, agreed in part, holding that account should
be taken both of the Old Norse forms and of the forms now
living in the popular speech.[50]

The contention between Munch and Aasen regarding the
orthography was sustained over a period of years.[51]   Despite
Munch's pleas for a liberal use of the more archaic forms,
Aasen in the *Ordbog,* as in the *Grammatik,* refused to disregard the modern dialects.   He was willing to employ Old
Norse forms and orthography, provided they could be found
in any living dialects, but, as he explained, he was describing
not a language of antiquity but a living language of the
present, and if he filled it with archaic forms, he might raise
a question about its authenticity.   Besides, as he candidly
admitted, many of the old forms were no longer known;
they could only be conjectured, and later information might
prove such guesses erroneous.[52]

[49] Munch, *Saml. Afh.,* vol. i, p. 153 *et seq.*

[50] *Det kgl. n. Vid.-Selsk. Skr.,* vol. iv, pp. 66, 67.

[51] It may be followed in T. Knudsen, *op. cit.,* p. 47 *et seq.*

[52] Aasen, *Ordbog over det norske Folkesprog,* p. vii. For a hearty
approval of his procedure see *Chra.-Post.,* 1850, no. 786.

But Munch was disappointed.[53]   Behind his argument in
this matter, lay the assumption that there were certain fundamental differences between the orthography of the Old
Norse and that of the Danish; the latter had lost, in time,
some of the markings of sound distinctions that had been
retained by the former.[54]   It seemed to him that Aasen, in
clinging to the established usage, had built his orthography
on an extraneous basis.   Munch considered that the Norwegian tongue had long enough been " tortured " by a
Danish spelling; [55] he would go back to a point five hundred
years earlier, throw off the " stiff laughable Danish confir-
mation gown," and put on " a national dress."   Had Aasen
clothed the popular speech in its proper, that is, Old Norse,
orthography, he would have made yet more strikingly evident the essential identity of the ancient and modern tongues,
and thus demonstrated more clearly that the pronunciation
of the contemporary peasant was the same as that of
ancient saga days.   Incidentally too, his dictionary would
have served for both Old Norse and modern Norwegian.[56]

Munch and Aasen had another occasion to argue this
question of orthography, in connection with the manuscripts for Landstad's ballad collection.   Landstad, following the advice of Munch, had borrowed heavily of the
Old Norse forms while Aasen kept urging him to approach
more closely to the modern ones.   Adducing his usual pragmatic reasons, Aasen strongly advised against too pronounced a trend away from the dialects.[57]   Apologizing for

[53] Munch, *Saml. Afh.*, vol. ii, p. 437 *et seq.*; *cf.* vol. i, p. 364 *et seq.*

[54] *Ibid.*, vol. ii, p. 439.

[55] *Ibid.*, vol. iii, p. 394.

[56] *Ibid.*, vol. ii, p. 441.

[57] *Maal og Minne*, 1926, pp. 2-3, 11-12. Letter of July 22, 1848 to
Landstad. On this editorial disagreement see further Gran, *Nordm. i. d.
nit. Aarh.*, vol. ii, pp. 303-4.

his reluctance to sanction a wide use of the ancient forms, he felt that he had perhaps an undue apprehension about going beyond the limitations of what flourished at present, but he felt constrained to insist that the basis and starting point must be the existing dialects.[58]   All of these, he argued, had varied from the Old Norse in some respects, and these variations, having some degree of similarity, really constituted the uniquenesses of the modern Norwegian which must be respected.[59]   Aasen, unlike Munch, was not seeking so much to " restore " a language as to take into wider use one already existing; he was concerned to establish that the dialect Norwegian had an individuality of its own, and to emphasize that it was distinct from the Old Norse and even from the modern Icelandic.[60]

As time went on, Aasen too, showed a growing preference for the Old Norse forms.   In his first attempts to create his new *landsmaal,* he respected the pronunciation of the present, but he kept in mind also " the original forms." [61]   He prepared a little reader in Old Norse,[62] and shortly after, in arranging a book of proverbs, felt attracted to the older forms.[63]   His growing tendency to follow the Old Norse as a standard was checked momentarily in 1858 when Prahl made a somewhat startling attempt [64] to clothe a piece of modern writing in very archaic Norse forms,[65] but the Old Norse trend was unmistakable in Aasen's reëditions of

[58] *Maal og Minne,* 1926, pp. 12, 31-2.

[59] *Ibid.,* 1926, p. 11.

[60] *Cf. Bergens Stiftstidende,* 1841, no. 67.

[61] Aasen, *Prøver af Landsmaalet i Norge* (Chra., 1853), p. iii.

[62] Aasen, *En liden Læsebog i gammel Norsk* (Chra., 1854).

[63] Aasen, *Norske Ordsprog, samlede og ordnede* (Chra., 1856), p. xxi.

[64] *Infra,* p. 313.

[65] On the positive side, *Dølen's* realist approach may have recalled him somewhat to the modern dialects. *Cf.* Garborg, Hovden and Koht, *op. cit.,* p. 153.

the *Grammatik* in 1864 and the *Ordbog* in 1873. Writing
as a champion of the *landsmaal* by that time, and anxious to
make this new medium more acceptable, he sought to show
that the living dialects on which it was built had an unmistakable unity. The first editions of both of his major
works, he explained, had failed to show this clearly enough
and so his efforts had brought the language " no real redress." But in the preparations of his second editions, the
Old Norse had sometimes supplied him with the norm he
needed to emphasize that unity.[66]

* * * * *

Aasen's investigations had established that the peasant's
speech, instead of representing the fragments of an otherwise extinct tongue, was a finished linguistic system in itself,
and this revelation suggested a program: to precipitate out
of the spoken dialects a written medium and thus give
Norway a truly national language.[67] There would be difficulties, recognized Aasen, for this popular speech had several
shortcomings; it had a restricted vocabulary, having been
used for generations to express only the peasant's narrow
circle of thought, and it had been for centuries without the
steadying influence of use as a written medium. But these
defects could be remedied and Aasen was convinced that the
popular speech had the potentialities to become a language of
culture. The vocabularies of the dialects might be lacking
terms that were needed in business and in specialized scholarship, but in this respect the popular speech was no worse off
than neighboring tongues had been, and like them it could
borrow from others.[68]

As an innovator Aasen was unusually cautious and he

[66] *Cf.* Aasen, *Norsk Ordbog med dansk Forklaring* (Chra., 1873),
pp. viii-ix.

[67] *Cf.* Aasen, *Det n. Folkespr. Gram.*, p. xi.

[68] *Maal og Minne*, 1917, pp. 10-12.

made it clear that he intended no immediate threat to the traditional Danish. He expressed himself as apprehensive of any sudden change and he assumed that Danish would long remain in official use.[69] At any rate, it must be left in complete freedom, just as there must be no compulsion about the new medium.[70] As an indispensable preliminary, he stressed the need for a thorough study of the language.[71] For a long time he seemed unable to decide on the plan he would follow in working out the new norm; several times he reiterated in his correspondence with Landstad that he had not yet decided on any plan.[72] He rejected the idea of selecting one of the more promising dialects to serve as a base; every dialect was lacking in some respect, not one was " perfect." [73] He decided to create a norm entirely new, incorporating what was good in the various dialects and drawing heavily upon the " best of them.[74] His norm would be artificial, he knew, but it would possess elements common to all the dialects. The forms adopted should be as familiar as possible to the people, that is, the anticipated medium should be built on the living dialects, mainly on those with the " best " and more " perfect " forms, those which most resembled the Old Norse. Aasen had no compunction about employing forms that were old, provided they were still in use, but the forms that were now extinct should not be adopted save for very good reasons.[75] The new medium might first be

[69] Aasen, *Skr. i Saml.*, vol. iii, pp. 61, 157, 167.

[70] *Ibid.*, vol. iii, pp. 11, 62, 125; *Maal og Minne*, 1917, p. 20.

[71] In order to avoid leaning on the established medium or on any one dialect. *Maal og Minne*, 1917, p. 20.

[72] *Ibid.*, 1926, pp. 30, 46.

[73] Aasen, *Skr. i Saml.*, vol. iii, p. 113; *cf.* Aasen, *Ordbog over det norske Folkesprog*, p. vi.

[74] *Cf. Maal og Minne*, 1926, pp. 45-6. Aasen to Landstad, April 16, 1852; *cf.* Aasen, *Skr. i Saml.*, vol. iii, p. 127.

[75] *Maal og Minne*, 1917, p. 10, *ibid.*, 1926, p. 45; Aasen, *Skr. i Saml.*, vol. iii, pp. 47, 133-4; *cf. Syn og Segn*, vol. xxviii, p. 1.

used for such " national " subjects as ballads, proverbs and folklore, whence one might pass on to employ it in simple descriptive sketches.[76]   Aasen planned a formal essay on the subject of the new language but he never prepared a final draft.   In that connection, some unusually full notations, packed with his pithy observations on the language situation, have been preserved.[77]

Aasen's first attempt to create a new medium, aside from the little dialogue sketch in 1849,[78] which really was couched in specific dialects, was his definitive effort [79] in 1853, employing a new norm patterned after no single dialect—a norm he called *landsmaal* (countryside speech).   He may have heard Keyser employ the term in lectures in 1847 [80] and he first used the word in his diary entry for June 1, 1851.[81]   He soon began to employ the new medium for various matters such as the difficult genre of drama,[82] and for a collection of proverbs.   In the latter instance, he dealt with materials which might seem best rendered in their respective dialects, but such a procedure would emphasize divergencies and so he deliberately chose to apply the new norm in order to emphasize the attribute of unity.[83]   He employed the new medium with increasing frequency in the later ' fifties and in the ' sixties.

The *landsmaal* thus launched did not quite live up to the promise which its name in one sense might connote; it

[76] *Maal og Minne*, 1917, pp. 19-20; Aasen, *Skr. i Saml.*, vol. iii, p. 61.

[77] " *Grundtanker til en Afhandling om en norsk Sprogform*," edited by K. Liestøl in *Maal og Minne*, 1917, pp. 4-21.

[78] " *En Samtale imellem to Bønder*," *Morgbl.*, 1849, no. 5; reprinted in his *Skr. i Saml.*, vol. ii, pp. 7-13.

[79] *Prøver af Landsmaalet i Norge*.

[80] Chr. Brinchmann, *National-forskeren P. A. Munch*, pp. 79-80, note.

[81] *Norsk Biog. Leks.*, vol. i, p. 58.

[82] In the play, *Ervingen*, reprinted in his *Skr. i Saml.*, vol. ii, pp. 20-65.

[83] Aasen, *Norske Ordsprog, samlede og ordnede*, p. xxi.

proved to be a language for something less than the whole
land. The base on which Aasen built was too restricted;
he did not employ equally the dialects of the entire country,
but in conformity with that characteristic romanticist premise [84] which classed the western dialects as more " perfect "
(i. e. more archaic, more like the Old Norse), he built very
heavily on such dialects, for instance, as those of Voss,
Hardanger and Sogn.[85] In this salient matter, he was yield-
ing to Munch's Old Norse orientation and giving his norm
a certain aristocratic slant somewhat at odds with the democratic and pedagogical purpose which he always professed;
his *landsmaal* would appeal especially to the educated who
could relate its forms to the Old Norse, but these specialists,
as he had complained in 1848, needed it least.[86] The preference for the western and central dialects gave his norm too
narrow a basis to make it truly national.

[84] *Supra*, pp. 280-81.

[85] *Prøver af Landsmaalet i Norge*, p. iv.

[86] *Maal og Minne*, 1926, p. 12. July 22, 1848 to Landstad.

CHAPTER XIX

Controversy

THE linguistic agitation in Norway entered a new stage in the 'fifties when the proposals of Knudsen and Aasen matured as definite programs. Each half of the decade had a particular controversy of its own. The first one raged about Knudsen's program and the second about that of Aasen. In the early 'fifties, the conservatives grew uneasy when certain developments seemed to portend an increasing use of Norwegian words in the established medium such as Knudsen had been urging. While the trend lacked cohesion, it might be thought of as the procedure of the moderates.[1] Asbjørnsen and Moe had to reconsider in what linguistic form to reproduce most faithfully the *Folke-eventyr* (1851-2) and Landstad had to make the same decision for his *Folkeviser* (1852-3). At the same time Knudsen was encouraging actors to use a "purer" Norwegian diction on the stage. The occasion which opened the controversy was Aasen's unprovocative comment[2] on the first issues of Vig's *Folkevennen*. Vig had been in a quandary regarding the style and vocabulary to choose for a venture intended to be so definitely popular.[3] Aasen, in a sympathetic vein, admitted the difficulty, and was glad to see that the editor's intention was to use simple words, understandable to the common people, and he approved of the elimination of "awkward and foreign" expressions. Vig planned to employ Norwegian and dialect words; Aasen thought that

[1] *Cf.* Knudsen, *Det norske maalstræv*, p. 234.

[2] *N. Tids. f. Vid. og Litt.*, 1851-2, pp. 217-43; reprinted in his *Skr. i Saml.*, vol. iii, pp. 24-56.

[3] *Folkevennen*, vol. i, p. 14.

this might prove helpful, but (taking the occasion to argue
for his own more radical plan) he did not regard it as ultimately satisfying.

The conservatives, ever guardians of the *status quo,* became indignant when such liberties were taken with the language, and came to feel that any attack on the traditional
medium was unsettling, and remotely a threat also to
their political hegemony and their social leadership. Their
chief spokesman, to our surprise, was P. A. Munch. We
have previously noted [4] that his intellectual responses could
be a bit chameleon-like. Though his premises might bear
him elsewhere, he shared with the particular social milieu
to which he belonged an apprehension about the disruptive
forces in the upheaval of 1848-50, and in the 'fifties these
apprehensions proved stronger than his academic enthusiasm
for a national language. As a matter of fact, he took it for
granted that the established medium should be maintained
unchanged, a premise which seemed to involve the continued
hegemony of the social classes then dominant; Munch, therefore, worked out an elaborate rationalization in their behalf
and in defense of their language.

He built his argument largely on the romanticist premises [5]
that between language and culture there existed a very
intimate bond and that cultures like languages might mix
but they did not readily fuse. He took the basic stand that
a language to be usable and practical, must modify its forms
in order to keep step with the march of culture, a " common
cultural necessity," he remarked, among all progressive
nations; [6] otherwise it would soon grow archaic and inadequate for modern purposes. Particularly must it develop away from its early complicated forms and take on

[4] *Supra*, p. 115.
[5] *Cf. supra*, p. 282 *et seq.*
[6] Munch, *Saml. Afh.*, vol. iii, p. 308.

flexibility (a contention that squared none too well with the view that language was essentially static). He explained elsewhere that this progression was facilitated whenever two languages " clashed " and neither gave way; in the encounter simpler forms were evolved, which left behind the stiff archaic forms that were inadequate for handling modern ideas.[7] The forms of a language revealed its linguistic age. One might identify a " younger " tongue by the extent to which it had dropped grammatical forms and suffixes and taken up independent particles.[8] By the same token, when a people's speech retained many archaic forms, this was a sign that such a people had yet far to travel on the path to modern culture.

Applying this line of reasoning to the situation at hand, Munch announced that the Old Norse had fallen completely behind and could no longer serve as a vehicle of modern culture. Gradually displaced as a written medium in the fourteenth and fifteenth centuries, first by the Swedish and then by the Danish, its development had been fully blocked. It had kept the involved constructions and had failed to take on flexibility, and in this archaic form it was fit to incorporate nothing beyond the culture of the fifteenth century.[9] But, some might say, there was the case of Iceland; it seemed to get along very well in the modern world with an ancient language. Munch, a bit later, pointed out, somewhat ineffectively, that its case was a little different; the Icelandic for centuries had been so well reworked to express what the Icelanders needed to appropriate of newer culture, that its clumsy grammatical apparatus had proven no inconvenience.[10]

[7] Munch, *NFH.*, vol. vii, pp. 597-8.

[8] Munch, *Saml. Afh.*, vol. iii, pp. 291, 306-7; *cf.* vol. i, p. 361.

[9] *Ibid.*, vol. iii, p. 313; *cf. Morgbl.*, 1858, no. 326.

[10] Munch, *NFH.*, vol. vii, pp. 598-99. That his respect for the anti-

For some of the patriots it must have been discomfiting to hear from P. A. Munch these strictures on the cherished Old Norse, the same Old Norse that he had so often lauded. But for these, Munch had a word of consolation. Flexibility in and of itself, he explained, did not make a language better in an absolute sense; it made it better only for its own age and circumstance.[11]   The neglect of the Old Norse and its failure to appropriate " the newer European language culture "[12] might seem to have been a great loss to Norway; on the contrary, things had worked out to Norway's advantage.   True, Norwegians of the fifteenth century had quite " unromantically " given up the " nationality of their language " but they had really displayed good judgment for they had done this to attain a higher culture.[13] Modern culture simply would not fit into the archaic Norwegian,[14] and Norway was fortunate that progress had reached her through the languages of her neighbors; since the Reformation, all cultural progress in Norway had come via the Danish.[15]   One might regret that the country's written medium was Danish but one could not change or deny the fact, and one had better feel resigned to it.[16]

Munch, as we noticed previously, attacked the tendency gradually to make the Danish over into Norwegian, branding this procedure as revolutionary and declaiming that nothing less than culture and civilization were at stake.

quarian qualities of the Icelandic was as great as it ever had been, is apparent from the tribute he paid to it as " the purest and most honorable remnant of our antiquity ! "   *Ibid.,* p. 599.

[11] Munch, *Saml. Afh.,* vol. iii, p. 308.

[12] Munch, *NFH.,* vol. vii, p. 597.

[13] Munch, *Saml. Afh.,* vol. iii, p. 312.

[14] *Cf. Chra.-Post.,* 1858, no. 334 and *Aftbl.,* 1865, no. 116.

[15] Munch, *Saml. Afh.,* vol. iii, p. 309.

[16] *Ibid.,* vol. iii, pp. 309, 313.

Thinking of language as something amenable only to its own inner laws and not to be tinkered with by human hands, he viewed Knudsen's attempt to bring the established medium closer to the Norwegian, as an effort to disregard the inheritance of the ages and to break the sacred bond of historical continuity. Munch insisted that Knudsen's proposal to build on the informal everyday pronunciation—a sort of linguistic " communism " [17]—was unsound, and that the tongue which he envisaged would be quite impractical and in very bad taste.[18] It would ultimately involve utilizing parts of the Old Norse (as preserved in the dialects), which, Munch admitted, had once been a magnificent language, but by this time it was as little adapted to modern usage as Latin or Greek; [19] a return to it now would be a retreat. Its lack of adequate expressions and its restricted circle of ideas would soon cramp civilized thought and depress those who used it to its own antiquated level.[20] Knudsen, said Munch, was really asking Norway to give up all that she shared in the common European development, and to go back to the cultural level of the fifteenth century. It would be far better, asserted Munch, to hold to the language now used, the established Danish, which could assure participation in European culture. From Munch's point of view, Norway's two languages must be kept as far apart as possible, and he vigorously opposed any attempt to bridge the chasm between the two; [21] far from lamenting the existence of that chasm, says Trygve Knudsen, he made its maintenance his program.[22]

[17] Munch, *Saml. Afh.*, vol. iii, p. 360.
[18] *Ibid.*, vol. iii, pp. 305, 326.
[19] *Ibid.*, vol. iii, pp. 291-2.
[20] *Ibid.*, vol. iii, p. 315.
[21] *Ibid.*, vol. iii, pp. 300, 394-5.
[22] *P. A. Munch og samtidens norske Sprogstrev*, p. 133.

It should be noted that Munch did not object to having the rural speech committed to writing, a procedure which he thought might well facilitate popular education and advance the study of Old Norse. But this achievement must be accomplished without violence to the " inner " nature of the language, and in any instance, he insisted, the medium created would not meet the demands of culture. One must go back to pick up the thread of development where it was left five hundred years previously. That Norway might well have two written mediums, he was willing to concede, if only they were kept sharply apart, so as not to violate the spirit or genius of either. The intimate connection that was supposed to exist between language and nationality, Munch here explained, was important only in the primitive stages of social development, but was no longer a factor of moment in the life of peoples of modern culture. The Norwegian nationality, for instance, was still intact though for centuries it had no literature and language of its own.[23] The net effect of Munch's argument was to rationalize the entrenched position of the established Danish and to substantiate the desire of the classes to keep at a distance the peasant's rustic vulgarity and boorish speech.

Munch's chief antagonist in this argument of the early 'fifties was Knudsen, and in 1853 the two carried on a labored discussion in the columns of *Morgenbladet*.[24] Knudsen, who argued[25] from a more empirical point of view, sought to break down the rigid barriers which Munch had erected between the two languages. The question, insisted Knudsen, was not an absolute but a very relative one. Languages varied in their development, not according to any " inner " command or " inner " laws but according to

[23] Munch, *Saml. Afh.*, vol. ii, pp. 616-17.

[24] Munch's articles are reprinted in his *Saml. Afh.*, vol. iii, pp. 272-301.

[25] *Morgbl.*, 1853, nos. 3, 4, 9, 11 with a rebuttal in nos. 147, 148, 149.

different external conditions. Their diverging paths were the result of innumerable concrete readjustments and they were not to be considered as the predetermined expression of any indefinable distinction in " spirit." Knudsen was particularly anxious to invalidate Munch's premise about the " genius " of a language. What counted, said Knudsen, was fidelity, not to any vague " spirit " of the language, but to its living usages and constructions. He was content to have Munch claim that Norway's written language was Danish, but he denied that this was true of the conversational Norwegian, even of that of the upper classes. These might speak a corrupt or a bad Norwegian but it certainly was not Danish,[26] and he reiterated that on this oral Norwegian should be built the hoped-for national language.

* * * * *

The moderates of the Knudsen trend continued their efforts to consolidate a program. Vig in 1856 argued extensively in *Christiania-Posten* and in pedagogical circles against the use of foreign and in favor of more domestic words. Knudsen the same year strengthened the moderate program by supplying it with a grammar in his *Haandbog i dansk-norsk Sproglære* ("Handbook of Dano-Norwegian Grammar "). Meanwhile, in connection with that broader romanticist resurgence of the later 'fifties,[27] the concern about a national language was intensified in several quarters. A case of extreme linguistic nationalism was manifested at Bergen in 1858 when Jan Prahl wrote his *Ny Hungrvekja*,[28] a somewhat romantic attempt to approach the Old Norse at once, supplying in a way, a practical demonstration of the procedure that might have pleased P. A.

[26] *Cf. N. Tids. f. Vid. og Litt.*, 1850, p. 205 *et seq.*; *Chra.-Post.*, 1852, nos. 1495, 1496.

[27] *Supra*, p. 65.

[28] Literally: new hunger-waker.

Munch.   The following year, at Christiania, a group which arranged the symposium entitled, *Det Unge Norge,*[29] lamented " the absence" of a national language which their generation might love and cultivate with " its whole heart," and spoke out forcefully on the indispensability of a national tongue.[30]   In the vigilant *Storting* of 1859 also, the language question was mooted and members debated whether the language in official use was Danish, Norwegian or Dano-Norwegian.[31]

But the most provocative advances in these years were registered by the *landsmaal*.   In 1858 it broke into two fields which belonged traditionally to the established Danish— belles-lettres proper and journalism.   Aasen aroused the conservatives and committed what seemed to some almost a sacrilege, when he translated the venerable literary treasure, Tegner's *Frithiofs Saga,* into *landsmaal*.   Even more disturbing was the fact that the new medium or a close relative of it brusquely invaded the field of journalism when Vinje launched his paper, *Dølen* " The Dalesman"),[32] and thus gave a definite impetus to the practical use of *landsmaal*.

Aasmund Olafsen Vinje (1818-70) was born in Øvre Telemarken.   In common with the other leading language reformers, Aasen, Knudsen and Vig, Vinje came of poor peasant and cotter stock (Munch was of the intelligentsia but after his reaction in the 'fifties he is hardly to be classed with the active reformers).   The cramped circumstances of Vinje's youth probably helped to give him that clear perception of realities which distinguished him, and made him

---

[29] *Supra*, p. 42.

[30] *Det Unge Norge*, p. 5.

[31] Liestøl, " *Ivar Aasen og 'Dølen'*," *Syn og Segn*, vol. xxviii, p. 4.

[32] It appeared very irregularly; at times, months passed without an issue.   For half a year in 1867 it was merged with *Vort Land. Cf.* Aasen, *Skr. i Saml.*, vol. ii, p. 209.

impatient of all shams. What took him beyond the narrow range of his low estate was his interest in study. He became first a school teacher and very much later he entered the University (1850). He decided upon the law, but his most persistent interests turned out to be journalistic and literary. His intellectual orientation is not easy to determine and it has been questioned whether he was basically a romanticist or a realist.[33] That he would consistently be either was pretty much excluded by the transitional nature of the period in which he was active, as well as by his marked sense of fairness which ever reminded him that any controversial matter was apt to have two sides. Both romanticism and realism colored his thought and it is interesting to see how completely at times he held to some of the premises that were central to romanticism. In his last important public appearances, he defended nationality in the metaphor of a universal " folk orchestra " in which every nationality must be left free to play its own distinctive instrument.[34] For a time, he had some intellectual difficulty with Scandinavianism, but came to see that what mattered most was that each of the three northern peoples should develop its own uniqueness.[35]

Vinje launched *Dølen* in a spirit of assertive nationalism, opposing Scandinavianism in any form. Norway, he insisted, could not draw closer to Sweden until the latter acquired some of Norway's political liberalism, while a

[33] K. Aabrek, "*Var Vinje romantikker eller realist,*" *Syn og Segn,* vol. xxxii, pp. 208-15; *cf.* J. E. Sars, *Samlede Værker,* vol. iv, pp. 306, 358-9 and Hj. Christensen, *Det nittende aarhundredes Kulturkamp i Norge* (Chra., 1905), p. 293.

[34] Vinje, *Om vaart nationale Stræv,* pp. 5, 25.

[35] For accounts of Vinje see: Koht, *Aasmund Olafsson Vinje, Stutt Livsskildring* (Chra., 1909) ; Koht, "*A. O. Vinje*" in Gran, *Nordm. i d. nit. Aarh.,* vol. iii, pp. 1-35; V. Vislie, *A. O. Vinje* (Bergen, 1890) ; J. E. Sars, *Samlede Værker,* vol. iv, pp. 299-359. O. Midttun, "*A. O. Vinje: 1818—6 April—1918,*" *Syn og Segn,* vol. xxiv, pp. 148-61, 230-40.

rapprochement with Denmark was yet more remote.   Both
neighbors must come to realize that Norway had been culturally distinguished long before either of the other two.   There
was at present, he explained, a " recreative " spirit coursing
through the entire nation and *Dølen* would help to give it
expression.   But what medium would best facilitate this?
Vinje decided upon a somewhat eccentric *landsmaal*,
which to some of the conservatives seemed little short of
outlandish.   Of late, he explained, a substantial portion of
the Norwegian people, in the towns especially, had unfortunately permitted its speech to be worn lop-sided (*skak-
kjoyrt i Munnen*) by the Danish.   But the popular speech
still retained the clarity and depth of thought which had
characterized also the literature of old, and there must be
a way leading to rehabilitation; *Dølen* with its broad popular
idiom meant to help in finding that way.[36]

The medium which Vinje had adopted was an approach
to Aasen's *landsmaal* though it differed somewhat.   Something, perhaps his sense for concrete realities, deterred Vinje
from rigorous adherence to Aasen's artificial norm, and he
chose to stay a little closer to the speech of the man in the
street [37] and to his own Telemark dialect.   His position on
the language question, as on other matters, is not easy to
define with exactness.   He wanted a language that would be
practical and at the same time indisputably Norwegian.   In
the early 'fifties he had been sympathetic with the Knudsen
tendency, but by 1858 he considered himself at one with
Aasen and the *landsmaal*.[38]   Yet he employed the latter only
with grave modifications.[39]   The *landsmaal* had too much

[36] *Dølen*, 1858, no. 1.

[37] *Cf.* K. Knudsen, *Det norske maalstræv*, pp. 141, 145.

[38] *Syn og Segn*, vol. xxxii, p. 211, note by O. M.

[39] *Cf.* V. Waschnitius, " *A. O. Vinjes Sprachentwicklung*," *Edda*, vol.
xiv, pp. 161-201.

finality as yet to suit him, a finality which he thought ought
to be left to the future. For the present he found it sufficient
that writers should color their diction with the idiom of
their several dialects; out of this varied usage would then
emerge the ultimate form of a truly national language.
However, his middle-of-the-road position netted him blows
from all directions. While one writer insisted that he had
conceded altogether too much to the speech of the countryside [40] another pronounced his medium really urban, the
speech of the suburbs.[41] Worse still, another called it
simply Danish and pointed to the hindrance and confusion
which its usage would involve for the development of " our "
literature.[42]

* * * * *

As the *landsmaal* threatened to become less academic and
more practical, the conservatives became seriously alarmed,
and while their attacks in the early 'fifties had been directed
mainly at Knudsen and the moderates, in the later 'fifties,
they levied their charges at Aasen, Vinje, and the supporters
of the *landsmaal* generally, whom we might call the radicals.
This time the leading spokesman for the conservatives was
M. J. Monrad, who warned against the practice of calling
the established medium Danish, lest this foster a negative
attitude which would " clip the wings " of all national enthusiasm. This misleading practice, he said, was in fact a
" confession of bankruptcy," and it helped to keep the true
Norwegian in disgrace. Monrad admitted that the established medium, if it were Danish, would be a menace to the
nationality, but it was really national; it had woven itself
so intimately into the traditions of every walk of life that it
must be considered Norwegian.[43]

[40] *Chra.-Post.*, 1858, no. 310.
[41] *Aftbl.*, 1858, no. 236.
[42] *Morgbl.*, 1859, no. 294.
[43] *Ibid.*, 1858, nos. 326, 336.

Like his predecessor, Munch, in the first half of the decade, Monrad insisted that the liberties being taken with the language involved a menace to culture and civilization. Through the established literary medium, he pointed out, Norway had appropriated all higher culture [44]—that culture which had left far astern, the *landsmaal* with its more " naïve " point of view.   Never, it was said in another connection, would the *landsmaal* displace the Danish; [45] more and more the speech of the common people on which it was based, was retreating to out-of-the-way places, and any attempt to employ it, as in the case of *Dølen's* " bastard tongue," would prove too restricted, and would help to keep the peasant in narrow localism.[46]   Sometimes the conservatives grew a bit obscurantist, taking refuge in a higher law.   It would not do, said one critic, to tamper with the development of language, whose directive forces were not human will or human ingenuity but natural development and " historical necessity."   Man was in no position to prescribe the future forms of language.[47]   Aasen's *landsmaal,* said Monrad, was in no sense an organic growth; [48] in fact the idea that the common speech could be made the general literary medium was fanatical and contrary to all laws of cultural development.

The most telling argument against the moderates as well as against the radicals, was the claim that only the established medium was adequate to the demands of culture.   Aasen had been aware from the outset that his *landsmaal* would fail to convince unless it could be shown to be adequate in

---

[44] *Ibid.*, 1858, nos. 287, 291.   *Cf.* also *Chra.-Post.*, 1858, no. 334.

[45] *Cf. N. Tids. f. Vid. og Litt.*, vol. vii, p. 367.

[46] *Morgbl.*, 1858, nos. 287, 291.

[47] *Chra.-Post.*, 1858, no. 335.

[48] But *" en Møkkurkalf af Leer med et Hoppehjerte,"* as Monrad said in an untranslatable phrase.   *Morgbl.*, 1858, no. 326.

this respect. He tried to demonstrate its adequacy by logic as well as by practical example. The popular speech, he conceded, had a limited vocabulary in some fields; for instance, it had a paucity of terms for the expression of abstract ideas,[49] but every cultivated language, after all, had to start as an untutored idiom [50] and, through gradual usage had to acquire the range and flexibility needed to express new and more discriminating thought. This it did either by fashioning new words out of roots of its own or by borrowing from another tongue;[51] the highly regarded Danish, for example, had kept up with the march of culture by the simple device of borrowing from abroad.[52] The popular speech, thought Aasen, had the potentialities to meet the demands that would be made upon it in this respect. True enough, it had retained many archaic forms but these really were no handicap, and those who so regarded them should recall that progress demanded not so much shorter grammatical forms — consider, for instance, the modern High German which had kept so many of its old forms [53]— but an increased vocabulary.

In the way of a pragmatic proof, Aasen began to use the *landsmaal,* first for very simple matters and then for subjects that were more difficult. Regarding its capacity to express abstract ideas, the judgments varied. While C. R. Unger, a sympathetic reviewer, thought Aasen had shown that the popular idiom was able to fashion new expressions [54] another was not much impressed by the abstractions.[55] These

[49] Aasen, *Det n. Folkespr. Gram.,* p. 2.
[50] *Ibid.,* p. x.
[51] Aasen, *Skr. i Saml.,* vol. iii, pp. 97, 121.
[52] *Ibid.,* vol. iii, pp. 140, 146-7.
[53] *Ibid.,* vol. iii, p. 165.
[54] *N. Tids. f. Vid. og Litt.,* vol. vi, p. 294.
[55] *Ill. Nyhbl.,* 1853, p. 104.

differences of opinion broadened into a controversy regarding the efficacy of the *landsmaal* as a medium of culture, and the task of defending it fell primarily upon Aasen, who did so in a number of articles.[56]

If Aasen were to make any headway in the argument he must show that the vital connection, postulated by Munch and now emphasized by others, between the established Danish and the present advanced state of culture in Norway, was not as important as many supposed; likewise he must disprove the shortcomings ascribed to the Norwegian in this respect. He made his chief attack by way of a redefinition of culture. The "classes," he explained, motivated frequently by nothing but a vain desire to distinguish themselves from the masses,[57] had identified culture largely with outward manners and speech, attributes which often were foreign. Lesser folk imitated their supposed betters and mistook superficialities for the essence of culture.[58] But culture, insisted Aasen, was something deep-seated, something close to the inner spirit; outward refinement in manners and speech were only the attendant frills. Culture did involve a refinement, but of intellectual and moral capacities; it included, on the one side, a broadening knowledge of the individual's physical and biological environment, and on the other, his attainment of a balanced judgment, trained to seek the truth without deferring to precedent or prejudice.[59]

Of course, culture was not to be confused with so-called progress, and to Aasen it was by no means incompatible

---

[56] See "*Om Dannelsen og Norskheden,*" *Folkevennen,* 1857, pp. 419-60; "*Brev om Kulturen,*" *Dølen,* vol. i, no. 16; "*Minningar fraa Maalstriden um Hausten 1858,*" *Dølen,* vol. i, nos. 18, 19, 21, 22, 23; "*Om Sprogsagen,*" *Ill. Nyhbl.,* 1858, nos. 45, 46. Reprinted in Aasen, *Skr. i Saml.,* vol. ii, pp. 169-174; vol. iii, pp. 66-128, 136-76.

[57] Aasen, *Skr. i Saml.,* vol. iii, p. 74.

[58] *Ibid.,* vol. iii, p. 73.

[59] *Ibid.,* vol. iii, pp. 69-70.

with a retention of the peasant's speech and manners. The continuance of these certainly did not involve, as some averred, the decline of culture and a calamitous return to ignorance, to rawness and pure barbarism.[60] Culture, being a matter of internal refinement, should rather help to keep the traditional speech and manners in repute;[61] these had belonged to the fathers and they were in no way foreign. The argument that in order to get a true national language, the nation must drop the cultural level of the existing literary Danish and go back four hundred years to begin where the Old Norse had left off, was just pure nonsense. The store of civilized knowledge of the present day was a common possession, said Aasen—a store not to be jeopardized by taking up a new or by reviving an old language.[62]

Aasen agreed that language had a very important connection with culture. It was important, not because some tongues possessed special qualifications for transmitting culture, but because culture should be brought to the people in the simplest and most familiar manner, that is, in their own language. On this point, he thought that the established Danish fell short; being alien to the common people of Norway and packed with foreign words, it encouraged " blind and foggy thoughts." The Norwegian people certainly did not need to depend on it for their culture,[63] which, he explained, would suffer in no way from the use of the new *landsmaal*.[64] Instead of being four centuries behind, the *landsmaal* was quite competent to acquire culture at its present level and disseminate its fruits.

Thus the argument went on; we have traced it far enough

[60] *Ibid.*, vol. iii, pp. 75, 119.

[61] *Ibid.*, vol. iii, pp. 105-6.

[62] *Ibid.*, vol. iii, pp. 153-4.

[63] *Ibid.*, vol. iii, p. 155; Aasen, *Norsk Grammatik*, pp. iv-v.

[64] *Cf. Maal og Minne*, 1917, pp. 16, 18.

to see how the conservatives in opposing first the moderates and then the radicals, tried to identify the retention of the established medium with the maintenance of the existing culture.

CHAPTER XX

CLEAVAGE

In the 'sixties the *landsmaal* gained its first adherents among intellectuals of urban antecedents. Some of these as Kr. Janson put it, came to feel their generation must work to inspire the people to desire, even to *demand,* the *landsmaal,*[1] though all were perhaps not as confident as he, that if the people did not want it, the undertaking would still succeed " if God wills it." But save in an isolated community like that in Gudbrandsdalen, where Chr. Bruun worked,[2] progress was necessarily slow.

A few of the intellectuals tried to make practical use of the new medium. The *landsmaal,* it was felt, should not be merely a fashionable sable for dress occasions but a sword to render good service.[3] Much had been written about the new medium; now it was time to write in it.[4] At the middle of the decade, Kr. Janson employed it[5] in writing a peasant novel and Werner Werenskjold used a modified *landsmaal,* close to the Telemark dialect, in a sample translation from the *Arabian Nights.*[6]

Not many could make practical use of the *landsmaal,* how-

[1] Kr. Janson, *Hvad vi Maalstrævere vil,* p. 42.

[2] Henrik Krohn, *Skrifter,* p. 28.

[3] *Svein Urædd,* 1869, no. 41.

[4] *Ferdamannen,* 1865, no. 1.

[5] " Driven to it," he said, by resentment at the sophomoric way in which Bergen rowdies made sport of visiting country folk. Janson, *Hvad jeg har oplevet* (Chra., 1913), pp. 96-7.

[6] *Salomons Laas.*

ever, and most of those interested had to be content to promote its cause chiefly by argument. They appealed to fellow educators and fellow intellectuals to take an active interest in the *landsmaal*. At Christiania, H. E. Berner and Chr. Bruun pleaded its cause in two successive weekly meetings of *Studentersamfundet*.[7] Hagbard E. Berner (1839-1920) from Søndmøre, later a politician and newspaper editor who sometimes took his patriotism quite literally,[8] had recently become interested in the new medium. In his speech before *Studentersamfundet* he insisted that the *landsmaal* issue was not a question of philology but a practical matter of nationality: "the Norwegian people," he announced, "demands that its national uniqueness be respected in every regard."[9]   Norwegians, he complained, were being instructed in a language which they never had learned to speak and the consequence was that they chose rather to be silent,[10] while their speech was being vulgarized by the urban Danish culture. The *landsmaal* signified an effort by the people to assert their nationality, and Berner asked that his fellow intellectuals lend it a sympathetic attitude. Christopher Arnt Bruun (1839-1920), subsequently a pastor and an early promoter of the folk high-school movement, had been influenced by the Grundtvigian trend[11] to look for a social and religious renewal through a sort of popular

[7] Oct. 27 and Nov. 3, 1866. The speeches were later printed as *To Foredrag om Maalsagen* (Chra., 1866).

[8] On the day that the Union project (which he opposed) was presented, he purchased fire-arms and joined a rifle corps, and on the occasion of the royal veto in 1880 he urged the further organization of armed popular defense units. *Norsk Biog. Leks.*, vol. i, pp. 481-84; Koht, "H. E. Berner," *Syn og Segn*, vol. xxv, pp. 259-66; Halvorsen, *Norsk Forf.-Lex.*, vol. i, pp. 236-7.

[9] Berner and Bruun, *To Foredrag om Maalsagen*, p. 4.

[10] *Ibid.*, p. 11.

[11] *Cf. infra*, p. 348.

renaissance.[12]   He asked that the classes, who prated [13] about their duty to culture and the homage which they owed to the literary medium, learn to respect the peasant and his culture.   Their hostility to the *landsmaal,* he declared somewhat bluntly, fed largely on the indifference to the countryman's welfare.[14]   They must realize that the *landsmaal* was not alone the concern of the peasant but their own cause as well, and that it demanded their support since it really involved Norway's national independence.[15]

Among the early proponents of the *landsmaal,* no little emphasis was laid upon the pedagogical and ethical arguments.   It was pointed out that the demand for the use of the popular speech was a just one; the peasant had a right to have his speech restored [16] and it was " a shameful injustice " to force on a people a language not only foreign, but ill-adapted " spiritually " to the folk uniqueness.[17]   Those who remarked that the peasant did not want his own language, were proving nothing, save that the Danish had become thoroughly familiar to him.[18]   According to the pedagogical argument, the peasant could be most effectively instructed in his own tongue—a point of view quite widely prevalent.   No later than the early 'forties one writer said it was illogical to expect that the Danish, adapted to voice the thoughts and feelings of Danes, should be adequate to express the ideas

[12] A foreign tour had made him sceptical of European culture, and he sought his ideals in ancient Hellas and Old Testament Palestine, adding to these an admiration for early Germanic life. *Norsk Biog. Leks.,* vol. ii, pp. 256-63; Halvorsen, *Norsk Forf.-Lex.,* vol. i, pp. 491-2.

[13] *Cf. Edda,* 1914, p. 157.

[14] Berner and Bruun, *To Foredrag om Maalsagen,* p. 52.

[15] *Ibid.,* p. 56.

[16] *Morgbl.,* 1852, no. 329.

[17] *Aftbl.,* 1865, no. 114.

[18] Kr. Janson, *Hvad vi Maalstrævere vil,* p. 30.

of the Norwegians.[19] In his plea to fellow intellectuals, Bruun dwelt much upon this line of argument. The cultured, he averred, must realize that what counted in this matter was the peasant's welfare; he must be permitted to get his enlightenment in a language not too profound or alien, and the only proper medium to give clear expression to his deepest thoughts and to his unique cultural life was the native language.[20]

In the western part of the country, the concern for a national language showed a perceptible trend toward the Old Norse. A group of Bergen intellectuals and middle-class folk approached the matter from a very patriotic, and in some respects, a very academic point of view. These folk thought that Aasen in his *landsmaal* was using a medium that was too modern. We have already noted the very archaic usages in Prahl's *Ny Hungrvekja*.[21] The central figure in the Bergen group was Henrik Krohn (1826-79), a merchant, who after losing most of his fortune in the crisis of the later 'fifties,[22] developed a philanthropic (and romantic) interest in the peasant. In the end he met disillusionment, for the countryman proved unresponsive and disinclined to accept " what was for his own good." [23] Krohn worked diligently to help to rehabilitate and preserve the culture of the peasant and sought to increase also the townsman's esteem for it; and it was his hope that both elements of the population would become deeply concerned about the rural language.[24] In general he approved Aasen's *landsmaal* and greeted the

[19] *Maal og Minne*, 1924, p. 147.

[20] Berner and Bruun, *op. cit.*, pp. 39-41, 58-9.

[21] *Supra*, p. 313.

[22] B. Bjørnson, *Bjørnsons Brev* (4 vols., Chra., 1912-21), vol. i, p. 356, note 93.

[23] Henrik Krohn, *Skrifter*, p. 29.

[24] *Cf.* E. M. Mohn, *Om Maalsagen og det Bergenske Maalstræv*, p. 31.

new edition of his *Grammatik* in more enthusiastic terms
than did most critics; [25] it was well adapted, Krohn thought,
to awaken and strengthen "faith in our linguistic, our
national, rebirth." He was especially pleased to see that
the *landsmaal* made some approach to the Old Norse and
he noted that Aasen had shown potentialities in it for
formulating abstract ideas.

*　*　*　*　*

That national romanticism, in some of its aspects, tended
to develop a measure of Danophobia has been previously
observed,[26] and we have now to note that this reaction
became very pronounced with the Bergen element, which
gave it expression in a tone more shrill and vituperative than
any heard earlier. The Danish influence, it was said, had
done irreparable historical wrong to Norway's language and
traditions, which still bore "open sores," traceable direct to
the period of "national infirmity." [27] Kr. Janson in his
Fraa Dansktidi ("From the Danish Period") referred to a
long series, an "entire litany," [28] of Danish sins under the
union. Denmark was severely criticized for her course in
connection with the events of the year 1814, a subject on
which Krohn was especially acrimonious. Brushing aside
the plea that Norway in 1864 should help Denmark as a
brother in need, Krohn demanded to know what sort of
fraternal love Denmark had shown in 1814 when she cava-
lierly disposed of Norway and kept the Norse colonies for
herself. Or again, what brotherly spirit had she manifested
in still clinging to her ill-gotten "booty," [29] that is, the old
colonies, Iceland and the Faroes. Not only had she torn

[25] *Aftbl.*, 1865, nos. 113, 114.
[26] *Supra*, pp. 135-40, 143-47, 153-56, 286-7.
[27] Henrik Krohn, *Skrifter*, p. 519.
[28] *Cf. Morgbl.*, 1875, no. 352 A.
[29] Henrik Krohn, *Skrifter*, p. 13.

these dependencies from their rightful connections but she was now mismanaging them. It was well known how the Danes could treat those who fell into their power and they had obviously learned nothing; at the moment (1871), they were trying to force an unwelcome constitution on the Icelanders.[30]

*   *   *   *   *

The publicists of the mid-century had said little of Iceland's modern political connections, a notable circumstance in view of the fact that they often spoke critically of Denmark and insisted on sharing Iceland's ancient culture. That the old *norrøn* empire was " torn to pieces " in the Treaty of Kiel naturally aroused some interest in Norway, but it appears to have stimulated no violent feelings.[31]   Later on, Henrik Wergeland, patriot and Danophobe, referred, in terms relatively mild, to the Danish retention in 1814 of the Norwegian possessions.[32]   In the early 'forties Ole Munch Ræder voiced a more vigorous disapproval. He designated what happened in 1814 a stupendous fraud and broached the subject of Iceland's separation from Denmark.   The future, he hoped, would give the Icelanders an opportunity to choose either complete independence or a freedom protected by Norwegian institutions. He also reminded Norway of a responsibility; she must not forget her debt to Iceland, until the latter was again "free and happy." [33]

Meanwhile, the interest in Iceland was on the increase at Bergen, where contacts with the island were more frequent. Krohn insisted [34] that the Norwegians themselves deserved

[30] *Ibid.*, pp. 445-46.

[31] *Cf.* Edv. Bull, *et al.*, *Det norske folks Liv og Historie,* vol. viii, pp. 229-32.

[32] *Cf.* his *Digterværker og Prosaiske Skrifter,* vol. i, p. 122.

[33] O. M. Ræder, *Den norske Statsforfatnings Historie og Væsen,* pp. 191-2.

[34] Henrik Krohn, *Skrifter,* pp. 445-6.

some reproach for having been inexcusably neglectful in 1814, when the matter of Norway's dependencies might have been easily adjusted " in its historical setting." In the actual circumstances, it was depressing to recall that not a single Norwegian had then mentioned Iceland or the Faroes.[35] " National thoughtlessness " had so prevailed that not one had recalled the brotherland of Snorre's birth, where some of the richest national treasures had been composed, and where the ancient tongue lived on in its purest and oldest form. It was " our own fault," said Krohn. " We must always remember with shame, that these peoples, torn from their true motherland, lay at the mercy of the Danes." Having wronged Iceland by forgetting her in 1814, Norway owed to her former dependency a " national responsibility." There might come a time to think of restitution even if it should involve the outright demand that Denmark abrogate her rule over the Norse descendants in " our old sagaland." [36] For the present, little could be done to loosen the political tie between Iceland and Denmark. But Norway and Iceland were akin, nationally and geographically, and something could be undertaken shortly to draw Iceland closer to Norway, especially as the Icelanders were anxious to establish more intimate trade relations.[37] In order to encourage these relations and thus help to restore " the broken bond " which had snapped apart in the days of Norway's " national infirmity," Krohn in 1870 formed at Bergen *Det Islandske Handelssamlag* ("The Icelandic Trade Association ") [38]

[35] This was a very erroneous statement, of course, in the light of the paragraph above.

[36] Henrik Krohn, *Skrifter*, p. 446.

[37] Several societies were being formed on Iceland to further this trade. *Bergensposten*, 1870, no. 109.

[38] Henrik Krohn, *Skrifter*, pp. 25-6, 445, 447.

The circumstance that the Icelanders were carrying on a serious agitation for political autonomy encouraged a few Norwegians to hope for eventual recovery of the former dependency.[39]   Norway and Iceland, it was said, formed a natural economic unit, while the island was only a burden to the Danish treasury.   Racially, Iceland was as much a part of Norway as Slesvig was of Denmark.   Now was the time, thought a writer in Bjørnson's organ, to negotiate peacefully for Iceland's annexation; if this result could be attained, it might be fittingly celebrated a few years hence (1872) at the millennial festival to commemorate Norway's political consolidation by Harold Fairhair.[40]

*   *   *   *   *

The intellectuals who became interested in the *landsmaal* in the 'sixties sought to coördinate and strengthen their labors through the organization of societies and the launching of periodicals.   Their earlier journalistic efforts were somewhat esoteric.   At Bergen, a manuscript medium called *Namnlaus* ("Nameless")[41] was first circulated privately. Three years later (1865), Krohn established a regular but not a very long-lived organ known as *Ferdamannen* ("The Traveller"),   ostensibly to further the education of "the common people,"[42] which, it was explained, could best be accomplished by using the "people's own speech," that is, a form of *landsmaal*.   At Christiania, the journalistic beginnings were more complicated.   Vinje's paper, *Dølen,* with its somewhat personal *landsmaal* had been appearing very irregularly since 1858.   For half a year in 1867 it was merged with the short-lived organ, *Vort Land* ("Our

[39] *Cf. Bergensposten*, 1870, no. 49; *Norsk Folkeblad*, 1870, p. 40.
[40] *Norsk Folkeblad*, 1870, p. 40.
[41] Kr. Janson, *Hvad jeg har oplevet*, p. 104.
[42] "*Til Læserne*," *Ferdamannen*, 1865, p. 1.

Country ")[43] a patriotic publication employing the established Dano-Norwegian. While its sponsors disapproved of the claims made for the *landsmaal* by the more extreme adherents,[44] they appreciated clearly its national implications and were generally sympathetic with the new medium. Not until 1868 did the Christiania enthusiasts launch a *landsmaal* organ proper, called *Svein Urædd* (" Svein Unafraid "),[45] whose editors, repelled somewhat by Old Norse usages in *Ferdamannen,* meant to employ a *landsmaal* that would be more practical and more adaptable to the whole country.[46] *Svein Urædd* ceased to appear in 1870, but there were other ventures at the capital, such as the short-lived *Andvake* (1871) and the very individualistic *Fram* (1871-3) of O. J. Fjørtoft.

*　　*　　*　　*　　*

In the 'sixties the efforts to promote the cause of the *landsmaal* through formal organization were centered in two large undertakings, one in Bergen and the other in Christiania. Both had somewhat irregular antecedents. At Bergen, an informal club was formed in 1862 and met on Saturdays to read and discuss the Old Norse; in this circle was passed about the manuscript, *Namnlaus,* referred to in the previous section. Among the members in this group were J. E. Unger, Velle, M. Nygaard, G. Greig, John Greig, and Kr. Janson,[47] while the most active of them all was Krohn, who

[43] Whose editors were Carl and H. E. Berner, J. C. Krogh, W. Werenskjold and J. E. Sars.

[44] *Vort Land,* 1867, June 16. Among those who attacked the *landsmaal* in 1867, a year of lively agitation, were Kjerulf, Ibsen, K. Knudsen and E. Mohn; Vinje, Krohn and Janson wrote in its defense.

[45] Edited by I. Schjøtt and L. Holst. Holst's mother was a sister of Henrik Krohn.

[46] *Cf. Svein Urædd,* 1869, no. 41.

[47] Kr. Janson, *Hvad jeg har oplevet,* p. 104.

later took the initiative in forming a permanent society.
Four days after his journalistic venture, *Ferdamannen,* had
lapsed, he circulated a prospectus in which he planned an
ambitious organization.   His intentions were not narrowly
linguistic or academic, but philanthropic and social.   Jaabæk
was just beginning to organize the peasantry into the *Bondevenforeninger* (" Societies of Friends of the Peasant "),
which Krohn and his circle thought altogether too narrowly
political and too utilitarian.[48] The peasant, it was felt,
needed something inspirational, and the stimulation of community feeling and love of fatherland might evoke much
that was desirable.   From these beginnings developed the
society known as *Vestmannalaget* (" The West Men's
Party ").[49] Paragraph I of the society's by-laws announced that the organization was intended to provide entertainment and to stimulate national feeling.   The second
paragraph dealt with eligibility and offered admittance to
every person who placed the " right " evaluation on the
landsmaal cause.[50] Meetings of the organization were to be
given over largely to programs of light entertainment, including folk dances, folk songs, popular readings and story
telling.[51] It was a paternalistic venture and its chief bene-
ficiaries were intended to be country folk; among the first
thirty-six persons who joined the society only *one* was a
peasant.[52]

The organization which was formed at Christiania in the

[48] Henrik Krohn, *Skrifter,* pp. 25, 520-21.

[49] T. Hannaas, *Vestmannalaget,* p. 16. Possibly its beginnings were
influenced by the example of *Døleringen* in Christiania. *Syn og Segn,*
vol. xxv, p. 283.

[50] Hannaas, *op. cit.,* p. 19.

[51] *Ibid.,* pp. 16-17. For some satirical comment on this aspect of the
matter see *Morgbl.,* 1868, no. 82.

[52] *Cf.* Hannaas, *op. cit.,* p. 17.

same year also had some informal predecessors.[53] In 1859
a little circle had met from time to time with Vinje, and in
the early 'sixties there were similar informal gatherings at
Hans Ross' or elsewhere, for the reading and discussion of
the *landsmaal*.[54] The most important group, brought together by Vinje,[55] was no doubt *Døleringen* ("The Dales-
mens' Circle"), whose members in 1867 published *Vort
Land*.[56] Finally in March, 1868, on the initiative of H. E.
Berner, steps were taken that led to the founding of *Det
norske Samlaget* ("The Norwegian Association"), which
was launched with a roster of 110 members,[57] and which has
had a long and distinguished history. Like its counterpart
at Bergen, *Det norske Samlaget* intended to carry on
much of its work through social gatherings. But it had
also the more academic purpose of encouraging the publication of materials in *landsmaal,* and the second activity soon
superseded the first; thus it came about that the Christiania
society neatly supplemented the work of *Vestmannalaget,*
which devoted itself almost entirely to social affairs (save for
the somewhat esoteric interest in the Old Norse).[58] *Det
norske Samlaget* became distinguished as a publisher and
patron of *landsmaal* and dialect literature.[59] Urban influences in the society forced a radical reorganization in 1902,
in such a way that two subdivisions were formed. One
section, *Landsmaalslaget,* was to further the *landsmaal,* and

[53] *Syn og Segn*, vol. xxiv, p. 95; vol. xiv, p. 229.

[54] Garborg, Hovden and Koht, *Ivar Aasen*, p. 164.

[55] *Cf.* Sars, *Samlede Værker*, vol. iv, p. 322.

[56] *Cf. Syn og Segn*, vol. xxv, p. 281.

[57] *Ibid.*, 1908, p. 225.

[58] *Cf. ibid.*, vol. xxiv, p. 96.

[59] *Cf.* S. Kolsrud, "*Skrifter utgjevne av det norske Samlaget 1868-
1918*," *Syn og Segn*, vol. xxv [p. 434 *et seq.*], paged separately as 1-33.
Cf. Syn og Segn, vol. xiv, p. 245.

the other, *Bymaalslaget,* sought to advance the townsman's *riksmaal,* though both agreed to promote "what is Norwegian." [60]

*   *   *   *   *

We have next to observe how the linguistic premises described in chapter seventeen were given a somewhat disturbing application in the 'fifties and 'sixties by the proponents of the *landsmaal,* who reached the conclusion that side by side in Norway lived two cultures and possibly two separate and distinct nationalities. It is necessary to recall that in romanticist thought, language, culture, and nationality, respectively, were regarded as generic, and endowed with a certain quality of homogeneity which precluded effective assimilation or amalgamation of one language with another or of one culture with another. [61] Likewise it is to be remembered that an intimate association was supposed to exist between language and nationality, between language and culture, and between nationality and culture. It had been made clear by the mid-century investigators that the country had a second language and a rural tradition; the logical deduction therefrom would be that it also had two cultures. [62] It came to be assumed that Norwegian society was thus fatally cleft. [63] Between the circles of culture and the genuine folk life there yawned "a fearful distance"; [64] the cultured seemed no longer able to think and write in "the spirit of the people." Under these conditions the two elements of the population could not have the proper reaction

[60] *Syn og Segn,* vol. xiv, pp. 251-2.

[61] *Supra,* p. 282 *et seq.*

[62] *Cf.* Kr. Janson, *Hvad vi Maalstrævere vil,* p. 8; E. Mohn, *Om Maalsagen og det Bergenske Maalstræv,* p. 6.

[63] Berner and Bruun, *To Foredrag om Maalsagen,* pp. 24, 32; Aasen, *Skr. i Saml.,* vol. iii, p. 13. *Cf. Norske Magasin,* vol. i, p. vii.

[64] *N. Tids. f. Vid. og Litt.,* vol. ii, p. 271.

on one another, and the country's spiritual resources were dissipated by the presence of "two hostile forces." [65] The same idea of two cultures lay behind Munch's fervid argument that the stage of a culture was intimately associated with the degree of progress attained by its language, which meant in Norway, that the peasant's speech represented a fourteenth century culture, and the established Dano-Norwegian a nineteenth century level of progress. A similar duality in culture was accepted by Bruun, but while Munch defended the Danish tradition, Bruun spoke for the culture of the peasant as he saw it still flourishing among the mountain valleys, a venerable heritage from the fathers, with a rich literary treasure and its own deep philosophy, which bred and matured noble and cultivated personalities. What a contrast, said Bruun, between this venerable and dignified tradition of the peasant, and the utilitarian, materialistic culture of the towns. [66] Out of the latter came nothing noble but only "deadness, ugliness and wearisome materialism"; as taken up by the peasant it often was identified with such superficialities as road improvement or better animal husbandry, or with such flippancies as whist-playing and polka-dancing. Berner noted that any intercourse between the two cultures always worked out to the detriment of the indigenous tradition. The foreign influence reduced the peasant's life to a plane of rawness and ugliness. [67]

But if Norway had two cultures, it must also harbor two nationalities, a conclusion that would follow from the romanticist assumption that a very intimate tie existed between culture and nationality. Then it must be asked, which culture and which nationality were indigenous and therefore truly national? Obviously they were those of the

[65] Kr. Janson, *Hvad vi Maalstrævere vil,* pp. 24-5.

[66] Berner and Bruun, *op. cit.,* pp. 27, 29, 45.

[67] *Ibid.,* pp. 11-12.

peasant. He was the original habitant of the country and the culture he had developed must be considered the country's own.[68] The romanticist investigators were quite agreed in their estimate of the peasant's national status. He essentially made up the Norwegian nationality.[69] The nationality proper must be sought in his estate, the " noblest part of the nation ";[70] the nationality of students and the bureaucracy was only of the salon or soirée variety.[71] " Israel itself," Wergeland had remarked, must be sought in the interior within the indigenous peasant stock; the burgher and official classes were the " Philistines " living in " Askalon and Gaza."[72] Munch sought the " real " Norway along the western coast and among the highlands of the interior, arguing that the eastern part of the country had early been affected by an alien Suedo-*gøthic* influence.[73] Ivar Aasen, with characteristic moderation, admitted that the peasants alone did not compose the nation but he insisted that they made up its largest and most significant part.[74]

*   *   *   *   *

When the peasant, after being toasted for a generation as the true Norwegian, at last began to think of taking the romanticists at their word, and developed his democratic movement, the cultured found themselves in a dilemma. Their teaching was proving a boomerang; if, as they had so often said, the peasant's nationality alone was genuine, then the cultured, as an alien element, had no warrant, no title, to share in the Norwegian nationality. But such a

[68] Aasen, *Skr. i Saml.*, vol. iii, p. 152.

[69] Keyser, *Efterl. Skr.*, vol. ii, pt. ii, p. 75.

[70] Munch, *Saml. Afh.*, vol. i, p. 386.

[71] " *Den Dannede Ungdoms Norskhed,*" *Morgbl.*, 1847, no. 47.

[72] H. Wergeland, *op. cit.*, vol. iv, pp. 451-2.

[73] Munch, *Saml. Afh.*, vol. iii, p. 267 *et seq.*

[74] Aasen, *Skr. i Saml.*, vol. iii, pp. 150-51.

conclusion they were loathe to accept and they sought to justify their position by redefining culture and by trying to show that their national lineage was also satisfactory. The ensuing argument, as L. Daae said, developed into "a paternity struggle." [75]

The *landsmaal* agitation, in taking seriously many of the flattering things said of the peasant, forced a fresh consideration of the relationship between nationality and cosmopolitanism. It is a matter of interest that this question had been touched upon a generation earlier. J. A. Hielm, who sympathized strongly with the rising Norwegianness in Wergeland's day, argued that the foreign must amalgamate with the "unique," or the national, to form something quite different, an entirely "new uniqueness." [76] The process was a delicate one, involving the danger that the cosmopolitan would outweigh the national and thus result only in a leveling conformity instead of a "new uniqueness." Hielm recognized that the cosmopolitan heritage could not be ignored, but each people must select of it only what might be in harmony with its nationality and its "spiritual" life; otherwise the nationality, as such, would gradually disappear.[77] Shortly after, A. M. Schweigaard of *Intelligentspartiet* defined the national as the specific and the unique after these attributes had been assimilated to and interpenetrated with the general "substance of culture." [78]

The implications of P. A. Munch's mid-century polemic with Knudsen were disturbing; he had identified modern culture with the maintenance of the established Dano-Norwegian, but since this was of foreign origin, the nationality

[75] *Morgbl.*, 1868, no. 54.

[76] *Alm. n. Maanedskr.*, vol. ii, p. 488.

[77] *Ibid.*, vol. ii, p. 470.

[78] *Cf.* E. Hertzberg, *Professor Schweigaard i hans offentlige Virksomhed*, p. 55.

of the cultured must also be foreign. Thus they seemed to have no right to share in the Norwegian nationality. Somehow it must be possible to show that they had such a right, and their case owed something to Monrad, who had argued that a measure of cosmopolitanism was not only harmless but positively necessary to nationality.[79] There was something one-sided about nationality, he explained, but also something universal. True progress was dependent upon participation in the working out of the universal, the eternal, the " Idea "—upon participation in a " world historic culture process " of give and take, wherein each nation took from the general store what suited it, and conversely donated its share of art and culture to the whole. Of course it would not do, as Monrad admitted, for a nationality to " desert " itself and go completely over to something new—that would be " suicide." But the nation should participate sufficiently in the cosmopolitan to be released from the one-sided and the transitory, that is, from the purely national. There was a particular danger in putting too much emphasis on what was uniquely Norwegian, at the expense of the universal.[80] Since there was a deeper harmony between nationality and cosmopolitanism the contradiction between them was therefore not conclusive, according to Monrad's argument, which thus provided a learned justification for the function of the cultured. In fact, by virtue of their special rôle in furthering the culture process, these ought possibly to be considered even *more* national than the peasantry.

As time went on, the cultured had to affirm more frequently their right to share fully in the Norwegian nationality. They argued that nationality must be something in which all could participate. The peasant and mountaineer by no means made up the whole nation and a collection even

[79] *Cf. N. Tids. f. Vid. og Litt.*, vol. vii, pp. 9-11.
[80] *Morgbl.*, 1858, no. 93.

of the " better " districts was not the entire country.[81]   The
rural folk, it was suggested, had perhaps been too much
admired; at any rate the townsman, while he may have
been " Danish " a generation previously, certainly was so
no longer.   Some of the younger intellectuals found corro-
borative evidence in history to show that the bureaucracy
likewise was mainly Norwegian.[82]   It could be demonstrated
that most of those who rose to official position were natives,
even after the overturn of 1660.   Hence it was an exaggera-
tion to place the peasant's nationality in absolute opposition
to the townsman's culture, or to speak of two nationalities
in the country, and it was very far-fetched to think of the
landsmaal agitation in terms of a Czechic or a Finnish
national renaissance.

Nevertheless, no amount of dialectic could argue away the
annoying fact that the presence of two languages weakened
the inner cohesion of the nationality.   Some, especially those
intellectuals who had espoused the cause of the *landsmaal,*
were inclined to urge reconciliation of the two elements.[83]
Neither the established medium nor the *landsmaal,* it was
remarked, was a full expression of the nationality.[84]   The
peasant had certain national elements, while the townsman
possessed others.   Both had once constituted a unity with a
common patriotism [85] that must somehow be recovered.   But
several of the *landsmaal* partisans were unrelenting and
demanded that the townsman get rid of his alien character
if he wished to be Norwegian.   Vinje took the stand that

[81] *Morgbl.,* 1858, nos. 287, 326; *Chra.-Post.,* 1858, no. 310.

[82] *Morgbl.,* 1868, no. 54.   *Cf.* K. Knudsen, *Det norske maalstræv,* pp.
158-60.

[83] Berner and Bruun, *op. cit.,* p. 51 ; *Chra.-Post.,* 1858, no. 310; *cf. Den
norske Rigstidende,* 1847, no. 27.

[84] Sars, *Samlede Værker,* vol. iii, p. 589.

[85] *Vort Land,* 1867, no. 15.

between the two languages and therefore between the two cultures there could be no fusion; in such a process one or the other would lose all of its essentials.   But let the towns-man once recognize that his culture was foreign and it would no longer be a " menace "; his consequent decision to assume the peasant's nationality would hasten the desired unity.[86]

* * * * *

Between the 'seventies and the close of the century the *landsmaal* agitation was gradually transformed into a broad social movement.   This development was due in large part to the success of the intellectuals in winning over to the *landsmaal* program important sections of peasant opinion. At first thought, it might seem that the peasant would, as a matter of course, unhesitatingly support a program aimed to rehabilitate his language, but the fact is that he had, at first, little or no interest in the matter.   For a generation he had been more concerned to rid himself of traditional and outworn usages and more anxious to catch up with modern progress.[87]   We have had occasion to note how the roman-ticists lamented the manner in which he recently was neglecting his traditions and his language.   Even his most distinguished political leader, Søren Jaabæk, arose in the *Storting* to pronounce the coming of the Danish language a fortunate thing for the country.[88]

That the peasant in the last decades of the century came to take the *landsmaal* seriously, was due to a combination of circumstances.   Something must be credited to the inordi-nate praise which romanticist writers for a generation had lavished on his language.   More significant were the propa-gandist activities of which we shall speak further in

[86] *Dølen*, 1859, no. 20.
[87] *Supra*, pp. 58-9.
[88] Garborg, Hovden and Koht, *Ivar Aasen*, p. 128.

the next chapter. A third factor, and an important one, concerned the exigencies of Norwegian politics in the ' sixties and 'seventies—circumstances which made the *landsmaal* issue a part of a broad democratic advance seeking to " liberate " the people, socially, culturally and even linguistically. Naturally it drew much of its strength from peasant support, and involved a rehabilitation of peasant influence and peasant culture.

These circumstances will be clearer when it is recalled that the growing democratic movement impelled the bureaucracy to seek additional support in unionist tendencies. In turn, patriots, who, like the group which in 1867 launched *Vort Land,* were apprehensive lest some encroachment be permitted on Norway's political independence, made common cause with the liberals who championed the democratic advance, and all spoke with increasing respect of the peasant. Any desire to promote the use of the peasant speech for written purposes was apt to mean increased support for the *landsmaal* program. Chr. Bruun appealed even to the conservatives, arguing that there was no real antithesis between the *landsmaal* cause and Scandinavianism, since the latter had use for all of the three peoples, each in its " full power." [89]

The purposes of the *landsmaal* proponents were gradually formulated into a program of broad, though somewhat vaguely defined, scope. At the mid-century M. D. Gjessing had suggested how within a generation (his proposals then seemed wholly chimerical), the speech of the peasant might be introduced into wide public use in elementary and higher schools, in university life and in literature.[90] As Gjessing conceived it, the change would come rather unobtrusively through persuasion, aided by " the strength of fatherlandic

[89] Berner and Bruun, *op. cit.,* pp. 56-7; *cf.* also p. 13.
[90] *Morgbl.,* 1852, no. 329.

love and the inner power of the language." The townspeople, he assumed, need not be forced to give up their language. As the democratic advance in the later decades moved forward to notable victories, the *landsmaal* naturally shared in its progress, its aims becoming politically articulate when sponsored by Sverdrup's party of the Left and, more recently, by the Peasant's Party. Much of the *landsmaal* advance has thus been associated with methods more brusque than those envisaged by Gjessing. A series of legislative enactments have been passed since the Left Party won its major victory over the bureaucracy and consolidated the principle of representative government (1884). Almost immediately a law (1885) proclaimed the principle of equality between the *landsmaal* and the established medium, by that time somewhat modified, and soon to be known as the *riksmaal*. Supplementary legislation made this intention effective, first and foremost in the educational system. The *landsmaal* was admitted to the elementary schools (1892), to teacher's training schools (1890), and to secondary schools or gymnasia (1896). At the University, a professorship in Norwegian folk language and folk literature was established in 1886 (filled by Moltke Moe) and in 1899 there was provided a separate professorship in the *landsmaal* proper (occupied by Marius Hægstad, a leader in *landsmaal* circles). In the common schools the *landsmaal* is now the medium of instruction in more than one-fourth of the nation's school districts.[91] In ecclesiastical affairs, it was employed on occasion in the 'seventies by Kr. Janson and later by others. Chr. Bruun, long a pastor of an old well-established congregation in the heart of

[91] There is a fairly extensive exposition of the progress made by the *landsmaal* during later decades in the recent study by Fritz Meyen, "*Riksmålsforbundet*" *und sein Kampf gegen das Landsmål* (Oslo, 1932), pp. 20-40.

Christiania, caused something of a stir in 1901 when he preached a sermon in *landsmaal*.[92]   In the publishing field the new medium is employed by many flourishing newspapers and periodicals.   Likewise the *landsmaal* has been recognized as valid for purposes of legislation and administration, and it has become a medium of some importance in business, especially in the western part of the country.

[92] Although the service at the altar was performed in the usual medium. *Cf. Syn og Segn*, 1908, p. 250.

PART V

CHAPTER XXI

The Heritage

As we look in this closing chapter to the continuing influence of national romanticism, we must note especially that after 1870 the attitudes of that romanticism flourished most, not among academic folk but among certain " lay " elements. It is quite true that some of the scholars of this later period, like the historian J. E. Sars or the folklorist Moltke Moe, were fair toward, and even sympathetic with, the chief bearer of those attitudes, the *landsmaal* movement; nevertheless their scholarship was distinguished not for its romanticist but for its realist orientation. Likewise among the generation of scholars active today, those who have been deeply influenced by the *landsmaal* tradition work in a spirit more critical than romanticist. It follows that while the historians, the folklorists and the philologists were much to the fore in our analysis of the mid-century decades, their successors can be pretty much disregarded in this chapter where, it should be borne in mind, we are not surveying the further growth of Norwegian nationalism at large, but only treating suggestively those aspects of it which have prolonged the ideology of mid-century national romanticism.

The chief heir to that ideology was the *landsmaal* movement, whose cause was championed by an increasing number of individuals and a growing variety of organized groups. We shall notice a few of those individuals who were representative of the movement. These aggressive " laymen," at times of an evangelistic and inspirational turn, such as Chr. Bruun or Lars Eskeland, have frequently chosen their

347

" texts " from the premises and conclusions of mid-century romanticism. In the field of group effort we shall note several popular movements which have promoted the *landsmaal* and related causes, and in connection therewith have simultaneously perpetuated many of the national romanticist attitudes. The most conspicuous in this regard have been the growing folk high schools, the language societies or *Maallagene,* and the young peoples' societies or *Ungdomslagene.* We may treat briefly of each in turn.

The folk high-school movement had been founded in Denmark by N. F. S. Grundtvig, in what we may term a spirit of Christian romanticism. The movement sought inspiration not only in the Christian heritage but also in the life of early Germanic days, and it spoke of recovering the old " northern power." The religious and patriotic teachings of Grundtvig influenced some religious circles in Norway, but his suggestion in the late 'thirties, that a folk high school be founded in Norway was not carried out before the closing 'sixties when romanticism was on the wane. Then the first schools were founded at Sagatun (1864), at Sell (1867) and at Sogndal (1871).[1] Their primary purpose was to inspire and enlighten the peasant; they may be thought of as one manifestation of the broadening democratic movement, and from the outset they espoused the cause of the *landsmaal.*

We may understand more clearly the spirit of the folk high-school movement in Norway from the attitudes of some of its leaders. During the early decades the outstanding figure in the movement was Chr. Bruun who had founded the school at Sell. He would impart "enthusiasm" (including therein a feeling of patriotism) to the peasants of the neighborhood. Many of them " did not know they had

---

[1] R. Stauri, *Folkehøgskulen i Danmark, Norge, Sverige og Finland* (Chra., 1910), p. 102 *et seq.*

a fatherland," but Brunn would teach them to love it, and would stimulate a reverence for its memories.[2]   Sometimes he grew impatient with his fellow clergy, when he thought that they did too little to link patriotism with religion.   For decades, he wrote, they had remained outside of the national awakening and their lack of interest had made " our national feeling alien to God." [3]   Few of them ever held any services in their churches on the 17th of May, the national holiday, and Bruun insisted that the commemoration of St. Olaf's martyrdom on Olsok [4] was important for both religious and national reasons.   He urged the clergy to take a more active rôle in the national movement; love of country was, after all, a part of the ethical ideal of Christianity.[5]

One of the most notable figures in the folk high-school movement has been Lars Eskeland (1867-   ),[6] who combines, as did Bruun, a deep religiosity with a fervent patriotism.   Eskeland has been very much attached to the history and the culture of medieval Norway.   He has often dilated on the theme of Norway's medieval glory and greatness and suggested that therein the Norway of the present must seek renewal.   He has frequently called attention to the supreme importance of national memories; a people which forgets its memories, he has maintained, commits " suicide." [7]   Eskeland has spoken of the folk high-school movement in terms

[2] Chr. Bruun, *Folkelige Grundtanker* (Hamar, 1878), pp. *32 et seq.*, 135, 322.

[3] *For Kirke og Kultur,* vol. iv (1897), pp. 366, 445.

[4] *Ibid.,* vol. iv, pp. 310-11; regarding Olsok *cf. infra,* p. 355.

[5] *Ibid.,* vol. v (1898), pp. 580, 588-9.

[6] Eskeland was superintendent of the folk high school at Voss for a generation, until forced to resign largely for reasons growing out of his somewhat conspicuous post-war conversion to Roman Catholicism. He continues his restless activity as a publicist.

[7] *Dagbladet,* 1926, Sept. 27; *Høgskulebladet,* 1923, pp. 102, 217-8; *Den Frilyndte Ungdomen,* vol. vii, pp. 17, 22.

that are strongly reminiscent of romanticism and of the rôle which it assigned to the Idea,[8] just as he feels that Norway's schools generally must espouse the *landsmaal* and discontinue the " mortal sin " of using Danish as a medium of instruction.[9]

A second movement which has helped to perpetuate the romanticist heritage has been that of the language societies, *Maallagene,* whose prototypes were *Vestmannalaget* and *Det norske Samlaget.*[10] Seeking to promote the wider use of *landsmaal,* this movement has been organized throughout the country in a network of local units, drawing support mainly from rural circles. A new impetus was given to their efforts by the events of 1905, when the political tie with Sweden was severed. Thereafter, since political independence was complete it seemed less defensible than ever that Norway should remain dependent upon Denmark in cultural matters and it was felt that renewed efforts must be made to displace the established language. In the endeavor to concentrate their energies, the various locals federated in a national league (1906) called *Norigs Maallag* which since has maintained a spirited agitation in favor of the *landsmaal.*[11]

A third bearer of the romanticist heritage, and one rather closely associated with *Maallagene,* has been the movement of the young people's societies or *Ungdomslagene.* Their program is aggressively nationalist, a fact which may be partly due to the circumstances associated with their beginnings. They were, at first, part of a movement to establish local volunteer rifle leagues, but in the 'eighties, when the practical training was left to the leagues, the propagandist

[8] *Syn og Segn,* vol. xxvii, p. 290.

[9] *Ibid.,* vol. xxx, p. 52.

[10] *Supra,* pp. 332-3.

[11] For its earlier period see Edv. Os, *Norigs Maallag,* 1906-1914 (Oslo [sic], 1915).

activities were separated out, and thus began *Ungdomslagene* proper. It is no accident that these have kept up an interest in the question of national defence [12] although their primary task has been to inform, or more specifically, to create, " a strong, self-assertive national will, politically, economically, culturally." [13] In the definitely romantic outlook of *Ungdomslagene,* considerable importance is ascribed to the national will. This will, it is said, after centuries of foreign domination in Norway was left " sick "; it had developed the obsequious spirit of the slave.[14] *Ungdomslagene* have sought to promote a national will, ready to subordinate every party and class consideration and to assert Norway's rights in the grim competition of nations.[15] The broader aim of *Ungdomslagene*—to prepare the youth of the country for active participation in later public life—is similar to that of the folk high schools, but the two movements differ in approach; the high schools rely upon a training touched by religious influences, while *Ungdomslagene* build their programs directly upon sociological and national considerations.

The three agencies mentioned, *Maallagene, Ungdomslagene,* and the folk high-school movement, have frequently coördinated their activities and shared the energies of many of their workers.[16] The most conspicuous example is perhaps that of Eskeland, who in the manner of the revivalist for more than a generation has moved among these circles as a sort of itinerant lay preacher, giving numerous patriotic

[12] Edv. Os, *Haandbog i lagsarbeid for Ungdomslag og Maallag* (Chra., 1922), pp. 21, 120-1.

[13] *Ibid.*, p. 22.

[14] Edv. Os, " *Nationale høgmaal,*" *Syn og Segn,* 1918, p. 87.

[15] *Ibid.*, p. 87.

[16] Among the men who early took part in the folk high-school movement, such as, Herman Anker, Olaus Arvesen, Chr. Bruun, Jac. Sverdrup, Olaus Thommesen, O. K. Ødegaard and Marius Hægstad, several later were active in the work of *Maallagene* and *Ungdomslagene.*

" sermons " and pleading the cause of the broader *landsmaal* movement.

*   *   *   *   *

The romanticist heritage of the *landsmaal* movement was strengthened and augmented in the 'nineties by a change in the outlook of some littérateurs and intellectuals. The realism of the two previous decades partially gave way to a neo-romanticism, which, although it did not prevail with the same ubiquity as its predecessor of the mid-century, subscribed to many similar premises. There may be noted an arresting correlation, on the one hand, between the change from romanticism to realism and then to neo-romanticism, and on the other, the successive rise and fall and rise again of interest in the activities associated with the *landsmaal* movement. The correlation was not too close, since the popular aspects of this oscillating movement would lag behind changes in the outlook of the cultured, yet it was pronounced enough to be instructive; it shows that when romanticism dominated, the *landsmaal* (and nationalist) energies were quickened more than they were when realism prevailed. The impulse which in the 'sixties had been imparted to the *landsmaal* cause was sustained to the middle of the 'eighties, but after the democratic forces had won in principle both the political and the linguistic victories in 1884 and 1885, there was a subsidence of interest until it was renewed again in the second half of the 'nineties. The careers of the two venerable societies, *Vestmannalaget* and *Det norske Samlaget,* are interesting in this connection; both lagged in their activities in the second half of the 'eighties and developed a remarkable vitality in the later 'nineties. From 1882 to 1896 there was no annual meeting in *Vestmannalaget* [17] and from 1890 to 1894 there was a similar hiatus in the affairs of *Det norske Samla-*

[17] T. Hannaas, *Vestmannalaget*, p. 132; *Den 17de Mai*, 1896, no. 27.

get.[18]   But in the second half of the decade both societies
renewed their activities, this time it may be noted, with more
emphasis than ever upon the popular and the unique in
folk life.   In *Vestmannalaget*, for instance, competitions
were arranged in such peasant arts as fiddling (1896), folk
dancing (1898) and wood-carving (1907).[19]   The rural
talent for dramatics was encouraged, and the beautiful
boat cavalcades of the picturesque Hardanger fjordal
wedding processions were revived. ⌊In connection with the
renewal of interest in the 'nineties, it is to be noted that a
daily paper, *Den 17de Mai,* to represent the *landsmaal* cause,
was established at the capital in 1894, and in the same year
steps were taken to launch *Syn og Segn,* a general periodical
employing the *landsmaal.*

Under the impulses of the 'nineties, the *landsmaal* movement took on more definitely the nature of a popular renaissance.   From the outset, its propagandists, refusing to think
of the *landsmaal* agitation merely as a linguistic matter, had
regarded it as a broad social movement.   The *landsmaal*, in
their minds, was to be not only an aim in itself, but a means
to further all that might promote a richer national life.[20]
The movement contemplated a renewal of Norwegian energies in every line of endeavor; it was broad enough to
include " all good national work." [21]   It envisaged a " renaissance of the *norrøn* people," seeking not only to rehabilitate the language and the culture of the peasant, but also
to recover so far as possible Norway's distinguished medieval
position in politics and the arts.   It sought release from
centuries of " mortification," and from the tutelage of an
alien culture.   This renaissance, said a writer in the 'seven-

[18] *Den 17de Mai,* 1894, nos. 59, 66; *cf. Syn og Segn,* vol. xxiv, p. 136.
[19] T. Hannaas, *op. cit.,* pp. 135, 163.
[20] *Svein Urædd,* 1869, no. 41.
[21] *Syn og Segn,* 1918, pp. 99, 102.

ties, meant to develop its own leaders and its own culture under the inspiration of the *norrøn* example.[22]

The revival has achieved some conspicuous successes in the arts, particularly in literature, a field wherein it has completely belied Monrad's early prediction, that the literary output in *landsmaal,* like that in the Gascon in France, never would make up more than a small part of the country's literature.[23] Beginning with Aasen's feeble efforts in the 'fifties, the writings in *landsmaal,* since the 'nineties, have grown to the dimensions of a literature.[24] Some of the creative work has been of a high order and one of the *landsmaal* writers, Olav Duun, has been seriously mentioned for the Nobel prize in literature.

The *landsmaal* movement, like the romanticism of the mid-century, has been inclined to think of language and of nationality as intimately associated, and possessed of fixed and static qualities. Arne Garborg, the littérateur pronounced language the most adequate expression of nationality;[25] when the language lapsed it was hardly possible to maintain the nationality.[26] Chr. Bruun, denying that the coming of Christianity had noticeably affected the national character, insisted that the latter remained the same as in heathen antiquity,[27] and a similar imperishable quality was claimed

[22] F. Hansen, *Om Maalsagen og Politikken* (Chra., 1873), pp. 8, 11, 23. Fritz Hansen (1841-1911) taught for a time at the Sagatun and Vonheim folk high schools.

[23] *Morgbl.,* 1858, no. 287.

[24] Jørgen Bukdahl, a Danish literary critic, has treated it in his *Norsk National Kunst* (1924) and *Det Skjulte Norge* (1926). There is a brief survey in English of this literary tradition by Rolf Thesen, "New Norwegian Literature," *The American-Scandinavian Review,* vol. xix, pp. 403-11.

[25] *Aftbl.,* 1876, no. 11; A. Garborg, *Den ny-norske Sprog- og Nationalitets-bevægelse* (Chra., 1877), p. 104 *et seq.*

[26] A. Garborg, *op. cit.,* p. 128.

[27] Chr. Bruun, *Folkelige Grundtanker,* p. 49; *cf.* also p. 297.

also for the language. The Norwegian tongue, says Os, lives on today just as pure in forms, constructions, and vocabulary, as ever under the ancient dynasty of Harold Fairhair.[28]

In connection with the tendency noted above to seek inspiration from Norway's glorious medieval period, we may consider the agitation for establishing the festival of Olsok (St. Olaf's Day, July 29th) as a day of national celebration. Landsmaal leaders have promoted it, including Kr. Bing [29] of the Bergen *Fjellmannalag* ("Mountaineers' Society"), and one local after another among *Maallagene* and *Ungdomslagene,* has made it a point to observe Olsok as a holiday. Since the World War, on a number of anniversary days there have been pilgrimages, partly religious and partly national in intent,[30] to the little church at Stiklestad, the scene of Olaf's last battle. In 1930, because of special circumstances, the entire nation capitulated momentarily and celebrated this day with unusual unanimity, when the 900th anniversary of the event which Olsok commemorates coincided with the dedication of the restored nave of the Trondhjem Cathedral.

In the 'nineties, an additional impetus—part of it academic but much of it national—was imparted to the interest in the historical remains and ruins which recalled the national greatness of medieval days. The most conspicuous manifestation was the restoration work expended on the Trondhjem Cathedral (which was of course by no means an exclusive *landsmaal* effort), but there were other undertakings as well. On the initiative of *Vestmannalaget* at Bergen, steps were taken to erect on the ruins of *Haakonshallen,* a dignified restoration of the stately royal hall of

[28] Edv. Os, *Norigs Maallag*, p. 74.
[29] *Cf.* Kr. Bing, *Olsoktradition* (Bergen, 1919).
[30] *Cf. St. Olaf*, 1917, p. 249; 1918, pp. 250-52.

the fourteenth century.[31]   In conjunction with a grand
assemblage of *Maallag* representatives from the entire
country, the completed structure was dedicated in the
summer of 1898.   During this season *norrøn* nationalism
was aroused to high pitch in Bergen; it was at this time that
the wider celebration of Olsok was advocated.   Meanwhile
the interest in restoration work persists among *landsmaal*
circles; to take only one example, *Rogalands Ungdomslag*
(" The Rogaland Young People's Society ") in recent years
has sought to stimulate interest in restoring the important
medieval monastic foundation at Utstein in the Stavanger-
fjord region.

*   *   *   *   *

The antipathy toward Denmark and the Danes fostered
by national romanticism, was retained and intensified in the
landsmaal movement.   In tones often bitter its spokesmen
criticize Denmark's conduct during the period of the Dano-
Norwegian union, and they heartily resent the fact that a
Danish cultural tradition has ever attained a foothold in Norway.   They have sometimes imputed to Denmark a deliberate intention to efface the flattering memories of Norway's
national greatness; how otherwise explain the way in which,
for instance, the graves of Norwegian royalty have been
despoiled,[32] or the treasures of the national archives transferred to Copenhagen (of course a matter of concern also to
other than *landsmaal* circles).[33]   Early in the period of union,
Denmark had sold or failed to redeem mortgages on some
of Norway's possessions in the west [34] (the Hebrides and

[31] Ready in 1895 at a cost of *kr.* 241,339.   T. Hannaas, *Vestmannalaget,*
p. 75.

[32] A. Haavoll, *Djupe Merke av danske vaapn svida* (Oslo, 1925), pp.
3-4.

[33] *Cf. supra,* pp. 155-6.

[34] *Den Frilyndte Ungdomen,* vol. vii, p. 20.

the Orkney Islands). It has been charged that Denmark
for centuries tried to suppress the Norwegian nationality,
and as a means to that end sought to curb or " thin out "
the Norwegian language; [35] she succeeded to the extent that
it was now difficult for Norwegians to speak freely with
their " kinsmen " on Iceland and the Faroes.[36] To an
alarming extent, Denmark with her bawdy literature (*grise-
literatur*) had corrupted the Norwegian reading taste; in
the post-war period, it was said, there was being distributed
in Norway more than three times as much Danish as native
reading material, and Norwegians were spending annually
(1923) for Danish reading matter, the sum of nine
million *kroner*. It was suggested that perhaps a tariff
would keep out some of this trash, so harmful alike " to
Norwegian morals, Norwegian culture, and Norwegian folk
character." [37]

Landsmaal circles have maintained that Denmark be-
haved very disgracefully when the two nations separated,
and these circles have no intention of ever forgetting the
" rape " of 1814. Vehemently they maintain that Denmark
in the Treaty of Kiel " stole " [38] from the crown of Norway—from " the most distinguished sea-faring folk on
earth—" [39] the colonial possessions of Iceland, Greenland and
the Faroes; and they use the word " stole " deliberately, insisting that these possessions always belonged to the Kingdom of Norway, and that Danish rulers had never claimed
title to them save in their rôle as Norwegian kings.[40] The

---

[35] Edv. Os, *Norigs Maallag*, p. 74.

[36] Haavoll, *op. cit.*, p. 7.   [37] *Ibid.*, pp. 13-15.

[38] *Cf. Den Frilyndte Ungdomen*, vol. vii, p. 20; *Høgskulebladet*, 1923,
p. 103; I. Handagard, *Grønland og Norge* (Chra., 1922), pp. 6-7.

[39] A phrase used by Eskeland in a lecture before *Grønlandslaget*, Feb.
21, 1927, which the author attended.

[40] Ræstad, *Grønland og Spitzbergen* (Chra., 1923), p. 9; I. Handagard,
op. cit., p. 60.

violence committed in 1814 remains " an open sore," [41] and
Norway, it is said, can never recognize that treaty.[42] The
situation would yet be bearable if Denmark after the separation had faced her new responsibilities properly, but her
colonial administration had been a failure. The Icelanders,
who lived " happy and prosperous " until 1814, had since
been dissatisfied with the attempts to remold them as
Danes,[43] and the experience of the people of the West
Indies, who now were better off under the rule of America,[44]
likewise disclosed the shortcomings of Danish rule. Denmark did no better in Greenland, for the Eskimoes were
quite " dissatisfied "; their interests were improperly looked
after, and Denmark might at any time decide to " sell " them
as she did the Norwegians in 1814 or the West Indian
natives in 1917.[45]

*   *   *   *   *

Certain aspects of Denmark's Greenland policy in the
post-war period have aroused indignant protests in Norway,
especially among the *landsmaal* circles. That policy has
occasioned a dispute between the governments of Norway
and Denmark, which now has been adjudicated by the
World Court. Here we may treat but briefly of the extent
to which the Norwegian point of view was complicated by the
attitudes of the *landsmaal* movement.[46] The dispute con-

[41] *Den Frilyndte Ungdomen*, vol. vii, p. 20; *Høgskulebladet*, 1923, p.
103; *cf.* a speech by I. Handagard at Sandefjord before *Norigs Maallag*
as reported by *Tidens Tegn*, 1927, Jan. 7.

[42] I. Handagard, *op. cit.*, p. 18; I. Handagard, *Skal Norge nu godkjende
Kielertraktaten?* (Porsgrunn, 1921), pp. 5, 12.

[43] *Den 17de Mai*, 1896, no. 45.

[44] I. Handagard, *Grønland og Fremmede Magter* (Chra., 1922), p. 7.

[45] E. Anker, *Grønland for Norge* (Chra., 1923), pp. 23, 31.

[46] The dispute has produced a voluminous literature. A bibliography
of titles from both sides of the controversy, up-to-date at the time of
its appearance, may be consulted in Gustav Smedal, *Opgjør og Forståelse
med Danmark* (Oslo, 1928), pp. 143-45.

cerned East Greenland, a coastal area north of Scoresby
Sound, which until recently was a No Man's Land but
gradually has come to have importance for Norwegian sea-
faring and whaling interests. The latter were naturally
indignant at an administrative order from Copenhagen in
1921 extending Danish sovereignty over this region; but no
less aroused were the *landsmaal* circles. A lively agitation
developed and a number of reasons were cited why Norway
should have been consulted prior to such a "high-handed
act." She, after all, had discovered the island [47] and she
had colonized it, not once or twice but three times; [48] she
had Christianized it and ruled it for centuries.[49] Her claims
were both legal and historic.[50] She must object to Danish
encroachment, because of certain moral obligations. She
owed this to future generations of her own people, whom she
had no right to exclude from a land which the Norwegians
had discovered and used for a thousand years.[51] She also
had duties to the poor Eskimoes, whose desertion at this
time would involve a sanction of their " imprisonment." [52]

In one phase of its Danophobia, the *landsmaal* movement, imbued with national idealism, has complained in a
tone of injured innocence that Denmark has played her rôle
for reasons of stark self-interest. She has pursued, it is
said, a selfish policy in the north, an " ice cold Arctic Sea

[47] I. Handagard, *Skal Norge nu godkjende Kielertraktaten?*, pp. 8-9.

[48] E. Anker, *Grønland for Norge*, pp. 8, 25-26. Ella Anker's father
was Herman Anker, who, together with Olaus Arvesen, both disciples
of Ole Vig, in 1864 opened the country's first folk high school at Sagatun.

[49] *Utenrikspolitikken*, 1923, p. 113; *Den Frilyndte Ungdomen*, vol. iii,
pp. 30-31.

[50] Handagard, *Grønland og Fremmede Magter*, pp. 13-14; *Fram*, 1924,
no. 3.

[51] E. Anker, *op. cit.*, p. 30.

[52] *Ibid.*, p. 31; *cf.* I. Handagard, *Folkesuværæniteten og Grønlands-
spørgsmaalet* (Porsgrunn, 1922), p. 8.

policy." She has no real concern for the " dissatisfied " Eskimoes; she really wants East Greenland for herself! [53] Contrast this with the altruistic motives of Norway, or rather, with the motives of the *landsmaal* movement, whose leaders plead with Denmark that she admit her wrongs in the north Atlantic and right them [54] and who explain that their concern for the peoples under Danish rule is not nationalistic, but internationalist; they profess to be interested in peace and in the rights of small peoples. [55]   In the case of the Eskimoes, for instance, the Norwegians might, if Denmark would but relax the rigor of her regime, come to their aid and coöperate with them " naturally." [56]

*   *   *   *   *

The eagerness to block Danish encroachment in East Greenland was but one phase of a larger program, according to which there is contemplated a rearrangement of political connections in the north Atlantic, a process of liquidation which will make the Norwegian Sea once again a *norrøn mare nostrum*.   The *landsmaal* movement looks forward to a partial " restoration " in some form, of the medieval Norse empire in the seas to the west, and it cannot forget that once upon a time there lived folk of *norrøn* race along almost every strand of those waters, although its leaders have to admit, that on some shores the descendants of this race have gone irrevocably over to other cultures; the speech of the English, for instance, has quite supplanted the older native tongue in the Orkney and Shetland Islands, although the Shetlanders know that they are northerners, and that right-

[53] I. Handagard, *Skal Norge nu godkjende Kielertraktaten?*, p. 12; E. Anker, *op. cit.*, p. 5.

[54] I. Handagard, *Grønland og Norge*, p. 14.

[55] *Ibid.*, p. 44.

[56] E. Anker, *op. cit.*, p. 23.

fully they ought to belong to Norway.[57]   More obviously, the earlier Norse identity has persisted down to the present in the Faroes and in Iceland.

In line with this outlook, there has developed a lively interest in *norrøn* coöperation (*norrønt samarbeide*) between Norway and the " lost " members of the *norrøn* stock, the peoples of the Faroes and Iceland.   These three, it is announced, are called to work together to preserve *norrøn* culture.   The agitation which looks to something like a *norrøn* renaissance has spread beyond the parental country to Iceland and the Faroes.   [A restless and untiring figure in promoting this *norrøn* irredentism has been Lars Eskeland.] As early as 1898 he had awakened *Vestmannalaget* to an active concern [58] for *norrøn* coöperation.   Ten years later when a hundred patriotic Faroese came to Bergen to pay their respects to *Norigs Ungdomslag,* Eskeland had a prominent rôle among the hosts,[59] and he was again a leading member when *Vestmannalaget* in 1911 arranged to repay the compliment by sending a delegation to the Faroe Islands.[60]   At gatherings of this character the *norrøn* race has been toasted over and over again; exhibits and contests have been arranged to display *norrøn* talent, and pilgrimages have been made to ruins and remains of one-time *norrøn* greatness.   Since the World War those interested in *norrøn* coöperation have begun to think in terms of permanent organization.   In 1924 a society called *Norrønalaget* was founded,[61] and just previously it had been proposed that a

[57] It was said recently, that in the Shetlands, Norwegian was spoken until eighty years ago. " *Lars Eskeland um ' norrønt samarbeid,'* " *Dagbladet,* 1926, Sept. 27.

[58] T. Hannaas, *Vestmannalaget,* p. 186 *et seq.*

[59] *Ibid.,* pp. 193-94; *Bergens Tidende,* 1908, nos. 178, 179, 181.

[60] *Cf. Bergens Tidende,* 1911, July 6.

[61] *Tidens Tegn,* 1924, Sept. 12.

fund be raised to promote the cultural coöperation of the three peoples.[62]   Eskeland suggested a livelier exchange of literary matter and thought that Bergen might become the seat of a *norrøn* university.[63]   The *norrøn* circles among the three peoples have found a common interest in the joint observance of Olsok as a national (or *norrøn*) holiday.[64]

The coöperation which is preached among the three *norrøn* peoples is usually intended to be cultural, but at times it takes on a political hue.   Both in the Faroe Islands and in Iceland, well entrenched political parties, championing programs looking toward autonomy or even independence, have on occasion given trouble to the Danish authorities.   The *norrøn* groups in Norway naturally sympathize with the political aims of these groups, and they find it difficult to view such troubles of Iceland and the Faroes as purely internal.[65]   Eskeland, it is true, has stated that the Norwegians have no desire to separate Iceland and the Faroe Islands from Denmark [66] but seek only to assure to both peoples a full right to administer their own affairs,[67] yet others wonder whether Norway " unfortunately " has not remained too passive in the issue between Denmark and the Faroese.[68]   There are deep political implications in the thought that among the three peoples around the Norwegian Sea, " Fate " may someday consummate a union.[69]

*   *   *   *   *

[62] By Ivar Tveit, *ibid.*, 1924, June 25.

[63] *Høgskulebladet*, 1923, pp. 104-5.   The income from the Snorre Fund which was donated by Norway to Iceland in 1930 on the occasion of the millennial festival, is used to support Icelandic students in Norway.

[64] Kr. Østberg, *Det Færøiske Folk* (Chra., 1923), p. 11; *Tidens Tegn*, 1923, Aug. 11; *Morgbl.*, 1926, Aug. 4.

[65] Cf. Ræstad, *Grønland og Spitzbergen*, p. 19.

[66] *Den Frilyndte Ungdomen*, vol. vii, p. 26.

[67] L. Eskeland, " *Island og Færoyane og Grønland,*" *Høgskulebladet*, 1923, p. 103; *cf.* also Handagard, *Grønland og Norge*, p. 13.

[68] *Fram*, 1924, pp. 4-5.   [69] *Tidens Tegn*, 1923, Sept. 13.

Of late the *landsmaal* movement has received no little support in its hope of a closer union among the *norrøn* peoples, from another quarter in Norwegian public life, that is, from the fishing, hunting, sealing and whaling interests. These interests have stimulated a newer imperialist impulse whose background is quite definitely urban, commercial and industrial. Their point of view has been ably championed by Albert Balchen (1874-   ), for instance, as editor of the financial weekly, *Tidsskrift for Bank og Finansvæsen* ("Review of Banking and Finance"), while the writings of those who dream of a new *norrøn* empire are frequently welcomed in the columns of the modern daily at the capital, *Tidens Tegn* ("Sign of the Time").[70] Materialistic whaling imperialism and romantic *norrøn* irredentism spring from diverse orientations, but they agree in some of their most important aims for a partial restoration of the *norrøn* influence in the north Atlantic.

The arguments of the imperialists, often concurred in by *landsmaal* leaders, naturally rest less on historical than on material considerations.[71] It is pointed out that everywhere about the scattered littoral of the Norwegian Sea, the *norrøn* race has rights of preëmption.[72] At present, Norway, the foremost of *norrøn* peoples is excluded from the major areas of Iceland and the Faroes and from a good share of Greenland. Is she then, it is asked, ultimately to be kept from every shore on the Norwegian Sea?[73] And that by Danes? In the East Greenland issue, large Norwegian interests were at stake, interests, it was pointed out, which affected all classes.

[70] Edited by Rolf Thommesen, son of Olaus Thommesen, who once was briefly connected with the folk high-school movement.

[71] Ræstad, *Grønland og Spitsbergen, passim;* I. Handagard, *Grønland og Norge*, p. 9.

[72] Illustrated graphically on a map of the north Atlantic in *Tidens Tegn*, 1924, Jan. 14.

[73] I. Handagard, *Folkesuveræniteten og Grønlands-spørgsmaalet*, p. 6.

Norway must have her own possessions across the sea if she is not to remain forever merely a carrying nation; she once had such possessions and they helped to rank her as a great dominion and a great power.[74]   Already the process of Norway's "reunion" with the Arctic Sea is begun.[75]   That it may involve force, has been suggested by the writer who has urged the Norwegian government to take advantage of the twenty-year period of the Greenland Treaty and build a Norwegian fleet which by 1944 may be large enough to make the Danes hesitate about provoking a conflict.[76]

Both *landsmaal* and imperialist groups have exerted their influence on the course of government policy.   It was in line with their programs that Norway in 1920 extended its sovereignty over Spitzbergen,[77] that No Man's Land, which even in a Norwegian school text of the later nineteenth century was regarded as Russian![78]   The same groups have strengthened the Norwegian government in its formal protests against Denmark's expansion into East Greenland, and when *landsmaal* circles felt that a *modus vivendi,* in the form of a twenty-year treaty, conceded too much to Denmark, they began a vigorous agitation throughout the country. While the treaty was pending in the *Storting,* speakers warned of this rising sentiment,[79] and it is interesting to note that in the final vote of 128 to 8 no less than five of the minority were farmers (*gaard-brukere*), and hence from the social group which has been most effected by the *landsmaal* agitation.   There was a similar opportunity to complicate

[74] *Ibid.,* pp. 5-6.

[75] *Cf. Tidsskrift for Bank og Finansvæsen,* 1924, p. 45.

[76] *Ibid.,* 1924, pp. 18, 34, 60.

[77] An act of duty [!] according to Werner Werenskjold, *Fra Spitzbergen* (Chra., 1923), p. 88.

[78] A. Hoel, "*Trues våre arktiske interesser?*" *Samtiden,* 1931, p. 243.

[79] *Stort. Forh.,* 1924, vol. vii, p. 700.

foreign policy early in 1927 when the *Storting* debated ratifi-
cation of the proposed mutual arbitration treaties among
the Scandinavian states. Only the Dano-Norwegian treaty
encountered any particular opposition and a good proportion
of this was inspired by *landsmaal* circles. Dreaming of
some restoration of the *norrøn* dominion, and resentful over
Denmark's possession of the national archives, these partisans demanded that before any arbitration treaty was
adopted there should be "a full adjustment " with Denmark.

The Greenland Treaty of 1924 was expected to run for
twenty years, but in the summer of 1931 the question of
sovereignty over East Greenland became a vital issue when
the Norwegian government avowed the act of some of its
citizens in raising the Norwegian flag and proclaiming Norway's sovereignty. Perhaps it was more than a coincidence
that this *fait accompli* in East Greenland was executed and
sustained but a few weeks after the Kolstad ministry took
power, the first time that full cabinet responsibility had de-
volved upon the party best oriented in *landsmaal* ideology,
that is, on the Peasants' Party. While the government's
decision to avow the act stirred the patriotism of the whole
nation, it naturally provoked the wildest rejoicing among
those circles which so long have dreamt of reviving the
norrøn dominion.

* * * * *

The course of Norwegian public life today is disturbed
by the presence of two rival national traditions whose developments have been conditioned by the old antagonism in
Norwegian society between the peasant and the upper classes.
The two might be spoken of as sub-nationalities, although we
shall refer to them as the rural and the urban traditions.
Both have been unevenly stimulated by historical movements
of the last century and a half. The period of the enlightenment, and the Rousseauean infatuation for the countryside,

was of more immediate importance to the urban tradition. Both trends were affected by developments of the revolutionary and Napoleonic era; in addition the peasant tradition received its first effective impulses from the lay religious movement of Haugianism which, rather incidentally, helped to disseminate the idea of national unity.[80] The period of national romanticism was significant for both traditions but proved to be of outstanding importance for that of the peasant. We have seen how, in that period, the cultured classes lavished their attention upon the peasant and through their investigations in history, folklore, and philology, worked out a characteristic ideology, so much of which was absorbed by the *landsmaal* movement. Investigators of the mid-century drew a charmed circle around the peasant's "backward" speech and culture in order to identify these more exclusively with nationality, and their efforts did something to block the leveling current of cosmopolitanism, which by the mid-century was lessening the differences between the mental patterns of urban dwellers and country folk. National romanticism, by identifying nationality so closely with the peasant and his culture, sharpened the chronic antagonism between town and country. Its premises fortified the attitude that the townsman and his tradition did not "belong," that the country harbored two languages and two cultures and possibly nurtured also two nationalities. National romanticism helped to stereotype the rural tradition in the *landsmaal* movement, and in provoking a reaction in the urban tradition, imparted to the latter a measure of cohesion, which is best identified in the *riksmaal* movement.

The modern line of cleavage between the *landsmaal* and *riksmaal* traditions is somewhat different from that which prevailed earlier between the peasant and the official and

[80] Koht, *Norsk Bondereising* (Oslo, 1926), pp. 335-54.

burgher. While the older alignment was pronouncedly social and economic, the newer cleavage has also a geographic aspect. Due in part to the somewhat restricted character of Aasen's *landsmaal* which favored the dialects of the west, the *landsmaal* tradition has consequently become most firmly established in the west. The eastern countryside, thus left to itself, has shown some disposition to follow the urban tradition. Bergen has been the leading center of *landsmaal*, or *norrøn* Norway,[81] as Oslo is that of *riksmaal* Norway, though it must never be forgotten that each tradition has partisans throughout the country.

The sense of a duality in national traditions is enhanced by the talk of a "hidden" Norway and by the attempt to point out differences in folk psychology between the eastern and the western part of the country,[82] and, likewise, by the desire to show that these spring from racial differences; it is suggested that an earlier brunette race lived in the west and that the blond Scandinavian after its arrival remained most pure in the eastern regions.[83]

The two traditions cherish in common many phases of the nation's history while on others they sometimes differ widely. Both rejoice over the rehabilitation of national independence in 1814 and its complete establishment in 1905. Likewise, there is something to inspire both in the medieval period of Norway's greatness,[84] but here they differ very

[81] *Cf.* E. Mohn, *Om Maalsagen og det Bergenske Maalstræv*, pp. 3, 24; *Morgbl.*, 1868, no. 82.

[82] *Cf.* the characterizations of J. Bukdahl, *Det Skjulte Norge*, p. 36 *et seq.*

[83] Concluding therefrom (somewhat unwarrantably it would seem) that for this reason Norwegians of the west have been reactionary, pietistic, prohibitionists (and *landsmaal* enthusiasts) while their eastern compatriots have been "progressive". A. M. Hansen, *Oldtidens Nord-mænd* (Chra., 1907), p. 129 *et seq.*

[84] Though on occasion the urban tradition can be quite critical. *Cf. Samtiden*, vol. xli, pp. 522-3.

much in emphasis, for the *landsmaal* movement makes that period the object of its special veneration.   It looks to national rejuvenation in the spirit of the generations that composed *Hávamál* and *Voluspá,* and fashioned the graceful nautical lines of the Gokstad and Oseberg ships or made Norway great and powerful in the glamorous day of Haakon Haakonssøn.   But in no matter do the two traditions differ so sharply as in their judgments on the centuries of the union with Denmark.   That union presents to the *landsmaal* heritage only disagreeable memories to be forgotten as completely as possible, while the *riksmaal* tradition finds that its deepest cultural roots go back chiefly to that period, which it considers not a day of decline but one of slow growth and preparation for independence.   The urban tradition has sought to rehabilitate this period, beginning (after the early efforts of Welhaven's circle) with the work of Birkeland and Aschehoug, while Sars, devoting a long career to the same purpose has made the Danish centuries mean something to the rural tradition.   With reference to the events in 1814 and thereafter, the two also differ in emphasis, in that the *landsmaal* tradition has given much attention to Denmark's " fraud " when she deceived Sweden into letting her keep Norway's colonial possessions.

The two traditions clash on a number of domestic issues. First and foremost, of course, they are at odds on the scope to be allowed to the *landsmaal* in various fields of public life. There are a dozen fronts on which this question has led to major engagements between the two opposing forces.   The extremists on one side will be content only with a linguistic unity which " restores " the *landsmaal* as " the single language of the realm." [85]   Those of the urban tradition feel that the entrenched position of the established medium justifies its continued hegemony.   The program to give Norway her

[85] Edv. Os, *Norigs Maallag,* p. 252.

own literary medium has amply justified Wergeland's early apprehension that it might cost a literary civil war.[86]   Sometimes the disagreement carries over to issues that seem a bit remote, as when a desire to render innocuous the incipient Lappish nationalist movement centering at Karasjok [87] leads to disagreement over the medium that should be taught to the minorities in the Arctic north.[88]

Within the last decade the two traditions have, on several occasions, clashed sharply on the issue of renaming towns and localities.   The *landsmaal* tradition wants to rehabilitate names now antiquated in order to associate modern Norway more closely with that of the *norrøn* period; in this matter too, it owes something to the heritage from mid-century scholarship.   The name of the capital city, Christiania, was once referred to by P. A. Munch as " a self-devised and half-barbaric name ";[89] Aasen agreed with the characterization, and went on to discuss the feasibility of a change.[90]   The *landsmaal* champions have found the Danish associations clinging to the word Christiania a standing challenge, and after a vigorous agitation, the name was discarded in 1924 for the medieval term Oslo.   It is to be noted that the change was heartily opposed by a substantial portion of the city's inhabitants.   More recently a similar agitation has centered about the word Trondhjem, and in 1930, this city was given its medieval name Nidaros.   But popular resentment in the city itself and in *riksmaal* circles generally, forced a suspension of this usage and the outcome

[86] H. Wergeland, *Digterværker og Prosaiske Skrifter*, vol. v, p. 259, or the same passage in his *Udv. Shr.*, vol. i, p. 312.

[87] Hidle and Otterbach, *Fornorskningen i Finmarken* (Chra., 1917) ; *Norsk Kirkeblad*, 1918, p. 39 *et seq.*

[88] O. Kyllingstad, " *Fornorskningen i Finmarken*," *Fraa Folkehøgskulen*, vol. vi, pp. 69-76.

[89] Munch, *NFH.*, vol. vi, p. 646.

[90] Aasen, *Skr. i Saml.*, vol. ii, pp. 204-6.

was a compromise in the word, Trondheim. Many citizens of Bergen, the country's second largest city, have been offended by a public use of the older designation, Bjørgvin. This tendency to change names has been manifest also in some lesser places; Fredrikshald, for instance, is once more Halden. Likewise, the newly acquired archipelago of Spitzbergen is now called officially by the vaguely identified saga designation, Svalbard, the " cold shore." In 1918 the designation of the provinces in Norway was changed from the Danish " *amt* " to the Old Norse " *fylke.*"

What helps to make agreement between the two traditions so difficult, is the fact that they differ widely on such fundamentals as the proper basis for nationality and a national culture. The *landsmaal* tradition continues to capitalize the results of mid-century scholarship which concluded that the peasant's culture and nationality were entirely autochthonous, preserving an unbroken lineage from remote saga days, and remaining uncontaminated by centuries of contact with foreign rule. Throughout it all, the folk spirit, true to the principles of its own being, kept the essence of its language, and sought its own unique expression in folk tale and folk dance, in balladry and song, in the wood-carver's art and in rural architecture. Near the close of the century it was stated that only the peasant had what really might be called a culture.[91] At any rate the idea that his is the only true national culture has become part of the outlook of the *landsmaal* movement, and it takes on added emphasis when there are references to the " chasm " in the Norwegian social order [92] as well as when a foreign critic such as Jørgen Bukdahl writes of the " hidden " Norway and of the indigenous creative life, which long was repressed by Danish culture.[93]

[91] *Den 17de Mai,* 1896, no. 27.

[92] *Cf. Samtiden,* vol. xi, pp. 152-4.

[93] J. Bukdahl, *Det skjulte Norge,* pp. 22-4.

The *riksmaal* or urban tradition, condemned by its opponents as alien, philistine, and Danish, has sought to defend itself as best it could.[94]   Being more urban, the tradition has naturally been more responsive to foreign influences, but it claims to be as Norwegian as its opponent.   Sars, among the earlier apologists, " denied the sharp cleavage and waved aside as " pure folly " all talk about two nationalities in the country.[95]   It has been observed that racially the urban element too, is mainly of peasant stock,[96] and it is denied that its language is foreign.   There is some tendency to consider the linguistic rivalry to be, not between two independent languages, but rather between two subordinate forms or two dialects.[97]   On occasion, the members of the urban tradition have reminded their opponents that even the *landsmaal* tradition is not simon-pure, but owes something to Danish influences.   It is pointed out that one of the agencies most active in support of the *landsmaal* tradition, that is, the folk high-school movement, had strong Grundtvigian antecedents, while the great literary champion of the *landsmaal,* Arne Garborg, was seriously affected by Kierkegaard.[98]   In a bitter tone, Charles Kent has pronounced the old peasant culture moribund and not worth saving.[99]   The counter offensive of the urban tradition is actively carried on through the organizations, *Riksmaalsforbundet* (" The *Riksmaal* Alliance ") and *Riksmaalsvern* (" Defense of *Riksmaal* ").

*   *   *   *   *

The legacy from the national romanticism of the mid-

[94] Sometimes in a manner quite vitriolic. *Cf.* G. Reiss-Andersen, " *Ormen lange og Målormen,*" *Samtiden,* vol. xli, pp. 502-23.

[95] *Samtiden,* vol. xii, pp. 104-5.

[96] *Morgbl.,* 1926, no. 233, p. 6.

[97] *Samtiden,* vol. xviii, p. 464.

[98] *Nordens Aarbok,* 1924, p. 140.

[99] *Vor Verden,* 1927, p. 154.

century thus remains to complicate present-day Norwegian affairs in several important respects.   There is no immediate prospect of eliminating the language controversy; each side naturally thinks that its tradition embodies what is most distinctive for the nationality, and feels that concessions should be made by the opposing side.   There are, of course, those who expect the two to carry on side by side in a spirit more and more conciliatory, and who look to an ultimate peaceful rapprochement—[100] an ideal which very likely may be furthered by the ambitious project (still in its early stages) for a scholarly dictionary of the words used by Norwegian writers in the last four centuries.   But even though the linguistic issue be resolved, there are other elements in the *landsmaal* heritage that may long prove disturbing.   In the realm of foreign affairs, for instance, the memories of national wrongs, whether fancied or real, may prove tenacious; they will have something on which to feed so long as Denmark holds any part of the old *norrøn* empire. The adverse decision (April, 1933) by the World Court in the East Greenland case may conceivably intensify the anti-Danish agitation in *landsmaal* circles.   Members of these circles will watch with interest the movements for autonomy in the Faroe Islands and they will await with some apprehension the reconsideration of Iceland's relation to Denmark and to the Danish crown in 1940.   The heritage of national romanticism has enriched not only Norwegian nationalism but Norway's cultural life in general but it has also been a disturbing factor, and the prospect is that it will continue to complicate certain aspects of Norwegian public life for some time to come.

[100] *Cf.* for example, *Samtiden*, vol. xii, pp. 116-17; vol. xx, pp. 25-26; vol. xxi, pp. 12-13; *Syn og Segn*, vol. xxiv, p. 144. Certain regulations in 1917 regarding orthography helped to emphasize what the two mediums had in common.

BIBLIOGRAPHY OF WORKS CITED

PRIMARY WORKS

Aall, Jacob, *Erindringer som Bidrag til Norges Historie fra 1800 til 1815.* 3 vols. Chra., 1844-45.

Aall, Jacob (editor), *Snorre Sturlesons norske Kongers Sagaer.* 3 vols. Chra., 1838-39.

Aasen, Ivar, *En liden Læsebog i Gammel Norsk.* Chra., 1854.

——, *Norsk Grammatik.* Chra., 1864.

——, *Norsk Ordbog med dansk Forklaring.* Chra., 1873.

——, *Det norske Folkesprogs Grammatik.* Chra., 1848.

——, *Norske Ordsprog, samlede og Ordnede.* Chra., 1856.

——, *Ordbog over det norske Folkesprog.* Chra., 1850.

——, *Prøver af Landsmaalet i Norge.* Chra., 1853.

——, *Reise-Erindringer og Reise-Indberetninger 1842-1847.* Edited by Halvdan Koht. Trondhjem, 1917.

——, *Skrifter i Samling.* 3 vols. Christiania and Copenhagen, 1912.

Allen, C. F., *Breve og Aktstykker til Oplysning af Christiern den Andens og Frederik den Førstes Historie.* Copenhagen, 1854.

Anker, Ella, *Grønland for Norge.* Chra., 1923.

Arentz, Hans, *Grundtegning af den fornuftige norske Patriotisme.* Bergen, 1787.

Árni Magnússons levned og skrifter. Udgivet af kommissionen for det Arnamagnæanske Legat. 2 vols. Copenhagen, 1930.

Asbjørnsen, Peter Chr., *Norske Huldre-eventyr og Folkesagn.* I-II *Samling.* Chra., 1845-48. Second edition, 1859-66. Third edition, 1870.

Asbjørnsen, Peter Chr, *Norske Folke-eventyr. Ny Samling.* Chra., 1871. Second edition. Copenhagen, 1876.

Asbjørnsen, Peter Chr. and Jørgen Moe, *Norske Folke-eventyr.* Chra., 1841-44. Second edition, with an introduction by Jørgen Moe and a long appendix of notes and variants. Chra., 1851-52. Third edition, 186[5-] 6. Fourth edition, 186[7-] 8. Fifth edition, 187[3-] 4. Note: The folk and fairy tales have been republished a number of times since the authors died, most recently as *Folke- og Huldre-eventyr. Norske kunstneres Billedutgave.* 2 vols. Oslo, 1932.

Aschehoug, T. H., *Statsforfatningen i Norge og Danmark indtil 1814.* Chra., 1866.

[Baden, Jacob], *Forsøg til en moralsk og politisk Catechismus for Bønderbørn.* Copenhagen, 1766.

373

Berner, H. E. and Chr. Bruun, *To Foredrag om Maalsagen.* Chra., 1866.

Berner, H. E. and J. E. Sars, *To Foredrag om Skandinavisme og Norskhed.* Chra., 1867.

Birckner, M. G., *Samlede Skrifter.* 4 vols. Copenhagen, 1798-1800.

Birkeland, M., *Historiske Skrifter.* Edited by Fr. Ording. 3 vols. Chra., 1919-1925.

Bjerregaard, H., *Den Syttende Mai 1824.* Chra., 1859. Reprint from *Morgenbladet,* 1859, no. 236.

Bjørnson, B., *Bjørnsons brev.* Edited by Halvdan Koht. 4 vols. Chra., 1912-21.

Bonnevie, Anders, *Nogle nødvendige Ord i Anledning af Tidsskriftet Saga.* Drammen, 1817.

Bruun, Chr, *Folkelige Grundtanker.* Hamar, 1878.

Brømel, August T., *Die Freie Verfassung Norwegens in ihrer geschichtlichen Entstehung ... ihrem Wesen und ihren Folgen.* Bergen, 1842.

Bugge, F. M., *Det offentlige Skolevæsens Forfatning i adskillige tydske Stater tilligemed Ideer til en Reorganization af det offentlige Skolevæsen i Norge.* 3 vols. Chra., 1839.

Bugge, Sophus, *Folkeviser fra øvre Thelemarken.* Copenhagen, 1859. Reprint from F. Barfod's *Folke,* I.

——, *Gamle norske Folkeviser.* Chra., 1858.

Daa, Ludv. Kr., *Bør Lærerne paa de høiere norske Skoler studere Old-norsk eller Hebraisk?* Chra., 1836.

——, *Om Nationaliteternes Udvikling.* Chra., 1869.

——, *Svensk-Norsk Haand-Ordbog.* Chra., 1841.

Daae, Ludvig, *Stortingserindringer. Utgitt for den norske historiske Forening.* Oslo, 1930—.

Dasent, Sir George Webbe, *Popular Tales from the Norse.* Edinburgh, 1850. Second edition, 1859.

Diplomatarium Norvegicum. Oldbreve til Kundskab om Norges indre og ydre Forhold, Sprog, Slægter, Sæder, Lovgivning og Rettergang i Middelalderen. Chra., 1849—.

Dunker, Bernhard, *Om den norske Konstitution.* Chra., 1845.

Engelstoft, Laurids, *Tanker om national Opdragelsen.* Copenhagen, 1808.

Falsen, Chr. M., *Geographisk Beskrivelse over Kongeriget Norge, og udsigt over dette Lands ældste Historie og Forfatning, som en Indledning til Norges udførligere Historie.* Chra., 1821.

——, *Norges Historie under Kong Harald Haarfager og hans mandlige Descendenter.* 4 vols. Chra., 1823-4.

Faye, Andreas, *Norges Historie til Brug ved ungdommens Underviisning.* Chra., 1831. Fourth enlarged edition. Laurvig, 1856.

——, *Norske Sagn.* Arendal, 1833. Second edition as *Norske Folke-Sagn.* Chra., 1844.

Foreningen til norske Fortidsmindersmærkers Bevaring. Aarsberetning, 1845—.

Foreningen til norske Oldskrifters Udgivelse afgiven i general forsamling den 2den Mai, 1850, Aarsberetning om.

Forhandlinger ved de skandinaviske Naturforskeres 10de Møde fra 4de til 10de Juli i Christiania 1868. Chra., 1869.

Garborg, Arne, *Den ny-norske Sprog- og Nationalitets-bevægelse.* Chra., 1877.

Grimm, Jakob and W. K. Grimm, *Briefwechsel der Gebrüder Grimm mit nordischen Gelehrten.* Edited by Ernst Schmidt. Berlin, 1885.

Grundtvig, N. F. S., *Til Nordmænd om en norsk Høi-Skole.* Chra., 1837.

Haavoll, Andreas, *Djupe merke av danske vaapn svida. Foredrag aat ungdomslag,* no. 26. Oslo, 1925.

Handagard, Idar, *Folkesuveræniteten og Grønlands-spørgsmaalet.* Porsgrunn, 1922.

——, *Grønland og Fremmede Magter.* Chra., 1922.

——, *Grønland og Norge.* Chra., 1922.

——, *Skal Norge nu godkjende Kielertraktaten? En klarlæggelse af det Grønlandske Spørgsmaal.* Porsgrunn, 1921.

Hansen, Andr. M., *Oldtidens Nordmænd, Ophav og Bosætning.* Chra., 1907.

Hansen, Frits, *Om Maalsagen og Politikken. Foredrag holdt i Vestmannalaget den 17de Septr. 1873.* Chra., 1873.

Hansen, Mauritz C., *Grammatik i det norske og danske Sprog.* Chra., 1828.

Hermes, Karl H., *De europæiske Staters Historie.* Translated by H. Lem. 2 vols. Chra., 1847-48. Pp. 511-28 on the northern states were by P. A. Munch.

Hidle, Johannes and Jens Otterbach, *Fornorskningen i Finmarken.* Chra., 1917.

Indbydelse til et Corresponderende Topographisk Selskab for Norge. Chra., 1791.

Indbydelse til et norsk Oldskrift Selskab. 1861.

Indbydelse til et Selskab for Norges Vel. Chra., 1809.

Janson, Kristofer, *Hvad jeg har oplevet.* Chra., 1913.

——, *Hvad vi Maalstrævere vil, og hvorfor vi vil det.* Chra., 1876.

Keyser, Rudolf, *Efterladte Skrifter.* 2 vols. Chra., 1866-67.

——, *Historisk heraldisk undersøgelse angaaende Norges Rigsvaaben og Flag.* Chra., 1842.

——, *Nordmændenes Religionsforfatning i Hedendommen.* Chra., 1847.

——, *Norges Historie.* 2 vols. Chra., 1866-70.

——, *Den norske Kirkes Historie under Katholicismen.* 2 vols. Chra., 1856-58.

——, *Samlede Afhandlinger.* Edited by O. Rygh. Chra., 1858.

Keyser, R., P. A. Munch and C. R. Unger (editors), *Speculum regale, Konungs Skuggsjá, Kongespeilet. Tilligemed et samtidigt Skrift om den norske Kirkes Stilling i Staten.* Chra., 1848.

Keyser, R. and C. R. Unger (editors), *Strengleikar eda Liodabok.* Chra., 1850.

Knudsen, K., *Haandbog i dansk-norsk Sproglære.* Chra., 1856.

——, *Det norske maalstræv.* Chra., 1867.

Det kongelige nordiske Oldskrift-Selskab. Norsk Afdeling. Program. 1848.

Krogvig, Anders, *Fra det nationale gjennembruds Tid.* Chra., 1915.

Krohn, Henrik, *Skrifter. Med fyreord av Kristofer Janson.* Bergen, 1909.

Landstad, M. B., *Folkeviser fra Telemarken.* Edited by Knut Liestøl. Oslo, 1925.

——, *Norske Folkeviser.* Chra., 185[2-] 3.

Lange, Chr. C. A., *De Norske Klostres Historie i Middelalderen.* Chra., 184[5]-7.

——, *Fortegnelse over de i Norge udkomne Bøger i Aarene 1814-1831.* Chra., 1832.

——, *Udtog af Norges, Sveriges, og Danmarks Historie.* Chra., 1841.

Larsen-Naur, Laura, *P. A. Munchs Levnet og Breve i Familiekredsen.* Chra., 1901.

Lindeman, L. M., *Halvhundrede norske Fjeldmelodier.* Chra., 1862.

——, *Ældre og nyere norske Fjeldmelodier.* 3 vols. Chra., 1853-67.

Lundh, Gregers F., *Bergens gamle Bylov.* Copenhagen, 1829.

——, *Specimen Diplomatarii Norvagici, etc. Prøve af et Norskt Diplomatarium, eller Samling af Documenter, henhørende til Kundskaben om det norske Folks Historie, Sprog, Sæder, Slægter og Rettergang ....Udgangen af det sextende Aarhundrede.* Copenhagen, 1828.

Malling, Ove., *Store og gode Handlinger af Danske, Norske, og Holstenere.* Copenhagen, 1777.

Moe, Jørgen, *Samlede Skrifter.* 2 vols. Chra., 1877.

——, *Samlede Skrifter. Hundredaarsudgaven.* Edited by A. Krogvig. 2 vols. Chra., 1914.

——, *Samling af Sange, Folkeviser og Stev i norske Almuedialekter.* Chra., 1840. Second edition: *Norske Viser og Stev i Folkesproget.* Chra., 1848. Third edition: *Norske Viser og Stev.* Edited by Hans Ross. Chra., 1870.

Mohn, E., *Om Maalsagen og det Bergenske Maalstræv.* Bergen, 1868.

Molbech, C., *Blandede Skrifter.* 4 vols. Copenhagen, 1853-56.

Munch, P. A., *Forn-Swenskans (Swæensku ok Gözku) och Forn-Norskans Norroenu) Språkbygnad, jamte ett bihang om den ældsta runeskriften.* Stockholm, 1849.

——, *Det gothiske Sprogs Formlære med korte Læsestykker og Ordregister.* Chra., 1848.

——, *Historisk-geographisk Beskrivelse over Kongeriget Norge (Noregs-veldi) i Middelalderen.* Moss, 1849.

[Munch, P. A.], *Kort Fremstilling af Aarsagerne til Krigen mellem Danmark og Tyskland.* Chra., 1848.

——, *Lærde Brev fraa og til P. A. Munch. Universitets-program. 2dre Semestret 1924.* Edited by Gustav Indrebø and Oluf Kolsrud. Chra., 1924. Vol. I covers the years 1832-50. Two more volumes are projected.

——, *Nordens Gamle Gude og Helte-Sagn.* Chra., 1840. Second edition: *Nordmændenes Gudelære i Hedenold.* Chra., 1847.

——, *Norges Historie i kort Udtog til Brug for de første Begyndere.* Chra., 1839.

——, *Norges, Sveriges og Danmarks Historie til Skolebrug.* Chra., 1838.

——, *Det norske Folks Historie.* Four parts in six volumes. Chra., 1852-59. Second series (*Anden Hovedafdeling*). *Unionsperioden.* 2 vols. Chra., 1862-63.

——, *Sagaer eller Fortællinger om Nordmænds og Islænders Bedrifter i Oldtiden.* Chra., 184[4-] 5.

——, *Samlede Afhandlinger.* Edited by Gustav Storm. 4 vols. Chra., 1873-76.

——, *Sammenlignende Fremstilling af det danske, svenske og tydske Sprogs Formlære.* Chra., 1848.

——, *Underholdende Tildragelser af Norges Historie, korteligen fortalte.* Chra., 1847.

——, *Verdenshistoriens vigtigste Begivenheder.* Chra., 1840.

Munch, P. A. (editor), *The Chronicle of Man and the Sudreys.* Chra., 1860.

——, *Norges Konge-Sagaer fra de ældste Tider indtil Aar efter Christi Fødsel 1177.* Chra., 185[7-]9.

——, *Saga Olafs konungs Tryggvasunar.* Chra., 1853.

Munch, P. A. and H. E. Schirmer, *Trondhjems Domkirke.* Chra., 1859.

Munch, P. A. and C. R. Unger, *Oldnorsk Læsebog.* Chra., 1847.

——, *Det oldnorske Sprogs eller Norrønasprogets Grammatik.* Chra., 1847.

Munch, P. A. and C. R. Unger (editors), *Fagrskinna.* Chra., 1847.

——, *Saga Olafs konungs ens Helga. Udførligere saga om Kong Olaf den Hellige, efter det ældste fuldstændige Pergaments Haandskrift i det store kongelige Bibliothek i Stockholm.* Chra., 1853.

——, *Den Ældre Edda.* Chra., 1847.

Munthe, Gerhard, *Noregr. Kart over det gamle Norge før Aar 1500. Efter gamle Sagaer, Jordebøger og Skind-breve.* Chra., 1840.

Nicolaysen, N., *Mindesmerker af Middelalderens Kunst i Norge*. Chra., 1854-55.

Nor: en Billedbog for den norske Ungdom. Arranged by P. Chr. Asbjørnsen, Bernt Moe, and Jørgen Moe. Chra., 183[7-]8. Second edition, 1843. Third edition, 1865.

Norges gamle Love til 1837. 5 vols. Chra., 1846-95. Vols. I-III (1846-49) were edited by Keyser and Munch; vols. IV (1885) and V (1895) by G. Storm and E. Hertzberg.

Norraena. En Samling af forsøg til norske National-Sange. Chra., 1821.

Norsk Folke-Kalender, eller Aarbog for nyttigt og underholdende. Chra., 1842—.

Norske Magasin. Skrifter og Optegnelser angaaende Norge og forfattede efter Reformationen. 3 vols. Chra., 1858-70.

Os, Edv., *Haandbog i lagsarbeid for Ungdomslag og Maallag*. New edition. Chra., 1922.

——, *Norigs Maallag 1906–1914*. Oslo (sic), 1915.

Østberg, Kr., *Det Færøiske Folk*. Chra., 1923. Reprint from *Ny Jord*, no. 7, 1923.

Rosted, Jacob, *Om patriotismens Væsen og Begreb*. Chra., 1811.

Ræder, Ole Munch, *Den norske Statsforfatnings Historie og Væsen*. Copenhagen, 1841.

Ræstad, A., *Grønland og Spitzbergen*. Chra., 1923.

Sars, J. E., *Samlede Verker*. 4 vols. Christiania and Copenhagen, 1911-13.

——, *Udsigt over den norske Historie*. 4 vols. Chra., 1873-91.

Schøning, Gerhard, *Afhandling om de Norskes og endeel andre nordiske Folks Oprindelse*. Soroe, 1769.

Thorpe, Benjamin, *Northern Mythology*. 3 vols. London, 1851-52.

Tønsberg, Chr., *Berømte Nordmænd. En Cyclus Mindeblade om fortjente Landsmænd i ældre og nyere Tider*, 12 nos. Chra., 1853-56.

——, *Norske Nationaldragter, tegnede af forskjellige norske Kunstnere og ledsagede med oplysende Text*. Chra., 1852.

——, *Norge fremstillet i Tegninger*. Chra., 1846-48.

——, *Norske Folkelivsbilleder*. Chra., 1854.

Det Unge Norge, 17de Mai 1859. Chra., 1859.

Vig, Ole. *Sange og Rim for det norske Folk*. Chra., 1854.

Vignir (W. Werenskjold), *Solomons Laas. Forteljing i Thelemaal, emna fraa Tusend og ei Natt*. Chra., 1866.

Vinje, A. O., *Om vaart nationale Stræv. Fyredrag holdet i Bergen til Intekt for taarnet paa Bergenhus*. Bergen, 1869.

Welhaven, J. S. C., *Samlede Digterverker. Jubilæumsudgave*. 4 vols. Christiania and Copenhagen, 1906-1907.

——, *Samlede Skrifter*. Eight volumes in four. Copenhagen, 1867-69.

Wergeland, Henrik, *Digterværker og Prosaiske Skrifter.* Edited by
H. Lassen. 6 vols. Copenhagen, 1882-4.
——, *Norges Konstitutions Historie.* Chra., 1841-43.
——, *Udvalgte Skrifter.* Edited by C. Nærup and J. E. Sars. Seven
volumes in four. Christiania and Copenhagen, 1896-97.
Note: Wergeland's works are being edited in a definitive edition as
Samlede Skrifter. Trykt og utrykt, by Herman Jæger and Didrik
Arup Seip. Oslo, 1918—.
Wergeland, Nicolai, *En sandfærdig Beretning om Danmarks politiske
Forbrydelse imod Kongeriget Norge fra Aar 995 indtil 1814.*
Christianssand, 1816. Second printing. Chra., 1817.

PERIODICALS AND NEWSPAPERS

Adressebladet. Tillæg til Almuevennen. Chra., 1855—.
Aftenbladet. Successor to *Krydseren.* Chra., 1855-1881.
Almeenlæsning. Maanedskrift for det norske Folk. Edited by P. A.
Munch. Chra., 1849.
Almindelig Norsk Maanedskrift. Chra., 1830-32.
*Annaler for nordisk Oldkyndighed. Udgivet af det kongelige nordiske
Oldskrift Selskab.* Copenhagen, 1836-63.
Arkiv for Nordisk Filologi. Vols. I-IV. Chra., 1883-88. New series.
Vols. V—. Lund, 1889—.
Avhandlinger fra Universitetets Historiske Seminar. Chra., 1914—.
Bergenske Blade. 1848—?
Bergensposten. 1854—. Merged with *Bergens Tidende,* 1894.
Bergens Stiftstidende. 1840—?
Bergens Tidende. 1868—.
Budstikken. Chra., 1808-1834. Series I, 1808-1814. Series II, 1817-
29. Series III, 1830-34.
Christiania Posten. Chra., 1848-1863.
Christianssandsposten. Christianssand, 1839—?
Christianssands Stiftsavis og Adresse-Contors Efterretninger. Chris-
tianssand, 1839—?
Den Constitutionelle. Chra., 1836-1847. Merged with *Den norske
Rigstidende* from 1847.
Dagbladet. Chra., 1869—.
Danmarks og Norges oekonomiske Magazin. 8 vols. Copenhagen, 1757-
1764.
Dansk Litteraturtidende. Copenhagen, 1811-1836.
Departements-Tidende. Chra., 1829-1921.
Dølen. Chra., 1858-1870.
Edda. Nordisk Tidsskrift for Literaturforskning. Chra., 1914—.
Ferdamannen. Bergen, 1865-68.
Folkebladet. Chra., 1831-33.

Folkevennen. Utgit av Selskabet til Folkeoplysningens Fremme. 48 vols. Chra., 1852-99.

For Ide og Virkelighed. Copenhagen, 1869-1873.

For Kirke og Kultur. Chra., 1894-1918. Continued as *Kirke og Kultur,* 1919—.

Fraa folkehøgskulen. Ymse stykke av norske høgskulemenn og Aarbok for den norske folkehøgskulen. 7 vols. Orkedalen, 1912-1919.

Fram. Eit vikebla for maalmenn og bondevenne. Chra., 1871-73.

Frey. Tidsskrift för vetenskap och konst. Uppsala, 1841-1850.

Den Frilyndte Ungdomen. Namsos and elsewhere, 1917—.

Fædrelandet. Copenhagen. A weekly, 1834-40, and a daily, 1840-1882.

Historisk-Philosophiske Samlinger. Udgivet af Selskapet for Norges Vel. 5 vols. Chra., 1811-13. Vol. IV, pt. i appeared at Copenhagen, 1813.

Historisk Tidsskrift (dansk). Copenhagen, 1840—.

Historisk Tidsskrift (norsk). Chra., 1869—.

Historisk Tidskrift (svensk). Stockholm, 1881—.

Hjemmet. Illustreret Maanedsblad til Oplysning og Underholdning. Chra., 1883-1887.

Høgskulebladet. Svorkmo, Fandrem, etc., 1904—.

Idun. Et Blad for Literatur og Kunst. Edited by A. M. Glückstad. Nos. 1-17. Chra., 1851.

Illustreret Nyhedsblad. Edited by P. Botten-Hansen (to 1861). Chra., 1851-1866.

Det kongelige norske Videnskabers-Selskabs Skrifter, i det nittende Aarhundrede. Copenhagen, 1813-1817. Trondhjem, 1824—.

Krydseren. Chra., 1849-1855. Continued in *Aftenbladet,* 1855.

Den lille Trondhjemske Tilskuer. Trondhjem, 1815-1817.

Literaturtidende. Published by J. Dahl. Nos. 1-20. Chra., 1845-46.

Maal og Minne. Utgit af Bymaalslaget. Chra., 1909—.

Maanedskrift for Literatur. Utgit av et Selskab. 10 vols. Copenhagen, 1829-1838.

Morgenbladet. Chra., 1819—.

Det nittende Aarhundrede. Maanedskrift for Litteratur og Kritik. Edited by G. and Edv. Brandes. 6 vols. Copenhagen, 1874-1877.

Nor. Tidsskrift for Videnskab og Literatur. Udg. av det Norske Studentersamfund. 3 vols. Chra., 1840-46.

Norden. Et Maanedskrift. Edited by J. Lieblein. 5 vols. Chra., 1866-70.

Nordisk Literatur-Tidende. Edited by Giödwad and Ploug. 1st (and only) volume. Copenhagen, 1846.

Nordisk Tidskrift. Edited by A. Sohlman. Stockholm, 1852-3.

Nordisk Tidskrift för politik, ekonomi och Litteratur. Lund, 1866-70.

Nordisk Tidskrift för Vetenskap, Konst och Industri. Utg. af den Letterstedska Föreningen. Stockholm, 1878—.

Nordisk Universitets-Tidsskrift. 10 vols. Copenhagen, Lund, Uppsala, and Christiania, 1854-64.

Nordmandsforbundet. Chra., 1908—.

Norsk Folkeblad. Edited by Bjørnstjerne Bjørnson. Chra., 1866-1873.

Norsk Kirkeblad. Chr., 1904—.

Norsk Tidsskrift for Videnskab og Litteratur. Edited by C. C. A. Lange (6th and 7th vols. by Monrad and Winter-Hjelm). 7 vols. Chra., 1847-55.

Den norske Folkeskole. Et Maanedskrift for Lærere og andre Opdragere. 4 vols. Chra., 1852-56.

Den norske Rigstidende. Successor to *Tiden.* Chra., 1815-1882.

Norske Samlinger. Edited by C. C. A. Lange. 2 vols. Chra., 1849-1860.

Norske Universitets- og Skole-Annaler. Chra., 1834—. Series 2, vols. I-VII appeared in 1842-57.

Norskt Maanedskrift. Edited by P. A. Munch, *et al.,* 6 vols. Chra., 1856-1860.

Nutid og Fortid. Et Hæfteskrift. Edited by Jacob Aall. 3 vols. Arendal and Christiania, 1832-36.

Ny Illustrerad Tidning. 1st series. 15 vols. Stockholm, 1865-1879.

Ny Illustreret Tidende. Chra., 1874-90.

Nyt Historisk Tidsskrift. Constitutes series two of *(dansk) Historisk Tidsskrift.* 6 vols. Copenhagen, 1846-56.

Runa. Antiqvarisk Tidsskrift. Stockholm, 1841?-1850.

Saga. Et Fjerdingaars-Skrift. Edited by J. St. Munch. 3 vols. Chra., 1816-20.

Samlinger til det Norske Folks Sprog og Historie. 6 vols. Chra., 1833-39.

Samtiden. Populært tidsskrift for literatur og samfundsspørgsmaal. Edited by J. Brunchorst and G. Gran. Bergen, 1890-99. Continued as *Samtiden. Tidsskrift for politik, litteratur og samfundsspørgsmaal.* Chra., 1900—.

Skilling Magasin. Chra., 1836-1891.

Statsborgeren. Chra., 1831-1837.

Stortings-Efterretninger 1814-1833. 3 vols. Chra., 1863-82.

Stortings Forhandlinger. Chra., 1815—.

Svein Urædd. Chra., 1868-1870.

Syn og Segn. Utgit av det norske Samlaget. Chra., 1894—.

Den Syttende Mai. Norsk landsmaalsavis. Chra., 1894—.

Tiden. Et offentligt Blad af blandet Indhold. 3 vols. Chra., 1808-1814. Continued as *Den norske Rigstidende.*

Tidens Tegn. Chra., 1910—.

Tidsskrift for Litteratur og Kritik. Edited by F. C. Petersen. 3 vols. Copenhagen, 1839-42.

Tidsskrift for Bank og Finansvæsen. Chra., 1915-1925?

Tilskueren. Nos. 1-104. 1824.

Topographisk Journal for Norge. 10 vols. Chra., 1792-1808.

Urda. Et norsk antiqvarisk-historisk Tidsskrift. 3 vols. Bergen, 1837-47.

Utenrikspolitikken. 2 vols. Chra., 1921-1923.

Den vestlandske Tidende. Arendal, 1832—.

Vidar. Et Ugeskrift udgivet af det Norske Studenter-Forbund. Chra., 1832-34.

Vor Verden. Chra., 1923-31.

Vort Land. Chra., 1867.

Secondary Works and Works of General Reference

Aschehougs Konversations Leksikon. 9 vols. Chra., 1920-1925.

Berge, Rikard, *M. B. Landstad.* Risør, 1920.

Beyer, Harald, *Henrik Wergeland og Henrich Steffens.* Chra., 1920.

Bing, Kr., *Olsoktradition.* Bergen, 1919.

Blanck, Anton, *Den nordiska renässansen i sjuttonhundratalets litteratur; en undersøkning av den "götiska" poesiens allmänna och inhemska förutsättningar.* Stockholm, 1911.

Borries, Kurt, *Die Romantik und die Geschichte. Studien zur romantischen Lebensform.* Berlin, 1925.

Brinchmann, Chr., *National-Forskeren P. A. Munch: Hans Liv og Virke.* Chra., 1910.

Bugge, Alexander, E. Hertzberg, A. Taranger, Y. Nielsen, Oscar Alb. Johnsen and J. E. Sars. *Norges Historie fremstillet for det norske Folk.* 6 vols. Chra., 1908-17.

Bukdahl, Jørgen, *Norsk National Kunst.* Copenhagen, 1924.

——, *Det skjulte Norge.* Oslo, 1926.

Bull, Edvard, Wilhelm Keilhau, Haakon Shetelig and Sverre Steen. *Det norske folks Liv og Historie gjennem Tiderne.* Projected in ten volumes of which six have appeared. Oslo, 1929—

Bull, Francis and Fredrik Paasche, *Norsk Litteraturhistorie.* Projected in five(?) volumes of which three have appeared. Oslo, 1923—.

Burgun, Achille, *Le Développement linguistique en Norvége depuis 1814. Christiania Videnskapsselskabets Skrifter.* 2 vols. Chra., 1919-1921.

Christensen, Hjalmar, *Det nittende aarhundredes Kulturkamp i Norge.* Chra., 1905.

Clausen, Julius, *Skandinavismen historisk fremstillet.* Copenhagen, 1900.

Daae, Ludvig, *Gerhard Schøning. En Biographi.* Chra., 1880.

Deutschbein, Max, *Das Wesen des Romantischen.* Cöthen, 1921.

Elster, Kr., *Illustreret norsk Litteraturhistorie.* 2 vols. Chra., 1923-24.

Elviken, Andreas, *Die Entwicklung des norwegischen Nationalismus.* Berlin, 1930.

——, "The Genesis of Norwegian Nationalism," *The Journal of Modern History* (Chicago, 1929—), vol. iii, pp. 365-91.

Erichsen, Valborg, *Henrik Wergeland i hans forhold til Henrich Steffens.* Chra., 1920.

Festskrift til Amund B. Larsen. Chra., 1924.

Garborg, Arne, Anders Hovden, and Halvdan Koht. *Ivar Aasen: granskaren, maalreisaren, diktaren. Ei Minneskrift um Livsverke hans.* Chra., 1913.

Gathorne Hardy, G., *Norway.* London, 1925.

Gjerset, Knut, *History of the Norwegian People.* 2 vols. New York, 1915. New edition. Two volumes in one. New York, 1927.

Gran, Gerhard (editor), *Nordmænd i det nittende Aarhundrede.* 3 vols. Chra., 1914.

Gran, Gerhard, *Norges Dæmring.* Bergen, 1899.

Halvorsen, Jens Braage, *Norsk Forfatter-Lexikon 1814-1880.* Chra., 1885-1908.

Hannaas, Torleiv, *Vestmannalaget i femti aar 1868-1918.* Chra., 1918.

Hansen, Hans, *P. Chr. Asbjørnsen: Biografi og Karakteristikk med supplerende Oplysninger om hans Samtidige.* Oslo, 1932.

Hayes, Carlton J. H., "Contributions of Herder to the Doctrine of Nationalism," *The American Historical Review,* vol. xxxii, pp. 719-36.

——, *Essays on Nationalism.* New York, 1926.

——, *The Historical Evolution of Modern Nationalism.* New York, 1931.

Heber, Lilly, *Norsk realisme i 1830- og 40-aarene. Et Bidrag til Intelligentspartiets historie.* Chra., 1914.

Heggtveit, H. G. and Rikard Berge, *Olea Crøger.* Risør, 1918.

Hertzberg, Ebbe, *Professor Schweigaard i hans offentlige Virksomhed 1832-1870.* Chra., 1883.

Ibsen, Henrik, *Samlede Verker.* Edited by Francis Bull, Halvdan Koht and Didrik Arup Seip. 20(?) vols. Oslo, 1928—.

Jæger, Henrik, *Illustreret norsk Literaturhistorie.* 2 parts in 3 vols. Chra., 1892-96.

——, *The Life of Henrik Ibsen.* Translated by Clara Bell. London, 1890.

——, *Literaturhistoriske Pennetegninger.* Copenhagen, 1878.

Jónsson, Finnur, *Udsigt over den norsk-islandske filologis Historie.* Copenhagen, 1918.

Kaufman, P., "Defining Romanticism: a Survey and a Program," *Modern Language Notes* (Baltimore, 1886—), vol. xl, pp. 193-204.

Knudsen, Trygve, *P. A. Munch og samtidens norske Sprogstrev.* Chra., 1923.

Koht, Halvdan, *Aasmund Olafsson Vinje. Stutt Livsskildring.* Chra., 1909.

——, *Norsk Bondereising.* Oslo, 1926.

Det kongelige Fredriks Universitet 1811-1911. 2 vols. Chra., 1911.

Krappe, Alexander H., *The Science of Folk-lore.* London, 1930.

Larsen, Alfred S., *P. Chr. Asbjørnsen. En literær-biografisk Skitse.* Chra., 1872. Larsen in 1880 changed his name to Sinding-Larsen.

Lassen, H., *Afhandlinger til Literaturhistorien.* Chra., 1877.

Liestøl, Knut, *Norske Ættesogor.* Oslo, 1922.

Lovejoy, Arthur O., "On the Discrimination of Romanticisms," *Publications of the Modern Language Association of America* (Baltimore, 1884—), vol. xxxix, pp. 229-253.

Meyen, Fritz, *"Riksmålsforbundet" und sein Kampf gegen das Landsmål. Ein Abschnitt aus Norwegens innerer Geschichte.* Oslo, 1932.

Moe, Moltke, *Samlede Skrifter.* Edited by Knut Liestøl. 3 vols. Oslo, 1925-27.

Nielsen, Yngvar, *Norges Historie efter 1814.* 3 vols. Chra., 1880-91.

Nordbø, Halvor, *Ættesogor frå Telemark. Skrifter utgitt av det Norske Videnskaps-akademi i Oslo.* Oslo, 1929.

Nordens Aarbok. Oslo, Copenhagen, Stockholm, 1921—.

Norsk Biografisk Leksikon. Chra., 192[1-]3—. The fifth volume has reached the name Helkand.

Portræter af mærkelige Nordmænd med korte Levnetsbeskrivelser. 2 vols. Chra., 1852-53.

Powell, A. E. (Mrs. E. R. Dodds), *The Romantic Theory of Poetry.* London, 1926.

Reynaud, Louis, *Le Romantisme: Ses origines anglo-germaniques.* Paris, 1926.

Schück, Henrik and Karl Warburg, *Illustrerad Svensk Literaturhistoria.* Third completely revised edition. 6 vols. Stockholm, 1926-1930.

Seip, D. A., *Norskhet i Sproget hos Wergeland og hans Samtid.* Chra., 1914.

Skavlan, Olav, *Henrik Wergeland. Afhandlinger og Brudstykker til en bredt anlagd monografi.* Chra., 1892.

Stauri, Rasmus, *Folkehøgskulen i Danmark, Norge, Sverige og Finland.* Chra., 1910.

Storm, Gustav, *Om den gamle norrøne Literatur.* Chra., 1869.

Sylwan, Otto, Fredrik Böök, Gunnar Castrén, and Richard Steffen. *Svenska Litteraturens Historia.* Part II. *Den Romantiska Tidsålderen.* New revised edition. Stockholm, 1929.

Vislie, V., *A. O. Vinje.* Bergen, 1890.

INDEX

A

Aall, Jacob, national patron, 82; 51, 93, 96, 98; on the constitution, 103; interest in history, 104; 206; use of Old Norse words, 267; 273

Aall, Nicolai, 206

Aasen, Ivar, Chapters XVII-XIX, *passim*; as a romanticist, 48; 58, 59, 65, 84; 233, note 65; 239; meeting with Landstad, 240; 273, 274, 276; sketch of, 289-92; memorandum of 1836, 290; dialects collected by, 291-2; working procedure of, 291-2; granted annuity, 292; personality, 293 *et seq.*; conservatism of, 294; philanthropic approach, 294-5; patriotic bent, 295; considered a dictionary for each dialect, 296-7; grammar, 297 *et seq.*; grammar, second edition, 303, 327; dictionary, 297 *et seq.*, second edition, 303; thoughts on *landsmaal*, 304-5; 307; review of *Folkevennen*, 307-8; 314; the *landsmaal* defended by, 318 *et seq.*; on political independence and a separate language, 337; 354; opinion of the name Christiania, 369

Abel, N. H., 79

Administrative order, Danish (1921), 359

Ældre Edda, Den. See Edda

Akershus, 166

Akers Church, 166

Amberg, 94

America, 41, 171

"*Amt*," the Danish word, 370

Ancient laws, 96, 141; arrangements for copying, 109-10, 151-2; editing of the, 157-8

Andvake, 331

Angles, Saxons and Jutes, 130

Anglesey, 172

Anglo-Gothic, in the Danish language, 284

Animal magnetism, 48

Anker, H., 351, note 16

Annaler for Nordisk Oldkyndighed, 118

Antiquités Russes, 144

Anthropology, used to support the idea of two nationalities, 367

Antipathy to Denmark. See Denmark, Danish language

Arabian Knights, translation of selection from, 323

Arbitration Treaty with Denmark, criticism of, 365

Archæology, 99

Archives, valuable finds in the, 141-2, 154; Norwegian records in Danish, 94, 151, 155-6, 356; chronic issue regarding, 156

Arentz, H., 22

Árni Magnússon, loan of records by, 155

Art, national culture and, 75-6

Arvesen, O., 351, note 16

Aryan hypothesis, 126; Moe perplexed by, 227

Asbjørnsen, P. C., 37; as a romanticist, 48; 53, 65, 68, 84; Chapters XII, XIII, XV, *passim*; stories in *Nor*, 204; meeting with J. Moe, 206; sketch of, 218-9; writes a "Natural History for Young People," 218; first folklore collecting, 219; grants-in-aid to, 222; collecting in the west and northeast, 225; explanation of his editing, 232, 233; claimed for realism, 249; characterizes folklore in decline, 253; as an editor, 259; foreign comment on style of, 260; 307

Aschehoug, T. H., 42, 368

Audunsson, T. See *Møllargutten*

"Memories," importance of national, 194, 209; 213-14, 349; Denmark's violence to Norway's national, 144, 356
Mengel, P. F., 157, note 28
Mesmerism, 48
Methodology, romanticist historical, 190 *et seq.*
Metternichian era, Norway and the, 25
Migration theory, the older, 123; the Norwegian School's, 124 *et seq.*; Scandinavianism and the, 150; decline of the, 133-4, 192
Moe, B., 204
Moe, J., the rôle of the Idea expressed by, 47; 48, 53, 54, 56, 58, 62, 63, 65, 78, 84, Chapters XII, XIII, XV, *passim*; sketch of, 205 *et seq.*; a national literature sought by, 209-10; linguistic proposal of, 211; grants-in-aid to, 222; 237; the Crøger MSS. and, 238-9; patriotic intent of, 226, 259-60; 307
Moe, Moltke, 342, 347
Mørch, Rev., 107
Møllargutten, 63
Mohn, E., 331, note 44
Molbech, Chr., 106, note 1
Molde, Aasen at, 290
Monrad, M. J., regarding nationality and the national Idea, 41, 69-71, 73, 74, 60; patriotic intent of, 86; folk tales reviewed by, 216; *landsmaal* attacked by, 317 *et seq.*; regarding cosmopolitanism, 73, 338; 354
Munkeliv Kloster, 166, note 70
Munkeliv Kloster Copibog, 162
Munthe, G., 93, 97, 104, 107
Munch, Andreas, 62, 109; fairy tales reviewed by, 222
Munch, J. Storm, 109, 267
Munch, P. A., Welhaven upheld by, 32-3; 48, 51, 56, 58, 60, 65; regarding unionism, 39 *et seq.*; 65, 80-1, 84; patriotic intent of, 85; 97; regarding pan-Germanism, 131; regarding Schleswig-Holstein and Scandinavianism, 132, 148-50; regarding the word *norrøn*, 136; Chapters V-XI, *passim*; sketch of, 109-111; intellectual orientation of, 111-15;

works of, 115-21; archives exploited by, 111, 152, 154, 156; Finnish nationalism analyzed by, 114; regarding nationality, 113, 284; Denmark and the Danes criticized by, 118, 143, 146; scenes of *norrøn* influence visited by, 173; Gothic tongue investigated by, 188; patriotic bias disclaimed by, 192-3; Faye's legends reviewed by, 202; 203, 212; 217, note 14; 224; folk tales reviewed by, 231; Crøger MSS. and, 238-9; 240; Landstad's ballads reviewed by, 243-5; 268; language proposal of, 269-70; 274, 276; modification of the Danish opposed by, 279-80; 281, 282, 284, 290, 293, 294; Aasen's grammar and dictionary reviewed by, 297 *et seq.*; Old Norse trend of, 299-301; advancing study of Old Norse, 312; Knudsen attacked by, 308 *et seq.*; culture related to language by, 308-9, 335; the "inner" nature of language respected by, 312; 314, 337; Christiania denounced by, 369
Mythology, Norse. See Norse mythology

N

Næss, 206
"*Namnlaus*," 330
Napoleonic era, 91
Narrators, folklore, 256-8
National character, Old Norse, 183; folklore and mythology reflect, 68, 227-8, 245; wide influence of the northern, 185; Christianity and the, 354
National culture, Wergeland and Welhaven regarding, 34; patriotic interest in, 74; interest in forging a, 77 *et seq.*; financial support of, 82
National feeling, in 'fifties and 'sixties, 42; romanticism and Norwegian, 44
National history, varying judgments on Norway's, 367-8
National holiday, Norwegian, 26, 355
National independence, language related to, 271; 285, 325